THE FLEET AIR ARM
AND THE WAR IN EUROPE
1939-1945

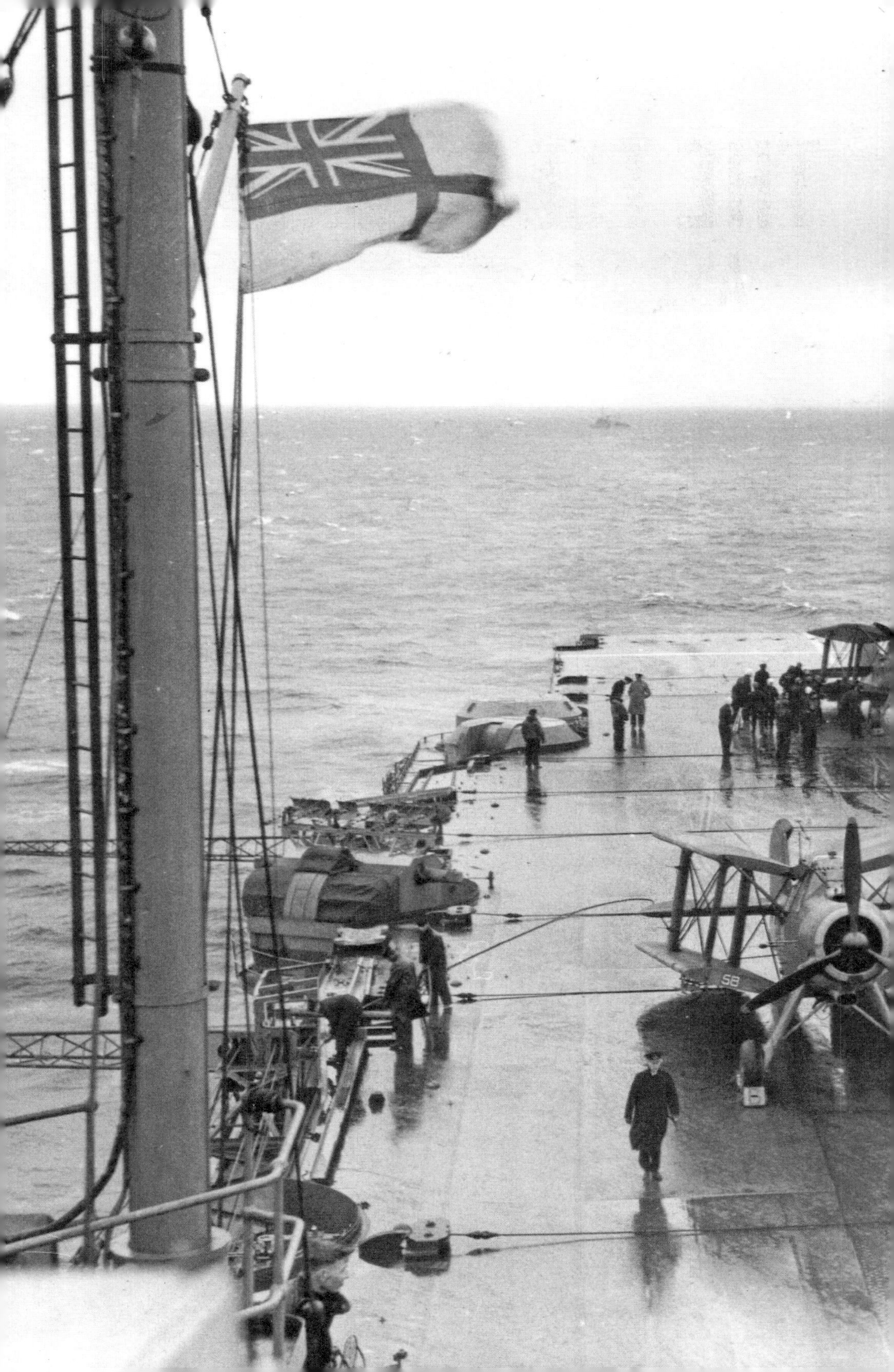

THE FLEET AIR ARM
AND THE WAR IN EUROPE
1939-1945

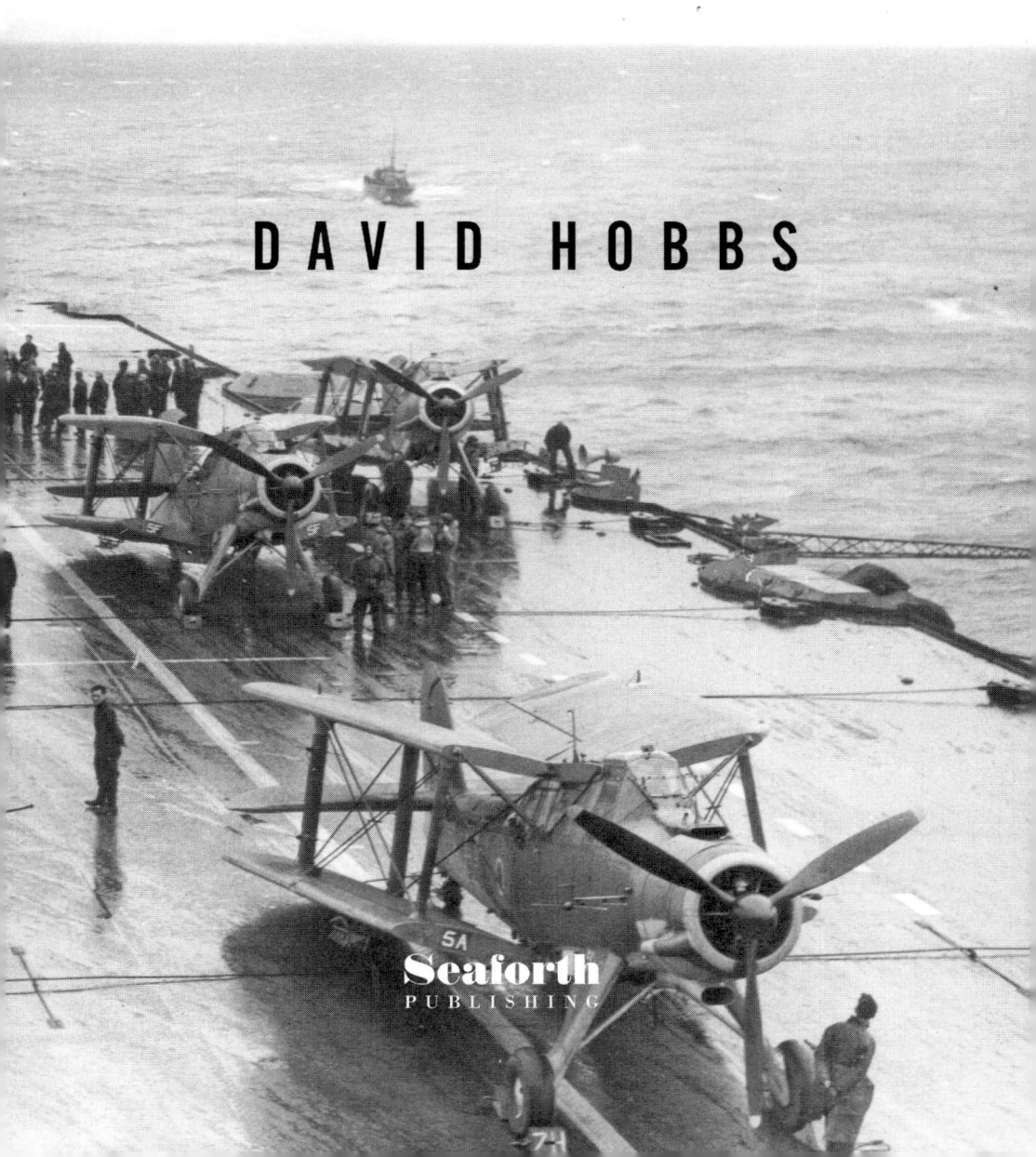

DAVID HOBBS

Seaforth
PUBLISHING

Copyright © David Hobbs 2022

First published in Great Britain in 2022 by
Seaforth Publishing
An imprint of Pen & Sword Books Ltd
47 Church Street, Barnsley
S Yorkshire S70 2AS

www.seaforthpublishing.com
Email info@seaforthpublishing.com

British Library Cataloguing in Publication Data
A CIP data record for this book is available from the British Library

ISBN 978-1-5267-9979-1 (Hardback)
ISBN 978-1-5267-9980-7 (ePub)
ISBN 978-1-5267-9981-4 (Kindle)

All rights reserved. No part of this publication may be reproduced or transmitted in any form or by any means, electronic or mechanical, including photocopying, recording, or any information storage and retrieval system, without prior permission in writing of both the copyright owner and the above publisher.

The right of David Hobbs to be identified as the author of this work has been asserted in accordance with the Copyright, Designs and Patents Act 1988

Pen & Sword Books Limited incorporates the imprints of Atlas, Archaeology, Aviation, Discovery, Family History, Fiction, History, Maritime, Military, Military Classics, Politics, Select, Transport, True Crime, Air World, Frontline Publishing, Leo Cooper, Remember When, Seaforth Publishing, The Praetorian Press, Wharncliffe Local History, Wharncliffe Transport, Wharncliffe True Crime and White Owl.

Typeset and designed by Mac Style
Printed and bound in Great Britain by TJ Books Ltd, Padstow

FRONTISPIECE: Albacores being ranged on a fleet carrier's flight deck. (*Author's collection*)

The Fleet Air Arm of the Royal Navy began the European conflict with limited numbers and obsolescent aircraft. Ships and aircraft of the necessary quality only entered service in the last two years of the war but despite these shortcomings, naval air squadrons fought with determination, skill and gallantry to achieve remarkable results that have often been undervalued by later generations. This book is dedicated to their memory.

Contents

Foreword viii
Acknowledgements ix
Glossary x

1	Introduction	1
2	The structure of the Fleet Air Arm in 1939	8
3	The first weeks of conflict	19
4	1940	31
5	1941	80
6	1942	128
7	1943	179
8	1944	197
9	1945	290
10	Retrospection	317

Notes 320
Bibliography 325
Index 329

Foreword

This book fills a gap in chronology left between my five earlier books on the development and history of the Royal Naval Air Service and its successor, the Fleet Air Arm. It describes the operations of naval aircraft from aircraft carriers of the Home Fleet and from airfields ashore in the European theatre of operations between September 1939 and May 1945. It does not include Atlantic convoy operations by aircraft from escort carriers and MAC ships allocated to Western Approaches Command; I intend to cover them in a future book. I believe that it is the first to describe Fleet Air Arm activities as an integral part of naval operations, including material drawn from documents that have never been published before. The description of the projected carrier operations in 1940 intended to cut the supply of Swedish iron ore exports to Germany from Lulea, Operation Paul, is an example. That said, there is inevitably a slight overlap between my description of early war operations in this book and those contained in my earlier book *The Dawn of Carrier Strike*. They are intended to stand alone for readers who have not read both books and, since naval aircraft were used during 1940 in ways that had not been foreseen, there is sufficient material to describe events from a fresh viewpoint.

The bulk of the text is drawn from research material that I have collected over the past three decades and, in addition to describing events, I have explained why they happened in the way that they did and analysed the results. Where I have made criticisms, they are based on opinions within the Admiralty at the time, sometimes augmented by my own views. I accept that hindsight gives a wider perspective but I have made full use of my own experience as a carrier pilot and good fortune in having met some of the men described or, at the very least, read those of their contemporary combat reports that survived.

As well as the story of the aircraft and their operations, I have tried to make this a story about people and have included personal accounts of some of their activities to add human interest. Wherever practicable, I have used the Fleet Air Arm Roll of Honour to name aircrew who were killed in action as a tribute to their memory.

David Hobbs MBE
Commander Royal Navy (Retired)
Alnwick
April 2021

Acknowledgements

As with my earlier book projects, I have been greatly encouraged and helped by my wife Jandy together with my son Andrew and his wife Lucyelle. Gathering the material that formed the background to the text of this book took a number of years in the Naval Historical Branch at its various locations in Empress State Building and New Scotland Yard in London and, to a more limited extent, its present location within Portsmouth Naval Base. I also carried out a great deal of research at the MoD Archive when it was at Hayes and was able to sift through a considerable amount of material while I was Curator of the Fleet Air Arm Museum at Yeovilton. I will always be indebted to David Brown, Christopher Page and Stephen Prince, Heads of the Naval Historical Branch at various times, for their unstinted support, as well as to Jenny Wraight, the Admiralty Librarian.

Most of the photographs came from my own archive. There were gaps, however, and I am grateful to Philip Jarrett and the Sea Power Centre – Australia, who were able to fill them from their own extensive collections. John de Lucy also kindly made images of his uncle, Lieutenant Bill Lucy DSO RN, and the *Königsberg* strike available. This publication contains Public Sector information licensed under the Open Government Licence v 1.0 in the UK. My thanks also go to Anthony Cowland, who painted the cover illustration, and Peter Wilkinson, who drew the maps.

Over decades of historical research in the margins of my naval career and full-time after it, I have been fortunate to discuss the development of naval aviation within the Commonwealth with many friends at historical gatherings in the UK, Australia, France and the USA. Besides stimulating my own thought processes, these have helped me to look at events from differing perspectives. Norman Friedman in the USA and David Stevens in Australia are among these, together with fellow council member of the Society for Nautical Research, the late Eric Grove. That said, of course, all errors or omissions in the text are entirely my own.

I continue to be very grateful to Rob Gardiner of Seaforth Publishing for his continued support; this book is the tenth on which we have co-operated and I have already started work on the eleventh.

David Hobbs

Glossary

1SL	First Sea Lord
2SL	Second Sea Lord
3SL	Third Sea Lord
5SL	Fifth Sea Lord
(A)	Air Branch Officer not qualified for executive duties
AA	Anti-Aircraft
AAA	Anti-Aircraft Artillery
ACNS	Assistant Chief of the Naval Staff
ADDL	Airfield Dummy Deck Landing
AED	Air Engineering Department
AEO	Air Engineering Officer
AFO	Admiralty Fleet Order
AIO	Action Information Organisation
AP(N)	Air Publication (Naval)
AS	Anti-Submarine
ASV	Air to Surface Vessel
Asdic	RN term for sonar before and during the Second World War
Avgas	Aviation Gasoline
BPF	British Pacific Fleet
BR	Book of Reference
BS	Battle Squadron
CAFO	Confidential Admiralty Fleet Order
CAM ship	Catapult aircraft merchant *ship*
CAP	Combat Air Patrol
CB	Confidential Book
C-in-C	Commander-in-Chief
CO	Commanding Officer
COS	Chiefs of Staff
CPO	Chief Petty Officer
CS	Cruiser Squadron
CVE	USN type designation for an escort aircraft carrier
DAD	Director of the Admiralty Air Department
DAM	Director of Air Material within the Admiralty

DCNS	Deputy Chief of the Naval Staff
DF	Destroyer Flotilla
DLCO	Deck Landing Control Officer (batsman)
DSC	Distinguished Service Cross
DSO	Distinguished Service Order
GP	General Purpose (bomb)
FDO	Fighter Direction Officer
FO	Flag Officer
FFO	Furnace Fuel Oil
HE	High Effect (bomb)
HF	High Frequency
HMS	His Majesty's Ship
hp	Horsepower
IFF	Identification Friend or Foe
kc/s	Kilocycles per Second
LA	Leading Airman
lb	pound
MAP	Ministry of Aircraft Production
MBE	Member of the Order of the British Empire
MID	Mentioned in Dispatches
MLA	Mean Line of Advance
MPA	Maritime Patrol Aircraft
MTB	Motor Torpedo Boat
MV	Motor Vessel
NA	Naval Airman
NAD	Naval Air Division (within the Admiralty)
NAS	Naval Air Squadron
Nm	nautical mile
OBE	Officer of the Order of the British Empire
PO	Petty Officer
PPI	Plan Position Indicator
RA	Rear Admiral
RAF	Royal Air Force
RCN	Royal Canadian Navy
RCNVR	Royal Canadian Naval Volunteer Reserve
RFA	Royal Fleet Auxiliary
RM	Royal Marines
RN	Royal Navy
RNAS	Royal Naval Air Station
RNAY	Royal Naval Air Yard
RNR	Royal Naval Reserve
RNVR	Royal Naval Volunteer Reserve
R/P	Rocket Projectile
R/T	Radio Telephone
SAP	Semi-Armour Piercing (bomb)
shp	shaft horsepower

SS	Steam Ship
TAG	Telegraphist Air Gunner
TBR	Torpedo Bomber Reconnaissance (aircraft)
Torpex	Torpedo explosive
TNT	Tri-Nitro Toluene (explosive)
TSR	Torpedo Spotter Reconnaissance (aircraft)
UK	United Kingdom
USA	United States of America
USN	United States Navy
USS	United States Ship
VA	Vice Admiral
VHF	Very High Frequency
VO	USN designation for an observation squadron
WS	'Winston Special' Convoy
W/T	Wireless telegraphy

1

Introduction

In September 1939 the Fleet Air Arm was a small but integral part of the Royal Navy that operated aircraft from aircraft carriers and other ships distributed across the world but mainly in home waters, the Mediterranean and the Far East. The Admiralty had only resumed full control of its air arm in May 1939 following the recommendation of Sir Thomas Inskip, the Minister for Defence Co-ordination in 1937. Before it, the Navy had suffered a period of dual control after the RNAS was subsumed with the Army's Royal Flying Corps into the new RAF in 1918. This had combined with the parlous state of the British economy after 1918 to influence the size and operational efficiency of the Navy's air element and the Washington Treaty of 1922 had limited both the number and size of capital ships in service with the navies of the UK, USA, Japan, France and Italy. Naval estimates were reduced, limiting the funding that would have allowed naval aircraft to reach their full potential. Throughout the interwar period the Air Ministry had the dominant say in all air matters[1] and it showed little enthusiasm for naval aircraft that would draw funds and design effort away from its myopic vision of warfare. It even forbade its own senior officers from having discussions with RN flag officers about aircraft and their use in naval operations, with the result that even those RAF officers who had begun their flying careers in the RNAS lost touch with naval tactics as they evolved in a period of rapid development.[2] All naval aircraft-related decisions had to be approved by the Air Ministry, and Winston Churchill typified the politicians' attitude when he wrote that 'the Air Ministry … is the repository of the science of aviation in all its branches … and is the supreme professional authority on aerial war as a whole'.[3] This attitude missed the fundamental truth that naval aircraft were the third dimension of a fleet at sea, fighting as part of it, and assumed without any basis of experience or evidence that aircraft would operate independently, unconnected with operations at sea or on land. In reality the RN had used aircraft, as their performance improved, to replace surface warships in reconnaissance and torpedo-attack tasks.

Argus in Plymouth Sound during 1938 after her conversion into a training carrier in Devonport Dockyard. The forward part of the flight deck was rebuilt and strengthened to support a hydraulic catapult capable of launching 12,000lb aircraft at up to 66 knots. (*Author's collection*)

The Air Ministry denied facts that contradicted its own theories and insisted that all future wars would be fought by bombers attacking their opponents' centres of population and industry. 'The bomber will always get through' became the Air Ministry mantra, accepted without question by politicians, and this policy had a profound effect on the allocation of resources during the rearmament period in the late 1930s. Since bombers would always reach their intended targets, the Air Ministry argued, there was little point in embarking high-performance fighters in aircraft carriers since they would be unable to stop them. Behind this absurd argument there was concern that if the ministry ever admitted that fighters provided a viable air defence option for the fleet, it would have to admit that its own bomber force would not always get through enemy defences and could not be the deterrent force accepted by politicians. In the late 1930s it was the UK Treasury, not the Air Ministry, that called for Fighter Command to be expanded as the myth of the bomber began to be realised.

The RN was fortunate that it had led the world in aircraft carrier design and construction and had ships in service, albeit the small prototype *Argus*, *Hermes* and *Eagle*, from 1918 onwards and the Air Ministry had to provide aircraft for them. At first these were types inherited from the RNAS flown by RAF pilots but their lack of knowledge about naval warfare led the Admiralty to set up a scheme for training naval officers as observers from 1921 together with ratings as telegraphist air gunners, TAG. The Trenchard/Keyes agreement of 1924 adopted the name Fleet Air Arm for the organisation that embarked aircraft in HM ships. Seventy-five per cent of its pilots were to be naval officers and, for those with the ability to think logically, the experiment of having a single, unified air force had already been recognised as a failure. The Fleet Air Arm was a naval entity, albeit with its ability to develop crippled by dual control. While embarked in a carrier, the aircraft came under the operational control of the aircraft carrier's captain or the flag officer in charge of its task force. Ashore the squadrons disembarked to RAF airfields, where they came

Hermes was too small to be an effective fleet carrier and should have been replaced. She is seen here recovering a Fairy IIID spotter/reconnaissance aircraft. Note the steam jet at the bow indicating a wind over the deck slightly to port of the centreline. (*Philip Jarrett collection*)

Furious in 1933 with Fairey IIIFs of 822 NAS overhead and on deck. The plane guard astern is a V and W-class destroyer. (*Author's collection*)

under the administrative control of the RAF, although observers and TAGs remained on board as part of the ship's company. RN pilots had to have an RAF rank in addition to their naval one, although they continued to wear RN uniform. This might not be the equivalent of their RN rank, thus a lieutenant RN relatively new to flying could be a flying officer RAF, the equivalent of a sub lieutenant RN. All maintenance was carried out by RAF personnel but aircraft handling was performed by parties of sailors, usually seamen, who were detailed off for this particular task. Some of them did so on a longer-term basis and became the basis of the aircraft handler branch formed during the Second World War. A good team of handlers could make the operation of aircraft smooth and efficient.

During this period the Admiralty specified the type of aircraft it wanted and, to be fair, the Air Ministry accepted that it had a duty to provide them, especially after 1924 when the Admiralty paid an annual sum from the Navy Estimates as grant-in-aid to cover their cost. The problem was the Air Ministry's insistence that carrier-borne aircraft must always be limited by the need to have airframes strengthened both for carrier operations and for launch by catapult from battleships and cruisers. This added weight, as did the requirement for naval radios, navigation equipment and, in some cases, observers and TAGs to carry out the range of operations for which some aircraft were intended. It never seems to have occurred to Air Ministry experts that land-based aircraft suffered limitations when viewed from a naval perspective. They were incapable of navigating accurately over the sea, communicating effectively with a fleet and in many cases lacked sufficient radius of action or endurance to be of use in distant fleet operations. Admiralty requests for specialised equipment such as a dive-bombing sight and improved aircraft depth charges were rejected by the Air Ministry for fear that funds and resources would be taken from its own bomber projects.

This outlook differed fundamentally from those in the United States and Japanese navies, which had not followed the British experiment of creating an independent air force. Both retained naval air arms after the Great War and recognised that carrier-borne fighters would need to oppose enemy aircraft of high performance when necessary. Both used long-range aircraft for open-ocean reconnaissance under fleet command and control. This integration of shore and ship-based naval aviation meant that their carrier-borne aircraft could concentrate on strike operations, whereas in the RN the lack of RAF co-operation meant that carriers had to use aircraft from their small air groups for reconnaissance, reducing the number of aircraft available for strike missions.

The fallacy that naval aircraft must suffer limited performance led to them being seen as a distinct sub-group of little value to the land-oriented operations that were only procured in relatively small batches and hence were less attractive than RAF contracts to much of the aircraft industry, although Fairey and Blackburn did specialise in naval aircraft. A more enlightened approach could have looked at compromise beyond the assumption that whatever aircraft the Admiralty wanted must have an inferior performance. The RAF was itself victim to the bomber lobby's claim of invulnerability. The lack of long-range-escort fighters as well as night fighters should have been addressed before the war and failure to do so had a significant impact on the British war effort. It is worth considering for a moment what might have happened in the Norwegian and early Mediterranean campaigns if the Fleet Air Arm had fighter squadrons equipped with an adequate fighter such as the Grumman F4F-4 Martlet in 1940. A folding-wing version of the Hurricane created from the outset by Hawker with an armament of four Colt-Browning 0.5in machine guns would have had a smaller radius of action than the Martlet but would still have made an enormous difference.

Unlike the transfer of the RNAS into the RAF in 1918, the handover of the Fleet Air Arm to full Admiralty control after the Inskip Award took just under two years and the RN had to recruit thousands of aircraft technicians as well as expanding the number of aircrew. Admiral of the Fleet Lord Chatfield deserves the credit for the award but even he failed to get Inskip to agree to the return of Coastal Command to RN control[4] since Inskip took the view that a land-based force operated by the RN to replace the command would detract from the ability to concentrate aircraft where they were needed in a time of crisis. In 1937 it was assumed that Coastal Command aircraft were basically bombers that could be used to supplement Bomber Command. It was also assumed that Bomber Command aircraft could be used to supplement Coastal Command, despite its aircrew having no training in the role, and its bombers having no suitable weapons and operating from airfields that were not in ideal locations. In the event both commands proved inadequate to provide the reconnaissance and anti-submarine capability required by the Home Fleet in 1940.

Attempts by the Admiralty to produce a reserve of naval pilots for the Fleet Air Arm to replace operational casualties were always considered unnecessary by the Air Ministry, which claimed that they could, if necessary, be provided from within the RAF's pool of manpower. In practice, the RN had to lend aircrew to the RAF after the outbreak of war; observers to teach squadrons how to navigate over the sea and

Swordfish of 823 and 825 NAS overflying *Glorious* in the Mediterranean during 1937. These were the first units to operate Swordfish. (*Author's collection*)

to recognise warships and fighter pilots during the Battle of Britain. In September 1939 the Admiralty struggled to recruit the necessary manpower to man new naval air squadrons as they were commissioned. There were never quite enough,[5] although young men from all over the Commonwealth volunteered for the RNVR Air Branch to add to the serving aircrew from the regular RN and those who had joined on short-service RN (A) commissions to fly. The Admiralty renamed its air element the Air Branch in 1939, although the term Fleet Air Arm remained in use throughout the war and was reintroduced officially in 1953. RN officers in the Air Branch who were not qualified for ship command had a gold letter 'A' for 'aircrew' in the executive curl of their sleeve rank lace, as did the growing number of RNVR officers. They referred to themselves as 'Branch Types', proud of their 'A' status. There were a few RNR aircrew officers but these were mostly ex Merchant Navy and, since they were capable of ship command, they had no 'A' in their inter-woven rank lace. Like RNAS officers before 1918, naval pilots all wore their 'wings' badge over their left sleeve rank lace. Observers had no flying badge until 1942, when the Admiralty introduced one to give them status when operating alongside the USN or RAF. The observers' badge was worn in the same place as the pilots' badge. Rating pilots were introduced before the war and initially they were instructed to sew their pilots' badges on to the right upper arm of their uniforms like other ratings' branch badges. This proved unpopular and they were subsequently worn in the same place as officers on the left sleeve. TAGs wore an Air Branch badge, a little aeroplane, on their right upper sleeve and their flying badge on the left cuff.

Before 1939 the Admiralty had anticipated a Jutland-style battle to destroy German heavy warships trying to break out into the Atlantic and fleet battle tactics were the focus of training in gunnery and flotilla tactics. Coastal Command was to carry out air patrols of the southern North Sea and British submarines were expected to patrol designated areas to intercept enemy warship movements. Fleet Air Arm aircrew were trained to find, fix and strike the enemy fleet so that the battle fleet could overtake and destroy it. This meant locating an enemy force at sea, shadowing it so that its position, course and speed were transmitted constantly and attacking it with torpedoes and bombs to slow it sufficiently for it to be brought to action on terms favourable to the Home Fleet. The RN torpedo bomber squadrons believed that they could sink enemy capital ships with their own weapons without the need for the big ships' guns. However, since aircraft had never done so under operational conditions in wartime there was an argument for maintaining faith in battleships until aircraft proved irrefutably that they could do so. That proof was to come at Taranto in November 1940.[6]

2
The structure of the Fleet Air Arm in 1939

On the outbreak of war the Fleet Air Arm was a very small force composed almost entirely of long-serving RN pilots, observers and TAGs supplemented by a growing number of RN (A) officers and the first RNVR (A) volunteers. There were too few maintenance personnel but the Admiralty was expanding their numbers as quickly as possible. The operational units available to the Home Fleet included the following aircraft carriers:

Ark Royal[1] Captain A J Power CVO RN
800 NAS 9 Skua Lieutenant Commander G N Torry RN[2]
803 NAS 9 Skua Lieutenant Commander D R F Cambell RN
810 NAS 12 Swordfish Captain N R M Skene RM
820 NAS 9 Swordfish Lieutenant Commander G B Hodgkinson RN
         1 Walrus

Furious Captain M L Clarke DSC RN
769 NAS 9 Skua Lieutenant Commander C A Kingsley-Rowe RN
816 NAS 9 Swordfish Lieutenant J Dalyell-Stead RN
818 NAS 9 Swordfish Lieutenant Commander J E Fenton RN

Based in Rosyth and used as a deck landing training ship from May 1939. No. 801 NAS was re-formed as a deck landing training unit, 769 NAS, for this task but became 801 NAS again in January 1940. No. 816 NAS commissioned on board *Furious* on 3 October 1940.

Courageous Captain W T Makeig-Jones RN
811 NAS 12 Swordfish Lieutenant Commander C S Borrett RN
822 NAS 12 Swordfish Lieutenant Commander P W Humphreys RN

Recommissioned after refit on 31 July 1939.

Ark Royal in early 1939 carrying out her work-up with Ospreys and Swordfish ranged aft. Note her two hydraulic catapults with the pronounced forward flight deck round-down between them. (*Author's collection*)

Furious as she appeared after her 1938–39 refit with a small island. Her original gun armament has been replaced by twin 4in mountings on either beam, on the former flying-off deck forward and right aft together with new directors and pom-poms. (*Philip Jarrett collection*)

Courageous as she appeared after her conversion to an aircraft carrier in 1928. Note the flying-off deck forward and the lack of arrester wires and catapults on the main flight deck; these were both fitted in 1933. (*Author's collection*)

Hermes Captain F E P Hutton RN
814 NAS   12 Swordfish   Lieutenant Commander N S Luard DSC RN

Recommissioned from reserve in August 1939.

Albatross   Lieutenant Commander J C Fison RN (Ret)
710 NAS   6 Walrus   Lieutenant Commander H L Hayes RN

Seaplane carrier recommissioned from reserve on 25 August 1939.

The aircraft in these squadrons were:

Fairey Swordfish, a three-seat biplane torpedo-spotter-reconnaissance aircraft powered by a single 750hp Bristol Pegasus XXX engine, giving a maximum speed in level flight of 125 knots. Its maximum take-off weight was 9,250lb and internal fuel capacity was 155 gallons of avgas in a main internal tank with a further 12.5 gallons in a gravity-fed tank, giving an endurance of four hours at 90 knots. A further 60 gallons could be fitted in an auxiliary tank in the rear cockpit or, without a torpedo, a 69-gallon overload tank could be fitted to the torpedo crutches to extend the endurance. Its primary weapon was a single Mark XII torpedo on centreline crutches with alternatives of a single Type A mine or up to 1,500lb of bombs or depth charges on centreline and under-wing hard points. It had one fixed Vickers 0.303in machine gun to the right of the pilot's cockpit with 500rpg and one 0.303in Lewis Mark IIIE or Vickers K gas-operated machine gun on a Fairey high-speed mounting in the rear cockpit with a number of replacement 47-round drum magazines stowed ready for use.

A float-fitted Swordfish of 700 NAS being lowered from the battleship *Malaya* with its engine running prior to a reconnaissance sortie. *Warspite*'s swordfish was exactly similar. The TAG is crouched over the pilot's cockpit ready to unhook the aircraft when it is afloat and the observer is in the aft cockpit. (*Author's collection*)

Blackburn Skua, a two-seat monoplane fighter/dive bomber powered by a single 890hp Bristol Perseus XII engine, giving a maximum speed in level flight of 198 knots. Its maximum take-off weight was 8,228lb and internal fuel capacity was 163 gallons of avgas, giving an endurance of four hours twenty minutes at 165 knots. Its primary weapon as a dive bomber was a single 500lb SAP bomb semi-recessed under the fuselage centreline. It had four 0.303in Browning front guns, two in each wing firing clear of the propeller arc, each with 600rpg. The TAG had a single flexibly mounted Lewis Mark IIIE or Vickers K machine gun with several spare 47-round drum magazines.

Supermarine Walrus, a three-seat boat-hulled biplane with a retractable undercarriage. Intended primarily for spotter-reconnaissance duties from battleships and cruisers but also capable of light bombing and anti-submarine search and strike. Powered by a single 775hp Bristol Pegasus II.M2 or VI engine, giving a maximum speed in level flight of 118 knots. Its maximum take-off weight was 8,050lb and internal fuel capacity was 150 gallons of avgas in two 75 gallon tanks, giving an endurance of five hours thirty minutes at 84 knots. Its defensive armament comprised two Vickers K-type 0.303in machine guns on flexible Scarff mountings; one

Skuas being catapulted from *Ark Royal* while she formed part of Force K searching for surface raiders in the South Atlantic during late 1939. (*Author's collection*)

Walrus K-9C of 715 NAS from the cruiser *Birmingham* in 1939 taxiing under the ship's crane for recovery. The TAG is sitting on the top wing waiting to grab the lowered hook. (*Author's collection*)

in the bow and another amidships. Ammunition was carried in circular 47-round drum magazines, one on each gun with three spares. There were underwing hard points for two 250lb or 100lb bombs or depth charges.

Gloster Sea Gladiator, a single-seat biplane fighter intended as a stopgap until sufficient Skuas became available. Powered by a single 840hp Bristol Mercury IX engine, giving 223 knots in level flight. Its maximum take-off weight was 5,420lb and internal fuel capacity was 83 gallons of avgas, giving an endurance of only two hours at 185 knots. Its only armament was four Browning 0.303in front guns, two in the lower wings firing clear of the propeller arc, each with 400rpg and two in the cowling forward of the cockpit, each with 600rpg, firing through the propeller arc with an interrupter mechanism that slowed their rate of fire.

Fairey Seafox, a two-seat biplane spotter/reconnaissance aircraft intended for operation from cruisers too small to operate the larger Walrus. Powered by a single 395hp Napier Rapier VI engine, giving a maximum speed in level flight of 110 knots. Its maximum take-off weight was 5,650lb and internal fuel capacity was 96 gallons of avgas, giving an endurance of four hours thirty minutes. Its defensive armament was a single 0.303in Lewis machine gun in rear cockpit with three spare 47-round magazines but it did have provision for two 100lb bombs on underwing hard points.

A Sea Gladiator of 801 NAS at RNAS Donibristle in April 1939 showing its faded pre-war markings. (*Author's collection*)

Torpedoes being wheeled out on their Admiralty-pattern trolleys for loading on to 822 NAS Swordfish at RNAS Hatston. They are live weapons with pistols and primers fitted. (*Philip Jarrett collection*)

The Fleet Air Arm's primary anti-surface vessel weapon in 1939 was the Admiralty-designed Mark XII torpedo, which had a warhead containing 388lb of TNT. Its total weight was 1,610lb and running depth could be adjusted in flight, although it was more commonly set before take-off when the nature of the target and its environment were known. Speeds of either 27 or 40 knots could be selected, giving maximum runs of 3,500 or 1,500yd respectively. The higher speed was almost always used in open water as the longer run associated with the lower speed gave targets more time to evade the weapon once it was dropped. It was propelled by a 'burner-cycle' engine developing 140hp started by high-pressure air from a chamber within the torpedo on release. This fed into an igniter and mixed with a atomised kerosene to produce a pressurised air/gas mixture at 1,000°C, which entered the engine cylinders via poppet valves and more fuel was injected into the cylinders, which ignited spontaneously to run the engine. A second compressed air bottle provided an air jet to run gyros, which kept the torpedo running straight and level. Heading was controlled by rudders and depth by elevators, both abaft the propellers to give maximum effect. Like all torpedoes, there were contra-rotating propellers driven by concentric shafts from a gearbox. If there had been only one, torque as it tried to turn against the pressure of the water would have rotated the smooth-surfaced torpedo rather than propelled it and contra-rotating propellers cancelled out this effect.

In 1939 the Fleet Air Arm used bombs designed by the Air Ministry for general applications, none of which had been specifically designed for use against warships. Their explosive content was Amatol, a mixture of trinitrotoluene, TNT, and ammonium nitrate. While relatively cheap to manufacture, it was less effective than later explosives and from 1940 development led to the formulation of more powerful substances including RDX/TNT (originally known as cyclonite), Amatex, Torpex for torpedo applications and Minex for mines. The bombs in RN use on the outbreak of war were categorised by their weight – 500lb, 250lb, 100lb and 20lb – and designated for specific purposes. General-purpose bombs, designated GP, had a charge to weight ratio of roughly 50 per cent, which was expected to make them suitable for a wide range of applications.[3] Semi-armour-piercing bombs, designated SAP, had a ratio of only about 25 per cent with a thicker steel casing intended to allow the weapon to penetrate a ship's hull before detonation. SAP bombs of up to 500lb were effective against lightly armoured warships such as destroyers but were of little value against heavily armoured capital ships, hence the Admiralty's emphasis on torpedoes. The 100lb bomb had a light casing and was intended as an anti-submarine weapon but was found to be almost totally ineffective, requiring a hit to cause any damage. The 20lb bombs were anti-personnel weapons that had virtually no value in a naval context.

The 0.303in Browning used in most British fighters weighed only 25lb, so the total gun weight in a Skua was 100lb. It had a muzzle velocity of 2,240ft per second and a rate of fire of 1,200 rounds per minute but the weight of each bullet was only 174 grains and they lacked penetrating power. Its maximum range was only 300 to 400yd, so fighter pilots had to close in to almost point-blank range in order to achieve the hits and penetration required to cause serious damage. This was dangerous when relatively slow fighters attacked faster bombers since they could easily be drawn into a stern chase where they were vulnerable to return fire.

The shore-based headquarters and drafting barracks for the Fleet Air Arm were both at RNAS Lee-on-Solent in Hampshire, which had been an RN Air Station during the First World War. It had only been handed over by the RAF and commissioned as HMS *Daedalus* on 24 May 1939. The adjacent Wykeham Hall accommodated Rear Admiral Naval Air Stations, RANAS, and his small staff. Other air stations handed over the by the RAF on 24 May were Worthy Down in Hampshire, HMS *Kestrel*, Donibristle in Fife, HMS *Merlin*, and Ford in Sussex, HMS *Peregrine*. Eastleigh in Hampshire was commissioned as HMS *Raven* on 1 July 1939 and Hatston near Kirkwall on the Orkney Island mainland on 2 October 1939.[4] These airfields were insufficient to meet the RN needs for advanced and operational training schools, facilities for squadrons to disembark for continuation flying when their parent ships were in harbour and a variety of second-line tasks including the provision of towed targets for firing practice and other fleet requirements duties. To fill this shortage, new naval air stations were being built under Admiralty contract at Yeovilton, HMS *Heron*; Arbroath, HMS *Condor*; St Merryn, HMS *Vulture*; Crail, HMS *Jackdaw*; and Machrihanish, HMS *Landrail*.[5]

On a short-term basis the Admiralty requisitioned the civilian airfield at Campbeltown in Kintyre for use until Machrihanish was completed and work began on a satellite for Hatston at Twatt on the Orkney mainland.[6] Disembarked squadrons also made use of some RAF bases and requisitioned civilian airfields on an opportunity basis.

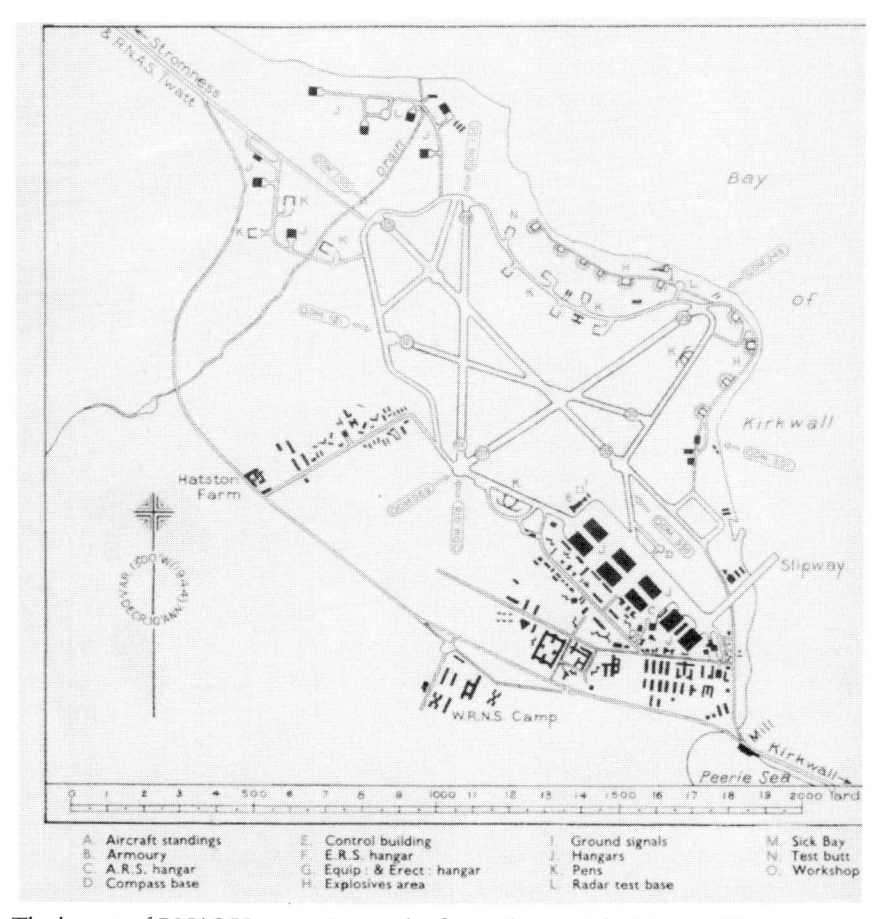

The layout of RNAS Hatston. It was the first military airfield in the UK to be built with hard runways rather than a grass surface. (*Author's collection*)

In September 1939 the Admiralty estimated that it had 226 aircraft in front-line units. This figure did not include new production aircraft that had yet to be issued to squadrons or those in service with second-line or training units based ashore. A small number were held in reserve to replace combat losses. Not all the aircraft listed were available to the Home Fleet as those in *Glorious* and *Eagle* were serving in the Mediterranean and Far East Fleets.

Swordfish	140
Walrus	45
Seafox	11
Sea Gladiator	12
Skua	18[7]
Total	226

On 3 September 1939 the RN had only 406 fully trained pilots with a further 332 under training. In addition to these, a number of men with previous pilot qualifications volunteered for the Fleet Air Arm and these required short refresher courses when they could be fitted into the operational flying schools. Some pilot trainees failed to meet the required standard but a proportion of these displayed sufficient airmanship and enthusiasm to be retrained as observers. Despite heavy losses in the first year of the war, therefore, about fifty pilots per month were qualified and the total number available rose to 764 by September 1940 with a further 635 under training.

When war broke out there were only 260 trained observers and the Admiralty regarded their shortage as acute. A further 248 were under training but shore-based front-line squadrons all had fewer than the number required in their scheme of complement. The Admiralty kept squadrons embarked in carriers up to complement but new units had to start with 25 per cent of their observer complement or less. About twenty-five observers a month were being qualified but early losses had a serious impact and by September 1940 there were still only 350 fully trained with a further 252 under training. As with pilots, a number of observers who had left the service volunteered to re-join on the outbreak of war.

The situation with regard to TAGs would have been satisfactory in 1939 had it not been for a shortage of telegraphists in the surface fleet that necessitated the mis-employment of TAGs as temporary replacements. The problem was overcome by training an expanded number of telegraphists, some of them at the TAG school at RNAS Eastleigh, allowing TAGs to return to their flying duties. In September 1939 there were 350 qualified TAGs with 210 under training. A year later the number of trained TAGs had risen to 554 with a further 192 under training. A number of TAGs who had left the service volunteered to re-join in 1939.

The inter-departmental agreement that followed the Inskip Award had made the RAF responsible for all elementary and basic flying training up to the standard required for the award of the pilots' flying badge or 'wings'. The Admiralty set up its own schools at naval air stations to teach specialised advanced and operational flying for naval pilots from 1939. With the exception of the Observer School, the RAF had previously refused to allow the Navy to set up schools at its airfields because it wanted to follow a policy of non-specialisation. That had led to aircraft carriers being mis-employed for every stage of naval pilot training, not just the final qualification in deck landing technique, and this had reduced the amount of time they could spend on operational development with the Fleet.[8] Until 1937 all RN pilots had been regular officers who volunteered to sub-specialise in flying duties but there were not enough, even if a high proportion of young officers volunteered. To resolve this problem the Admiralty trained ratings as pilots and the first course of twenty arrived at Number 1 Flying Training School at RAF Leuchars on 9 May 1938 to begin Number 41 Naval Pilots' Course,[9] the last in the sequence of courses that had begun in 1924.[10] Subsequent courses began a new series starting with Number 1 on 27 June 1938. These were all made up with both officers and ratings and were carried out at Elementary and Reserve Flying Training Schools at Sywell, Rochester, Yatesbury, Netheravon, Gravesend, Peterborough, Desford, Shawbury, Castle Bromwich, Elmdon and Sydenham. The number of schools gives a clear idea of how large the overall British flying training organisation had become during this period of expansion. Number 2 Pilots' Course began on 2 January 1939 concurrently at Sywell, Yatesbury, Rochester and Netheravon and comprised thirty-nine officers and nineteen ratings.

A short-service commission scheme for officers was introduced in February 1938. Volunteers were expected to serve for a minimum of seven years, which could be extended and, once qualified, they were commissioned as midshipmen or sub lieutenants depending on age. At the same time as the new Air Branch was announced, a new form of pilot's badge or 'wings' was introduced; still worn over the left sleeve lace, the new badge superimposed a crown above the foul anchor, which was surrounded by a laurel wreath with Albatross wings to either side as in the earlier badge. The same 'wings' are still worn on the left sleeve of blue uniform jackets today. The Admiralty realised that when war did come its Air Branch would need aircrew in unprecedented numbers and an Air Branch of the RNVR was established in 1938. Number 1 RNVR (A) Pilots' Course began at Desford in May 1939 with twenty-five students. They wore the wavy gold lace of the RNVR with the letter 'A' woven into the curl and when war broke out this group was at Hyères in the south of France for deck landing training in *Argus*. Once qualified they were appointed to front- and second-line squadrons in the same way as RN and RN (A) aircrew.

3

The first weeks of conflict

On the outbreak of war, Home Fleet aircraft carriers were ordered to carry out anti-submarine patrols to provide cover for the many merchant ships approaching the British coast before the convoy system could be fully implemented.[1] Coastal Command had to admit that its own resources were inadequate to do so, with most aircraft based on the UK's east coast where they expected to search for German surface ships. They lacked the mobility to move closer to the western approaches to British ports. *Ark Royal* was deployed to the north-west approaches under Home Fleet operational control.[2] The recently recommissioned *Courageous* and *Hermes* deployed to the south-west approaches under the operational control of the new Western Approaches Command based in Plymouth. Their embarked squadrons had been given no specialised anti-submarine training and it was not yet appreciated that the 100lb AS bomb was virtually useless.

The loss of Courageous

These tactics proved extremely dangerous and on 14 September *Ark Royal* was narrowly missed by torpedoes fired by *U-39* but her screening destroyers subsequently detected the boat and sank it. That afternoon the British merchant ship *Fanad Head* was attacked by the surfaced *U-30*. Three Skuas of 803 NAS were flown off *Ark Royal* to attack it but two of them were lost in the explosion of their own bombs. Both observers, Petty Officers G V McKay and J Simpson RN, were killed but the pilots survived and were taken on board *U-30* as prisoners of war. On 17 September *Courageous* was sunk by *U-29* with the loss of 518 of her ship's company.[3] She sank in less than fifteen minutes but a study of the 2011 Fleet Air Arm Roll of Honour shows that, of these, Air Branch losses amounted to only four observers, two pilots, a single TAG and eighteen air technical ratings. Things might have been far worse for the fledging air arm but twenty-four Swordfish were lost, including the aircraft that were airborne at the time the carrier sank. Both 811 and

Principal Home Fleet Area

Barents Sea
Tromsø
Kirkenes
Petsamo
Vaenga
Murmansk
Narvik
odö
Lulea
SWEDEN
Archangel
lamsos
ıdheim
FINLAND
ESTONIA
SOVIET RUSSIA
LATVIA
LITHUANIA
Baltic Sea
NY
POLAND
0
400 miles
0
400 km
CZECHOSLOVAKIA
AUSTRIA
HUNGARY
ROMANIA

Unfortunately this image of *Courageous* is of poor quality but it shows the pall of smoke and sparks emanating from her funnel seconds after she was hit by torpedoes from *U-29* on 16 September 1939. A Swordfish in the landing pattern is visible just ahead of the bow. (*Author's collection*)

Men can be seen abandoning ship as *Courageous* rolls to port and sinks. Out of the 1,260 men on board, 518 were lost including her captain. (*Author's collection*)

822 NAS were temporarily disestablished and their survivors allocated to other units. The lost aircraft represented 17 per cent of the front-line RN Swordfish force.

The first enemy aircraft shot down by a fighter
The surviving carriers joined cruisers to form hunting groups searching for enemy surface raiders, operations that culminated with the Battle of the River Plate in December 1939, during which the Seafox catapulted off *Ajax* played an important part. However, before *Ark Royal* could

join Force K to search for raiders in the South Atlantic with *Renown*, she sortied with the Home Fleet on 25 September after the C-in-C, Admiral Sir Charles Forbes, learnt that the submarine *Spearfish* had been damaged off the Horn Reef and was unable to dive. The 2nd Cruiser Squadron extricated her with cover provided by the flagship *Nelson* with *Rodney*, *Hood*, *Repulse*, *Ark Royal* and destroyers. *Rodney* and *Sheffield* were among the first RN warships fitted with Type 79Y air warning radar, which was capable of detecting aircraft out to 70 miles from the fleet at 10,000ft. On 26 September the fleet was returning to Rosyth, 180 miles east of Aberdeen, after *Spearfish* had been rescued when there was a report at 1100 from a Swordfish on anti-submarine patrol that a Dornier Do 18 flying boat was shadowing the fleet. *Rodney*'s radar detected groups of enemy aircraft 80 miles to the south-east and action stations were sounded. *Ark Royal* ranged nine Skuas, which were launched in groups of three at intervals, briefed to drive off the shadower. The first group was from 803 NAS led by Lieutenant Commander Cambell with his senior observer Lieutenant M C E Hanson RN. Lacking accurate position information, they had to carry out a visual search for the shadower made difficult by its dark camouflage paint scheme as it flew low over the sea. They found and engaged it but it flew off when attacked.

It was subsequently learnt that *Rodney* had been tracking the shadower on radar and had passed ranges and bearings to the C-in-C in *Nelson* by

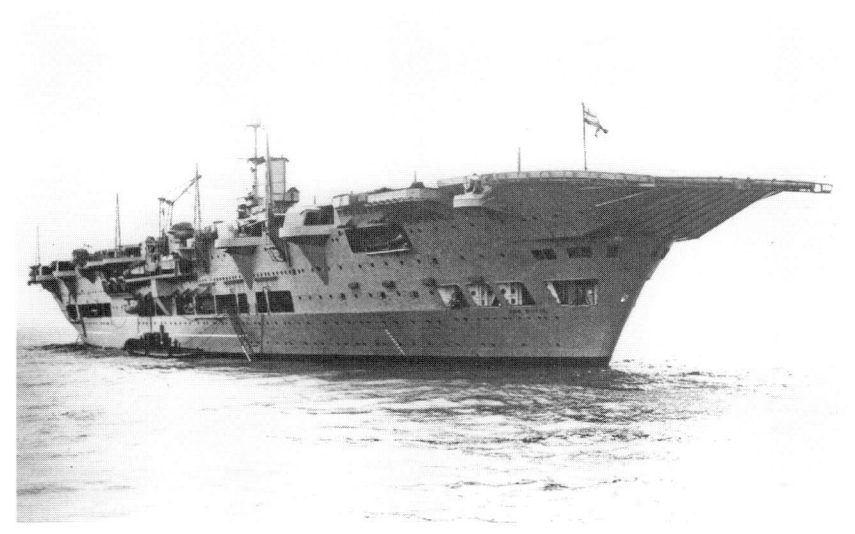

Ark Royal's after round-down was a purely aerodynamic shape intended to smooth the airflow over the deck. In aircraft operating terms, however, it was a wasted space that could not be used to park or range aircraft. (*Author's collection*)

The first German aircraft shot down by a fighter in the Second World War; Lieutenant B S McEwen's 'kill', a Do 18, being abandoned by its crew and photographed from *Somali*. Note the dinghy just left of the aircraft's hull. (*Author's collection*)

flag signals but these had not been passed on to *Ark Royal*. Tight security had surrounded anyone with any knowledge of radar's capabilities and, perhaps for this reason, Admiral Forbes and his staff had completely failed to appreciate its value in directing fighters to intercept enemy aircraft. As the shadower made off to the south-east, the Skuas fired several long-range bursts, which they thought might have damaged it and the Admiralty subsequently received a report that a damaged Do 18 had landed in Dutch territorial waters after failing to get back to its base at Borkum Island. The second section, also from 803 NAS, was flown off at 1130 led by Lieutenant B S McEwen RN with Petty Officer B M Seymour RN as his observer. They were directed towards a second group of shadowers by an improvised system that now made use of *Rodney*'s radar, passing ranges and bearings to *Ark Royal*, which then relayed them to the aircraft by Morse W/T. Although the data rate was slow, fighters were directed towards their targets and the lack of height information did not matter because shadowers operated at low level. This section gained visual contact and split up to engage individual enemy aircraft. McEwen made a firing pass at a Do 18 and was manoeuvring for a second when he saw that it had come down on the water with a crew member waving white flying overalls as a signal of surrender. The four-man crew was rescued by the destroyer *Somali*, which then sank the aircraft with gunfire. This was the first German aircraft to be shot down by any British fighter in the Second World War.

German shadowers continued to probe the force, however, and the third section, led by Lieutenant E D G Finch-Noyes with Petty Officer C J E Cotterill as his observer, was flown off at 1230 and directed towards another Do 18, which they chased away from the fleet but fired out all their front-gun ammunition. The enemy made a series of very tight low-level turns as each Skua made its firing pass and got away. The shadowers had reported the fleet's position and an attack by bombers followed at 1420. Having failed to grasp the potential offered by radar to direct his fighters against enemy bombers while they were still beyond visual range, Admiral Forbes thought that they could not make interceptions until the enemy was within visual range and still thought of gunnery as the fleet's best means of defence. This led him to order *Ark Royal* to strike down all her aircraft into the hangar, including the fighters, and to drain them of fuel to reduce the risk of fire. Coming so soon after McEwen's combat victory, this caused surprise in *Ark Royal* but she was ordered to close the battleships to add her guns to the fleet's barrage fire. Speaking to the Royal Aeronautical Society after the war when he was himself an admiral, Cambell was asked when RN attitudes to the use of fighters for fleet air defence had changed. He replied that it was when bombs fell on the Home Fleet on 26 September 1940.

At 1420 five Heinkel 111 bombers had approached at 6,000ft above patchy cloud cover. Four of them dropped their bombs outside the barrage and withdrew, but one, flown by Lieutenant Adolf Francke, singled out *Ark Royal* for a glide-bombing attack with his single 1,000kg bomb. He achieved a near miss and, although he never claimed to have done so, the German propaganda used this attack as the basis for the first of many claims to have sunk her. Other attacks followed and *Hood* received a glancing blow on the quarter from a bomb that caused no damage. Cruisers were subjected to poorly co-ordinated, high-level attacks from about 12,000ft, which achieved no hits. The fleet's anti-aircraft fire proved to be as ineffective as the bombing and Admiral Forbes noted in his action report that control personnel were clearly unprepared. Critics might have added that his own performance had been little better.

Operations by naval air squadrons based ashore
The Admiralty War Memorandum (Germany) of May 1937[4] designated Rosyth as the main base for the Home Fleet's North Sea Force, although three battlecruisers and two aircraft carriers were to be based in Scapa Flow. Supplement Number 1 issued in August 1938 envisaged war with both Germany and Italy and saw the Force split between Rosyth and Scapa, with battleships at the former and battlecruisers at the latter. However, Supplement Number 2 issued in September 1938, just before the Munich

A Martlet of 804 NAS on alert, parked next to the control tower at RNAS Hatston in 1940. It was one of several F4F-3s diverted to the RN from an original French order when France surrendered. The aircraft to the left of the building is a Sea Gladiator, also on alert. (*Author's collection*)

crisis, left the choice of a main base to the C-in-C Home Fleet. He chose Scapa Flow, a decision confirmed by the Admiralty's War Memorandum of January 1939, which described Scapa Flow as the primary base for the North Sea Force. The Air Ministry had taken the view that Scapa Flow was too remote to be threatened by German bombers but in early 1939 it changed its opinion and stated that the Luftwaffe could drop 446 tons of bombs in one day on Scapa Flow or roughly half that amount every day over a sustained period. Existing Air Ministry plans for the air defence of Great Britain included Edinburgh, Rosyth and the area around the Firth of Forth but not the Orkney Islands. RAF Fighter Command stated that it was hard pressed to meet its existing commitments and was not able, therefore, to cover the Orkney Islands in the immediate future. Air defence of the Home Fleet in its main base would have to be undertaken by the Navy's own aircraft disembarked from carriers to suitable airfields ashore. No. 803 NAS disembarked its Skuas to RNAS Hatston near Kirkwall in the Orkney Islands on 1 October 1939 and, at the First Lord's instigation, 804 NAS was formed with Sea Gladiators, at Hatston, at the end of November 1939 tasked with the defence of Scapa Flow. Other RN fighter squadrons would follow during 1940 and, when airborne, naval fighters were controlled by Fighter Command's 14 Group, which had a sector headquarters at Wick.

The Air Ministry's pre-war belief that high-performance, shore-based enemy aircraft would not be much concerned with British warships at sea was shown to be totally erroneous during this period. The C-in-C Home Fleet summed up the depressing state of affairs in a letter to the Admiralty[5] in which he stated that '... the Fleet Air Arm was assigned a limited role before the war and I appreciate that the design of aircraft ... was in consequence ... directed towards developing types of aircraft best suited for operation from carriers against enemy ships at sea'. He went on to mention the misplaced theory that carrier-borne aircraft must be inherently inferior to land-based types but added that during the early months of the war this had resulted in the frustration of his pilots, who felt unable to achieve much with their existing equipment. As the Fleet Air Arm found itself having to face a growing number of unforeseen tasks opposed by superior enemy aircraft, frustration was turning to exasperation. This, he said, was 'not so much a criticism of their employment ... but there is no getting away from the fact that the Walrus, Swordfish and Skua ... are the slowest aircraft of their respective types in the world'.

By 1940 Forbes felt compelled to inform the Admiralty that 'so far as the war in home waters is concerned it has to be acknowledged that the occupation of Norway by Germany is a definite restriction on the useful operation of aircraft carriers. This has been met in part by the establishment of an air striking force at Hatston which has now become an integral and central part of our naval strategy. Hatston is in fact deputising for a carrier in the area in which the operation of a carrier is likely to be unprofitable.' While Forbes admitted that RAF Coastal and Bomber Commands were constitutionally responsible for providing land-based reconnaissance and strikes, he firmly expressed the opinion that neither was equipped nor trained to deliver the forms of attack that were best suited to sea warfare: torpedo strikes and dive-bombing. He therefore asked as a matter of urgency for better British or American fighters to be based at RNAS Hatston, including Spitfires, to defend the base and for the provision of a strong naval air striking force at the same air station supported by suitable modern fighters. He further recommended that the equipment of all carriers should, in future, include fighters procured from the USN, at least until the Fairey Fulmar became available. American naval fighters were, he believed, superior to those designed in Britain.

The Admiralty's Naval Air Division, NAD, used early war experience to prepare the *Fleet Air Arm Manual of Operational Training* in 1940. It contained details of courses in disciplines ranging from torpedo and bombing attack, air combat including air-to-air firing and air-to-ground firing, and others such as signals, navigation, reconnaissance and gunnery spotting. It also contained details of the standard bombing and air firing exercises with their systems of marking and the methods used to analyse navigation exercises. The details of pilots' elementary, intermediate and advanced flying training were continued in publications issued by the Air Ministry, which retained responsibility for them. Pilots' operational training was an Admiralty responsibility from 1939 and course details for fighter, torpedo, seaplane and deck landing instruction were listed by the Admiralty in *The Training of Fleet Air Arm Flying Personnel*, which also contained observers' and TAGs qualifying course details. Despite the acute shortages of observers at this time, restrictions on flying over the North Sea and English Channel because of German air activity caused the Admiralty to move observer training from the UK to RNAS Piarco in Trinidad.

Aircraft in development for service in 1940

Several aircraft were under development or destined for service in the Fleet Air Arm at the end of 1939 and due to enter squadron service in 1940.

The **Blackburn Roc** was a two-seat monoplane fighter powered by a single 890hp Bristol Perseus XII engine, giving a maximum level speed of 196 knots. When fitted with floats, its poor performance deteriorated

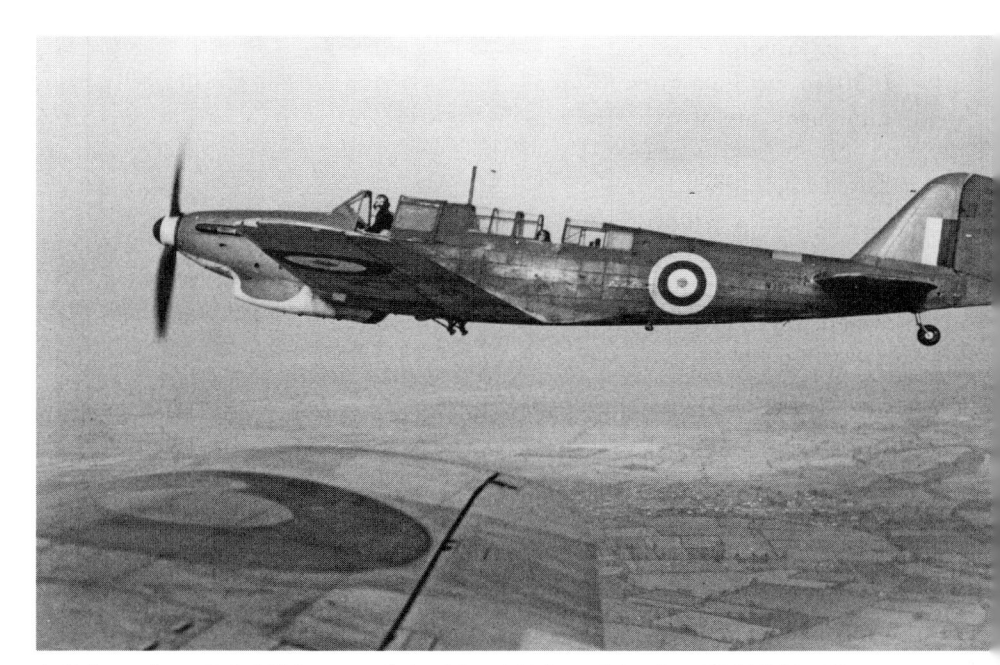

A Fulmar from 761 NAS, part of the Naval Fighter School at RNAS Yeovilton. (*Author's collection*)

A formation of four Rocs. (*Author's collection*)

still further. Maximum take-off weight was 8,000lb and internal fuel capacity was 163 gallons of avgas, giving an endurance of four hours twenty minutes at 118 knots. Armament comprised four Browning 0.303in machine guns in an electrically operated Boulton Paul 'A' type gun turret aft of the pilot's cockpit with 600rpg. It proved a complete failure in service and was soon withdrawn, many finding a useful role as target tugs.

The **Fairey Albacore** was a three-seat, biplane torpedo/dive bomber/reconnaissance aircraft powered by a single 1,085hp Bristol Taurus XII engine, giving a maximum level speed of 140 knots. Maximum take-off weight was 12,500lb and internal fuel capacity was 193 gallons of avgas, giving an endurance of six hours at 100 knots. Its principal strike weapon was a single 1,610lb Mark XII torpedo with alternative loads of a single Type A mine, three 500lb bombs, six 250lb bombs or four depth charges. It had a single 0.303in Browning front gun in the starboard lower wing and a single 0.303in Vickers K gun on a flexible mounting in the rear cockpit with several spare 47-round drum magazines.

The **Fairey Fulmar** was a two-seat monoplane fighter powered by a single 1,300hp Rolls-Royce Merlin XXX engine, giving a maximum speed in level flight of 216 knots. Maximum take-off weight was 10,700lb and internal fuel capacity was 155 gallons of avgas with provision for a 60-gallon overload tank. Endurance on internal fuel was three and a

Albacores ranged on a fleet carrier ready to be flown off. (*Author's collection*)

half hours at 200 knots. Armament was eight 0.303in Browning machine guns, four in each wing firing clear of the propeller arc with 500rpg. It also had provision for one 250lb bomb under each wing.

The **Grumman Martlet** was an American-designed and built single-seat, monoplane fighter powered by a single 1,200hp Pratt & Whitney Twin Wasp S3C4-G engine, giving a maximum level speed of 265 knots. Maximum take-off weight was 6,607lb and internal fuel capacity was 144 US gallons of avgas, giving an endurance of five hours at 215 knots. Armament was six 0.5in Colt-Browning M2 machine guns with 240rpg, three in each wing firing clear of the propeller arc. Mark I Martlets were the non-folding equivalent of the USN F4F-3 from a batch originally ordered for the French Navy. The Mark II had folding wings and was the equivalent of the USN F4F-4, ordered specifically for the RN.[6]

4

1940

Following the loss of *Courageous* and the deployment of *Ark Royal* to join *Glorious* in the Mediterranean, the shortage of carriers in the Home Fleet led to some squadrons operating from shore bases, like those at RNAS Hatston. Others operated from RAF bases in southern England.

Naval fighter squadrons operating ashore

Both 803 and 804 NAS had operated from RNAS Hatston in the air defence role from late 1939.[1] From February 800 NAS operated from Hatston to escort both UK coastal convoys and others to and from Norway. No. 801 NAS operated from both Wick and Hatston from March 1940 to protect ships of the Home Fleet anchored in Scapa Flow and the convoys. Sorties consisted largely of patrols and the investigation of radar contacts on unidentified aircraft. There was an air attack on Scapa Flow at 1950 on 16 March and all of 804 NAS took off in great haste but failed to make contact with the enemy in the gathering gloom. Their recovery was difficult because runway lights had been switched off to prevent enemy bombers from seeing them. Captain R T Partridge RM commanded 800 NAS and from April 803 NAS was commanded by his old friend Lieutenant W P 'Bill' Lucy RN, described by Partridge as 'a fine officer and, as far as I could see, completely fearless'.

No. 803 NAS' activities during this period were described in my earlier book *The Dawn of Carrier Strike* but I will include them here for continuity. Patrols over the sea lasted over four hours, close to the Skua's maximum endurance. Bill Lucy always flew with his senior observer, Lieutenant M C E Hanson RN, and other pilots flew with rating observers or TAGs.[2] Sometimes directed to merchant ships under attack by Heinkel He 111 bombers, they could dive on them to chase them off but their lack of level speed usually prevented them from catching and destroying them. Whenever he could, Lucy returned to ships that had been attacked and flew low past them to boost morale. He was often rewarded by the crew coming on deck to wave their thanks. He was more successful than other Skua pilots and told Partridge that he always patrolled as high as the cloud base would allow so that he stood a good chance of having a height advantage over enemy bombers to enable him to catch them in a dive. He never opened fire until the last moment, so that he gained the maximum number of hits in what might be his only firing pass as enemy bombers jettisoned their bombs and fled. The Skua's reflector gunsight helped pilots to estimate their aim-off and getting as close as possible to the target further simplified it and ensured the largest number of hits. In level flight the He 111 was faster than a Skua, so once the advantage from the dive was lost, the fighter slid astern into the area covered by the bomber's defensive fire. With only four rifle-calibre machine guns and sufficient ammunition for about twelve seconds' fire, something vital had to be hit to bring any aircraft down or even to damage it. It was usual to make the enemy cockpit the point of aim, hoping to incapacitate the pilot, but hits on engines or their liquid cooling systems could also be effective.

Lieutenant W P Lucy DSO RN, the first British pilot to achieve five or more air victories in the Second World War. (*John de Lucy collection*)

On 20 March a section of Skuas from 800 NAS were escorting convoy ON 21 to Norway when it was attacked by ten He 111s at 1850. Lieutenant E W Taylour RN, with Lieutenant R S Bostock RN as his observer, was leading Petty Officer H A Monk and his observer, Leading Airman M Hall. Taylour fired 1,860 rounds and drove off the bombers but Monk suffered gun jams and only fired 300. Lucy and Hanson were returning from another convoy escort sortie on the same day at 1940 when they saw a merchant ship being strafed by an He 111. Lucy made two attacks on it, firing 1,600 rounds; his windscreen was covered in oil from the bomber's damaged engines and he saw its undercarriage come down as it evaded into cloud, so he knew that he had damaged it. Coastal Command's 18 Group reported a day later that the Germans had tried to contact a missing aircraft until midnight without success and this had been assessed as Lucy's Heinkel. This was his first combat victory and the Admiralty signalled that 'their Lordships have heard with great pleasure of the successful manner in which Fleet Air Arm Skuas protected the ON convoy yesterday'. The *Daily Telegraph* took up the story under the headline 'Three British planes rout ten Nazis'.

The German invasion of Norway

In retrospect, it seems remarkable that the Home Fleet had no operational carrier available on 9 April when German forces invaded Norway and Denmark. *Ark Royal* had been sent to the Mediterranean to join *Glorious* and carry out aircrew training in its relatively safe waters. *Furious* had just completed a refit and was not yet fully worked up. Her two Swordfish squadrons, 816 and 818 NAS, were disembarked for weapons training at RNAS Campbeltown and the Skuas of 801 NAS were at what was then still an RAF airfield at Evanton on the Cromarty Firth.[3] Geoffrey Till made the point in *Air Power and the Royal Navy* that Admiral Forbes did not consider *Furious* to be a part of his fleet[4] on 7 April, a significant oversight that would have consequences. Anchored off Greenock, she had not embarked 801 NAS since its re-equipment with Skuas in January and this squadron's availability was complicated by the fact that while at Evanton it was under the operational control of Fighter Command, which had to give permission for its release. *Furious*' log shows that Sunday, 7 April was a quiet day and on Monday, 8 April hands were painting ship and loading ammunition. Two days in which 801 NAS could have moved to Campbeltown had been wasted when the Admiralty eventually ordered the ship to sail. Captain T H Troubridge RN reacted at once but considered his fighter squadron to be 'too far off to comply with what was obviously an urgent order' and so he sailed without it. Whatever sort of action the C-in-C thought his fleet was going to fight, it would have to do so without fighters embarked. Urgent preparations for sea began at 1700 and she passed through the Clyde boom at 0020 on 9 April heading around the Mull of Kintyre for an anchorage off Campbeltown, which was reached at 0405. Swordfish squadron personnel and stores were embarked from a patrol vessel and a tug by 0730, when she weighed anchor and moved out to sea to land on the two squadrons, escorted by *Maori*, *Ashanti* and *Fortune*. The recovery was complete by 1030 and *Furious* headed north through the Minches at her best speed to rendezvous with *Warspite* off Muckle Flugga, the most northerly of the Shetland Islands. A short delay would have allowed 801 NAS to be embarked and included fighters in the Home Fleet's force off the Norwegian coast a fortnight earlier than those that eventually arrived in *Ark Royal* and *Glorious* after they were recalled from the Mediterranean. With hindsight it was an act of folly to sail without fighters embarked but on that day the scale of enemy air attack was completely underestimated and a valuable opportunity lost.

Furious and her escort joined the Home Fleet off Bergen at 0745 on 10 April and Admiral Forbes ordered her to prepare her aircraft for a torpedo attack on enemy cruisers reported to be in the harbour but cancelled the order when he decided to move his heavy ships away from waters that were already being dominated by the Luftwaffe. Instead, he decided to use them to attack enemy warships reported in Trondheim.[5] On the same day Hatston showed its value as a 'static aircraft carrier' by launching a strike force of sixteen Skuas from 800 and 803 NAS led by Lucy to attack the cruisers in Bergen. They had been seen by an RN observer flying in an RAF reconnaissance aircraft on 9 April. The Admiralty had, at first, thought that German warships were trying to break out into the Atlantic but when it was realised that they were carrying troops to Norway's Atlantic ports alternative attack plans followed each other in quick succession. A strike against ships in Bergen by cruisers was dismissed as too dangerous and when the C-in-C moved *Furious* north with the battleships it fell to sixteen Skuas of 800 and 803 NAS from Hatston to carry out the strike. It was planned by Lucy and Hanson on the evening of 9 April, with every aircraft armed with a 500lb SAP bomb. They would be operating at the extreme limit of their radius of action but were helped by the lack of adverse wind on both the outbound and return flights.

Königsberg on fire and sinking alongside the Skoltegrund Mole in Bergen after being hit by Skuas of 800 and 803 NAS on 10 April 1940. (*John de Lucy collection*)

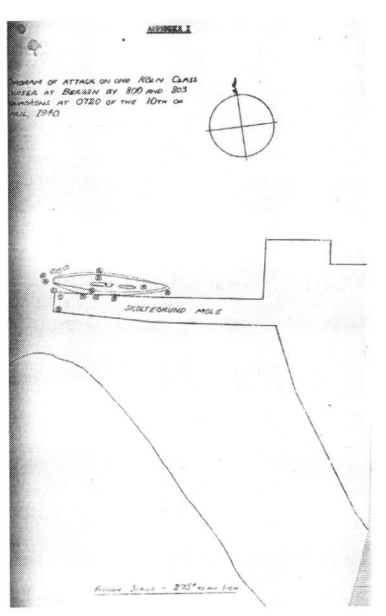

Lieutenant Lucy's bomb plot, originally attached to his action report on the *Königsberg* strike. Note that even the near misses would have caused considerable damage, especially those that fell between the mole and the hull. (*Author's collection*)

After taking off in the dark, the Skuas arrived over Bergen at dawn and found the cruiser *Königsberg*, which had been damaged the day before by a Norwegian coastal gun battery, alongside the Skoltegrund Mole. They achieved complete surprise and carried out their dive-bombing attack on her out of the sun. Every bomb was either a hit or a near miss and the burning cruiser rolled to port and sank. She was the first major warship in history to be sunk by air attack. One Skua crashed into the sea on the return flight, either because the pilot succumbed to injuries or as the result of damage suffered from hits by enemy anti-aircraft shells, and its crew, Lieutenant B J Smeeton RN and his observer Midshipman (A) F Watkinson RN, were lost. Lucy and Partridge were awarded the DSO, Hanson and Lieutenant Commander G Hare RN, Partridge's observer, the DSC and there were a number of other awards.[6]

At 0350 on 11 April *Furious* turned into wind to carry out the first torpedo strike operation in history to be flown from the deck of an aircraft carrier.[7] Every Swordfish was flown off, starting with the nine aircraft of 816 NAS at 0409, followed by the nine aircraft of 818 NAS from 0448. They were all armed with torpedoes and their objective, laid out in *Furious*' Operation order Number 1, was to attack *Blücher*- and *Köln*-class enemy cruisers reported at anchor in Trondheim Roads. The squadrons were led by their commanding officers, Captain A R Burch RM and Lieutenant Commander P Sydney-Turner RN. Burch led 816 NAS down through scattered cloud over Trondheim at 0519. The German cruisers had gone and the only vessels in sight were merchant ships but after a search they found what appeared to be a small cruiser at anchor in Skorjen Fjord south of Agdenes Light at 0549 and Burch decided to attack it. Conditions were ideal and the first torpedo ran true but detonated after only 400yd. At least one other torpedo detonated prematurely and all tracks appeared to stop 500 to 600yd short of the target, which had, by then, been identified as a destroyer.

After their return to *Furious,* the aircrew studied a large-scale chart, which showed that the torpedoes had probably grounded on shoals at the mouth of the inlet in which the target was anchored. Since they had been briefed to attack ships in Trondheim, this chart had not been shown to the aircrew. The results were disappointing and it was clear that only the latest information about time-sensitive targets such as warships had any value. Too much reliance had been placed on reports by RAF aircraft, which were out of date by the time they had been relayed from Coastal Command to the Home Fleet and then by the C-in-C to *Furious* in his signal 1410/10. It was also appreciated that the choice of weapon in coastal waters or in other specialised conditions needed more careful consideration and bombs might have been a better option. NAD regarded

An 816 NAS Swordfish from *Furious*, armed with a torpedo, crossing the Norwegian coast on 11 April 1940 as part of the strike force briefed to attack enemy ships that were believed to be in Trondheim. (*Author's collection*)

torpedoes as better ship-killing weapons than bombs but their tactical use needed to be considered against local conditions. Littoral warfare had not been studied in any great detail before 1939 and both tactics and weapons had to evolve with experience.

The briefed target for 818 NAS was a cruiser reported in Trondheim, part of the stale intelligence listed in the C-in-C's 1410/10. No cruisers were seen but an enemy destroyer was found heading up the fjord towards the port and Sydney-Turner set up an attack from its starboard quarter. Two torpedoes were thought to have exploded under the target's stern and it was assessed as damaged. The less-than-ideal launch position had been accepted so that surprise and time were not squandered trying to gain a better position. Given the draft of the briefed target, the torpedoes were set to run at 20ft but two were altered in flight to 12ft before the destroyer was attacked. They all used the high-speed setting and duplex pistols. All eighteen Swordfish returned safely and landed on from 0630. Later in the day two Swordfish of 816 NAS carried out a reconnaissance to see what was really in Trondheim and to attack targets of opportunity. One was armed with four 250lb bombs and the other with two 250lb bombs and eight 20lb bombs; the latter were anti-personnel weapons of no use against warships but were included to give a range of options. After photographing the harbour, they found the destroyer that had been attacked earlier and carried out a dive-bombing attack from its port beam, an approach angle less likely to be successful than one along the ship's axis. The bombs were dropped together in a single pass but none of them hit the target, which was seen to be getting under way hastily. As they turned towards the sea they were followed by a German seaplane, showing how vulnerable the fleet was to shadowers of even modest performance in the absence of fighters, but they managed to evade it before coasting out by flying low through mountainous terrain.

After recovering these aircraft, *Furious* headed north with the Home Fleet for operations off Narvik, where Captain Warburton-Lee's destroyer flotilla had been in action a day earlier. *Valiant* gained radar contact at 1500 on enemy aircraft approaching the fleet and they were seen at 1540. *Furious* opened fire at 1543 but hit nothing in the ensuing hour-long air-sea battle despite having fired 500 rounds of 4in and a considerable quantity of close-range ammunition. The bomber attack from high level was also ineffective, indicating a lack of training against ships. On 12 April *Furious* flew off eight aircraft of 818 NAS followed by nine aircraft of 816 NAS briefed in the ship's operation order Number 2 to bomb enemy destroyers that had survived the encounter with Warburton-Lee's flotilla on 10 April. All were armed with four 250lb and six 20lb bombs but encountered bad weather with a cloud base down to 300ft in the fjords, although it rose to 2,800ft over Narvik. Sydney-Turner had briefed his pilots to carry out low-level attacks because of the forecast cloud base but as they manoeuvred into attacking positions it lifted and the element of surprise was lost. However, they all pressed home their attacks with determination. Enemy fire from destroyers and light guns ashore began as the first aircraft began their shallow dives but three hits were claimed on destroyers, with more on the Narvik ore quay. Sydney-Turner was shot down but he and his crew were rescued by *Grenade*, as was Sub Lieutenant (A) S G J Appleby RN and his TAG. As they flew up Vestfjord, 818 NAS passed the returning aircraft of 816 NAS but as they approached Narvik the weather deteriorated with visibility down to 200yd in a heavy snowstorm and a cloud base down to 100ft. Despite these appalling conditions, they managed to turn back in the confined fjord and were recovered safely.

On 13 April *Furious'* aircraft took part in the Second Battle of Narvik. Admiral Whitworth entered the fjords in *Warspite* with nine destroyers and the Swordfish were briefed to search Vestfjord for enemy warships and U-boats ahead of the surface action group and to attack enemy positions in Narvik itself. *Warspite*'s own Swordfish was catapulted off with Lieutenant Commander W L M Brown RN as observer and Petty Officer F C Rice RN as pilot and they flew up and down the fjord, which was 40nm long, locating enemy warships and warning Admiral Whitworth of the danger they posed. One of these was *Erich Koellner* in Herjangsfjord, positioned to fire torpedoes at the British ships as they passed. Forewarned, the British destroyers approached the danger point at high speed with their guns and torpedo tubes already trained to starboard and smothered the German ship with fire. Later, Brown and Rice saw a U-boat at the head of Herjangsfjord and attacked it with their two 100lb bombs. One bomb was seen to pass down the boat's open forward hatch before exploding and they saw the hull of *U-64* cocked up into the air as it sank with members of its crew swimming for the shore. Admiral Whitworth wrote that he doubted whether 'a ship-borne aircraft had ever been used to such good purpose'; Brown was awarded the DSC and Rice the DSM.

Furious had flown off air patrols from 0630 and the main strike force of nine aircraft was flown off at 1220. All were armed with four 250lb and eight 20lb bombs. It comprised aircraft from both squadrons led by Captain Burch. Initially the weather was bad with low cloud at 500ft, heavy rain and occasional snow showers, which forced the aircraft to fly in extended line astern along Vestfjord, but as they approached Barøya island the weather improved dramatically at 1323 with visibility increased to 5 miles and a cloud base at 1,500ft. Five minutes later *Warspite* and her destroyers opened fire and the Swordfish arrived over the scene of action at exactly the same time. Pilots picked individual destroyers and attacked them in 60-degree dives from just below the cloud base. Two hits were claimed and the air attack combined with the battleship's fire to destroy the enemy force. Two Swordfish were lost, from which one crew was recovered but the other from 818 NAS were killed in action. They were Sub Lieutenant (A) G R Hampden RN together with his observer Sub Lieutenant (A) L C Franklin RN and TAG Naval Airman RF Dale RN. A third Swordfish was damaged but returned with the others through the bad weather along the coast, flying low over a storm-lashed sea for 60 miles to reach *Furious'* briefed recovery position at 1553.

Patrols were flown on the next day after *Furious* was ordered to operate with a small destroyer escort under the orders of the Flag Officer Narvik, Admiral of the Fleet Lord Cork and Orrery. One of these patrols found

Furious flying off a strike of Swordfish. (*Sea Power Centre – Australia*)

enemy aircraft operating from the frozen Lake Hartvig and a nine-aircraft strike led by Captain Burch with aircraft from both squadrons was flown off to attack them. Two aircraft were armed with two 250lb bombs to see what effect these would have on the ice and the remainder with eight 20lb bombs, which, it was thought, would have a greater impact spread than a smaller number of larger bombs while still damaging aircraft parked in the open. Attacking runs were made from an initial point 5nm west of the lake with pilots selecting one aircraft as their target and releasing all their bombs in a single pass from a 40-degree dive at 700ft. At least two direct hits were seen and most bombs fell sufficiently close to have caused damage. Four pilots used their front guns to strafe parked aircraft and reported a number of hits. The flattened ice that constituted the runway was rendered unserviceable by bomb hits and the 250lb bombs caused large holes to appear. One Swordfish was forced to ditch after damage from anti-aircraft fire but its crew was rescued by *Zulu*. Four others were damaged with some of their crews injured but all the remaining aircraft landed safely at 2200, well after dark. *Furious* had to switch on her flight deck lights to aid recovery.

Furious anchored off Tromsø at 0600 on 16 April with only 27 per cent fuel remaining. The Norwegian naval authorities proved most helpful and a lighter containing 1,000 tons of FFO was brought alongside at 1500 but they had no way of pumping the fuel into the carrier. An ingenious solution was provided by the Tromsø Fire Brigade, which donated two fire engines and these pumped the oil at an acceptable rate, but refuelling was not completed until early on 18 April. FO Narvik had not communicated with the ship and it was not even known for certain where he was, so

Captain Troubridge decided to fly patrols over the Narvik area. At 1350 a German bomber carried out two slow and deliberate attacks undeterred by gunfire and in the last of these two near misses caused shocks that were felt throughout the ship and damaged the starboard inner high-pressure turbine. On 19 April more fuel was taken on from RFA *War Pindari* after 0200 but later in the day the threat of air attack forced her to break off and head for the open sea. By 20 April *Furious* had only nine serviceable aircraft left but instructions were eventually received from FO Narvik tasking her to fly reconnaissance missions over Narvik and Vestfjord. These were flown but limited by low cloud, 60-knot winds and heavy snow. If his aircraft were to make any useful contribution to military operations in Narvik[8] Captain Troubridge realised that he had to move his ship into a position where aircraft would not have to overfly mountains to reach the port and so he moved to an area west of the southern Lofoten Islands, from which they could approach Vestfjord low over the sea. The disadvantage was a transit of 150nm to and from Narvik, which left his aircraft only an hour on task. However, a major assault was planned for 22 April and FO Narvik considered it highly desirable that as many aircraft as possible should support it.

The new area was reached at 0300 on 22 April in a blizzard under solid cloud cover but by 0800 patches of blue sky were visible and a ripple flying programme was begun that aimed to keep one or two aircraft over Narvik continuously, which, it was hoped, would discourage the Luftwaffe from dropping supplies to the beleaguered German garrison. They were armed with four 250lb bombs and pilots were briefed with targets to attack if no higher-priority target of opportunity was found. One aircraft was shot down by anti-aircraft fire and another, flown by Lieutenants A T Darley and D Sanderson RN with Naval Airman T Dwyer as TAG, had to return flying west along Vestfjord at 50ft just below the cloud base in a visibility of less than 2 cables[9] in heavy snow. He eventually landed on safely but was so exhausted that he had to be lifted out of the cockpit. The appalling weather forced later aircraft to turn back and continued attempts to fly were clearly not worth the risk, so *Furious* headed for Vaags Fjord, where the port outer high-pressure turbine was found to be unserviceable. The C-in-C was informed and his staff ordered the shaft to be disconnected, leaving her with only two serviceable shafts out of four. The weather remained bad with visibility less than one cable and on 24 April *Furious* was ordered to return to the UK for urgent repairs.

Thus ended a deployment that had seen an aircraft carrier in prolonged action for the first time in history and Captain Troubridge's report showed how the theory of peacetime operations had evolved into the harsh reality of war. Interestingly, he felt that it had been Admiral Forbes' order to fly in bad weather on 12 April that was the catalyst for further bad-weather operations since it had given aircrew confidence in their ability. Confidence was also bolstered by the navigating officer's ability to place the ship in its pre-briefed recovery position on every occasion. The limitations caused by the lack of fighters led Troubridge to regret, bitterly, that he had not requested a delay to embark 801 NAS and he believed that events might have turned out differently if Skuas had been available to intercept enemy bombers. He also believed that the Swordfish was too slow to carry out attacks safely in daylight, pointing out that seventeen out of his eighteen aircraft had been hit at some time by enemy fire and it was fortunate that no more had been lost. Troubridge made a number of well-considered recommendations ranging from the need to embark more comprehensive map coverage of land areas over which aircraft might need to operate to the need for more general-purpose bombs. The volume of signal traffic had shown the need for a second cypher book in aircraft carriers because his decoding team had frequently been overloaded while they struggled with their single volume. This had led to delays of more than four hours in clearing signal traffic, which was quite unacceptable. Another practical point, quickly grasped, was the vital need for a specialised aircrew debriefing team. Before Norway, returning aircrew had informed the captain and commander 'Air' about the perceived success or failure of their mission but off Norway in April 1940 the captain and his flying staff were far too busy operating the ship and generating new sorties to give sufficient attention to this important task and the wealth of debriefed material was often so varied that it would 'require the analysing powers of a King's Counsel' to gather a full picture from it'. The last paragraph of Troubridge's report[10] cannot leave the reader unmoved:

> It is difficult to speak without emotion of the pluck and endurance of the young officers and men, some of them Midshipmen, who flew their aircraft to such good effect. Once their baptism of fire had been successfully undergone their morale and spirit rose as each obstacle was in turn successfully surmounted. All were firing their first shot, whether torpedo, bomb or machine-gun, in action and many made their first night landing on 11 April. Undeterred by the loss of several of their shipmates, their honour and courage remained throughout as dazzling as the snow covered mountains over which they so triumphantly flew.

While *Furious* was in action, Hatston had continued to mount Skua attacks against Bergen to limit the flow of German material into Norway. No. 801 NAS had arrived from Evanton on 12 April and took part in a strike led by Partridge that destroyed a warehouse, presumably being used to store ammunition. There was still an element of surprise, aircrew felt they were getting to know the target area well and were keen to carry out a third attack despite the increasing risk from fighters. It was led by Lucy and took place on 14 April, with pilots briefed to reduce the number of harbour berths at which the Germans could unload equipment. Aircraft of Dick Partridge's 800 NAS arrived over Bergen under lowering cloud at 0700 and hit a ship alongside the Dokskier Jetty with their 500lb bombs, causing considerable damage. No. 803 NAS aircraft arrived at 0745 but by then the weather had deteriorated and only Lucy's Blue Section got through. Red and Green Sections lost touch, jettisoned their bombs and returned to Hatston. Despite the appalling weather, Lucy and Hanson led two other aircraft to attack a transport ship on the other side of the Skoltegrund Mole to that on which *Königsberg* had been sunk on 10 April. Lucy attacked from a shallow dive below cloud, releasing his bomb at only 350ft. It was seen to hit and started a fire on the inboard side of the ship that spread to the jetty. He stayed low over the water and strafed a flying boat, which was seen to be on fire as he left the harbour. Blue 2, Lieutenant A B Fraser Harris RN with Leading Airman G S Russell, bombed the same ship from only 200ft and also obtained a hit. Blue 3, Captain E D McIver RM with Leading Airman A A Barnard, having followed his leader gallantly through low cloud and falling snow, was shot down while making his attack and his aircraft was seen to crash into the harbour in flames from about 300ft. Both McIver and Barnard were killed.

Against the odds, surprise had been achieved for the third time and accurate bombs dropped on ships alongside the two jetties. Two ships alongside the Skoltegrund Mole had been sunk, which, with the sunken cruiser, achieved the aim of reducing the number of berths available to the Germans for landing stores and equipment. The two ships alongside the Dokskier jetty were estimated as damaged, together with the jetty itself. After these three attacks it was clear that further set-piece attacks would be too costly and operations were limited to two armed reconnaissance sorties briefed to attack enemy supply ships found in Bergen or its approaches, each comprising two Skuas, which split up near the Norwegian coast. These sorties ended the strike operations mounted by Skuas from Hatston in the early part of the Norwegian campaign but it should be borne in mind that the three squadrons had also remained responsible for coastal convoy defence and for the defence of the Home Fleet base at Scapa Flow. The determination with which every mission was carried out speaks volumes about the devotion and adaptability of the aircrew and maintenance personnel.

Operation DX

Far from providing ubiquitous air cover as it had said it would before the war, the RAF now declared that it was unable to do anything unless the Navy provided ships to move its aircraft to Norway and the transport ships needed to carry the fuel, ammunition, maintenance personnel and the logistic support needed to sustain them in action.[11] They also required the Army to construct temporary airfields and troops to protect them. In contrast, the advantages of the aircraft carriers that the RN had fought so hard to develop were clear. They were mobile airfields equipped with their own technical and logistic support. Unfortunately for the troops on the ground in Norway, these advantages had been dismissed over the previous two decades by the Air Ministry, which had followed its own concepts of warfare with little attention paid to the requirements of the Admiralty and War Office. *Ark Royal* and *Glorious* were recalled to join the Home Fleet and arrived in Scapa Flow on 23 April to refuel before embarking their fighter squadrons and sailed at 1315. Vice Admiral Wells, Vice Admiral Aircraft Carriers, VAA, flew his flag in *Ark Royal*. His force was to provide fighter protection for the Allied expeditionary forces being landed in Namsos and Åndalsnes, which were intended to remove the Germans from Trondheim, the key to central Norway, in a linked series of events designated as Operation DX. It was also to protect Allied shipping and attack enemy aircraft, airfields and shipping in the Trondheim area. An RAF Gladiator squadron was to be ferried from the UK to a position where it could be landed to operate from the frozen Lake Lesjaskogvann inland from Åndalsnes.

Admiral Wells selected an area for his force to operate that would allow three Skuas to be maintained on CAP over both Namsos and Åndalsnes throughout the lengthening hours of daylight while other aircraft attacked targets in Trondheim. It was not known when Lesjaskogvann would be ready for the Gladiators and, frustratingly, the RAF pilots said that their navigational skills were insufficient for them to navigate from the sea to their new airfield. Skuas had, therefore, to be kept ready to lead them ashore and locate their airfield for them. The Home Fleet's orders for DX specified that flying operations were to begin on 24 April but, somewhat optimistically, they were expected to cease when the Gladiators were established ashore. The carrier task force took up a position equidistant from Namsos, Trondheim and Åndalsnes.

Embarked Aircraft, Operation DX, 23 April 1940

Ark Royal	Captain C S Holland RN
800 NAS	9 Skuas and 2 Rocs
801 NAS	9 Skuas and 3 Rocs
810 NAS	12 Swordfish
820 NAS	9 Swordfish
Ship's Flight	1 Walrus for SAR duties

Glorious	Captain G D'Oyly-Hughes DSO DSC RN
802 NAS	9 Sea Gladiators
803 NAS	11 Skuas
804 NAS	9 Sea Gladiators
263 RAF Squadron	18 Gladiators

The flying programme on 24 April was ambitious but heavy snow showers disrupted it. CAP fighters from *Ark Royal* made their landfall at Bud at 1635, where they found better weather and extreme visibility. Two aircraft suffered engine failures and ditched near their carrier but both crews were rescued by destroyers. *Glorious* flew off blue and red flights of 803 NAS led by Lucy, each comprising three Skuas. They set heading at 1639 and, after crossing the coast, headed up Romsdalen Valley, where they encountered a Heinkel He 111 flying in the opposite direction. Both sections attacked it with front guns and it was seen to crash. At 1810 a second Heinkel He 111 was seen and attacked by individual aircraft, the flights having become split up during the first attack. This aircraft was also hit, jettisoned its bombs and dived away from the fighters. An RAF officer on the ice at Lesjaskogvann confirmed seeing the both Heinkels crash. At 1900 Lucy led his aircraft over Åndalsnes to show troops on the ground that, at last, they had fighter cover and all six aircraft landed on safely by 2030. The risks involved in operating these aircraft up to 200 miles from the carriers were shown

Hangars burning at Vaernes airfield on 25 April 1940 photographed by the observer in an 820 NAS Swordfish. (*Author's collection*)

when Lucy's aircraft 'F' was found to have been hit five times by return fire from the bombers but fortunately not seriously. Admiralty signal 1530/24 ordered *Glorious* to fly off the Gladiators to Lesjaskogvann at 1700. They were ranged as soon as the last Skua had left the deck and flown off in two groups, each led by a Skua; both arrived safely. By the time 803 NAS was recovered there was little daylight left and it was decided to postpone offensive sorties against Trondheim until the next day, a decision reinforced by Admiralty signal 1947/24 received at 2300, which ordered that even if the Gladiators were able to operate on 25 April the carriers were to maintain CAPs over Namsos and attack objectives near Trondheim.

On 25 April the first range on *Ark Royal* comprised eight Swordfish from 810 NAS led by Captain N R M Skene RM flown off at 0300. It was followed by a second range of six Swordfish from 820 NAS led by Captain A C Newsom RM, all armed with four 250lb SAP bombs and eight 20lb HE bombs. The first attack was to be by 810 NAS on the frozen lake Jonsvatnet. One suffered an engine failure after take-off and ditched but the remaining seven found the lake empty. Once more the intelligence on which the strike briefing had been based was found to be stale and Skene led his aircraft to the alternate target, Vaernes airfield. A column of black smoke was seen rising from it at 0520, coming from a hangar destroyed by 820 NAS' attack. Newsom's pilots carried out a dive-bombing attack from 5,000ft and hit aircraft and installations together with a hangar next to the one destroyed by 820 NAS. Two aircraft failed to find *Ark Royal* on their return and ditched, the crew of one being rescued by the destroyer *Maori*. The other crew, Lieutenant A A Pardoe RN and Petty Officer L M Lloyd RN, both of 810 NAS, were killed. Vaernes had been 820 NAS' primary target and it was approached from the north-west across the eastern end of Aasen Fjord. Pilots attacked targets in pre-briefed strips across the airfield to avoid confliction, flying from west to east with thirty seconds between sub-flights. Direct hits were made on the westernmost hangars and on both paved runways and huts at the northern side of the airfield. Newson's aircraft suffered an engine failure and ditched before it landed on but he and his crew were picked up unharmed by a destroyer and the remainder were recovered safely.

Five 803 NAS Skuas led by Lucy were launched from *Glorious* at 0315, all armed with one 250lb and eight 20lb bombs and briefed to attack seaplanes reported to be moored in Trondheim harbour. After arriving at 0440 they dive-bombed nine twin-engined floatplanes moored in the south-west corner of Trondheim Roads. This time the intelligence was not stale and once down at low level they strafed the seaplanes with front guns before re-forming. As they headed towards the coast, Lieutenant Fraser-

Harris had to make a forced landing in the shallow, partially frozen, water of Sujorn Fjord near a village. He and his TAG were seen to climb out of the aircraft uninjured. The remainder were back on board *Glorious* by 0715. Three more Skuas of 803 NAS led by Sub Lieutenant (A) G W Brokensha RN were flown off at 0415 with the same bomb load, briefed to search fjords south of Trondheim for enemy warships. If none were found they were to attack any shipping found in the harbour itself. Two oilers were seen at pipeline terminals at Thamshavn, near the southern end of Orkedale Fjord, but they flew on hoping to find warships. When none were found they returned to the oilers, dive-bombed them and set them on fire at 0700 before joining up with a group of five Skuas and four Swordfish from *Ark Royal* for mutual protection. They landed on from 0735.

He 115 floatplanes in Trondheim photographed by Lieutenant Hanson shortly before he and Lieutenant Lucy dived to strafe them on 25 April 1940. (*Author's collection*)

Ark Royal had flown off nine Skuas of 801 and 800 NAS led by Lieutenant Commander H P Bramwell RN, the CO of 801 NAS, at 0420. They were armed with the standard mix of 250lb and 20lb bombs in addition to their front guns and briefed to use the larger bombs on shipping and small ones on floatplanes. This strike encountered heavy snow showers and their approach was made over a thin layer of broken cloud in line astern ready to attack as soon as a target was seen. No warships were found and so Bramwell attacked two large merchant vessels at anchor with a classic dive-bombing attack in which bombs were seen to straddle their targets. One direct hit, probably from a light bomb, was seen on the stern of one vessel and both were then strafed. Two aircraft searched further afield and found a Junkers Ju 88 and a damaged Heinkel He 111 on a frozen lake; both were strafed and the Ju 88 seen to be hit.

Once all the strike aircraft had departed the force, three 800 NAS Skuas were launched at 0455 for CAP over Namsos. They were directed by the radar-equipped cruiser *Calcutta* on to a Heinkel He 115 twin-engined floatplane, which was attacked and damaged. *Ark Royal* launched a further three Skuas of 800 NAS led by Partridge to replace them at 0610.

They found no enemy aircraft and after their recovery the task force moved away from the coast and Admiral Wells signalled the C-in-C that DX had been completed and that his task force was returning to Scapa Flow due to the shortage of fuel in the screening destroyers. Admiral Forbes replied immediately that DX was not over and that replacement destroyers would be provided. The Allied intervention in central Norway lacked overall cohesion and the failure to keep Wells informed about what was required from him was an example. There was also insufficient information coming from the military command ashore for the fleet to gain a full picture of what was required from it. The serviceability, or otherwise, of the Gladiators at Lesjaskogvann was unknown but it now appeared that they had made little difference as far as the Army in contact with the enemy was concerned. They had no means of carrying out controlled interceptions, no practical command and control facilities and, probably, no very clear idea of how they could contribute to the situation on the ground from their temporary accommodation on a frozen lake.

Urgent calls for air support were received overnight from the expeditionary force headquarters in Åndalsnes. Since there were too few Skuas to cover Namsos as well, the carriers began to operate closer to Åndalsnes, a decision subsequently endorsed by Admiral Forbes. No strikes were planned but *Ark Royal* and *Glorious* flew off CAP Skuas at two-hourly intervals throughout the day, while Sea Gladiators from *Glorious* flew CAP over the fleet. The first Åndalsnes CAP launched at 1000 comprised six Skuas of 801 NAS led by Bramwell. The radar-equipped cruiser *Curacoa* was stationed close inshore to provide both fighter direction and anti-aircraft gunfire. At 1145 three Heinkel He 111 bombers were seen closing on Åndalsnes and CAP Skuas attacked them. Bramwell saw his front guns hit the starboard engine of one enemy bomber, which caught fire, and his wing man scored hits on the port engine. It was seen to crash into a snow drift. A second Heinkel was last seen losing height with smoke and oil pouring from it and the third fled. None of the Skuas were damaged and all landed on by 1330. A further CAP was flown by three Skuas of 803 NAS from *Glorious* led by Lucy with Hanson as his observer. They arrived over Aalesund at 1231 and at 1308 a formation of Heinkel He 111s was seen at 12,000ft, slightly above them. Lieutenant Filmer broke away to carry out an individual attack, after which he was seen to be diving away leaving a trail of smoke. Lucy, with Lieutenant Christian as his wing man, positioned himself on the bombers' starboard beam and engaged them but they turned south-east and dived away after a few rounds had been fired at them. One was seen to drop out of formation before they disappeared from sight at 1335. Filmer's Skua came down near Aalesund; he was subsequently rescued but his TAG, Petty Officer Baldwin, had been killed by return fire from the bombers. By 1350 Lucy's depleted section was over Åndalsnes at 12,500ft when they saw a Dornier Do 17 flying west. As they turned to intercept, a Heinkel He 111 was seen several thousand feet below moving in to attack a ship. This was a better target and Lucy dived on to its port quarter followed by his wing man and both opened fire at short range. Lucy carried out a second firing pass and saw the Heinkel crash into the fjord at 1412. Both Skuas had fired out their ammunition and they returned to *Glorious*, landing on at 1540. This was Lucy's fourth 'kill' but after his debrief he learnt from his air mechanics that his aircraft had been hit six times and one bullet had damaged the hydraulic system, a second had penetrated the front engine casing and a third had punctured the port main-wheel tyre. Taken with the fact that 7Q had been shot down by return fire, this was cause for concern but it failed to deter Lucy and his contemporaries from close-range attacks to gain the best chance of a kill.

The next CAP by three 800 NAS Skuas from *Ark Royal* led by Partridge was flown off at 1410 and saw two Heinkel He 111s over Åndalsnes, one level with them and another lower. Partridge went for the lower one and fired out all his ammunition to no visible effect. Sub Lieutenant B H Hurle-Hobbs RN engaged the higher aircraft and also failed to score hits. The third Skua flown by Petty Officer J Hadley RN attacked the lower Heinkel but was seen to break away violently and lose height. His observer, Petty Officer W Crawford RN, informed Partridge that his pilot had been wounded in the face but had elected to re-join the leader rather than force-land. Having fired out their ammunition, the three aircraft returned to *Ark Royal* and landed on from 1615. Hadley's windscreen had been smashed by return fire and he had been wounded by the splintered glass.

A further CAP of three Skuas from 803 NAS led by Sub Lieutenant Brokensha established an orbit over Åndalsnes from 1718. It had not been due to launch until 1830 but urgent signals were relayed by the sloop *Flamingo* from the military commander ashore, stating that if incessant Luftwaffe attacks could not be halted the position of his troops would be untenable. A double CAP of six Skuas was, therefore, ranged with aircraft from both 800 and 801 NAS and flown off at 1700 led by Lieutenant Finch-Noyes. No enemy aircraft were encountered until 1905, when a single Heinkel He 115 floatplane was seen flying south along the coast at 4,000ft. Three Skuas attacked it in turn and saw its rear gunner cease firing; fuel poured from the port float after their bullets hit. Long bursts were fired at the engines, which were seen to hit, but the Skua's lack of a 'killing' weapon was never more emphatically demonstrated as the damaged enemy aircraft was last seen heading for

Trondheim. As the carrier task force moved to the north-west for the night, reports came in that showed how grave the situation ashore had become. The Gladiators had been wiped out and the Admiralty ordered VAA to continue flying CAPs over Åndalsnes on 27 April. Admiral Forbes signalled that the Army hoped to construct new airfields for RAF fighters but *Ark Royal* was to maintain CAP over the expeditionary force while *Glorious*, which had less endurance, returned to Scapa Flow after another day's flying to refuel. Again, there was a clear lack of cohesion between the Admiralty War Room and the C-in-C Home Fleet. Admiral Wells decided to concentrate his remaining Skua assets and 803 NAS was instructed to re-embark in *Ark Royal* at the first opportunity on 27 April. The Royal Navy's small air arm was now recognised as the only means of providing fighter cover for an expeditionary force on foreign soil faced by a tactical air force designed and equipped to support its own military operations. Inadequately equipped and without the personnel reserves the Air Ministry had always argued that it would never need, the Fleet Air Arm now had no choice but to fight on doing the best it could. Three Skuas of 801 NAS were launched at 0800 on 27 April led by Lieutenant R L Strange RN to CAP over Åndalsnes. His wing man, Sub Lieutenant P E Marsh RN, saw two Heinkel He 111s in a valley below them and Strange ordered him to attack while the others positioned themselves for a quarter attack. Marsh saw his bullets hit and the enemy aircraft crashed into a wood. The other Heinkel took violent evasive action and got away despite having being hit.

At 0930 *Ark Royal* lookouts spotted a shadowing aircraft low on the horizon and a radar report from *Curlew* confirmed the presence of enemy aircraft. Three Sea Gladiators of blue section 804 NAS led by Lieutenant R M Smeeton RN were flown off *Glorious* to intercept them, quickly joined by an aircraft of 802 NAS that had been on CAP. They identified the shadower as a Heinkel He 111, which dived to sea level at full throttle but was attacked in turn by all four Sea Gladiators. Only Sub Lieutenant (A) R R Lamb RN got into a position close enough to see his bullets hit from 350yd astern of the enemy. After a long burst the bomber pulled up and then dived back to sea level, trailing brown smoke from the starboard engine. After another long burst, smoke came from the port engine but there was no reduction in its speed. Further bursts caused the aircraft to fly erratically and it actually glanced off the surface of the sea but managed to fly on. Norwegian intelligence subsequently confirmed that it crashed on landing at Stavanger. A second Åndalsnes CAP was flown off at 1035 by the only four serviceable Skuas left in *Glorious'* 803 NAS, led by Lucy. They split into blue and yellow sections at 1125 but Lucy's Blue saw no enemy aircraft and returned to the fleet at 1430. On arrival

An oil tanker left on fire by Sub Lieutenant Brokensha of 803 NAS' dive-bombing attack. (*Author's collection*)

overhead they were ordered to land on *Ark Royal*. Yellow section led by Sub Lieutenant Brokensha attacked a Heinkel He 111 that was seen bombing Åndalsnes at 1240. It jettisoned its remaining bombs and evaded to the south-east. Diving on to it, Brokensha saw his bullets strike the fuselage and starboard engine and his wing man, Lieutenant L A Harris RM, hit the port engine and they saw the aircraft crash. They too were instructed to land on *Ark Royal* so that all serviceable Skuas were now concentrated in her.

Three Skuas of 800 NAS led by Partridge were flown off 1230 and almost at once they saw a Heinkel He 111 bombing a British warship near Bud. Sub Lieutenant Hurle-Hobbs carried out a full-deflection beam attack while Partridge and Taylour gained height. The bomber turned away to the south but the three Skuas gave chase and continued to attack and saw it crash. Partridge's engine was hit by return fire and he was forced to carry out a dead-stick landing on a frozen lake not far from where the Heinkel came down. Both he and Bostock, his observer, were unhurt and the remaining two Skuas landed on safely at 1540. At 1515 *Ark Royal* launched five Skuas from 800 and 801 NAS with flights led by Finch-Noyes and Bramwell. Near Åndalsnes they saw a convoy of British ships being attacked by two Junkers Ju 88s. The Skuas followed the bombers into their dives, with Bramwell and his wing man concentrating their fire on one of them. They saw both its engines on fire but broke off when a number of Heinkel He 111s were seen and all five Skuas climbed to gain attacking positions. Individual combats followed in which the Skua crews used both their front and rear guns. None of these bombers got close enough to attack the convoy but bursts of anti-aircraft fire from it indicated more Heinkels approaching from the north, which were attacked by the Skuas in a series of combats that broke up the enemy formations. After pilots had fired out their front gun ammunition they made dummy attacks on the bombers to keep them away from the convoy for a further fifteen minutes. Four enemy bombers were confirmed shot down out of thirty engaged and this had been the Fleet Air Arm's largest and most successful air combat to date. The Skuas all landed on safely by 1820. A German airman rescued from the water by a destroyer claimed that five Heinkels had actually been shot down.

A further CAP of three Skuas from 801 NAS led by Lieutenant (A) W C A Church RN was flown off at 1645 and saw a single Heinkel He 111 over Åndalsnes at 1735. It dived away and the Skuas were drawn into a stern chase. Church's aircraft was hit by return fire and seen to burst into flames; within seconds the engine detached from the fuselage and the aircraft was seen to crash vertically into the sea, killing Church and his observer Sub lieutenant (A) D G Willis RN. The remaining two Skuas flown by Lieutenant R C Hay RM with Petty Officer H Kimber RN as his wing man, engaged the bomber and shot it down, after which they returned to the spot where Church had come down but saw nothing on the sea surface but a partially inflated life raft and a petrol slick. They landed on at 1855 and at 1930 VAA ordered the task force to move to a position from which strikes could be launched against Trondheim at dawn on the following day, Sunday, 28 April. *Ark Royal* ranged a strike force of Swordfish, six each from 820 and 810 NAS, the former led by Lieutenant R N Everett RN and the latter by Captain N R M Skene RM. All were armed with four 250lb GP bombs, six 20lb HE bombs and two 25lb incendiary bombs, and they began to take-off at 0305. A second strike was ranged comprising seven Skuas of 800 and 801 NAS, each armed with a single 250lb SAP bomb and eight 20lb HE bombs. The six Swordfish of 820 NAS approached Vaernes airfield from the north in the grey light before sunrise, opposed by intense short-range anti-aircraft fire. Bombs were dropped from diving attacks on barrack blocks north of the airfield at 0532 and hits were observed with every type of bomb. Several Swordfish were damaged but all six landed on by 0615. The other swordfish of 810 NAS made a dive-bombing attack from 0443 on the same barracks but Lieutenant D F Godfrey-Fausset RN broke away to attack a hangar, which he destroyed. Three aircraft received minor damage but all six landed on safely by 0610. The Skuas were briefed to attack shipping in Trondheim with warships as first priority, using lighter bombs against floatplanes. They achieved tactical surprise over the harbour with no anti-aircraft fire until the first two Skuas had completed their attacks. No warships were seen so they attacked four merchant ships and eighteen floatplanes found moored in the harbour. At least one direct hit was observed on the ships and others on the floatplanes together with near misses that would have caused damage. Six Skuas returned to *Ark Royal* and landed on safely by 0635 but one, flown by Midshipman (A) L H Gallagher RN with NA G W Halifax as his TAG, became detached, failed to find the carrier and returned to land on a frozen lake near Åndalsnes. Once safely down, Gallagher found a damaged RAF Gladiator and used his initiative to transfer avgas from it to fill his own tanks. He obtained a Norwegian school atlas, took off and used it to navigate across 350 miles of sea to Sullom Voe in the Shetland Islands, where he refuelled again and flew on to RNAS Hatston.

Throughout the forenoon of 28 April, VAA received urgent calls for air support from Molde, Åndalsnes and convoy TM1. Three Skuas of 803 NAS' blue section led by Lucy were flown off launched from standby at 1105 and coasted in over Bud. At 1218 they saw a Junkers Ju 88 below them bombing a British escort vessel and Lucy dived on it but it saw him and made off at high speed. He tried a beam attack but the bomber was too fast and after a short, inconclusive, burst of fire he broke off. Sub Lieutenant Brokensha failed to get into a firing position but Petty Officer A G Johnson managed to carry out a quarter attack, which slid into a stern chase because of the enemy's speed, but he managed to hold a good, if brief, firing position astern of it at 270 knots and fired a series of short bursts, which he saw hit. The Junkers jettisoned its bombs and dived away but crashed on the west side of an island.

At 1245 three high Heinkel He 111s were seen but Johnson, who was detached, had sufficient momentum to pull up and carry out an urgent attack, firing out his front-gun ammunition at one of the bombers, which jettisoned its bombs and escaped to the south. Lucy, with Brokensha as his wing man, climbed for position and carried out successive attacks from astern on one of the others. Its starboard engine stopped, the undercarriage came down and it was seen to tip over and crash into a valley. At 1310 Lucy and Brokensha returned to Åndalsnes, where they saw a Junkers Ju 88 but its high speed prevented them from engaging it. At 1320 Lucy saw eight Heinkel He 111s level with him and he attacked the starboard-wing aircraft. Successive attacks were made until it caught fire and crashed into the sea. While Hanson sent a warning message to the fleet at 1345, Lucy got into a position above and slightly ahead of the

The German supply ship *Bahrenfels* sunk on the southern side of Skoltegrund Mole on 12 April after a dive-bombing attack by 800, 801 and 803 NAS with 500lb bombs. The warehouse on the mole is burning. (*Author's collection*)

enemy formation leader. He carried out a head-on attack, only ceasing fire to break away at the very last moment and pull up into an 'Immelmann' manoeuvre to maintain his height advantage. The effect was dramatic as the enemy formation broke up and jettisoned their bombs. Brokensha picked an individual target and fired out his front-gun ammunition into it, watching it disappear into cloud with its starboard engine stopped. Lucy attacked the only Heinkel that was still heading towards the fleet and saw it turn away and jettison its bombs before flying into cloud as he ran out of ammunition. Johnson, still over Molde, saw the retreating Heinkels coming at him from seaward and, with no front-gun ammunition left, positioned his aircraft so that Leading Airman F Coston RN could engage one with his rear gun. They both saw a long burst of fire hit and set the port engine on fire; the bomber dived steeply into cloud but was not seen to crash. All three Skuas returned safely to *Ark Royal*. Lucy's two kills were his fifth and sixth and both were credited to him by the Admiralty but the achievement was not announced to the public. He was not only the first pilot in the Royal Navy to achieve the five kills that would have brought him 'ace' status in the USN during the Second World War, he was the first pilot from anywhere in the British Commonwealth to do so. He was the outstanding pilot of the early war period and his achievements deserve far greater recognition than historians have given him.

The Luftwaffe grew in strength daily and now knew where the carrier task force was operating. At about midday on 28 April, *Curlew* gained radar contact on enemy aircraft closing from the south-east. Minutes later three Junkers Ju 88s were seen but only two pressed home their attack through the anti-aircraft barrage, selecting *Ark Royal* as a target. No ships were damaged but in *Glorious'* absence *Ark Royal*'s Rocs were being used for fleet air defence. Three were scrambled from deck alert at 1215 but they only found an He 115 floatplane that had been guiding the bombers towards the fleet. They drove it off but lacked the speed to chase it and they landed on to refuel and rearm at 1330. The same aircrew and aircraft were launched again at 1430 against another shadower, this time a Heinkel He 111. Again they drove it off but none got the turret gunner into a position from which he could open fire and it escaped.

By noon VAA was concerned at the scale of operations his fighter pilots were committed to and he signalled Admiral Forbes to say that after five successive days in action they were showing signs of strain. Operation DX had proved a greater commitment than envisaged and he proposed withdrawing *Ark Royal* to the north-west for two days' rest before recommencing operations that might have no end in sight. Forbes approved and after the last aircraft were landed on at 1615 the task force headed away from the bomber threat. A further signal from the C-in-C ordered *Ark Royal* to recover replacement fighters from Hatston on 30 April. A later amendment ordered *Glorious* to embark the replacement fighters but weather delayed the process. The situation became even more complicated when military commanders ashore signalled that their position was no longer tenable and that plans to evacuate Åndalsnes and Namsos were being hastily prepared. At first these required the evacuation of both to begin on the night of 1/2 May but the situation at Åndalsnes became so critical that the withdrawal there was advanced to the night of 30 April. Fighter cover during the daylight hours of 1 May was, therefore, vital and it could only be provided by the carriers.

At 0400 on 1 May 1940 three Skuas of 801 NAS were flown off *Ark Royal* to cover Åndalsnes and the evacuation shipping. No enemy aircraft were seen but at 0445 repeated calls for help from

Oil tanks at Florvag near Bergen on fire after an attack by Skuas. (*Author's collection*)

the Army led to three more Skuas of 801 NAS being flown off to CAP over the town. They, too, failed to find any enemy aircraft but at 0700 *Valiant*'s radar detected shadowers and three Rocs were flown off to intercept them. One chased an enemy aircraft, thought to be a Junkers Ju 87 dive bomber, but failed to catch it and the others saw nothing. At 0751 a Junkers Ju 88 dived out of the sun and dropped a bomb that missed *Ark Royal*'s port quarter; it was not seen until the last moment and not engaged by anti-aircraft fire until it was flying away. At 0755 another Junkers Ju 88 carried out a dive-bombing attack on *Ark Royal* and dropped a bomb, which fell only 50yd astern and there were further unsuccessful attacks.

Glorious re-joined the force at 1005 with the eighteen Sea Gladiators of 802 and 804 NAS embarked plus twelve Swordfish, three Skuas and a Roc as replacements for combat losses. An RAF signal to VAA was relayed by C-in-C Rosyth, the link between the RN and RAF communication systems, to confirm that RAF long-range Blenheim fighters would CAP over Åndalsnes from 0600 on 2 May. Since the first two Skua CAPs had seen no enemy air activity, VAA moved his task force north to cover for the evacuation of Namsos, due to start that night, which was beyond the range of RAF Blenheims operating from the UK. Repeated attacks were made on the carriers by enemy bombers and the Sea Gladiator CAP was doubled. Anti-submarine patrols by Swordfish were maintained, the requirement for turns into the light southerly wind at high speed to launch and recover them slowing task force progress to the north. Between 1100 and 2130 *Glorious* maintained six Sea Gladiators on CAP with three more on deck alert. Yellow section of 804 NAS led by the CO Lieutenant Commander J C Cockburn RN was airborne between 1215 and 1415 but saw no enemy activity. Blue section led by Lieutenant Smeeton intercepted and damaged one Heinkel He 111 at 1520 and drove off a second at 1600. From 1523 to 1610 high-level attacks were carried out on the fleet by enemy bombers that kept the sun behind them and were not seen until they dropped their bombs, all of which missed.

At 1630 804 NAS red section took off led by Lieutenant R M P Carver RN with Lieutenant D C E F Gibson and Sub Lieutenant M F Fell RN as his wing men. A series of chases under radar direction ended at 1800 when they intercepted and damaged a Heinkel He 115 shadower. At 1800 blue section from 802 NAS led by Lieutenant J P Marmont RN was scrambled from deck alert and 804 NAS' yellow section led by Cockburn were launched early at 1815 to give nine fighters airborne to oppose hostile aircraft seen on radar. Cockburn's section saw six Ju 87s 3 miles away on an opposite course and attacked them, firing in short bursts. Cockburn then ordered his section to break off as he assumed that the fleet's anti-aircraft guns would engage the enemy. They failed to do so because the single-engined Junkers were misidentified as friendly but one was shot down by Marmont and a melee ensued during which ships' gunners fired at every aircraft in sight including the Sea Gladiators but no ships were hit. In addition to their single 'kill' the fighters broke up bomber formations but radar direction failed because *Valiant* passed a stream of bearings and distances, many of which were actually the CAP fighters, and the embryo fighter direction organisation was clearly overwhelmed.

This had been the most testing day for the fleet's air defence organisation and lessons were learned that would have application throughout the war. Cockburn believed that operations on 1 May had brought out three important points: the Sea Gladiator lacked the necessary performance, and naval fighters needed heavier armament and much greater endurance than the Sea Gladiator to prevent the carrier from having to turn constantly into wind to maintain CAP stations. The adoption of any USN fighter would resolve these shortcomings. The scale of enemy air attacks concerned VAA and he signalled that the orders he had been given were no longer capable of fulfilment. Admiral Forbes agreed and directed the carrier task force to return to Scapa Flow and redistribute its aircraft. Rocs had proved virtually useless and all were landed for second-line duties ashore. Once again Skua squadrons were to be concentrated in *Ark Royal*.

Admiral Wells listed twenty enemy aircraft destroyed by the fleet's fighters during DX but post-war analysis of German records revealed that of the five Heinkel He 111s claimed on 27 April only one had in fact been shot down and the other four probably damaged. Whatever the actual number, the enemy bomber formations had been broken up and no ships had been hit or damaged. Gunfire had only shot down one enemy aircraft. *Ark Royal* had sailed with twenty-one Swordfish and eighteen Skuas, with four of each being lost, and *Glorious* had lost five Skuas. By later standards these losses were not heavy but in April/May 1940 they represented a significant percentage of the RN's small number of aircraft and they were a new experience. The Fleet Air Arm had committed all its five fighter squadrons to DX and attempted to cover the expeditionary force for days on end within range of enemy bombers and in waters threatened by U-boats. Under these new circumstances the success achieved by the Skua squadrons was remarkable. At first they achieved few 'kills' but as pilots gained experience they learnt to use high diving speed to catch the bombers and their first pass usually inflicted sufficient damage to slow them to speeds within the Skua's reach. The first sure sign that the fighter pilots were gaining the ascendancy came on 27 April when several bombers were shot down and all others driven off. It was ironic that the Army commander ashore chose this day to write that 'our

Frequent unconfirmed reports by his pilots that they had successfully attacked an aircraft carrier led the commanding officer of Kampfgeschwader 100 to place this club with nails imbedded in it and the accompanying warning outside his office at Trondheim. Translated into English it reads 'whoever now again sights and reports an aircraft carrier will be beaten to death with this if he has not 1. photographed her 2. sunk her. Signed Commander KG 100'. (*Author's collection*)

own air was conspicuous by its absence'. RN aircraft had undoubtedly reduced the weight of bombs dropped on the ill-fated expeditionary force in central Norway and the Germans gained a respect for aircraft carriers that was to influence all their future naval operations.

The end of the Norwegian Campaign

German forces in Narvik had been cut off from sea-borne support by the RN but Luftwaffe Junkers Ju 52 transport aircraft provided sufficient logistic support for them to hold out against encircling Allied forces. Three carriers took part in operations off Narvik, two of which ferried the RAF fighters, which eventually managed to operate with some success from Bardufoss.[12] On 4 May *Ark Royal* sailed with 800, 801 and 803 NAS' Skuas forming part of her air group and she operated aircraft every day until 19 May, when she refuelled at Tromsø. On 3 May *Glorious* embarked eighteen RAF Hurricanes and the Walrus of 701 NAS from Greenock; both types being craned on board from lighters. She sailed on 14 May in company with *Furious*, which ferried RAF Gladiators to Norway and arrived off Narvik on 18 May. There 701 NAS was disembarked to Harstad. Bad weather prevented the Hurricanes from being flown off and they were still on board when *Glorious* had to return to Scapa Flow to refuel on 22 May. On 24 May she returned to Norway and flew off the Hurricanes, initially to Skaanland, on 26 May. *Ark Royal*'s Skuas escorted them and gave them cover until they were able to move to Bardufoss. *Glorious* lacked the fuel to carry out sustained operations this far north and so on 30 May she returned to Scapa Flow. Once the RAF fighters were declared operational, *Ark Royal* also returned to Scapa Flow but returned in early June when the Allied governments decided to evacuate Narvik, only days after its capture, because of the deteriorating situation in France and Belgium. *Ark Royal*'s Skuas shot down six enemy aircraft during this period, damaged a further eight and drove off many more. Five Skuas were shot down but only one crew was killed in action, Lieutenants Lucy and Hanson.

On 14 May *Ark Royal* provided fighter cover for the forces advancing on Narvik and the second CAP of the day comprised three Skuas of 803 NAS led by Lucy with Hanson, as usual, in his rear seat. His wing men were Lieutenant T E Gray RN with Leading Airman A Clayton and Petty Officer A H Glover RN with Naval Airman S G Wright. They orbited Narvik for an hour until a report was received that the battleship

Glorious turning into wind to fly off RAF Hurricanes to Skaanland on 26 May 1940, photographed from her plane guard destroyer. The Swordfish just visible at the front of the range was flown off to lead them ashore and provide navigational assistance. (*Author's collection*)

Resolution was being attacked by a single Heinkel He 111. Lucy led his section towards it, climbing to 17,000ft and after seeing the enemy aircraft they chased it to the south for about ten minutes without getting into a firing position and Petty Officer Glover became detached. A further report was received from *Resolution* that it was firing at another bomber but then things happened quickly. Five enemy aircraft were seen approaching from the east at 18,000ft. Lucy and Gray split and attacked the leading pair head-on to break up the formation, after which they turned to attack from astern. Lucy's attack had set one Heinkel's port engine on fire and he engaged the second pair as they dived; Gray saw him closing to almost point-blank range to ensure hits but then he swung away and the Skua appeared to flash only 50ft above the water. Gray then fired a 'good burst and observed port engine smoking in one machine' but then broke off his own attacks to search for his leader. He saw wreckage including a Skua tail unit and dinghy off Trangy Island. There was no sign of either Lucy or Hanson in the water but Gray flew across the fjord and communicated with the destroyer *Whirlwind* off Ransundet, which he then led back to the crash site where debris was still floating. *Whirlwind* recovered Lucy's body but found no sign of Hanson. As was normal, Bill Lucy was given a naval burial at sea some hours later and so both he and Hanson have no known grave but the sea. Lieutenant William Paulet Lucy DSO RN is commemorated on the Fleet Air Arm War Memorial at Lee-on-Solent, Hampshire, on Bay 1 Panel 2. Lieutenant Michael Charles Edward Hanson DSC RN is commemorated on the same panel.

Allied forces captured the town of Narvik on 28 May and advanced along the railway line that carried iron ore from Sweden during the winter. The ore quays, electric power supplies and the railway line were sabotaged and then preparations were made for withdrawal. Air cover for the expeditionary force was provided by the Hurricanes and Gladiators at Bardufoss but the C-in-C Northern Norway asked for the Home Fleet to cover the final stages of the withdrawal. Accordingly, *Ark Royal* and *Glorious* arrived off the Norwegian coast on 2 June. *Ark Royal* was to provide fighter cover but *Glorious*, with its more limited endurance, was tasked with recovering as many RAF fighters as possible and had only a small air group of its own. Rather than destroy their aircraft, the RAF pilots had asked to be allowed to attempt to land on *Glorious* and there was a general consensus that every available fighter would soon be needed in the UK. Whether this handful of fighters was worth risking a valuable aircraft carrier in dangerous waters without its full air group is a moot point and not one that should have been taken as lightly as it apparently was.

The six Walrus of 701 NAS operating from Harstad had conducted a spirited campaign, carrying out missions that even the type's greatest admirers would hardly have considered possible a month earlier. These included overland tactical reconnaissance, bombing, VIP transport and close air support. On 6 June they dive-bombed an enemy-held harbour and both dive-bombed and strafed German troops and their vehicles. The withdrawal from Narvik was better planned and executed that any other aspect of the ill-fated campaign. Store ships and troop transports arrived in Harstad on 2 June and were loaded with minimal interference from the enemy. They sailed on 7 June with 10,000 Allied troops embarked and considerably more equipment than the Army had expected to save. Some 15,000 troops had sailed before that in six large troopships on 4, 5 and 6 June, also without interference from the enemy, and on 7 June fighters from *Ark Royal* took on the air defence task as the RAF fighters flew out to *Glorious*. Ten Gladiators and seven Hurricanes were all that had survived at Bardufoss and they landed on successfully, demonstrating that landing modern high-performance monoplane fighters on an aircraft carrier was entirely practical. The last men of the expeditionary force were evacuated on 8 June and *Ark Royal* landed on five of the 701 NAS Walrus on 7 June before joining the convoy and reaching home waters safely.

On 7 June *Glorious* asked permission to leave the Narvik area with a screen of only two destroyers, fewer than on her previous transits of the North Sea, in order to return to the UK independently and this was granted by VAA. At the time, no troopships or store ships had been lost or damaged on their passages to and from Vestfjord and only one in central Norway but, unknown to the Home Fleet, a German task force

Hurricanes being flown off *Glorious* on 26 May 1940. (*Author's collection*)

comprising the battlecruisers *Scharnhorst* and *Gneisenau* with the heavy cruiser *Hipper* was at sea heading for northern Norway. Their movements went undetected by Coastal Command reconnaissance aircraft and no warning was given to either Admiral Forbes or Admiral Lord Cork and Orrery that they were at sea. Surprisingly, *Glorious* had no reconnaissance aircraft airborne and no strike force ranged ready for immediate launch when she was encountered by this enemy force at 1600 on 8 June. As soon as the German ships were seen, she turned away and increased speed while the destroyers *Ardent* and *Acasta* laid a smokescreen, but she had been caught completely unaware and vulnerable. By 1740 *Glorious* had been hit repeatedly, rolled to starboard and sank with the eventual loss of over 1,500 men. After his Board of Enquiry, the C-in-C Rosyth concluded that, '*Glorious* appears to have been caught unprepared for action and to have been unsuspecting of enemy forces in her vicinity and no evidence has been obtained as to why this state of affairs existed.' The full reasons probably died with her captain and will never be fully explained.

The Norwegian campaign ended with two attempts to attack *Scharnhorst* after she was damaged by a torpedo fired by *Acasta* on 8 June. She put into Trondheim for temporary repairs, where she was located by an RAF reconnaissance aircraft. A raid by Bomber Command on 11 June was ineffectual and the Admiralty ordered *Ark Royal* to carry out a dive-bombing attack on her with Skuas. A launch position 170nm from Trondheim was selected and the Admiralty and Coastal Command agreed that four Beaufort bombers would carry out a synchronised attack on the fighters based at Vaernes and six Blenheim long-range fighters would escort the Skuas. Difficulties were foreseen by NAD, including the almost continual daylight this far north in June and the long overland transit after crossing the coast, which would allow the enemy defences to be alerted. The synchronisation of different air striking forces controlled by different headquarters with land-based aircraft flying from distant bases and only the sketchiest idea of what was going on would be difficult, if not impossible, to achieve.

Fifteen Skuas from 800 and 803 NAS took part in the strike, led by Lieutenant Commander J Casson RN, who had replaced Lucy in command of 803 NAS. They were flown off shortly after midnight and carried out a standard dive-bombing attack with 500lb SAP bombs before heading back down the fjord towards the sea chased by enemy fighters. In his report on the attack VAA wrote that he believed that the task force had reached the flying off position undetected but that the decision to send only fifteen Skuas was based on the fact that only fifteen of the available pilots now had experience of dive-bombing and other Skuas had to be retained to maintain CAP over the task force. In the prevailing light wind, fifteen was also the maximum number that could be flown off in a single range fully loaded. The aircrew were briefed that Blenheims would give them fighter support during the attack and that the Beaufort attack on Vaernes would not take place earlier than 0200. At 0305 *Ark Royal* altered course into the light southerly wind but by 0345 only seven Skuas had returned. The last CAP Skua landed on at 0550, when course was altered to the west to return to Scapa Flow in accordance with the C-in-C's signal 0518/13.

It is difficult to judge whether the Beauforts' attack on Vaernes, actually carried out before the Skuas' arrival, served to distract attention from the dive bombers' approach or whether it alerted the enemy. Many enemy fighters were certainly over the anchorage when the Skuas arrived but this may have resulted from their being reported during their long passage from the coast. There was no doubt that the Skuas' attack had been pressed home courageously in the face of intense anti-aircraft fire and fighter opposition. With one exception, all the survivors escaped at low level. The exception was Sub Lieutenant Brokensha, who circled the area twice to see if he could help anyone. The Blenheim fighters failed to arrive until after the Skuas had left the coast and in his covering remarks on the attack, Admiral Forbes wrote that surprise had been unlikely since it was reasonable to assume that the Skuas were reported by coast watchers at least twenty minutes before they arrived over the target. From the eight Skuas that failed to return, ten aircrew became prisoners of war and six were killed in action. Those who became prisoners included both squadron commanding officers, Casson and Partridge. Those killed in action included Partridge's observer, Robin Bostock, Midshipman Gallagher, who had refuelled his Skua from a crashed Gladiator and been awarded a DSC and an MID, and Lieutenant Finch-Noyes, who had been awarded a DSC and two MIDs.

On 21 June 1940 *Scharnhorst* was reported to be at sea returning to Germany from Trondheim after completion of its temporary repairs, and on learning of this the Operations Officer at RNAS Hatston planned a daylight torpedo attack on her by six disembarked Swordfish of 821 and 823 NAS,[13] neither of which had recent torpedo-attack training. They succeeded in intercepting her after a flight of 240nm, in itself no mean achievement, and attacked in the face of heavy anti-aircraft fire, which shot down two of their number. Unfortunately their inexperience showed: they had not set up co-ordinated approaches from different directions and all their torpedoes missed. It had been the first ever attack of its kind by torpedo aircraft against a capital ship at sea and when the survivors turned for home, they were at their limiting radius of action. In his subsequent report, Admiral Bell-Davies described the attack as a gallant failure by an inadequate force.

Operation Paul

The attacks on *Scharnhorst* marked the end of the Norwegian campaign but another operation had been approved that, had it been carried out, could have significantly changed the course of the war. German imports of iron ore from Sweden in 1938 amounted to 22 million tons but the British blockade after September 1939 was estimated to have prevented 9 million tons from reaching Germany.[14] The ore was vital to the enemy war effort and as soon as Churchill became First Lord of the Admiralty he pressed the War Cabinet to sanction disruption of this traffic. In summer it was shipped across the Baltic from Lulea in Sweden to German ports but in winter the northern Baltic froze over and the ore was taken by rail to Narvik, from where it was shipped down the Norwegian coast to Germany. Churchill was frustrated to learn that enemy iron ore ships made most of the voyage through Norwegian territorial waters where international law protected them from interception and proposed laying minefields to force them out into the open sea where they would be intercepted. The War Cabinet did not agree and the French opposed the idea, fearing reprisals. The Winter War between the Soviet Union and Finland complicated matters but the British Cabinet eventually gave permission for a minefield to be laid off Norway on 3 April 1940. The Admiralty designated the project as Operation Wilfred and planned to declare three areas as mined; one in Vestfjord, another off Bud further south and a third off Stadlandet still further south. Mines were laid in Vestfjord by the destroyers *Esk*, *Impulsive*, *Icarus* and *Ivanhoe* on 8 April, the day before the German invasion of Norway, and the minelayer *Teviot Bank* laid mines off Stadlandet. No mines were laid off Bud. By then these minefields had only short-term value as the northern Baltic would soon be ice-free, allowing German ships to use the Baltic largely free from British interference. To counter this, Churchill proposed to 'bottle up Lulea' in order to prevent the bulk export of iron ore from Sweden to Germany.[15] The Admiralty designated this project as Operation Paul.

On 12 May the Chiefs of Staff discussed Paul's feasibility and instructed the Joint Planning Sub Committee, JPSC, to consider its strategic implications.[16] Lulea was beyond the range of any aircraft in Bomber Command and it was immediately clear that only carrier-borne aircraft would be capable of carrying out the task. On 14 May Churchill, Prime Minister since 10 May, ordered Paul to be put into effect within three weeks and the Naval Staff's Director of Plans, Captain C S Daniel RN, began detailed planning. Despite the deteriorating war situation in both France and Norway, Churchill kept up the momentum and he minuted to General Ismay, his Military Advisor, on 24 May that 'it is essential that the largest possible number of mines should be laid in the approaches to Lulea. Let a plan be prepared for laying mines by flights from aircraft carriers.'[17]

Admiral of the Fleet Sir Dudley Pound, 1SL, briefed the Chiefs of Staff on progress with Paul on 5 June. He said that sixty Swordfish had been fitted with long-range fuel tanks in the observers' cockpits, giving them a theoretical range of 600nm. Six aircraft thus fitted had flown from RNAS Hatston to lay a minefield off Stavanger, flying a total distance of 520nm, and it had been found that engine lubricating oil, not fuel, had been the limiting factor. Two aircraft with relatively old engines had suffered engine seizures after lubricating oil ran out and had been forced to ditch after five and six hours' flight respectively. Both crews were rescued and the remaining four had returned safely to Hatston. It was, therefore, concluded that the maximum radius of action from a carrier at which the aircraft could practically be tasked to lay their mines was 250 miles. For their aircraft to reach the approaches to Lulea, carriers would have to operate either close to the Lofoten Islands or near Bodø and Vestfjord. Both locations would be liable to attack once the Luftwaffe established aircraft at Bodø, Skaanland and Bardufoss. Pound also stated that he expected losses to be heavy and said that he was prepared for fifteen of the sixty strike aircraft being prepared to be lost together with their aircrew. The Foreign Office minuted that there might be unfavourable reactions in the United States but, surprisingly, offered little comment about the probable effect on public opinion in Sweden. Overall, the feeling was that there would be significant losses for little overall gain and that Paul would incur adverse political reactions from Finland, Sweden, the Soviet Union and the USA. On 6 June Pound agreed at a Chiefs of Staff meeting that the JPSC should be instructed, in consultation with the Foreign Office, to examine alternative plans 'having particular regard to the effect that the operation might have from the political point of view'.[18] He did not mention that a day earlier he had signalled C-in-C Home Fleet and VAA instructing them to prepare to carry out Paul.

The original plan devised by Captain Daniel and his team went into considerable detail and included charts of the Gulf of Bothnia where the mines were to be laid and both the Barents and Greenland Seas where the carriers might launch their aircraft. The proposed wording, in Swedish, of warning pamphlets was also included. Descriptions of the approaches to Lulea from the Admiralty pilot were detailed and the scale of potential German air intervention was estimated. The aim was simply expressed as being 'to stop the export of iron ore from Lulea by means of attack from carrier-borne aircraft'. It was anticipated that a force of three carriers would carry out the operation with cover and escort being provided by forces arranged by the C-in-C Home Fleet. The three carriers selected were *Ark Royal* with thirty Swordfish and eighteen Skuas embarked; *Glorious* with twenty-four Swordfish and twelve Skuas embarked and *Furious* with twenty-four Swordfish and nine Sea Gladiators. On the day the operation was to be carried out, the flying programme would comprise an initial launch of six Swordfish and six fighters for a surface search in the vicinity of the task force and CAP. An hour later thirty-six Swordfish were to be flown off in the first wave, within which thirty were to be armed with mines and six with pamphlets. The latter were also to photograph the minelayers as they made their drop. An hour later a further thirty-six swordfish were to be flown off, of which twenty-four were to be armed with mines and twelve with torpedoes to attack ships under way near the port. Fighters were to be launched at regular intervals to fly CAP over the task force and to escort Swordfish. Zero hour for the first launch was to be at 0030 if the task force was operating from the area of Varangerfjord and 0100 if operating from the area of And Fjord.

Mines were not to be dropped in less than 25ft of water and preferably in more than 30ft. Nor must they be dropped in depths greater than 12 fathoms, using charts to check the briefed drop positions. Mines must be dropped from the lowest practicable height, not more than 250ft, and at an airspeed less than 100 knots. They should be laid more than 300ft apart and totals of fifty-four, thirty-three or eighteen should be laid depending on whether three, two or one carrier took part. Pamphlets were written in Swedish that translated as: 'Lulea Harbour is mined. Abandon your ship immediately as it will shortly be torpedoed. Do not remain on the quays.' They were prepared in bundles of 750 double sheets or 1,500 single sheets that each weighed 5lb. The aircraft flare tube was generally to be used to drop them but 'it seems that they can be thrown over the side with a medicine ball action'. Tables gave the predicted endurance of the Swordfish and Skua. The former had an internal fuel capacity of 167 gallons with 65 gallons in the auxiliary tank, giving a total of 232 gallons. Usage was calculated at an average of 30 gallons per hour at 92.5 knots, giving an endurance of seven hours forty minutes and a range of 630nm. The Skua had internal tankage of 166 gallons and used 27 gallons per hour at 120 knots, giving an endurance of six hours five minutes and a range of 640nm. Since they could not fly at the Swordfish's low speed, however, the Skuas could not stay close to the strike aircraft throughout their sortie despite their similar range.

Signal logs were regarded as temporary documents at the time and few have survived but the preparatory signal is in a file in the Admiralty Library. It was handwritten without (i) as the first paragraph heading and timed at 1655 on 5 June addressed to C-in-C HF, copy to VAA. It said:

(i) Preparations are to be put in hand for carrying out Operation Paul as soon as possible on completion of Operation Alphabet [the withdrawal from Narvik] using *Ark Royal* and *Furious*.
(ii) Following Squadrons will be available – 800, 803, 810, 820, all already embarked; 821 at Hatston and 822, 816 and 818 at present operating under Coastal Command [RAF].
(iii) Mines and aircraft will be embarked at Clyde except for 821 squadron which will be embarked from Hatston.
(iv) Plan is to be modified as follows (a) torpedoes are NOT repetition NOT to be used. (b) Fighters will NOT repetition NOT accompany TSRs [Swordfish] (c) Pamphlets NOT repetition NOT to be dropped. (d) Further signal follows regarding 812, 816 and 818 squadrons.[19]

The modifications mentioned reveal that both recipients had already been made aware of the original plan by signal. Torpedo attack on loaded ore ships that had left Lulea had been considered but would not have been possible because even by early June the ice was not yet clear from the port's approaches.

Events following the evacuations of expeditionary forces from Dunkirk and Narvik moved quickly but the progress of deliberations over Paul can be traced through surviving signals in the Admiralty Library and a War Office file in the National Archive at Kew.[20] These reveal that the C-in-C Home Fleet was told that the greatest importance was attached to Paul but, in view of the risk to aircraft carriers operating close to the Norwegian coast, it was now to be carried out by just eighteen aircraft operating from a single carrier, *Ark Royal*, rather than the three in the original plan. Each Swordfish was to carry a single Type A Mark 1 mine and they were to be flown off near Vestfjord, after which the carrier was to retire to the west at high speed. After laying their mines, the Swordfish were to return to the area off Norway, where they were to ditch alongside destroyers left in the area to rescue the crews. However, Pound subsequently signalled that 'if VAA considers that *Ark Royal* can maintain her position for aircraft to land on he should amend these orders'. An entry in the Naval War Diary in the Admiralty Library made reference to Admiralty signal 0043/8 June, which stressed that recent experience in Norway did not support the suggestion that the carrier should remain close to the coast. It also mentioned that the value of the minefield would 'largely depend on whether the enemy had evolved a satisfactory counter to the Type A mine'.[21] Amendments to Paul orders were signalled to the C-in-C in Admiralty signal 2033/8 June, by which time *Glorious* and her escorting destroyers had been sunk and *Ark Royal* was on her way back to Scapa

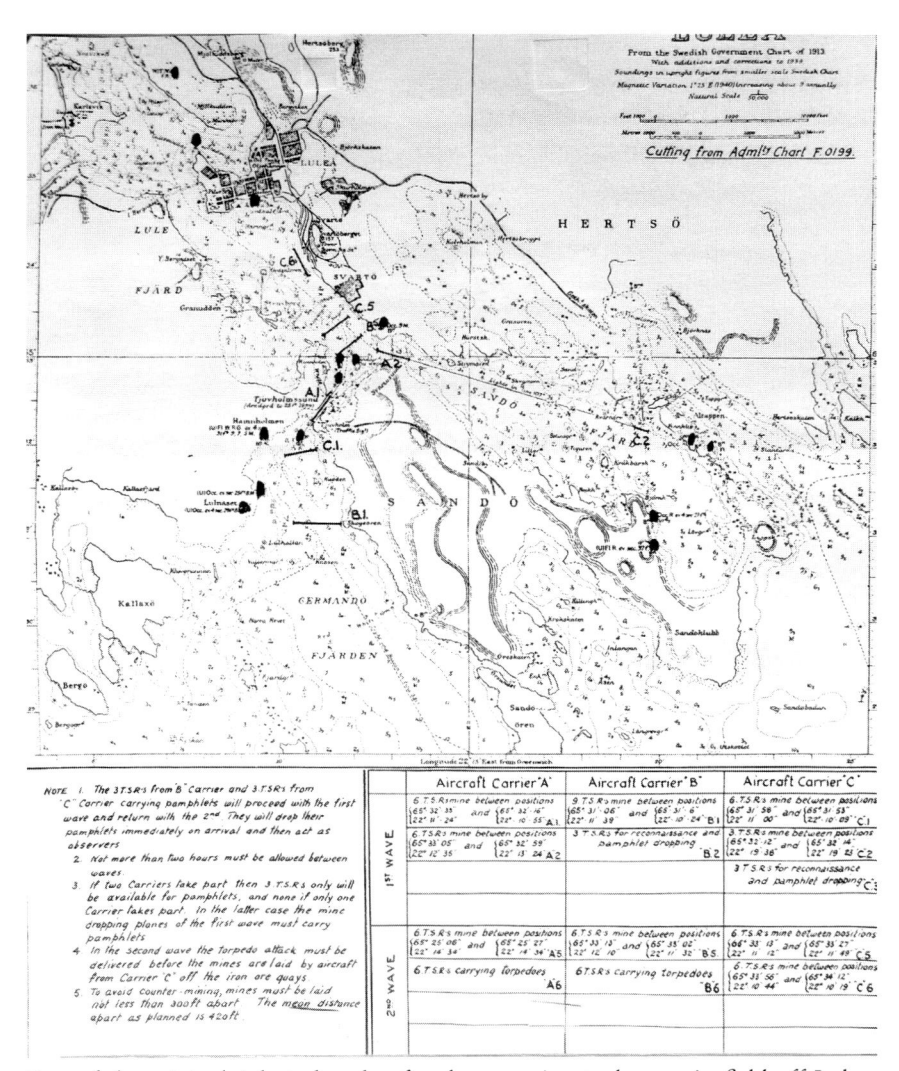

Part of the original Admiralty plan for three carriers to lay a minefield off Lulea, Operation Paul, in 1940. (*Author's collection*)

Flow. There copies six and seven of the full operation order were taken on board their flagships for the C-in-C and VAA.

With the Admiralty reference M/P.D. 08704/40 dated 8 June 1940 and categorised as Most Secret, this document described the original attack to be carried out by three carriers launching a total of seventy-eight Swordfish, of which sixty would lay mines and the remainder would drop pamphlets over the port that were intended to warn the Swedish authorities about the minefield and the reasons for laying it. This was the basic document that had already been extensively amended by signal. The Chiefs of Staff met again on the evening of 9 June and were told that the JPSC had advised against it but Captain Daniel stated that the order had already been given. Despite this, the operation could not have taken place any earlier because Lulea was only just becoming clear of ice. Later that evening the First Lord, A V Alexander, Pound and Churchill met specifically to discuss Paul. Despite some argument it was finally agreed that the operation must go ahead but it was not to be. The BEF had been evacuated from Dunkirk, the French Army was in full retreat and the French government had declared Paris an open city. Italy declared war on Britain and France and the Germans captured more iron ore resources in Lorraine than Britain could hope to blockade in the Gulf of Bothnia. The C-in-C Home Fleet's staff completed a revised plan for *Ark Royal* to launch eighteen long-range Swordfish from a position 60 miles north-east of Tan fjord but they lacked the range to return to the carrier and would have had to land in Sweden or Finland after laying their mines. Admiral Forbes signalled the Admiralty in HF 1253/16 June 1940 asking whether or not the operation was to proceed but there is no surviving reply in the National Archive or the Admiralty Library. On 18 June *Ark Royal* was ordered to proceed to Gibraltar to join Force H. Operation Paul had obviously been forgotten amid the pressure of events elsewhere.

Although they are not fitted with long-range tanks in their rear cockpits, these Swordfish at RNAS Hatston are loaded with the same Type A mines that would have been dropped off Lulea in Operation Paul. (*Author's collection*)

The signal, handwritten by a telegraphist, from the Admiralty to the C-in-C Home Fleet, copied to VAA, ordering preparations for Operation Paul to be put in hand. (*Author's collection*)

If it had been carried out, a modified Paul could have prevented iron ore ships from leaving Lulea for a short period until the mines were swept but it would have needed to be re-sown at frequent intervals to remain effective and this would not have been possible. The decision to use carrier-borne aircraft certainly recognised their strategic value and should have alerted the War Cabinet to some of the many shortcomings of Bomber Command but it would have incurred crippling losses of aircraft and aircrew that the Fleet Air Arm could not afford, especially at a time when the MAP was suspending the development and production of naval aircraft. Worse, just as relations with France were soured by the attack on Mers-el-Kébir, Anglo-Swedish relations would have suffered for decades after what would have been seen as an act of unprovoked aggression against a neutral nation. Whatever short-term benefit the War Cabinet thought it might achieve, it is fortunate that Paul was never carried out.

The Battle of Britain

After the fall of France, German air attacks on the British Isles were thought by some to be the precursor to an amphibious assault. Those who think so fail to take into account the facts that the German surface fleet had been reduced significantly by the losses incurred during the Norwegian campaign and the German armed forces had made no preparations for amphibious operations on the scale that would have been necessary. The Allies needed 4,000 vessels, the Mulberry prefabricated harbour and numerous other important elements to make the D-Day landings in

Normandy four years later a success. By comparison, the Germans had nothing but canal barges and tugs and their temporary removal from the waterways of Europe actually hurt enemy industry to a greater extent than Bomber Command could have achieved. What really happened was that for the first time the Luftwaffe had encountered serious opposition that prevented it from achieving air dominance. Moreover, the RN's ability to dominate the Channel was so obvious to the German high command that Admiral Raeder commented that the German Navy could never have matched the British and that in 1940 the Luftwaffe lacked the weapons and skills needed to attack the British fleet.[22] Air attacks on warships in daylight obviously had to be taken seriously but it must be remembered that unlimited German air power subsequently failed to prevent the RN from withdrawing British troops from Norway, Dunkirk, the Channel ports, Greece and Crete, and nor did it prevent the RN fighting relief convoys through the hostile Mediterranean to Malta and Tobruk. Is it really likely that the world's largest navy fighting in defence of its homeland would have been any less successful? In 1944 Grand Admiral Raeder wrote that he had consistently held the view that British naval power made the risk of attempting to mount an invasion too great.

Despite its mantra in the 1920s and '30s that bombers would always get through to their targets, the RAF belatedly embraced the requirement to provide fighter defences for the UK at government insistence. By 1940 it had a viable command and control system based on that created by Brigadier E B Ashmore of the Royal Flying Corps in 1917 but with the addition of radar. During the period known as the Battle of Britain the Admiralty was asked to provide Fleet Air Arm pilots to make up shortfalls in Fighter Command and twenty-three RN pilots were lent to the command, many of them midshipmen and sub lieutenants (A) straight from training.[23] The RAF subsequently took steps to recognise aircrew who flew fighters during the battle but not maintenance personnel or fighter controllers. The definition of the award criteria, however, led to controversy for many years after the first announcement was made in an Air Ministry Order of 24 May 1945. This stated that a silver-gilt rosette would be awarded, to be worn on the ribbon of the 1939–1945 Star. It was to be made as an 'immediate' award to pilots or recognised members of aircrew who had flown at least one operational sortie with an accredited unit controlled by Fighter Command between 10 July and 31 October 1940. Two naval fighter squadrons, 804 and 808 NAS, met this criteria when they operated in defence of Scapa Flow[24] and they were included in the list. Thirty-four pilots served in these two squadrons and their number was added to the twenty-three pilots lent to the RAF who flew Hurricanes and Spitfires.

The badges of two naval air squadrons, 804 and 808 NAS, appear among others on the Battle of Britain Memorial on the Embankment in London. They can be seen at the bottom right of this photograph. (*Andrew Hobbs collection*)

Subsequent iterations of the criteria proscribed the award of the rosette to aircrew who flew in any aircraft other than a fighter, thus ruling out men who had flown missions for Bomber and Coastal Commands as well as the gallant Skua, Swordfish and Albacore crews who attacked the ports where invasion barges were being gathered by the enemy as well as those who laid minefields off the French coast. The chosen dates also ruled out fighter operations in defence of the Dunkirk evacuation. A final iteration of the criteria was issued on 9 November 1960, twenty years after the battle, in which 804 and 808 NAS were still included. Paul Beaver, who researched the subject for his book *Forgotten Few*, draws attention to the fact that confusion over the exact entitlement has led to some naval pilots' names appearing on the London Embankment and Capel-le-Ferne memorials who do not meet the 1960 criteria.[25] Wing Commander Allen, himself a Battle of Britain fighter pilot, calculated that a total of 2,543 pilots had qualified for the rosette when he carried out research for his book *Who Won the Battle of Britain?* He made no specific reference to the fifty-seven RN pilots but noted that the overall total included twenty-two Australians, ninety-four Canadians, 147 Poles and thirty-seven Czechs. Surprisingly, in view of the huge number of targets presented to Fighter Command by the Luftwaffe in the period covered by the criteria, more than 1,000 aircraft on some days, Allen found that very few RAF pilots had amassed high scores of enemy aircraft destroyed. He found that only seventeen pilots had been credited with more than ten 'kills' and the highest score was achieved by Sergeant Pilot J Frantisek DFM, a Czech, who was credited with seventeen. A Pole, Flying Officer W Urbanowicz

DFC, was credited with fourteen. Allen ascribed this overall lack of achievement to several factors including the poor tactical training of RAF fighter pilots before 1940 and the lack of hitting power inherent in the British fighters' 0.303in machine guns. The US Colt-Browning 0.5in machine gun would have been considerably more effective but by mid-1940 British fighters were being mass produced with their obsolete armament and their replacement with more effective weapons would have caused delays. Allen found that less than 15 per cent of pilots who fought in the Battle of Britain could claim a German aircraft destroyed and, based on random sampling, only about 12 per cent of these could realistically have achieved two kills. Only about 7 per cent would have destroyed four or more enemy aircraft. The inadequate priority given to the tactical training of fighter pilots before 1939 and the failure to study German tactics during their participation in the Spanish Civil War were the root cause. Taken against these figures, the RN pilots loaned to Fighter Command did remarkably well, with four pilots, Sub Lieutenants (A) F Dawson-Paul, A G Blake, R J Cork and R E Gardner RN, achieving five or more kills, which would have given them 'ace' status in the USN.

After the event the Battle of Britain acquired legendary status, although those who describe it as a victory fail to explain how the Luftwaffe was able to bomb London every night or destroy a succession of cities including Plymouth and Portsmouth. As with most legends, there is some factual basis but those who emphasise the sacrifices made by 'the few' often forget or pay insufficient attention to the sacrifices made by many others, not least the British public who bravely carried on with their daily lives despite suffering air raids virtually every night. Anthony Cumming wrote in *The Royal Navy and the Battle of Britain*[26] that during the period covered by the battle criteria, 1,730 Merchant Navy personnel were killed bringing critical supplies to the UK. To the nation's shame they were classified as non-combatants, despite having bravely gone into harm's way under attack from U-boats, enemy surface raiders and long-range bombers. During the same period Fighter Command lost approximately 540 men and the entire RAF lost fewer men in combat than the Merchant Navy. Cumming identifies a strong argument for a memorial that identifies the defence of the UK in 1940 as a national effort in which Fighter Command had a role to play but was certainly not the only factor. At least Air Chief Marshal Sir Hugh Dowding GCB GCVO CMG, Commander-in-Chief of Fighter Command in 1940, recognised the true, joint, nature of the battle in a 1942 newspaper article[27] in which he said that air power had become an essential adjunct of sea power. It would have been even more accurate to admit that it was British sea power that had prevented a German invasion in 1940 aided by the whole of the RAF and the British population. Also, as Churchill was quick to realise, the presence of the BEF back on British soil, albeit after the loss of much of its equipment, with reinforcements arriving from the Commonwealth and countries that had been overrun, made the UK a very much more difficult place for the enemy to invade after June 1940.

Aircraft carrier operations

With *Ark Royal*'s departure to the Mediterranean, the only operational carriers available to the Home Fleet were *Furious* and the elderly *Argus*. The new *Illustrious* was completed on 25 May 1940 and after a short period of trials she sailed for Bermuda, where she worked up in sea areas that were relatively safe from U-boat attack. Her air group comprised 815 and 819 NAS with Swordfish and 806 NAS, the first unit to be equipped with the Fairey Fulmar fleet fighter. After a brief spell in Scapa Flow, she sailed in August to reinforce the Mediterranean Fleet.[28]

Argus had no air group after her return from training duties in the Mediterranean and on 27 June she ferried 701 NAS' Walrus to Iceland, where it was to carry out anti-submarine patrols. On 12 August she sailed from the UK with twelve RAF Hurricanes, which were eventually flown off to reinforce Malta in two ranges of six, each being led by an RN Skua. A similar ferry operation was carried out in September and in November *Argus* delivered thirty crated RAF Hurricanes to Takoradi on what was then the Gold Coast, where they were assembled and flown across Africa to Egypt.[29] A further ferry mission to Takoradi was carried out in company with *Furious*. After the end of the Norwegian campaign, *Furious* crossed the Atlantic at high speed with £18 million worth of gold from British reserves to be stored in Canada. On her return voyage she ferried forty Grumman Martlet and Brewster Buffalo fighters plus a package of spare parts for the RN back to the UK.[30] During this period she embarked 816 and 825 NAS with a total of eighteen Swordfish, six Sea Gladiators from 804 NAS and six Skuas of 801 NAS at various times.

More offensive operations resumed on 7 September with a sweep off the coast of Norway, during which *Furious* launched three groups of aircraft briefed to attack any shipping encountered.[31] Force A comprised nine Skuas of 801 NAS, each armed with a single 250lb GP bomb and eight 20lb HE bombs. Force B comprised six Swordfish of 816 NAS each armed with six 250lb GP bombs and six 20lb HE bombs. Force C comprised six Swordfish of 825 NAS with the same weapons load as Force B. The weather was not good, with the surface wind gusting between 25 and 35 knots, heavy rain squalls and visibility only 3 to 5 miles. One sub-flight of Force A found and attacked a small supply ship alongside a jetty with a warehouse. Both ship and warehouse were hit and the former was believed to have been left in a sinking condition. Force B found nothing but Force C located and attacked a supply ship, although it failed to hit it. Another sweep was carried out on 22 September and a strike force of ten Swordfish and six Skuas was flown off *Furious* to attack shipping and shore targets in Trondheim by moonlight.[32] Four Swordfish were from 816 NAS and six from 825 NAS, all armed with torpedoes. The six Skuas of 801 NAS were armed with a single 250lb bomb. Again the weather was bad, with cloud over the coast down to 700ft and extending all the way up to 7,000ft. The torpedo force became separated but two aircraft attacked a small auxiliary warship in one of the inner leads. They failed to hit it. The Skuas dive-bombed two merchant vessels at anchor, fuel tanks and a jetty but all their bombs missed since the low cloud limited the height from which they could dive. One Skua and five Swordfish failed to return but the Skua and two Swordfish were reported as having landed in neutral Sweden.

The last in this series of strikes by *Furious*' air group was carried out on 16 October when a total of eighteen aircraft carried out a night attack on Tromsø.[33] Six Swordfish of 816 NAS were armed with five 250lb GP bombs, seven 25lb incendiary bombs plus a single flare and briefed to attack oil tanks close to the shore. Two aircraft attacked the correct target but only claimed near misses, which started some fires. The remaining four Swordfish were from 825 NAS, armed with six 250lb GP and two 20lb HE bombs with six incendiary bombs and flares. Their briefed target was a seaplane station and most of their bombs fell accurately on target, causing fires and damage to the slipway and seaplane mooring area. Six Skuas from 801 NAS, each armed with a single 500lb SAP bomb, were briefed to attack shipping found in or near Tromsø. In poor visibility one sub-flight found nothing but the other located and attacked a medium-sized merchant vessel, unfortunately without hitting it. As the aircraft returned to *Furious* the visibility deteriorated, eventually dropping to just over a mile. One Skua failed to return and was reported as having landed in Sweden. In November *Furious* ferried thirty-four RAF Hurricanes from Liverpool to Takoradi and then a further forty RAF Hurricanes and twelve RN Fulmars to Takoradi in company with *Argus* during December. On her return to the UK she began a refit in Belfast.

One other action involving an embarked aircraft is worthy of mention. On 17 October the cruiser *Newcastle* and her escorting destroyers engaged enemy destroyers between the Scilly Islands and Ushant. *Newcastle*'s Walrus was flown off and provided valuable spotting and situation reports on the enemy force. It also sent a prompt and accurate report of enemy torpedoes that allowed the RN warships to avoid them successfully. These valuable reports continued throughout the action despite the fact the Walrus was itself being attacked by an enemy Do 17. When the Walrus was ordered to land, the enemy aircraft carried out a final attack and wounded the pilot but, despite this, he landed safely close to the cruiser and the damaged aircraft was hoisted inboard.[34]

Operations by naval aircraft from airfields ashore

After the German offensive on the Western Front began on 10 May the RAF sought urgent reinforcement from naval air squadrons[35] because it found itself facing a broad range of tasks that were essentially naval in character and its airmen had no experience or training in this type of warfare. The Admiralty made several naval air squadrons available, including some that had recently formed for the new *Illustrious* and *Formidable*. These included two fighter squadrons, 801 NAS with Skuas and 806 NAS with both Skuas and Rocs, which operated over the English Channel under the orders of Coastal Command rather than Fighter Command. They had several successful combats, particularly when they surprised Ju 87s attacking shipping. Unfortunately 806 NAS' first sortie from RAF Detling proved to be a disaster in which the enemy played no part. White section was briefed to patrol in the area between the North Foreland and Dunkirk on 28 May. One aircraft piloted by Midshipman (A) J Marshall RNVR with leading Airman A G Jones as TAG, failed to get airborne and crashed into trees at the edge of the airfield. The remaining two were over the Goodwin Sands at 0915 when they were

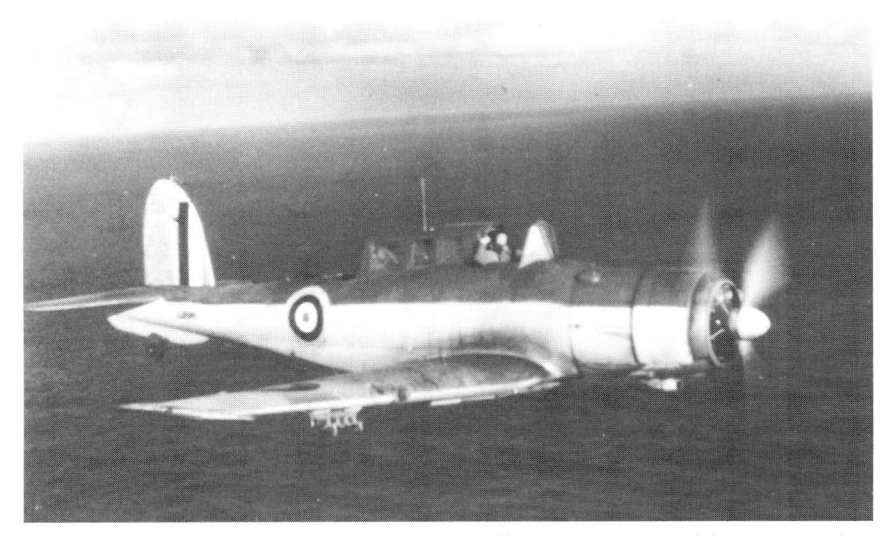

A Skua flying low over the North Sea. It is difficult to understand how RAF pilots off Dunkirk could have mistaken Skuas for Bf 109s. (*Author's collection*)

attacked by RAF Spitfire pilots, who mistook them for German Bf 109s. Lieutenant C P Campbell-Horsfall RN with his observer Petty Officer Clare were shot down but rescued by a destroyer. Midshipman (A) G S Hogg RNVR was damaged but able to fly back to RAF Manston, where he carried out a wheels up landing. His TAG, Naval Airman A G Burton, was killed.

After disembarking to RNAS Hatston from *Furious*, Skuas of 801 NAS carried out a series of attacks on targets in Norway. The first was on 24 July together with six Swordfish of 823 NAS, also from Hatston, following a report from an RAF reconnaissance aircraft that enemy ships were at sea 250nm from the air station off the coast of Norway. The Swordfish were armed with torpedoes and after a night flight in showery weather they located a group of ships in line astern at dawn. One doubtful hit was obtained on the last ship in the line. The Skuas failed to locate the enemy ships and after its analysis of the operation, NAD took the view that some of the Skuas should have been used to search for, relocate and shadow the enemy. While still at Hatston, 801 NAS went on to carry out further strikes on shipping off the Norwegian coast. Notable among these were two attacks on petrol storage tanks at Dolvik on 7 and 28 August respectively. As a result of these, the Admiralty believed that all three tanks had been destroyed, a blow to the enemy's logistics. A further attack was carried out on 9 September by nine Skuas, each armed with a single 250lb GP bomb and eight 20lb HE bombs. One sub-flight attacked a ship alongside in Haugesund but failed to hit it; one bomb did hit the jetty about 20yd from the ship, however. Another sub-flight attacked a merchant ship in ballast that was under way. They, too, failed to get hits but a single bomb burst only 20yd off the ship's port side. One aircraft attacked what the pilot believed to be an enemy encampment of twelve huts, three of which were destroyed. One Skua failed to return and its crew, Petty Officers A G Clayton RN and H C Kimber RN, were reported as killed in action.

During the Dunkirk evacuation 825 NAS, which had been disembarked from *Glorious* to make space so that aircraft could be ferried from Norway, carried out a remarkable series of operations from RAF airfields at Bircham Newton and Detling. These included night reconnaissance of the French coastline now held by the enemy, attacks against enemy military transport and gun positions, spotting the fall of shot for cruiser bombardments of the French coast, strikes against enemy MTBs, and other short-notice attacks on enemy forces as they gathered near the coast. All of these were pressed home gallantly and achieved success. On some sorties they had fighter escort but by no means always. Between May and November seventy sorties were flown by Swordfish of 812 and 815 NAS and Albacores of 826 NAS laying mines in enemy-controlled waters. These were all flown at night and they suffered remarkably few casualties. The first into action was 812 NAS deployed to RAF Bircham Newton on 22 April, where it came under Coastal Command operational control as a replacement for obsolescent RAF Vildebeest torpedo bombers to form an east coast strike force. It was equipped with some of the long-range tanks prepared for Operation Paul and given the task of minelaying. The mines were Type A Marks I, II, III or IV, each of which weighed 2,000lb, 400lb more than a Mark XII torpedo. They were referred to as 'cucumbers' and were carried in the standard torpedo crutches, but when loaded with both a mine and the long-range fuel tank the aircraft were heavily overloaded and unable to climb above 6,000ft. The squadrons used differing tactics, the most common being to fly to the target area at night in formation and then dive to about 600ft, at which height the mines were dropped without a parachute. Moonlight nights were needed to aid navigation to the laying area and for accurate positioning once there. At first there was little opposition but later the Germans began to position small ships with anti-aircraft guns, known as flak ships, near potential targets but these had little deterrent effect. After dropping their mines, the aircraft got away at very low level, an important tactic given the slow rate of climb of the Swordfish. As they dived below 5,000ft, pilots throttled back their engines to 1,600rpm and glided at 65 knots, at which speed they could not be heard, and they were seldom located or tracked by searchlights.

The tactics used by 826 NAS differed in that its aircraft took off and flew to the laying area independently to allow greater freedom of manoeuvre, but in all other respects they were similar. The dropping position was approached above 5,000ft, which was considered to be beyond the range of small-calibre anti-aircraft guns and beneath the effective hitting range of controlled guns of heavier calibre. The mine was dropped from a low-speed glide and the engine was not opened up until the aircraft was clear of the drop position. If there was low cloud the aircraft were navigated to a landfall clear of the target and, when certain of their position, the aircrew climbed to just below the cloud base and then carried out the lay as normal. During this period, 812 NAS laid more mines than any other squadron, 320 by the end of February 1941. The Admiralty estimated that 97 per cent of these had been dropped in exactly the right position. The squadron also carried out fifteen night bombing raids on enemy-held ports.[36]

Up to the end of August naval aircraft were credited by the Admiralty with shooting down thirty-four German aircraft and the number of kills continued to rise. On 11 September six Albacores of 826 NAS joined RAF Blenheim bombers to attack enemy shipping in Calais. They were intercepted by eighteen Bf 109s but three of these were shot down by the Albacores' TAGs. One Albacore was forced down into the sea and another crashed on landing as a result of the damage it had received but both crews survived. The successful action resulted in a congratulatory letter to the First Lord from the Secretary of State for Air.

The tasks allotted to Fleet Air Arm aircraft attached to the RAF during the latter part of 1940 included attacks on enemy-occupied French and Dutch ports. Targets included ships and barges, E-boats and other enemy light craft, port infrastructure including fuel tanks and ships alongside. Between them, 812 and 829 NAS carried out six night bombing raids on Brest and Lorient with a combined total of thirty-four aircraft, only one of which was lost to enemy action. Other attacks by 812 and 815 NAS Swordfish together with 826 and 829 NAS Albacores were carried out armed with 250lb GP bombs during this period on a variety of targets. Two other weapons of particular interest were used in some of these strikes; these were 'B' bombs and mines with bomb fuses. The former were first used in an attack on Den Helder in Holland on 30 May. They were delivered in diving attacks, dropped short of the target and were then expected to float up under the hull and detonate, upon which they would break the ship's back. They proved unreliable, however, and were not used again. The use of mines with bomb fuses, known as 'Tims', came about because of the shortage of British bombs with large explosive-to-weight ratios. They were expected to have an effect four or five times greater than a 250lb bomb and were used extensively in attacks on ports after the Admiralty modified sufficient mines for this role. The squadrons mentioned above together with 818 NAS' Swordfish also flew on anti-submarine patrols during their time under Coastal Command control and escorted convoys in the narrow waters near the Thames Estuary, the Dover Strait and the English Channel. In all these operations they had to operate in the face of enemy fighter opposition and their time ashore demonstrated both the unusual qualities of the aircraft and the skill of the crews who flew them. Between them the naval squadrons had successfully attacked enemy motor transport columns, tanks, oil installations, ammunition dumps, gasworks and barges. They also hit and damaged a power station, a pontoon bridge and both gun and searchlight batteries, docks, airfields, military headquarters, railways and their rolling stock, roads and warehouses. Two E-boats and a merchant ship had been damaged. Bombardment spotting was successful on three out of four occasions, two of which were at night. Photographic reconnaissance sorties provided valuable material and the minelaying operations were particularly successful. All these tasks were beyond anything the aircrew had been trained for and great credit is due to them for taking the fight to the enemy at a most difficult time.

Reconnaissance to give strike planners situational awareness of the enemy's strength and intentions was vital but the RAF lacked both the resources and training to provide all that was necessary. To help fill this gap two Walrus squadrons were employed after the evacuation from Norway on local reconnaissance, anti-submarine patrols, photographic flights and other duties, freeing Coastal Command aircraft for longer-range work. The first of these, 701 NAS, was established in Iceland on 27 June and operated for four months in conditions of bad or rapidly changing weather and local magnetic disturbances. They gave considerable assistance to the northern cruiser patrol, which formed part of blockade operations against Germany. The other Walrus unit was 700 NAS, made up with aircraft disembarked from ships of the Home Fleet, which was used on similar duties from Sullom Voe in the Shetland Islands between August 1940 and March 1941.

A number of RN observers were lent to Bomber Command to make up for the organisation's inadequate knowledge of operations over the sea. One of these was Commander G A 'Hank' Rotherham RN, who expressed surprise that the Wellington-equipped squadron in which he found himself saw no need to practise bombing, learn about ship recognition or find out whether their briefed targets were still where a reconnaissance aircraft had said they were anchored hours or even days before a sortie. In autumn 1940 he was serving in NAD and was asked about the reliability of Coastal Command patrols since the readiness ordered for anti-invasion destroyers was reliant on the accuracy of their reports. Rotherham decided that the only way to be sure was to fly on such a patrol himself to see what was normal[37] and he arranged to fly in a Hudson from Bircham Newton. The aircraft was equipped with radar and was briefed to do two night runs 100 miles out sea in the general direction of Denmark with a track spacing of 20 miles. On take-off the operator told him that the radar was unserviceable but none of the crew seemed concerned. The first run was carried out at low altitude searching visually but the second was carried out at 15,000ft and departed the planned track in order to fly over Holland looking for something to drop a bomb on. When one of the crew saw a night fighter they turned and flew back to base. Once back at the Admiralty, Rotherham looked at the night's anti-invasion patrol reports from Bircham Newton, which stated that his aircraft had conducted a radar search on two runs without detecting anything. He pointed out that this had not been the case; the credibility of Coastal Command's searches was called into question and the Admiralty reduced the anti-invasion destroyer forces from four hours' notice for steam to two.

5
1941

The new year brought with it no new aircraft carriers for the Home Fleet. The armoured carriers *Illustrious* and *Formidable* had both been deployed to the Mediterranean Fleet and the completion of *Victorious*, intended to be the second of the class, was delayed by the slow delivery of armour plate and gun mountings. She was not completed until 29 March 1941.[1]

Taking stock

As the new year progressed, the production of aircraft for the RN actually decreased because the MAP failed to give adequate priority to meeting the Navy's urgent need for new aircraft.[2] Its first minister, the press magnate Lord Beaverbrook, soon established a reputation for overruling the services his Ministry was meant to serve and the Admiralty became concerned. The directing staff of the new ministry did not at first include any naval members and so, as a matter of urgency, the Admiralty's Director of Air Material, Captain M S Slattery RN, was appointed to fulfil a dual appointment as a full member of the Air Supply Board. He was a pilot who had qualified with number 1 course in early 1925 and flown a variety of aircraft types. One of his first actions was to complain that Fulmars and Albacores were still excluded from the priority list and the MAP was forced to agree that it must accept responsibility for meeting Admiralty requirements in research, experiment and development matters as well as the supply of airframes, engines, spares, equipment and armament. It also accepted that the Admiralty had an absolute right to determine the types of aircraft, engines and equipment to be procured for the Fleet Air Arm and that it would allocate the necessary proportion of the available resources to do so in line with government policy. Any question of priority that now arose was be resolved by discussion between the respective staffs and gradually this became effective. The MAP also agreed to set aside capacity for the repair of naval aircraft, engines and equipment that were beyond the capacity of RN repair yards under Admiralty control, and that the Navy and Air Force could, by mutual agreement, exchange aircraft, engines and equipment as they saw fit, informing the MAP subsequently that they had done so. Lastly, the MAP accepted that the Admiralty alone would decide the relative priority to be accorded to Fleet Air Arm materiel and its distribution. This arrangement took time to implement but was a considerable improvement that continued with very little change until the end of the war.

One other important change in air operations over the sea had been agreed in late 1940. Dissatisfaction at the lack of priority given to Coastal Command by the Air Ministry led A V Alexander, the First Lord, to demand immediate increases in its strength. He was supported by Lord Beaverbrook and their combined submissions evolved, after consideration by the defence committee, into a request for the complete transfer of Coastal Command to the RN. Alexander observed that 'to suggest that ships should be under one command and aircraft under another would be equivalent to suggesting that battleships should be commanded by one man and destroyers by another'. The First Sea Lord explained that reliance on Bomber Command for the provision of air striking forces at sea constituted a significant weakness because its crews were not trained or equipped for such operations. If the small number of bomber squadrons lent to Coastal Command were transferred to the Navy, their crews could receive long-term specialised training in naval warfare that would enhance their performance. The Chief of the Air Staff opposed such a change which, he said, would cause the RAF 'to suffer a disastrous blow to its esprit de corps'.[3] The Cabinet Committee tasked with investigating the Admiralty and MAP submissions decided, in the end, not to transfer the command to the Navy. It did, however, agree to increase the strength and operational efficiency of the command and stated that 'for all operational purposes it should come under the control of the Admiralty'. This important change had been announced by the Prime Minister on 10 December 1940 and he added that 'as the function of Coastal Command is that of co-operation with the Royal Navy. the operational policy of the Command must be determined by the Admiralty'. This was a political compromise and the argument for full Admiralty control of all maritime air matters remained irrefutable but the C-in-C of Coastal Command was Air Chief Marshal Sir Frederick Bowhill, a former naval officer who had begun his flying career with the RNAS. He maintained a good working relationship with his naval colleagues and matters were thus resolved.

In early 1941 the effective expansion of the Fleet Air Arm's operational strength continued to be limited by several factors that the Admiralty tried its best to overcome. The expansion of aircraft maintenance arrangements still required the entry and training of a large number of technical ratings as well as the completion of new air yards and air stores depots. Considerable extra shore accommodation at naval air stations was required to allow for the formation and preliminary training of new naval air squadrons before they could be considered fit to be embarked operationally. In principle, the new naval air stations such as Yeovilton and Crail, which opened as the fighter and torpedo/bomber schools in 1940, were to be used as accommodation bases for the formation of new squadrons, generally of the type with whose principal function the school was concerned. Thus, for example, at Yeovilton new fighter squadrons were formed. At such air stations the squadrons generally carried out their working up practices and standardised operating procedures were introduced for them.

Recruitment of RN air mechanics and artificers had been begun when the Inskip Award handed full control of the Fleet Air Arm back to the Admiralty but at the outset their training had been carried out at RAF establishments. The RAF had generously lent 1,350 maintenance personnel to the Navy in May 1939 and by the outbreak of war the RN had trained a total strength of 3,000 air maintenance ratings. Eight hundred RAF personnel volunteered to transfer to the Navy in 1939 and one complete entry of 200 RAF apprentices did the same before completing their training. The first purely naval aircraft maintenance ratings were former seamen and stokers who had volunteered for cross-training. Many of these were still awaiting courses on the outbreak of war. By 1941, however, the various training schemes were beginning to produce results and growing numbers of technical ratings were coming forward. Later on a number of WRNS ratings trained as aircraft mechanics for service with second-line squadrons ashore, freeing men for service at sea.

By 1941 NAD was able to reflect that, despite their shortcomings and the very small numbers available, the contribution of Fleet Air Arm aircraft to the naval war effort had been of a consistently high standard. The Swordfish had done particularly well considering its unremarkable biplane design and its versatility and robust qualities came in for special comment. It could operate from the deck in the most severe weather conditions and had remarkable load-carrying capacity for its size. These, together with its general reliability, had proved to be its outstanding qualities during the first year of the war and were to continue into 1941. The fleet's fighters had been inadequate in number and, prior to the entry into service of the Fulmar, deficient in many of the qualities they required. The Skua fighter/dive bomber had earned its place in history, sinking the *Königsberg* in the latter role, but it lacked both speed and firepower. The Roc turret fighter had been a failure in its intended role and was soon relegated to second-line duties. The Walrus had played an important part in reconnaissance and anti-submarine patrols since the long-range types of aircraft capable of carrying out such tasks were not widely available.

The Admiralty appreciated that the tactical training given to aircrew prior to 1939 had been concerned mainly with hypothetical fleet-versus-fleet encounters but the many unexpected tactical uses to which naval aircraft had been put during the first full year of the war led to important changes being made in the training squadrons, especially for fighter pilots. In general, however, the sound basic air and naval training given to all types of naval aircrew enabled them to adapt to the new conditions quickly and successfully. The use of crash barriers to allow a deck park had been a success, although the most important lessons learnt in 1940 had been the requirement for the forward and after round-downs to be replaced by flat extensions to the deck that would allow larger numbers of aircraft to be embarked on the deck park and operated when they became available, and the need for larger lifts in new construction. The latter would allow larger and heavier aircraft to be struck down into the hangar.

Operations against enemy surface raiders

The early months of 1941 saw a number of sorties by German warships and auxiliary cruisers intended to disrupt British shipping in the Atlantic and naval aircraft played a part in countering them. In the last few days of 1940 the cruiser *Admiral Hipper* had made contact with the convoy WS 5A about 600nm off Cape Finisterre. It had an ocean escort comprising *Berwick*, *Bonaventure* and two sloops but the main element of the convoy, WS 5, was escorted by *Dunedin* and included the aircraft carriers *Furious* and *Argus*, which were carrying RAF fighters for the reinforcement of Malta and the Middle East via Takoradi.[4] *Berwick* and *Hipper* exchanged fire but the former's Walrus was damaged by blast in the opening salvo and could not be flown off to spot the fall of shot. Once again, Admiralty advice that spotting aircraft should be flown off before action was joined to avoid such damage had been disregarded. The carriers were not as valuable as they would have been if their employment as aircraft transports had not robbed them of their capacity for offensive action. *Argus* had her hangar loaded with crated Hurricanes but had two Swordfish embarked intended for anti-submarine patrols. Presumably, because she had previously been a training carrier and the aircraft were not expected to operate in the strike role, she had no torpedoes on board. *Furious* also had her hangars full of Hurricanes; she did have torpedoes in her magazines but no Swordfish to carry them. She did have six Skuas of 801 NAS embarked, however, and three of these were flown off to locate the enemy cruiser, which could not be seen from this element of the convoy. *Argus* flew off her two Swordfish, which were then recovered on *Furious* and armed with torpedoes. The Skuas orbited the force while this was happening, ready to act as a search and escort force to support the

Swordfish. The weather deteriorated, however, and *Hipper* disengaged, having received some damage. It may be that her captain had concerns that Force H or Force K, which included *Formidable*, would be close enough to launch air strikes. On this sortie *Hipper* had sunk only one merchant ship.

The lack of effective air reconnaissance over the North Sea meant that the Admiralty lacked information about enemy warship movements in early 1941 and the C-in-C was further handicapped by the lack of an aircraft carrier in his battle force. The Admiralty had responded to the surface raider threat by using 'R'-class battleships and, sometimes, battlecruisers to support North Atlantic convoys and the German task force commander, Admiral Lutjens, had strict instructions when he was at sea from February to avoid action with a convoy that was escorted by a battleship armed with 15in guns. In such cases he elected, when his embarked reconnaissance aircraft located a heavily escorted convoy, to shadow from a distance and send short messages to the headquarters ashore in the hope that the situation would be grasped sufficiently for U-boats to be homed onto the convoy. This is what happened on 7 February when he was at sea in *Scharnhorst* with *Gneisenau* in company off the Canary Islands and recognised *Malaya* with a convoy. He turned away but the convoy was attacked by two U-boats, which sank five merchant ships. Lutjens continued to shadow in conditions of low visibility but on 8 February one of *Malaya*'s escorting destroyers sighted the German ships and the battleship immediately catapulted its Walrus. *Malaya* and *Gneisenau* exchanged fire briefly but the enemy broke away and headed west at high speed, shadowed by the Walrus, which sent a series of valuable reports. It was soon evident that *Malaya* lacked the speed to close the enemy and the aircraft was eventually recalled. However, in the prevailing low visibility it became uncertain of its position and had to land on the sea. It was found and taken to Tenerife by a Spanish merchant ship. Two days later *Rodney* and *Ark Royal* took over the convoy escort and the German battlecruisers made no further attempt to engage it.

Later in February every available capital ship, including *King George V*, *Rodney*, *Renown*, *Malaya*, *Ark Royal* and the 'R'-class battleships were at sea in the Atlantic supporting convoys against the growing number of sorties by enemy surface raiders. On 15 March *Scharnhorst* and *Gneisenau* intercepted several Allied tankers, which had sailed independently, Lutjens deciding to make prizes of three and sink the others. Two of these ships managed to send raider reports, however, and the Admiralty ordered *Rodney* and *King George V* to proceed to the area. *Rodney,* the nearest, actually intercepted *Gneisenau* a day later, after she had sunk ten ships out of a stream of south-going merchant ships.

Her arrival had been too late, however, and her speed too slow to force an action, with contact lost after sunset. Before the German ships could return to Brest they were sighted by a reconnaissance aircraft from *Ark Royal* at 1730 on 20 March roughly 600 miles west-north-west of Cape Finisterre. This contact illustrates the limitations of reconnaissance by a single aircraft, however, since it was operating at a considerable distance from its carrier. *Ark Royal*, with *Renown* in company, was 150 miles to the south-east and dusk was falling. The prevalent low visibility prevented both night shadowing and a long-range attack on the German warships, and unfortunately Force H was unable to regain contact in daylight. On 21 March an RAF reconnaissance aircraft located the ships as they entered Brest, one of nine aircraft launched early that morning to search for the ships based on *Ark Royal*'s report.

Apart from the loss of British shipping, this operation was important because it taught lessons about the tactics needed in capital ship ocean warfare and these proved valuable during the subsequent operations against the *Bismarck*. The most important of these was the realisation that aircraft carriers were of critical importance in locating enemy surface raiders as well as carrying out torpedo attacks against them. Inputs from the Admiralty's war room, where information from a range of sources was gathered and fused, were also recognised as being an important factor. By the middle of May 1941 convoys in the North Atlantic were threatened by surface attack and U-boats as well as Focke-Wulf Condor bombers operating from western France. Winston Churchill observed that the situation was one that 'would subject our naval strength to a trial of the first magnitude'. *Scharnhorst* and *Gneisenau* were at their operating base on the flank of the north–south convoy routes and two other powerful warships, *Admiral Scheer* and *Admiral Hipper*, had just completed a series of destructive operations in the North and South Atlantic and returned unscathed through the Denmark Strait to their home base. A powerful new enemy battleship, *Bismarck*, was believed to be almost ready for operations, as was the new cruiser *Prinz Eugen*.

Destruction of the Bismarck

The timing of the German Operation Rheinübung,[5] a sortie into the Atlantic by *Bismarck* and *Prinz Eugen* to attack British convoys, was ideal from a German perspective. Germany had seized control of the entire European seaboard from the Pyrenees to the North Cape and its intervention in the Balkans in April had quickly overwhelmed Yugoslavia and Greece. British Commonwealth forces had been evacuated from Greece and on 20 May a German airborne invasion of Crete had begun that, in the space of ten days, led to a further evacuation of British forces and grievous losses to Admiral Cunningham's Mediterranean Fleet. In the Atlantic, U-boat attacks on convoys were causing grave anxiety and the recent sorties by *Scharnhorst* and *Gneisenau* had sunk twenty-two merchant vessels. More positively, Britain had weathered the critical winter months of 1940–41 despite the protracted bombing that Fighter Command had failed to prevent and a closer relationship was developing with the USA. However, on 20 May Admiral Sir John Tovey, now C-in-C Home Fleet, had only *King George V* and her recently completed sistership *Prince of Wales* with him at Scapa Flow together with *Hood*, flagship of Vice Admiral L E Holland, VA Battlecruiser Squadron. These were the only capital ships fast enough to stand a chance of engaging the major German units. *Argus* was occupied with training and ferrying and was no longer regarded as an operational carrier; *Ark Royal* was at Gibraltar with Force H and *Eagle* was in the South Atlantic. *Illustrious* and *Formidable* had both been damaged in the Mediterranean and *Furious* was ferrying RAF aircraft to the Middle East. The only aircraft carrier immediately available to the Home Fleet was *Victorious*, completed on 29 March and commissioned into the RN on 16 April prior to sea trials and a move to Rosyth, where she was fitted with Admiralty-supplied items. There was no time for her to be worked up and on 14 May she arrived in the Clyde, where she was loaded with forty-eight crated Hurricanes for shipment to the RAF in Malta[6] as part of troop convoy WS 8B. Admiral Tovey's fleet also included the 2nd Cruiser Squadron under Rear Admiral A T B Curteis, CS2, which comprised *Galatea* (flag), *Aurora*, *Kenya* and *Neptune* and nine destroyers. The 1st Cruiser squadron under Rear Admiral W F Wake-Walker, CS1, was deployed across the gaps through which German warships might try to break into the Atlantic. *Norfolk* (flag) and *Suffolk* covered the Denmark Strait, *Manchester* and *Birmingham* the gap between Iceland and the Faroe Islands. The battlecruiser *Repulse* was in the Clyde standing by to escort WS 8B.[7]

The original German plan had been to deploy a task force comprising *Bismarck*, *Prinz Eugen*, *Scharnhorst* and *Gneisenau* into the Atlantic during the new moon period at the end of April. *Gneisenau* was to sail first and carry out diversionary attacks between Cape Verde and the Azores to draw British ships south away from the others. In the event damage to the two battlecruisers in Brest caused by RAF bombing was sufficiently serious to prevent them from sailing with the two new ships and neither *Bismarck* nor *Prinz Eugen* were ready in April. Rheinübung was, therefore, modified to include only these two ships. Six tankers, a stores ship and two merchant reconnaissance ships were deployed into waiting positions in the Atlantic on 17–18 May from where they could provide logistic support. *Bismarck* and *Prinz Eugen* sailed from Gotenhafen in the Gulf of Danzig at 2130 on 18 May and were joined by a powerful escort of destroyers and anti-aircraft ships on the morning of 19 May. They passed through the Great Belt shortly before midnight on 19 May and at 1500 on 20 May they were seen and reported steaming north out of the Kattegat, probably by the Swedish cruiser *Gotland*, which had passed them. Whether or not it was her that originated the information, the fact that *Bismarck* was at sea was passed to the British Naval Attaché in Stockholm and signalled to the Admiralty at 2100. At 0900 on 21 May *Bismarck* and her consorts entered Kors Fjord and anchored near Bergen.

The Admiralty requested intensified air reconnaissance of the southern North Sea and at 1330 on 21 May an RAF aircraft sighted what the pilot reported as two *Hipper*-class cruisers in Bergen. Analysis of his photographs subsequently identified one of the ships as *Bismarck*, the Admiralty was informed and the war room passed the information to Admiral Tovey. Tovey was dubious, however, since he considered it unlikely that a German force intended to sortie against the Atlantic convoy routes would put into a harbour as vulnerable to British air reconnaissance as Bergen, which was only 270 miles from Scapa Flow. This failure was one of the major lessons drawn from Rheinübung by the German Naval Staff, which appreciated that greater importance should have been attached to the element of surprise. Despite his doubts, Tovey ordered Admiral Holland in *Hood* with *Prince of Wales* and the destroyers *Electra*, *Anthony*, *Echo*, *Icarus*, *Achates* and *Antelope* to sail from Scapa Flow and cover 1 CS' cruisers in the Denmark Strait. They passed the Hoxa Boom, the main gate through the net defences for capital ships entering and departing Scapa Flow, at 0052 on 22 May. The cruiser *Arethusa* was in Hvalfjord in Iceland and was placed at CS 1's disposal. *Manchester* and *Birmingham* were ordered to refuel from RFA tankers in Skaalefiord in Iceland and then resume their patrol. *King George V*, 2 CS and the remaining destroyers in Scapa Flow – *Active*, *Punjabi* and *Nestor* – were brought to short notice for steam. The Admiralty cancelled the sailing of *Repulse* and *Victorious* to join WS 8B and they were placed under the orders of the C-in-C Home Fleet. Captain H L StJ Fancourt RN, the commanding officer of RNAS Hatston, was ordered to deploy 828 NAS to Sumburgh, where it was to prepare for a torpedo attack on *Bismarck* in Bergen.

The RAF was requested to attack the ships in Bergen and despatched a mixed force of eighteen Whitley bombers and Hudson light bomber/ reconnaissance aircraft to do so on the night of 21/22 May. They found the coast shrouded in fog; only two aircraft reached Kors Fjord and they saw nothing. The weather deteriorated on 22 May with cloud down to 200ft over the North Sea. Over the North Atlantic aircraft reported cloud down to 300ft and visibility less than 1,000yd, and Coastal Command declared itself unable to fly the reconnaissance sorties requested by the Admiralty to confirm whether the enemy ships were still in Bergen or had sailed. Fully understanding the importance of this information, Captain Fancourt decided to send one of his own aircraft to find out. He selected a Martin Maryland, one of two operated by the Fleet Requirements Unit, 771 NAS, to tow sleeve targets used for the Home Fleet's anti-aircraft gunners to practise their skills. Both aircraft, AR717 and AR720, had been part of a batch ordered for the French Air Force but had been transferred to the RAF after the French armistice with Germany. Seven were allocated from the RAF to the RN in October 1940. The Maryland had two 1,050hp Pratt & Whitney Twin Wasp engines, which gave it a maximum speed of 264 knots at 12,000ft. Its service ceiling was 29,000ft and it had a radius of action in excess of 500 miles, making it an ideal reconnaissance aircraft that was difficult for enemy fighters to intercept.[8] Fancourt hoped that the Maryland reconnaissance would fix the *Bismarck*'s position accurately enough for 828 NAS to mount an attack on the night of 22 May but he also wanted to pass on information to the Admiralty and Admiral Tovey. Lieutenant N E Goddard RNVR, 771 NAS's senior pilot, volunteered to fly the aircraft, taking with him his two regular TAGs, Leading Airmen J W Armstrong and J D Milne. Before volunteering for the RNVR he had been chairman of the Gloucester Flying Club and had a wealth of varied flying experience. The day-to-day duties of 771 did not require observers to fly in their aircraft but, fortunately, RNAS Hatston's executive officer was the same Commander Rotherham who had reported to NAD on the inadequacy of Coastal Command's anti-invasion patrol. He was one of the most experienced RN observers[9] and volunteered to fly with Goddard. Hank Rotherham left a very good account of this historic flight in his autobiography *It's Really Quite Safe*.[10]

The Maryland was designed for a crew of four, with the observer sat in an extensively glazed nose section. The pilot's cockpit was above and behind him, the two positions separated by a bulkhead. The telegraphist sat in another isolated compartment situated behind the pilot and the fourth crew member, who doubled as a rear gunner, or winch operator on the aircraft's more normal fleet requirements sorties, occupied a ventral position just behind the wing training edge. Communication between these positions was by intercom but this had proved so unreliable that Goddard had had a speaking tube installed between the pilot's cockpit and the telegraphist. The two aircraft had no navigational aids but Goddard had ensured that compass swings had kept them in perfect condition. Rotherham telephoned Coastal Command to ask for information about Bergen and was warned that it had efficient radar to guard against an

Martin Maryland AR717, side letter 'U' of 771 NAS based at RNAS Hatston; the aircraft in which Commander Rotherham and Lieutenant Goddard flew their critical reconnaissance mission to Bergen to discover that *Bismarck* had sailed. (*Author's collection*)

approach from the west and an airfield to the north that operated fighters. His informant also told him that the weather was awful and considered too bad for flight. Given the prospect of an enemy-held coast shrouded by low cloud, Rotherham decided to use the tried and trusted technique of selecting a landfall well to the south of Bergen so that even if it could not be identified, there would be no doubt about which way to turn. Lieutenant Commander G A Tilney RN, Hatston's operations officer, helped with the planning and produced a photograph of an island off the Norwegian coast, which Rotherham selected as his initial point, IP. Goddard and Rotherham agreed that they would have to cross the North Sea at low level, preferably below 1,000ft, for two reasons. It would enable them to remain below the radar coverage as long as possible and, as important, if Rotherham could see the waves they would help him to gauge the direction and strength of the wind and keep his dead-reckoning plot as accurate as possible. They agreed that if they came under fire they would climb into the cloud cover and took their departure from Fair Isle, which was halfway between the Orkney and Shetland Islands, as this gave the shortest direct run to the IP.

After an uneventful take-off in AR717 they overflew Fair Isle in clear weather with 220 miles to run but after a while the cloud cover became darker and lower and the wind increased steadily. Goddard was forced to fly lower so that Rotherham could keep the surface in sight until they were below 50ft in reducing visibility. This was too much of a strain and they decided to climb, clearing the cloud tops at 3,000ft. After a period of relative calm, they descended to check the surface wind but conditions were no better and they had to climb again. A further attempt ended when Rotherham saw the sea just below them and shouted that they must climb immediately. Goddard had not seen the water at all but Rotherham was at least able to estimate that the wind had increased and veered. As they neared the point where they must descend to find the IP, their luck changed as the cloud broke up. They descended to 1,000ft without difficulty and a few minutes later their island IP appeared dead ahead after what had been an impressive feat of navigation. At that point the intercom failed but at least it had worked long enough for Rotherham to guide his pilot to the IP and he did at least have two buttons that operated red and green lights in the cockpit and, after their thorough planning, Goddard knew exactly what to do once they made landfall. They flew at low level through the fjords to the photographed anchorage position and found it empty. Goddard then flew on to examine every fjord and inlet and even Bergen harbour itself to see if the ships had moved there. There was no sign of them but the Maryland came under a considerable amount of anti-aircraft fire and Goddard dived across the harbour heading for the fjord that led to the open sea at over 300 knots. Crossing a spit of land at about 100ft, they flew directly over a gun position and Milne opened fire on it, scattering its crew.

With no intercom, Rotherham wrote down his vital report 'Battleship and cruiser have left' on a signal pad and pushed it through a hole in the bulkhead to Goddard, who relayed it to Armstrong through the cockpit voicepipe.[11] Because of the message's urgency, Rotherham instructed that it was to be transmitted in plain language and Armstrong first tried to do so on the Coastal Command reconnaissance frequency. He got no response, however, and so on his own initiative he retuned his set to the 771 NAS target-towing frequency and disturbed the normal tranquillity of fleet requirements work with his emergency call, a succession of three Os or long dashes in Morse code, which cleared the air of all other traffic. Upon receipt of the signal, Hatston informed Admiral Tovey by telephone[12] and the Admiralty operations room by teleprinter. The Maryland landed first at Sumburgh, where some slight damage to the aircraft was discovered, including a shattered a window close to Goddard's head that had been hit by an anti-aircraft round. Rotherham was immediately called to a telephone to speak to Commodore E J P Brind RN, the C-in-C's chief of staff. Confirmation was given that the ships were no longer in Bergen and Brind asked if Rotherham had searched to the north; Rotherham said no and explained that this had been due to the presence of fighters at the airfield to the north, which would certainly have been alerted by the anti-aircraft fire over Bergen and were thus in a position to shoot the Maryland down before its vital message was transmitted. Commodore Brind rang off and the remaining ships of the Home Fleet slipped and sailed for what was to become one of the most dramatic naval actions in history.

On returning to Hatston, Rotherham was handed a copy of a signal from the C-in-C that read, 'Congratulate you most heartily on your daring and successful reconnaissance and you have the thanks of myself and the fleet for giving us the opportunity of making contact.'

Rotherham was awarded an immediate DSO; Goddard an immediate DSC and Armstrong a DSM. Milne, who had fired at the enemy gunners, got nothing but a vote of thanks from the remainder of his crew. Rotherham subsequently met Captain R A B Edwards RN, who had been in the Admiralty operations room at the time and recalled that somebody had just said 'if only we had a naval aircraft to get through the weather' when Rotherham's report was handed in. It was not that the Maryland's crew were more skilful than their RAF contemporaries, although Rotherham probably had more over-water navigation experience than anyone they had available. The difference was simply that the naval aircrew had a much better appreciation of the enormous importance of what they were doing, the vital need to locate the enemy and pass on information that would help the Home Fleet to bring *Bismarck* to action.

King George V left Scapa Flow at 2245 on 22 May with *Victorious*. Because the latter had been prepared for a ferry mission, she only had the nine Swordfish of 825 NAS and six Fulmars of 800Z NAS embarked, the former intended for anti-submarine protection while on passage and the latter to act as guides to lead the RAF Hurricanes to Malta. Like their ship, neither of these squadrons was fully worked up and their

Commander G A 'Hank' Rotherham RN. The observer's badge was not introduced until some months after this photograph was taken so his left sleeve shows no indication of his aircrew qualification. (*Author's collection*)

inclusion in the Home Fleet's front line shows how widely the Admiralty had had to cast its net to assemble the necessary forces. Other ships in the C-in-C's battle group included the cruisers *Galatea, Aurora, Kenya* and *Hermione* and the destroyers *Inglefield, Intrepid, Active, Punjabi, Nestor, Windsor* and *Lance*. The last-named was forced to return to Scapa Flow with boiler trouble soon after sailing. The destroyers *Legion, Saguenay* and *Assiniboine* joined the C-in-C from Western Approaches Command on 23 May with *Repulse*.

Bismarck and *Prinz Eugen* had left Bergen at 1945 on 21 May, heading north at 24 knots, and were thus well to the north when Rotherham and his gallant crew searched the fjords around Bergen. Admiral Lutjens had decided to use the Denmark Strait and his two warships arrived at its northern entrance at noon on 23 May. All that day the Home Fleet had headed west in weather so bad that the Coastal Command air patrols requested by the C-in-C could not be carried out but at 2032 on 23 May, when the C-in-C's flagship was 230 miles north-west of the Butt of Lewis, a signal was received from CS 1 that *Bismarck* had been located. On that day the ice on the Greenland side of the Strait stretched some 80 miles from the coast and there was a minefield off the north-west coast of Iceland. The weather conditions were unusually clear over the pack ice and the sea for 10 miles beyond it but the remainder of the Strait was shrouded in mist as far as the Icelandic coast. At 1922, as the Arctic twilight drew on, *Suffolk* had been steering south-west when she sighted the two German ships 7 miles away skirting the edge of the Greenland pack ice, 55 miles north-west of Iceland's North Cape. Her enemy report was picked up by CS 1, who closed and gained contact himself before reporting the enemy's position, course and speed to the C-in-C, who had not received *Suffolk*'s initial report. CS 1's signal was also received in the Admiralty operations room, which rebroadcast the information to every ship taking part in the hunt. With strong winds from the north-west, conditions were not suitable for either cruiser to fly off its Walrus to shadow and *Suffolk*'s aircraft was actually blown off its catapult and damaged.

Throughout the night of 23/24 May, Admiral Holland's force steamed at 27 knots heading 285 degrees to intercept and engage the enemy. At midnight the cruiser reports put *Bismarck* 120 miles north of *Hood*'s position, steering approximately 200 degrees, and it was anticipated that contact would be made soon after 0140 on 24 May. The British ships went to action stations and battle ensigns were hoisted but at 0031 the cruisers lost contact in a snowstorm and Holland signalled to *Prince of Wales* that if the enemy were not in sight by 0210 he would probably alter course to the south until contact was regained and that he intended *Hood* and *Prince of Wales* to engage *Bismarck*, leaving *Prinz Eugen* to

Norfolk and *Suffolk*. There is no record of this signal being transmitted to the two cruisers, nor was it received by them. *Prince of Wales*' Walrus was prepared ready for catapulting and her commanding officer, Captain J C Leach MVO RN, intended to launch it but visibility deteriorated rapidly and instead it was defuelled and stowed away in its hangar. At 0205 Holland ordered a change of course on to 200 degrees and made a visual signal to his destroyers that they were to carry out a search to the north but it was not taken in by all of them. At 0247 *Suffolk* regained contact as visibility increased to about 12 miles. By 0450 *Hood* was steaming at 28 knots on a heading of 240 degrees and Captain Leach ordered his Walrus to be refuelled and prepared for flight. A delay followed, caused by the discovery that water had contaminated the ready-use fuel supply, and the Walrus was still on the catapult when action commenced. It was damaged by splinters and was jettisoned into the sea, unfortunately playing no part in the action that followed. The first degree of action readiness was ordered at 0510 in the Arctic twilight and at 0535 a vessel was seen on the horizon to the north-west bearing 335 degrees. It was *Bismarck* 34,000yd away with *Prinz Eugen* ahead of her.

At 0537 Holland turned his force 40 degrees towards the enemy by blue pendant to close the range and at 0552 *Hood* opened fire, initially at the leading enemy ship, not the *Bismarck*[13] as the range decreased to 25,000yd. *Prince of Wales* opened fire a minute later but suffered problems with her main armament, which still had contractors' working parties on board trying to rectify manufacturing defects. At 0555 Holland ordered his ships to turn two points (22½ degrees) to port by blue pendant to open their 'A' arcs. At 0600 a further 'two blue' signal was ordered by flags but as she began to turn, *Hood* was straddled by *Bismarck*'s fifth salvo and literally blown apart by explosions. Three or four minutes later her shattered hull had sunk, leaving only three survivors, some wreckage and a pall of smoke. *Prince of Wales* had to alter course to starboard to avoid the wreckage but *Bismarck* quickly shifted target on to her at 18,000yd and at 0602 a 15in shell hit her bridge and killed or wounded most of the personnel on it but not the captain. At about the same time she was hit below the waterline aft. Captain Leach elected to turn away behind a smokescreen at 0613 and the after turret continued to fire but its shell ring jammed. This put two of its four guns out of action until 0720 and the other two were made serviceable at 0825. She had fired only eighteen main armament salvoes and was clearly not in a position to continue the action alone with her badly malfunctioning gunnery system.

The catastrophic loss of the famous *Hood*, known and admired throughout the British Commonwealth, had been a grievous blow but *Bismarck* had received two significant hits, one of which had destroyed a dynamo and caused some flooding in the port boiler room. The second hit was in the forward part of the ship by a shell that entered the port side and exited on the starboard side over the armoured deck, piercing oil fuel tanks and causing her to leave a trail of oil behind her. Her maximum speed was reduced by extensive flooding in her bow compartments. When *Hood* blew up *Norfolk* was 15 miles to the north closing at 28 knots and at 0630 CS 1 ordered *Prince of Wales* to follow at her best speed while he maintained contact. The destroyers *Echo*, *Electra*, *Icarus* and *Achates* were ordered to search for survivors. At 0757 *Suffolk* reported that *Bismarck* had reduced speed and appeared to be damaged, and at 0810 a reconnaissance Sunderland from Iceland reported that she was leaving a broad slick of oil behind her. Admiral Wake-Walker had to decide whether to resume the action and, after consideration, he decided that the hit on *Prince of Wales*' bridge, the technical problems with her main armament and the limitation on speed forced by her flooding aft made her unfit for further action. He decided to continue shadowing but not force an action. Admiral Tovey in *King George V* was still 360 miles to the east but the Admiralty took steps to bring more ships into action. *Rodney*, 550 miles south-east of *Bismarck*, was ordered to leave the ships she was escorting and head towards the enemy. *Ramillies* was ordered to leave convoy HX 127 from Halifax and place herself to the west of the enemy and *Revenge* was ordered to leave Halifax and head towards the enemy. The cruiser *Edinburgh* was ordered to close the scene of action as a potential relief shadower.

During the afternoon *Bismarck* made two attempts to shake off her shadowers by turning sharply west in a squall while her consort continued to the south. Both attempts failed and a southerly course was resumed. Admiral Lutjens informed German Group Command West that loss of fuel now compelled him to head for the Normandie Dock in St Nazaire, the only dry dock on the French Atlantic coast large enough to take *Bismarck*. Admiral Tovey appreciated that the enemy ships' superior speed might allow them to escape and he ordered a torpedo attack by *Victorious*' Swordfish. Tovey was aware, given 825 NAS' lack of recent practice, that this was a big ask but he wrote in his subsequent report that it was carried out 'with splendid gallantry and success'. At 1440 on 24 May *Victorious* was ordered to close to a position within 100 miles of *Bismarck* for the attack, after which she was to remain in contact if possible. Position, course and speed reports of *Bismarck*'s progress were received from *Norfolk* and *Suffolk*, and *Victorious*' force obtained a sun sight to fix its own position at 2000 so that the strike could be planned with reasonable accuracy. The carrier's operations team calculated from this data that she could not get within 100nm until 2300 and with a

Swordfish of 825 NAS ranged on *Victorious* with torpedoes loaded ready for their strike against *Bismarck*. (*Author's collection*)

strong wind blowing from the north-west, navigational accuracy would deteriorate as time elapsed. It was decided, therefore, to fly off the nine strike aircraft while they were still 120 miles from their objective and at 2208 *Victorious* turned into wind on a heading of 330 degrees and reduced speed to 15 knots to fly off 825 NAS led by Lieutenant Commander (A) Eugene Esmonde RN. There was considerable deck movement but it took only two minutes for the aircraft to get airborne into a leaden sky with extensive, scudding clouds and rain.

All nine aircraft were fitted with ASV Mark II radar, 825 NAS having been the first unit equipped with it, and the observers were still learning how to make the best use of it. The *Bismarck* action was its first operational use by naval aircraft.[14] The set's transmission and reception used Yagi arrays on the outer port and starboard forward interplane struts, each mounted 15 degrees off the aircraft centreline to give wide coverage. They were not movable and only covered the aircraft's forward hemisphere. ASV Mark II worked on 176 MHz in the VHF range. It had a beam width of 150 degrees and theoretical ranges could be selected from one to 35 miles dependent on sea state, although under the stormy conditions in the Atlantic on that night contact was unlikely at the maximum range. Contacts appeared on an 'A' scan display in the observer's cockpit. This showed a triangular area of sea return at the bottom with a vertical line above with contacts appearing on it. The range of the contact could be calculated from the height of its 'blip' above the bottom and its bearing left or right of the nose could be deduced from whether the greater part of the 'blip' was to left or right of the line, an indication of which aerial had the stronger signal. The observer could instruct the pilot to turn until the 'blip' was centred in the beam as the range reduced until the target could be seen visually for an attack to commence.

The nine Swordfish flew towards the reported position of *Bismarck* through extensive cloud cover with a base at 1,500ft[15] and at 2330 the leader gained ASV contact at 16 miles fine on the port bow. Shortly afterwards the contact was seen through a break in the clouds and positively identified as *Bismarck* on a course of 160 degrees at an estimated 28 knots. Esmonde turned his squadron to the south with the intention of working his way round to an attacking position from ahead but this alteration took the target outside the coverage of his aircraft's radar and contact was lost. Unfortunately a rain squall caused visual contact to be lost as well at this moment but during a turn back on to north the shadowing cruisers were seen and informed by flashing light that a torpedo attack was imminent. *Norfolk* replied, helpfully, that *Bismarck* was 14 miles on her starboard bow; at 2350 Esmonde's observer gained radar contact on a target estimated to be in the right place and he led the squadron down below the cloud cover to attack. At the last moment the target was identified as a US Coastguard cutter lying stopped in the water and the attack was aborted. *Bismarck* was 6 miles away to the south and saw the aircraft as they broke cloud. Realising that an attack would soon follow, she fired a box barrage, which was continued throughout the attack.

Esmonde had intended to attack on the enemy's starboard bow with his sub-flight, leaving the port side to his number two and three sub-flights, but his starboard lower aileron was hit by anti-aircraft fire and he ordered his sub-flight to drop their torpedoes from the position they were in off the port bow. The second sub-flight leader set up an attack on the port bow but he was not happy with it and, staying at low level, he led his aircraft into a better position. It was a torpedo from this sub-flight that appeared to cause a water splash and spurt of black smoke that led to a hit being claimed. Number three sub-flight leader also got into a good dropping position but one of his aircraft lost contact in cloud and never saw the target. Dropping ranges varied between 600 and 1,200yd, with the majority at 1,000yd. The torpedoes were set to run at 40 knots at a depth of 31ft and fitted with duplex pistols. The attack was well executed and deserved success but whether any of the torpedoes did in fact hit is open to debate. German records examined after the war revealed that *Bismarck*'s violent manoeuvring to avoid the torpedoes, together with her heavy firing, increased the damage to her number two boiler room, which flooded completely and had to be abandoned. The aircraft all got away at low level but continued to be fired upon out to a range of 7 miles.

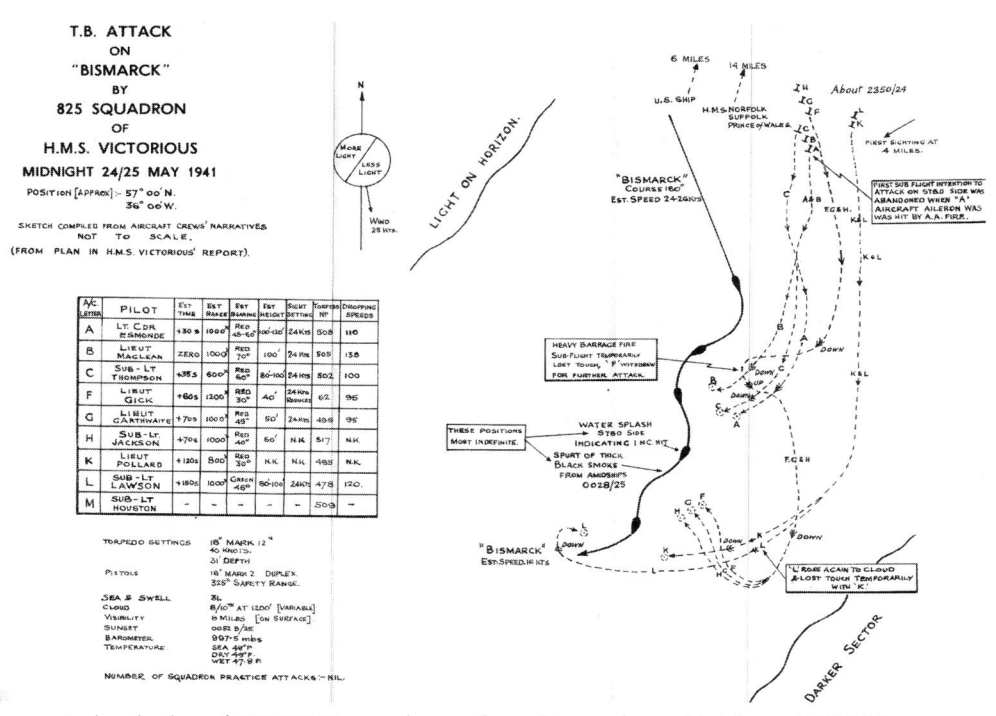

A sketch plan of 825 NAS' torpedo attack on *Bismarck* at midnight on 24/25 May 1941 drawn from *Victorious*' action report. (*Author's collection*)

Night was falling as the strike force returned to *Victorious*[16] and, unfortunately, her Type 72 aircraft homing beacon failed, a rain squall hid the ship and the strike force missed her at first in the darkness.[17] They had to be directed to the ship by radar and the beams of signal projectors were shone into the air to guide them towards the deck. All nine landed on safely by 0201 on 25 May. A Fulmar, one of two flown off at 2300 to shadow the enemy, reported seeing the column of smoke rising from *Bismarck* that was taken to be a torpedo hit and two further Fulmars were flown off for shadowing duties at 0105. The two Fulmars flown off at 2300 were still missing and lights were shone until 0250, when all hope that they might still be airborne was given up. One of their crews, Lieutenant B D Cambell RN with his observer Sub Lieutenant (A) M G Goodger RNVR, were never seen again but the other crew subsequently had an interesting tale to tell that John Hoare recounted in his autobiographical *Tumult in the Clouds*.[18] This crew comprised Lieutenant (A) F C Furlong RNVR and his observer Sub Lieutenant J E M Hoare RCNVR. Before joining the Air Branch of the RNVR, Frank Furlong had been an amateur jockey and had won the Grand National in 1935 on *Reynoldstown*. Knowing that they might have to fly that night in appalling weather, they both took precautions; Furlong 'borrowed' a small, single-pilot dinghy from one of the RAF pilots destined for West Africa who would no longer need it and Hoare filled a flask with brandy and put it in his hip pocket. He also stuffed Penguin editions of Evelyn Waugh's *Decline and Fall* and *Vile Bodies* into the pockets of his monkey jacket. The two Fulmars on standby had their engines warmed through but were kept in the hangar because of the stormy conditions on the flight deck. Hoare had his doubts about their aircraft's radio tuning and its compasses had not been swung since their issue to the improvised 800Z NAS for use as guides to lead the assembled RAF Hurricanes to Malta. Once they were ordered to launch, Hoare described how the ship turned into the gale to launch the Swordfish and then the Fulmars were ranged to be launched after a short pause. His 'bits and pieces' – Bigsworth chart board, compasses, protractors, pencils (sharpened at both ends), erasers and so forth – were already in the observer's cockpit and Commander H C Ranald RN, Commander 'Air', cheerful as ever, just said, 'Off you go; there will be beer and sandwiches for you in the wardroom when you get back.' Cluttered in Irvine jackets, Mae Wests, flying helmets and gloves they clambered into their cockpits and then:

> … the grey reality of ship, sea and sky was pretty overwhelming. From the entrance to the island people waved. The engine roared, Commander 'Air' flagged us, we moved slowly along the deck downhill, then faster and faster seeing island and gun sponsons passing and as the bows rose ahead of us we sailed off up into the sky and away. We drew breath, set course, noted times, synchronised watches and looked out.

The cloud base was at about 200ft and they flew just below it, in and out of snowstorms, sometimes skirting a particularly heavy one so that they could maintain their visual search. Their outbound leg was to be for two hours and almost at the turning point they both thought they saw *Bismarck* beyond a snow shower and turned towards it. When the snow cleared the sea surface appeared empty and they were left wondering if it had been a hallucination; certainly a brief glimpse, if that is what it was, did not merit a sighting report that might send the fleet in a wrong direction. An expanding square search failed to find any further trace and they set heading back to *Victorious*. Two hours later they knew they were in trouble. *Victorious*' homing beacon was off the air and they failed to see her in the darkness and low cloud. The observer of *Kenya*'s Walrus, a course-mate of Hoare's, later told him that they were heard flying overhead and a searchlight shone upwards to guide them but they did not see it. The official endurance of the Fulmar was four and a half hours but after nearly five hours:

> Frank Furlong said we'd better come down while we still have an engine and we checked our ditching drill ... and slowly motored down into wind. I fired Verey lights to give Frank a glimpse of where the water was. Open everything that opens said Frank and when we come down go straight into the dinghy. Stand by. There was a bit of a thump, a long pause when nothing happened, then a real thump and we were down.

The Fulmar's dinghy, a big round one, inflated at once and came alongside; Frank stepped into it dry shod and held it while he loaded the emergency rations. Hoare had to swim a few strokes but brought with him the 'borrowed' dinghy. In seconds, as their aircraft sank, they were 'rocketing up and down in enormous seas'. Frank inflated the 'borrowed' dinghy and they stood it at an angle of 45 degrees to act as cover against the broken water, which would otherwise have completely flooded them. It proved to be an invaluable asset. Hoare reckoned later that three things saved them; first Frank's immaculate ditching, then the shelter provided by the second dinghy. Third, and running counter to all later survival training, was Hoare's flask of brandy:

> ... at dawn we each had a modest mouthful. It went down ... like a river of fire ... then seemed to spread through the entire cold and weary framework of our bodies and for a moment there was peace. A moment later, in perfect synchrony, we leaned over the side and threw up ...

They thought that their only hope was the search that *Victorious* would surely mount for them and the ship did indeed do so but lost a Swordfish in the process. It ditched and after its pilot, Lieutenant J M Christian RN, and his two crew members got into their dinghy they encountered the surviving crew of a Norwegian ship in their lifeboat. They seemed to be sailing in what he considered to be the wrong direction, however, and he declined to join them. He and his crew were later picked up off Iceland and the Norwegians were, apparently, never seen again.

By the afternoon of 26 May the weather had improved, the swell had moderated and visibility was good. So good in fact that Hoare saw a smudge of smoke on the horizon that grew into a funnel and mast, then the superstructure and finally the hull of a merchant ship, which saw them and turned towards them. Painfully, but with many helping hands, they managed to climb a Jacob's ladder and were safe, or as safe as they could be in a single ship on passage across the Atlantic. She was the Canadian Pacific fast freighter *Beaverhill*, which had sailed in convoy from St John New Brunswick for Liverpool but when news broke that the *Bismarck* was on a raiding mission in the Atlantic she had been detached to sail independently at her best speed. When she found Furlong and Hoare she was, therefore, several hundred miles north of the track she would otherwise have taken. She could not break radio silence and so neither *Victorious* nor their next of kin knew of their rescue until the customs authorities at Holyhead were informed some days later.

About three hours after 825 NAS' torpedo attack the shadowing cruisers lost contact with *Bismarck*. *Suffolk* was fitted with a Type 284 gunnery range-finding radar in addition to the Type 279 intended for surface search. The former provided both range and accurate bearings but the latter, because of its wide beam width, lacked accuracy and it was difficult to discriminate between separate contacts at roughly the same range. However, using the Type 284 in this way did involve continuous training of the director control tower on which it was mounted since it did not have a rotating aerial. This was not normally considered advisable for more than a few hours at a time but her commanding officer, Captain R M Ellis RN, decided that the risk of a breakdown could, with due safeguards, be accepted in order to make the best tactical use of the set.[19] He and his navigating officer devised a suitable drill and the radar operators, gun director crew and surface plotting team had practised the technique during the previous weeks but there was a definite limit on how long it could be sustained. Among the many awards announced after the *Bismarck* action, Ordinary Seamen (Radar) C F Tuckwood and A J Sinker of *Suffolk* were both awarded the DCM for their work in the action and relief crews of the Type 284 'to whose zeal and skilful operation of their equipment the success of the low visibility shadowing by its aid was due'. This had been one of the first prolonged uses of radar in a surface action by the RN.

At 0229 on 25 May *Bismarck* was tracked bearing 192 degrees from *Suffolk* at 20,900yd and its speed had dropped to 20 knots. Captain Ellis was sufficiently confident to resume zig-zagging and at 0306 the enemy was relocated on the same bearing and *Suffolk* turned on to the outward leg of a 30-degree zig-zag, which was to last ten minutes. When she turned back, contact was not regained and as the minutes passed it became clear that *Bismarck* was lost. Admiral Tovey considered that the loss of touch had been caused primarily by overconfidence; the radar had given such consistently good results and had been used so skilfully that it had engendered a sense of false security. *Suffolk* had got used to shadowing from the extreme range of her Type 284 and had lost touch on those parts of the zig-zag that took her furthest from the enemy. *Bismarck* had evaded by turning sharply to starboard as the cruiser had altered to port and had been out of range by the time she turned back. *Suffolk* signalled at 0411 that contact had been lost.

At 0800 *Victorious* flew off seven Swordfish to search for the enemy and joined a line of search herself with the cruisers of 2 CS. None of them made contact. An Admiralty DF bearing, attributed to *Bismarck*, was received but drawn on the general operations plot too far to the north in *King George V*, giving Admiral Tovey the misleading impression that the enemy was heading back to the North Sea. To counter this he turned his force on to 055 degrees at 27 knots at 1027 on 25 May, actually heading away from the *Bismarck*'s real position. *Victorious* landed on six of her Swordfish at 1107. The seventh had ditched close to an abandoned ship's lifeboat, which was well stocked with provisions and water. The aircrew spent nine days in it before being seen and rescued by a merchant vessel. At this stage the Admiralty ordered Force H to proceed to sea on the assumption that *Bismarck* was heading for Brest and as 25 May progressed opinion in the Admiralty operations room hardened in favour of the battleship heading for a French Atlantic port. Unknown to the Admiralty, however, *Prinz Eugen* had parted company with *Bismarck* at 1914 on 24 May with instructions to carry out independent cruiser warfare against British shipping but machinery defects forced her to return, undetected, to Brest after refuelling in mid-Atlantic. She was eventually seen in Brest by air reconnaissance in early June.

On 26 May the 4th Destroyer Flotilla led by Captain P L Vian DSO, D 4, which had been escorting the troop convoy WS 8B, was ordered to join the C-in-C Home Fleet and so too was the battleship *Rodney*. The heavy cruiser *Dorsetshire* was ordered to leave the Sierra Leone-bound convoy she was escorting and head towards the C-in-C at her best speed. As Force H headed north, deteriorating weather forced it to reduce speed to 17 knots and its escorting destroyers were sent back to Gibraltar. *Ark Royal* flew off ten Swordfish on anti-submarine patrols and further aircraft to search for the enemy. She was pitching into a north-westerly gale and the after round-down was estimated to be rising and falling through 56ft or more. Aircraft were sliding across the spray-drenched deck as they were ranged and flying operations under these conditions were a considerable achievement. Further search Swordfish were flown off before the first aircraft were recovered from 0930.

Spirits throughout the fleet had been low at dawn on 26 May but at 1030 a Catalina of 15 Group Coastal Command sighted *Bismarck*. Its flash report was received in *King George V* at 1043 and *Renown* at 1038, and there was elation after its position was plotted and showed her to be well to the west of Force H. A refined, more accurate, position was transmitted forty-five minutes later when Swordfish 2H piloted by Sub Lieutenant (A) J V Hartley RN, with Sub Lieutenant (A) P R Elias RN as his observer and Leading Airman N Huxley as TAG, from *Ark Royal* located *Bismarck* and found it to be 25nm east of the position transmitted by the Catalina. Seven minutes later 2F, flown by Lieutenant (A) J R Callender RN with Lieutenant P B Schonfeldt RN and Leading Airman R Baker, also located Bismarck.[20] This placed the enemy battleship 690 miles west of Brest but Admiral Tovey's force was 130 miles to the north, too far away to intercept *Bismarck* unless she could be slowed by a further air torpedo attack. At 1154 *Bismarck* broke radio silence to report that she was being shadowed by enemy 'land planes', indicating that there was a British carrier within range. From then until 2320 that night *Ark Royal*'s Swordfish, working in pairs, continued to shadow the enemy. Admiral Somerville's Force H was ordered to close *Bismarck* and keep in touch but *Renown* was not to engage the enemy battleship alone. *Ark Royal* was to position herself within 50 miles of *Bismarck* and launch a series of torpedo attacks. The Catalina's report had also been received by Captain Vian, D 4, who found himself only 30 miles astern of the enemy battleship. Knowing that the C-in-C would wish him 'to steer to intercept the enemy', Vian altered course to the south-east in order to close and, if possible, attack *Bismarck*.

Rodney joined *King George V* at 1806 on 26 May approximately 90 miles north of *Bismarck* but the two battleships' fuel states were critical. *King George V* had only 32 per cent remaining and *Rodney* reported that she would have to turn for the nearest UK base at which she could refuel at 0800 on 27 May. Speed had to be reduced to a more economical 22 knots, forcing the C-in-C to accept that unless the enemy's speed could be reduced it was no longer possible to force an action. Everything, therefore, depended on *Ark Royal*'s Swordfish and a strike force of fifteen Swordfish was ranged and armed with torpedoes. However, the aircrew were not briefed that the cruiser *Sheffield* had been detached at 1315 by Admiral Somerville with orders to shadow *Bismarck*. Apparently he did so because weather conditions had become particularly bad and Sub Lieutenant Elias, the first observer to return from shadowing, had said at his debrief that he was not absolutely certain whether the ship they had been following was a battleship or a heavy cruiser. This introduced an element of doubt, which led to the strike force torpedoes being fitted with duplex pistols set to run at only 30ft. The signal to detach *Sheffield* had been transmitted visually but not repeated to *Ark Royal*. A signal reporting *Sheffield*'s new task was transmitted to the Admiralty and copied to *Ark Royal* but it had still not been decoded in the carrier when the aircraft took off. Once it had been decoded a warning signal was transmitted urgently to the aircraft at 1620 but by then it was already too late.

Ark Royal's embarked squadrons on 26 May 1941

807 NAS	12 Fulmars	Lieutenant Commander (A) J Sholto-Douglas RN
808 NAS	12 Fulmars	Lieutenant Commander E D G Lewin RN
810 NAS	12 Swordfish	Lieutenant Commander M Johnstone DSC RN
818 NAS	9 Swordfish	Lieutenant Commander T P Coode RN
820 NAS	9 Swordfish	Lieutenant Commander J A Stewart-Moore RN

The strike force took off from 1450 but one aircraft suffered a broken flying wire and had to recover immediately. The remaining fourteen formed up and flew through the extensive cloud cover towards the reported position of *Bismarck*. Only the leader's aircraft had been fitted with ASV radar and in the prevailing conditions of cloud and bad visibility great reliance had to be placed on it. With no knowledge that there was any other ship in *Bismarck*'s vicinity, the observer in the leading Swordfish gained contact on a ship within 20 miles of its briefed position and guided his pilot into an attacking position above the low cloud base. The strike aircraft dived out of the cloud at 1550 and eleven had released their torpedoes before they realised that the ship they were attacking was *Sheffield*. To his credit, Captain C A A Larcom RN of *Sheffield* immediately appreciated what was happening, ordered maximum speed, turned hard away from his previous course and ordered his anti-aircraft gunners not to open fire. Fortunately she was not hit; two torpedoes exploded as they hit the water and three detonated harmlessly astern; the remainder all missed. *Bismarck* itself was 15 miles to the south and, somewhat chastened, the aircrew flew back to *Ark Royal*. On their way they saw 4 DS about 20 miles west of Force H, the first intimation of their proximity. This failure of task force command had nearly led to a disaster but a valuable lesson had been learned. All the strike aircraft were recovered by 1720, refuelled and rearmed as quickly as possible for a further strike. Meanwhile, *Sheffield* took up a shadowing position 10 miles astern of the enemy battleship and relief Swordfish from *Ark Royal* confirmed that the enemy in sight was definitely *Bismarck*. In view of the apparent failure of the torpedoes' duplex pistols in the first strike, possibly because of the rough sea conditions, they were replaced with contact pistols and set to run at 22ft.

At 1910 on 26 May *Ark Royal* began to launch her second strike, deploying four Swordfish from 818 NAS, four from 810 NAS and seven from 820 NAS. They formed up into two groups, each of three sub-flights in line astern. They were briefed to contact *Sheffield* first to be directed by her on to *Bismarck* but they encountered thick cloud and as they climbed through it the groups got split up. There was a force six wind from the north-west and three-quarter cloud cover. *Bismarck* clearly knew that Swordfish were shadowing her and that a strike must follow. There was little point, therefore, in maintaining radio silence and the aircraft made frequent transmissions so that *Sheffield* could use its direction-finding equipment to home them on to her. She was seen at 1955 but then lost again. Visibility improved and she was seen again at 2035 for long enough to inform the aircraft by flashing light that the enemy bore 110 degrees from her at 12 miles. The strike force then took departure from her overhead at 2040 in sub-flights, each of which flew in line astern formation. As they neared the enemy the cloud became thicker with a base at 700ft and several aircraft became detached.

At 2047 the three Swordfish of sub-flight number one dived through the cloud and saw *Bismarck* 4 miles to the south-east downwind of them. They were joined by a single aircraft that had become detached from sub-flight number three and they climbed back into the cloud together before making their attacking dives at 2053 on the enemy's port beam, immediately coming under fire. They dropped their four torpedoes together and assessed one of them to have hit. Sub-flight number two lost contact with the first in cloud and one of their own number lost contact with the rest. One of the other two was fitted with ASV and attacked out of cloud on a radar bearing. They found themselves on their target's starboard beam under intense fire when they dropped and one of their two torpedoes was assessed as a probable hit. The third aircraft of this sub-flight returned to *Sheffield*, got a fresh range and bearing of the enemy and then carried out a determined attack on its port bow under heavy fire. This crew also believed that their torpedo had hit. Sub-flight number four followed number three into cloud but encountered icing conditions at 6,600ft and dived into a clear area at about 2,000ft, where they were joined by the second Swordfish of number three sub-flight. *Bismarck* was seen firing at number two sub-flight to starboard and so they worked their way around her stern, diving through a low patch of cloud to attack simultaneously from the port side. They dropped their four torpedoes but unfortunately none was seen to hit. As their attack developed, they too came under heavy fire and Swordfish 4C was later found to have been hit by more than 100 pieces of shrapnel. Both pilot and TAG were wounded but they managed to fly back to *Ark Royal*.

Two aircraft of number five sub-flight lost contact with each other and the other sub-flights in cloud but pressed home their attacks with great determination. They climbed individually to 7,000ft before encountering icing conditions and then dived towards the estimated position of the enemy. Swordfish 4K emerged from cloud at 1,000ft and saw the enemy downwind, then climbed back into cloud under fire but saw a torpedo hit *Bismarck*'s starboard side through a gap. After reaching a position on the battleship's starboard bow, 4K opened out to 5 miles and then flew back in again just above the waves to drop its torpedo just outside 1,000yd. The crew deserved success but unfortunately they saw that their weapon had not hit. The other lone Swordfish from this sub-flight made two attack attempts under heavy fire but was eventually forced to jettison its torpedo and return to the carrier. The two aircraft of number six sub-flight attacked individually. The first attacked from the starboard beam and dropped its torpedo at 2,000yd without success. The second lost sight of the enemy, then returned to *Sheffield* for a new range and bearing before returning to search for *Bismarck* at sea level. It was eventually driven off by anti-aircraft fire and did not attack.

This strike was over by 2125 after thirteen torpedoes had been dropped and two jettisoned. The aircrew thought that two hits had been obtained but after their debrief *Ark Royal* signalled to Admiral Somerville at 2213 that there had been 'one hit amidships'. This was amplified at 2240 with a second report that there had been 'a second hit on starboard quarter' and it was this hit that had sealed *Bismarck*'s fate. At 2140 she turned to port and fired six accurate 15in salvoes at *Sheffield*, none of which hit but a near miss killed three men and seriously injured a further two. Minutes later, 4 DS was seen approaching from the west and its destroyers held contact and carried out a series of torpedo attacks through the night of 26/27 May, which were later described by the C-in-C as 'a model of their kind'. In *Ark Royal* aircraft were made ready for a further torpedo strike at dawn.

Bismarck could no longer steer; the hit on the starboard quarter had damaged her propellers, wrecked the steering gear and jammed her rudders. The steering room was flooded and although divers managed to get into it and centre one rudder, the other proved to be immovable. After turning a complete circle, she headed erratically into the prevailing wind at about 8 knots, unable to avoid the approaching British battleships as they steamed down from the north. She stopped occasionally when hit by destroyers' torpedoes. At 0115 Force H turned south to keep roughly

20 miles south of *Bismarck* to leave a clear approach for the battle fleet. *Ark Royal* had a strike force of twelve Swordfish ready at dawn and it was flown off at 0915 while heavy gunfire could be heard to the north as *King George V* and *Rodney* engaged the enemy. There was a clear horizon and the Swordfish had no difficulty locating *Bismarck* but by then they were no longer needed, she was a wallowing hulk, settling in the water and on fire. The battleships had already departed, leaving the cruisers *Norfolk* and *Dorsetshire* to finish her off. *Norfolk* fired four torpedoes at 1010 at an estimated range of 4,000yd, two of which were reported as hits. *Dorsetshire* fired two torpedoes from *Bismarck*'s starboard side at 1025 from a range of 3,600yd and one of these was seen to explode under the bridge, while the other was thought to explode further aft. At 1036 a final torpedo was fired into the port side from 2,600yd and this also hit. At 1040 she heeled over to port and sank by the stern. *Dorsetshire* and *Maori* picked up survivors while Swordfish searched for U-boats.

Survivors subsequently claimed that the ship had been scuttled on her captain's orders once it became clear that she could not escape and it might never have proved possible to prove whether it was the scuttling charges or the many hits by shell and torpedo that had sunk her. However, in 2001 an expedition by the underwater explorer David Mearns located the wrecks of both *Hood* and *Bismarck*. The state of *Hood*'s wreckage revealed the true extent of the damage she had suffered when blown apart by internal explosions. *Bismarck*'s wreck was also interesting; it had hit the bottom on the side of an underwater volcano and slid for over half a mile down an incline. In his book describing the expedition,[21] David Mearns made the following observations about *Bismarck*'s sinking:

> Never before had anyone been able to say precisely how effective these torpedo strikes had been in damaging Bismarck below her armour belt. Because she had avoided so many of the earlier torpedo attacks and had seemingly shrugged off all those that did not reach her hull, with the sole exception of the fateful strike on her rudders, perhaps people were led to believe that Bismarck was immune to torpedoes. We can reveal for the first time that she was not. Our investigation along both her starboard and port sides shows most definitely that Bismarck was mortally wounded by the British torpedoes. In total we found four gaping torpedo holes – two on the starboard side and two on the port side – that were clearly sufficient to sink Bismarck, without the aid of additional water ingress due to the scuttling charges. The locations of the torpedo holes – firstly, abreast the conning tower, starboard side, secondly abreast the rear AA gun director, starboard side, thirdly abreast the bridge port side

and fourthly, slightly abaft the turret 'Caesar' – match well with the eyewitness testimonies. The second and third torpedo holes were probably enlarged in the course of Bismarck's slide down the volcano slope, but there is a distinct possibility that the third hole was by two strikes from Norfolk and Dorsetshire. The first hole was probably from a Dorsetshire strike that exploded against the hull and distorted the armour plates immediately above. The position of the fourth hole suggests that it was from the Ark Royal Swordfish on 26 May, causing far more damage than anyone realised, thus explaining the flooding that caused Bismarck's list to port ... The scuttling action taken by the Germans may have hastened the inevitable, but only by a matter of minutes. However [Admiral] Tovey's unfortunate radio transmission to Vice Admiral Somerville on board Renown 'Cannot get her to sink with guns' which was timed some five minutes after she had actually sunk ... initiated the lingering idea that British guns were not up to the job. The ironic truth is that they were.

Hunting down Bismarck's supply ships

Unaware that *Prinz Eugen* had suffered defects with her new machinery and been forced to head for Brest, *Victorious* and *Ark Royal* were able, at various times, to use their aircraft to search for her and the German supply ships that were still at large.[22] *Eagle* and *Nelson* covered the area west of the Cape Verde Islands and the carrier aircraft achieved a degree of success in their searches. Having refuelled in the Clyde and taken on board another load of RAF Hurricanes for Malta, *Victorious* was heading for Gibraltar with Convoy WS 8X on 4 June when a patrolling 825 NAS Swordfish sighted and stopped the enemy supply ship *Gonzenheim* 200 miles north of the Azores. The cruiser *Neptune* was detached to board and capture the ship but before it could arrive its crew fired scuttling charges and sank their ship.[23] The tanker *Esso Hamburg* was intercepted by the destroyer *Brilliant* and *Gedania* was captured by *Neptune*.

At 0700 on 6 June *Eagle* had two Swordfish airborne on anti-submarine patrols to protect the cruiser *Dunedin*, which was refuelling at sea, when one of them sighted a lone merchant ship 30 miles north-west of the carrier steering north.[24] When challenged, the ship identified itself as the Norwegian *Kristiana Fjord* but she altered course to the west and increased speed. From the known description of the ship it was clear that this was not the vessel's true identity and at 0950 a strike force of Swordfish armed with 500lb bombs was flown off but failed to locate it. In fact the ship had altered course again but, anticipating that this might have been the case, *Eagle* flew off four search aircraft at 1315, each armed with two 500lb bombs. One of these, Duty 'B', sighted the enemy at 1439 and transmitted a flash report, following this with an amplifying signal at 1510. These were received by Duty 'D', which was 100 miles away, and Duty 'F', which was 150 miles away, but not by the nearest aircraft, Duty 'C'. Duty 'B' continued to shadow the enemy, assuming that the other aircraft would join him, but when they did not do so he ordered the ship by flashing light to close *Eagle*. The other aircraft had actually returned to the carrier and landed on. When the ship showed no signs of obeying Duty 'B's order, the TAG was instructed to fire his machine gun across the ship's bow but it responded by increasing speed. At 1700 Duty 'B' dive-bombed it but missed and at 1728 the ship, which was in fact the German *Elbe*, made an SOS transmission in German plain language. Her captain had probably already decided to scuttle his ship. At 1550 *Eagle* flew off a further strike force of five Swordfish, each armed with two 500lb bombs, and these sighted *Elbe* at 1725. The ship was stopped and on fire with its crew abandoning it. Instructions to turn on to south were ignored and so the aircraft bombed *Elbe*, obtaining a single hit on number three hold and three near misses. She was left in a sinking state but a subsequent search for lifeboats found nothing.

Further success for *Eagle*'s Swordfish followed on 15 June; they were carrying out a surface search at 1215 when E5B sent a flash report after sighting a single merchant ship.[25] Minutes later the aircrew, Midshipman (A) W L Hughes RNVR his observer Sub Lieutenant (A) P A Denington RNVR and TAG Leading Airman N C Wills, sent an amplifying report describing the contact as a tanker. They closed the ship, later identified as the tanker *Lothringen*, and ordered it to stop by flashing light. It failed to do so and the TAG fired a burst across its bow. This was answered by machine-gun fire, which damaged both the fuselage and wings of the Swordfish, proving that it was indeed an enemy vessel, Hughes dive-bombed it with his two 250lb SAP bombs, both of which hit. He also strafed the ship with his front gun, while Wills engaged it with the rear gun. By 1350 the ship was turning circles, leaving a thick pall of smoke behind it, but E5B was getting low on fuel and had to return to the carrier. Its place in contact with *Lothringen* was taken twenty minutes later by E5K flown by Sub Lieutenant (A) C R Camidge RNVR, his observer Sub Lieutenant (A) W H Lett RNVR and TAG Leading Airman F A Dean. They found the ship to be steering erratically and leaking oil but it was flying two white flags from the foremast and a white sheet was waved from the bridge. As they watched, an attempt was made to lower a boat but to prevent any attempt to scuttle and abandon the ship Camidge and his TAG machine-gunned the boat and they saw it dropped into the water with only one man in it. They proceeded to machine gun all the lifeboats, which had the desired effect of keeping the crew on board. Repeated requests for the ship's real nationality were finally answered by flashing light with 'German' in plain language. Three more Swordfish joined E5K to circle the ship and keep watch. At 1335 *Dunedin* was ordered to close *Lothringen* and, if possible, to board it and take it as a prize. She arrived at the ship at 1725 having seen the aircraft circling overhead and proceeded to put a party on board, which eventually took the ship to Bermuda. They found the German merchant navy crew co-operative but the small Kriegsmarine party much less so. They had set six scuttling charges but none of them had been detonated and the boarding party were able to make them safe. This had been one of the few occasions when a ship surrendered to an aircraft.

The strikes on Petsamo and Kirkenes

The German attack on the Soviet Union on 22 June 1941 came as a surprise to the British government and had inevitable repercussions on strategy.[26] By then the Home Fleet was centred on two battleships together with the aircraft carriers *Victorious* and *Furious*, four cruisers and about twenty destroyers, but it was frequently required to provide ships for tasks outside its operational area. *Victorious*' part in ferrying RAF Hurricanes to Malta is an example. Churchill immediately saw the value of providing unstinted support for Britain's unexpected new ally and ordered the C-in-C Home Fleet to investigate the possibility of deploying a task force into the Arctic, which would be of 'enormous value' to Soviet resistance. Although Churchill had been a staunch supporter of the RAF, especially its Bomber Command, he now found that the force whose existence he had advocated so strongly was actually incapable of immediate strategic operations at the ranges necessary to be of any use in northern Norway or the adjacent Russian littoral. As he should have realised if he had thought back to his days as First Lord of the Admiralty when the RNAS had first demonstrated its potential, only aircraft carriers had the strategic capability to deploy over large distances and strike at short notice when they arrived. Unfortunately the years of dual control between 1918 and 1937, in which Churchill had been a willing participant, meant that while the Navy had a growing fleet of modern carriers, it lacked the number and types of aircraft it needed for the strategic role Churchill now expected it to perform. Both the US and Japanese navies showed later in 1941 what British naval aircraft would have been capable of achieving if only politicians between the wars had not taken such a negative view of their importance.

As a first step, Admiral Tovey sent the newly promoted Rear Admiral Vian to reconnoitre the Russian port of Murmansk at the head of the Kola inlet 2,000 miles from Scapa Flow. Besides being the only ice-free port in north Russia, it was linked to Moscow by rail, allowing the relatively fast movement of logistic supplies sent by the UK to aid the Soviet armed forces in their fight against the common enemy. Vaenga lay on the eastern shore of the inlet and the Soviet naval base at Polyarnoe lay on the western side near its entrance. Vian found that the Kola inlet lacked sufficient anti-aircraft defences and other facilities necessary for it to be considered as a potential British fleet base. It was only a few minutes' flying time from German airfields near the ports of Kirkenes and Petsamo. Both were to the west of the Kola Inlet; Kirkenes on the north coast of Norway near the Finnish border and Petsamo on the narrow, northern stretch of Finnish coastline between Norway and Russia.

Any operation intended to aid the Soviet Union in the short term had only one option open to it, the passage of merchant ships loaded with war material in convoys escorted as strongly as possible around the North Cape to the Kola Inlet, but many adverse factors had to be taken into account. German-occupied Norway had airfields spread along its entire coastline as far east as Kirkenes. Enemy reconnaissance aircraft frequently overflew Scapa Flow and would know when the Home Fleet was at sea. In winter there was no real daylight in the Barents Sea and weather conditions could be appalling. In spring, when the Arctic sea ice

Albacores being ranged on *Victorious*. Note the steering arm attached to the tail wheel of the aircraft nearest the camera; instructions for how to turn it would be shouted by the leading aircraft handler in charge of the move. (*Author's collection*)

reached its southern-most limit, there was little sea room for manoeuvre. There was continuous daylight in summer but also intermittent fog that was difficult to predict. Given the lack of RAF strategic mobility, its aircraft were of no value in the Barents Sea and defence against air attack would have to be provided by the Home Fleet's own fighters and anti-aircraft guns. Carrier operations would be difficult and dangerous in these conditions.[27]

While the first arrangements to provide the Soviet Union with weapons were finalised, Churchill wanted to fulfil his pledge to support the Soviet Union as soon as possible and in July Admiral Tovey was informed by the Admiralty that the Soviet government had asked for British forces to attack German troop transports reported to be moving into the Petsamo–Kirkenes area from more southerly Norwegian ports. The only British force capable of doing so was the Home Fleet and the C-in-C was ordered to make preparations for an attack on both ports with aircraft embarked in *Victorious* and *Furious*. Admiral Tovey expressed his dislike of such an operation in the Arctic summer since it seemed to him that 'the risk to which the carriers, aircrews and oilers would be exposed during this operation ... was out of all proportion to the most optimistic estimate of the results they could achieve'. There was every likelihood that the slow Swordfish and Albacore strike aircraft would be intercepted by high-performance fighters, against which they would stand little chance even if escorted by Fulmars. He suggested an alternative plan in which enemy shipping in the Norwegian littoral further to the south could be attacked but this was not accepted. Churchill insisted that from the point of view of Britain's new relationship with the Soviet Union it was essential that a strike against enemy shipping and territory in the Petsamo area was carried out as soon as possible. A strike by the two carriers was to be organised with a task force made ready to sail from Scapa Flow no later than 21 July.

Both the Admiralty and the C-in-C were only too well aware that *Victorious* had still not been able to work up fully since commissioning in the days before the *Bismarck* action and that *Furious* had been employed on ferrying duties for some weeks with no chance to practise normal carrier flying and strike drills. The latter's 817 NAS had only been commissioned in March and was inexperienced in torpedo attack; many of its pilots were new and had been given no chance to qualify in deck landing prior to the embarkation because *Argus* had been used ferrying RAF aircraft to Gibraltar and West Africa. This state of unpreparedness had to be accepted by Admiral Tovey and the considerable political pressure that he was under can be deduced from the fact that he did so. The subsequent strike against Kirkenes and Petsamo was designated Operation EF by the

Home Fleet. The task force assigned to it was designated as Force P and commanded by Rear Admiral W F Wake-Walker, CS 1, flying his flag in *Devonshire*. It was organised in two divisions, each with one aircraft carrier, one cruiser and three destroyers:

First Division	Second Division
Devonshire	*Suffolk*
Victorious	*Furious*
Inglefield	*Intrepid*
Icarus	*Echo*
Escapade	*Eclipse*

The strike force from *Victorious* consisted of twelve Albacores from 827 NAS led by Lieutenant Commander J A Stewart-Moore RN, all armed with torpedoes, and a further eight Albacores of 828 NAS led by Lieutenant Commander L A Cubitt RN, also armed with torpedoes. Nine Fulmars of 809 NAS[28] led by Lieutenant Commander V C Grenfell RN flew as escort. The strike force from *Furious* consisted of six Swordfish of 812 NAS armed with torpedoes and three others armed with six 250lb GP bombs and eight 25lb incendiary bombs each, led by Lieutenant Commander W E Waters RN. Six Albacores of 817 NAS were armed with torpedoes and a further three with the same bomb load as the three bomb-armed aircraft of 812 NAS, led by Lieutenant Commander D Sanderson RN. Escort for this force was provided by six Fulmars of 800 NAS led by Lieutenant Commander J A D Wroughton RN but, unlike the fighters from *Victorious*, these were armed with four 20lb HE bombs in addition to their front guns to enable them to attack targets of opportunity on the ground. Four Sea Hurricanes of 880 NAS led by Lieutenant Commander F E C Judd RN provided CAP cover for Force P while the strike forces were away.

The briefed objective for the strike forces was to sink German ships; aircraft from *Victorious* were to attack Kirkenes and those from *Furious* were to attack Petsamo; the different weapon loads offering options since no prior reconnaissance had been possible to assess the actual targets in the harbours. If no shipping was found, the aircrew were briefed to attack the iron ore plant at Kirkenes and the jetties and oil tanks at Petsamo. Force P sailed from Scapa Flow on 23 July and refuelled at Seidisfjord in Iceland on 26 July. The two cruisers' Walrus aircraft flew local anti-submarine patrols while the ships were in the fjord as a U-boat had been reported in its vicinity but no contacts were made. *Suffolk*'s Walrus also escorted the minelayer *Adventure*, which was carrying mines to Archangel, to the limit of its endurance. After leaving Seidisfjord, Force P encountered frequent fog patches and a low cloud base that prevented flying but which allowed the force to remain undetected by German reconnaissance aircraft. Unfortunately, as the force neared its planned flying off position 80 miles north-east of Kirkenes at 1330 on 30 July the sky cleared and it was immediately located by an He 111, which was heard transmitting a contact report shortly afterwards. This removed any chance of achieving surprise and gave the enemy at least an hour's warning of the impending attack. Admiral Wake-Walker considered cancelling the operation but, aware of the political importance attached to it, he decided to continue and at 1400 *Victorious* flew off her twenty strike aircraft from a single range and *Furious* flew off nine strike aircraft and four Sea Hurricanes. A second range comprising twelve Fulmars, nine for strike escort and three for force CAP, was flown off *Victorious* at 1418, followed shortly by the balance of nine strike aircraft and six Fulmars from *Furious*.

Twenty Albacores and nine Fulmars set heading from *Victorious* for Kirkenes and nine Swordfish, nine Albacores and six Fulmars set heading from *Furious* for Petsamo. By then all the aircrew knew that the enemy had been forewarned and that stiff opposition could be expected. *Victorious'* aircraft found that their track took them directly towards bright sunlight and 809 NAS failed to see or join up with their strike aircraft. As they went 'feet dry' crossing the coast 809 NAS' aircraft were engaged by heavy anti-aircraft fire near the target area. They had been briefed to fire four red Verey lights, the German recognition signal for the day, to deceive the enemy defences but German records studied later by the Admiralty included a report by the Commander of the seaward defences that said the lights had not been of the shade used by the Germans and the gunners never doubted that the aircraft were hostile. On the other hand, Captain H C Bovell RN of *Victorious* noted in his own letter covering the aircraft combat reports that 'on three occasions enemy aircraft approaching to attack withdrew when this signal was fired and that one enemy aircraft even replied with a pyrotechnic signal'. In all probability the signal did actually cause a degree of confusion that the defence commander had not been anxious to admit. Lieutenant Commander Grenfell, having failed to join up with the Albacores, decided to orbit the target area at 4,000ft to draw enemy fire away from the strike aircraft as they attacked. The gunfire ceased abruptly when a mixed force of about nine Bf 109 and Bf 110 fighters attacked the Fulmars and a number of individual combats ensued. Two Bf 110s and one Bf 109 were claimed to have been shot down for certain; one by Lieutenant Commander Grenfell and the other two by Sub Lieutenant (A) J Cooper RN with his observer Sub Lieutenant (A) A E Wilkinson RNVR. Two Fulmars were lost, one of which was seen to carry out a forced landing under control. Leading Airman L E Barrow of 809 NAS was recorded as missing, killed in action on that day.

While the fighter combat was developing, *Victorious*' Albacores only found the gunnery training ship *Bremse* and two medium-sized merchant ships in Kirkenes harbour, all of them under way. All three were attacked and the latter two were seen to be stopped and on fire as the aircraft withdrew. As they did so, the Albacores were attacked by Bf 109, Bf 110 fighters and, surprisingly, several Ju 87 dive bombers. The latter type was reported by intelligence to be armed with extra forward-firing machine guns and possibly cannon for use against vehicles on the Russian front and this armament made them a formidable adversary for slow biplanes like the Swordfish and Albacore. German records revealed that the Ju 87s had just returned, or been recalled, from operations over the front line and had not even been refuelled when they attacked the strike aircraft. During the combats that followed the enemy's arrival there were some remarkable incidents, including that of Lieutenant J N Ball RN and his observer Lieutenant B J Prendergast RN from 827 NAS in Albacore 4K. They stayed low over the water as they withdrew and were attacked more than thirty times. In every one of these Prendergast's skilful conning instructions enabled Ball to take effective avoiding action and their aircraft was never hit. Eventually one Ju 87 pilot became so frustrated at getting no results from stern and quarter attacks that he selected his flaps down and dive brakes open to reduce speed and came at 4K from ahead and slightly above it. On seeing this, Ball took the opportunity to fire a zero-deflection burst with his single front gun into the enemy aircraft, which broke up and crashed after a few seconds. After returning to *Victorious*, armourers counted the number of rounds remaining in 4K and found that only eighty-seven had been fired. Mechanics also found that no enemy bullet had hit 4K. Both Ball and Prendergast were awarded the DSC for their gallant action. In his action report Lieutenant Commander Stewart-Moore, the commanding officer of 827 NAS, wrote that this had been 'a classic example of cool thinking and complete co-operation between pilot and observer … the enemy were undoubtedly waiting for us in force; the fact that Ju 87s were employed as fighters against the TSRs while their faster aircraft held off our small fighter escort shows that they had a fair idea of what was coming. They seem to have put every available aircraft into the air.' It also seems that, unlike so many of Britain's wartime leaders, the Germans had appreciated from the outset that RN aircraft embarked in their carriers were the only strike assets with sufficient strategic reach to attack them in this remote area that had suddenly become strategically important.

In another combat, this time between a Fulmar of 809 NAS and a Bf 110, Leading Airman P P Ford beat off the enemy aircraft's attack with a hand-held Thompson sub-machine gun after opening his canopy. These guns had been issued to Fulmar observers as much to boost their morale as to offer any chance of lethal effect. Captain Bovell wrote that his aircraft had returned from the strike 'bloody but unbowed'. Eleven Albacores and two Fulmars had been lost and a further eight damaged, some of them severely. The only one to return unscathed had been Ball's 4K. Against this two Bf 110s, one Bf 109 and one Ju 87 were claimed as destroyed. Admiralty analysis of German records revealed that the Germans had intercepted this strike with four Bf 110s, nine Bf 109s and nine Ju 87s. Of these they admitted losing one Bf 110 and one Ju 87 destroyed but claimed to have shot down twenty-seven British aircraft. They also admitted the loss of one merchant ship in ballast and a damaged jetty.

The strike from *Furious* found the harbour at Petsamo to be empty and the torpedo-armed aircraft had to attack their alternate targets, jetties that were made of wood and thus easily repairable. The aircraft armed with bombs proved more useful and they attacked planned objectives including shipyard installations and oil tanks. Minor damage was inflicted on the former and at least one oil tank was claimed to have been set on fire. Two small craft were claimed to have been damaged. German reports admitted hits on jetties, the steamer *Rottvar* sunk and several empty oil tanks rendered unserviceable. Fighter opposition over Petsamo consisted mainly of Bf 109s but was on a smaller scale than Kirkenes and there were, therefore, fewer casualties. One Fulmar and one Albacore were shot down and one Fulmar force landed just before reaching the objective. One crew, not named in *Furious*' combat report, was thought to have eventually reached Soviet-held territory in their dinghy but this was later found not to be the case. At the planning stage it had been intended to use the cruisers' Walrus amphibians for combat rescue but after Force P was detected it was decided that conditions were too dangerous to risk such vulnerable aircraft and they were not used. Two TSRs were severely damaged, one was slightly damaged and so too was a Fulmar, but all four managed to land on safely. No enemy aircraft were claimed as destroyed and since none appeared until the strike aircraft were withdrawing, 800 NAS Fulmars attacked ground targets with their tiny bombs. NAD subsequently criticised the choice of weapons for these aircraft, noting that the 20lb bomb was obsolescent and had a negligible effect on anything but personnel, which could have been attacked more effectively with the aircraft's eight front guns. Carriage of the bombs would have adversely affected the Fulmar's performance, the light series carriers contributing to drag even after the bombs were dropped.

Seventeen aircrew were listed as killed in action by the Admiralty during EF. They were Lieutenant MG McKendrick RN of 827 NAS, Lieutenant (A) E E Hughes-Williams RNVR of 828 NAS, Sub Lieutenant

(A) E S Burke RNVR of 800 NAS, Sub Lieutenant (A) J J R Davies RN of 828 NAS, Sub Lieutenant (A) F J G Gallichan RN of 800 NAS, Sub Lieutenant (A) D R McKay RNVR of 828 NAS, Sub Lieutenant (A) J G Patton RNVR of 828 NAS, Midshipman (A) E A Mills RNVR of 827 NAS, Petty Officer J F Black of 800 NAS, Leading Airman L E Barrow of 809 NAS, Leading Airman J Beardsley DSM of 800 NAS, Leading Airman C F Beer of 828 NAS, Leading Airman D W Corner of 828 NAS, Leading Airman E P Fabien of 828 NAS, Leading Airman A Fox of 828 NAS, Leading Airman F Sharples of 827 NAS and Leading Airman H J R Wade of 827 NAS.

The combined RN aircraft losses for EF were twelve strike aircraft and four fighters, a heavy price to pay for what CS 1 conceded to be disappointing material results. Captain A G Talbot RN, the commanding officer of *Furious*, best summed up the operation when he noted that his squadrons had carried out their plan without a hitch but it had been a bitter blow to find that they had come 2,000 miles to attack a harbour without a single real military objective in it. He also noted that 809 NAS's fighters had carried on an undisciplined running commentary on R/T in plain language that continued after the strikes began to return to Force P, possibly giving away the fleet's position.[29] These comments were taken

The wind when this photograph was taken was so high that *Victorious* had to steam downwind to allow this Albacore to take off from bow to stern into an acceptable relative wind over the flight deck. (*Author's collection*)

seriously by the Admiralty, which gave instructions that R/T security was to be stressed at the Naval Fighter School at RNAS Yeovilton.

In his report to the C-in-C Home Fleet and the Admiralty, CS 1 made three pertinent points that needed to be addressed before any similar strike operation was undertaken. Operation EF had been planned in a hurry before either carrier was fully ready, so before any future operation all the forces taking part must be fully prepared. Better intelligence was needed if targets of any value were to be located and attacked. German ships carrying supplies to the front line in northern Russia could have been strung out between Narvik and Kirkenes. Lastly, CS 1 thought that the flag officer and his staff would have been better situated in a carrier during air operations. Admiral Tovey agreed and added that he believed that attacks by low-performance aircraft in broad daylight where fighter opposition was likely could only achieve results commensurate with their losses if complete surprise was achieved. To this end he felt it would have been better to have attacked during the night, even in this region of perpetual daylight, in the hope that the enemy would be less alert. This would also have avoided the attacking force heading directly into the sun. On a positive note, he was encouraged by the enemy's failure to find and attack Force P as it withdrew. On this point the failure of the Ju 87s to refuel before intercepting the strike is interesting. It may account for their reluctance to follow the battered strike forces out to sea on their return to the carriers, although German records state bluntly that '… the British warships could not be found again later owing to fog …' The C-in-C ended his review of the operation by writing that:

> The gallantry of the aircraft crews, who knew before leaving that their chance of surprise had gone and that they were certain to face heavy odds, is beyond praise. The conduct of the operation by the Rear Admiral Commanding 1st Cruiser squadron, the handling of the ships by their commanding officers in most difficult conditions, the keenness and efficiency of all officers and men, especially of the deck handling parties in the carriers,[30] are much to be commended. I trust the encouragement to the morale of our Allies was proportionately great.

The last word on EF should go to Rear Admiral A L St F Lyster, now 5SL, whose analysis was to be very much heeded in later operations of this kind. Three months after EF he wrote a minute in its Admiralty file under the sub-heading 'The necessity for adequate fighter protection for TSR aircraft if a daylight attack has to be carried out'. In it he commented that *Victorious* had flown off nine Fulmars to protect twenty strike aircraft and *Furious* had flown off six to protect eighteen. In his opinion, given the known strength of enemy air opposition, these proportions were too low and if no more Fulmars were available the number of strike aircraft should have been reduced. In any case, he considered the number of strike aircraft to have been disproportionate to the possible number of targets. He attributed the fact that *Furious*' strike aircraft had got away virtually unscathed to the enemy's fighter concentration at Kirkenes. He also expressed the view that adequate protection of the strike aircraft depended on their escort making contact with them before they reached the target area. In the event, *Victorious*' fighters had failed to make contact for whatever reason and disaster had followed. From this he concluded that, since the distance from the carrier to a likely target could not be reduced, adequate protection of the strike force could not be left to chance. This sound advice had a profound effect on the planning and composition of future RN air strike operations.

Admiral Wake-Walker considered that a second strike in the Petsamo–Kirkenes area was not a practical proposition with the number of aircraft that he had left. He therefore ordered Force P to withdraw to the north once it was clear that there was no hope of any more aircraft returning. The force was not relocated by the enemy and nor was it ever attacked but heavy W/T traffic was intercepted, believed to emanate from German destroyers off Tana Fjord. Early on 31 July, therefore, CS 1 ordered a single Fulmar to carry out a reconnaissance of the fjord to see if it was being used as an anchorage for enemy supply ships. The aircraft had its

A running range of Fulmars on *Victorious*. Chock men are in place ready to pull them clear so the launch is imminent. (*Author's collection*)

distinguishing marks painted out in order to make it less conspicuous in the twilight conditions. An hour and a half after being flown off, the Fulmar returned and reported that the entrance to the fjord was being patrolled by four two-engined aircraft and because of these it had been impossible to press home the reconnaissance. By then *Furious*' low fuel state was a cause for concern and CS 1 ordered it to detach to Seidisfjord. Before it departed, however, a number of serviceable strike aircraft were transferred to *Victorious* with the idea of using them to attack targets in the region of Tromsø and while the crossover was taking place a Do 18 flying boat was seen approaching, too low to have been detected by radar. Red Section of 880 NAS was immediately flown off, flown by Lieutenant Commander Judd and Sub Lieutenant (A) R B Haworth RNVR, and they shot the aircraft down in a well-executed bow attack. *Furious* detached at midnight on 31 July while Force P was 40 miles north-east of Bear Island; it arrived at Seidisfjord to refuel on 3 August and returned to Scapa Flow on 5 August.

CS 1 ordered *Victorious* to prepare for possible strikes against enemy shipping between Tromsø, Hammerfest, Honningsvaag and Tana Fjord, and his resolve was strengthened by the C-in-C's signal 0357B of 1 August with an appreciation that there were no enemy fighters west of Kirkenes. Notwithstanding that, however, Captain Bovell considered that a further daylight attack by TSR aircraft carried too much risk and so, rather than discuss the possibility by signal, CS 1 transferred his flag to the carrier in *Devonshire*'s Walrus. After talking the matter through, they agreed to carry out an armed reconnaissance of Tromsø with three Fulmars. They hoped that this would keep the enemy apprehensive and uncertain of Force P's intentions in the far north. Several pairs of Fulmars were flown off *Victorious* at this time to intercept enemy aircraft detected by radar but the ship's direction team was not yet fully worked up and no interceptions were made.

Early on 4 August the three Fulmars were flown off from a position 100nm from Tromsø briefed to attack a seaplane station[31] and any shipping in the vicinity. They were each armed with four useless 20lb bombs that did little but reduce the aircraft's top speed and endurance. Two of them returned at 0315 to report that the section leader, Lieutenant H D Mathew RN, had been shot down while attacking two armed trawlers near Tromsø. A parachute had been seen but it was later learnt that Mathew had been killed and his observer, Sub Lieutenant (A) R A Burroughs RNVR, had been taken prisoner. German sources revealed that neither trawler had been hit. No information about shipping was gathered and this proved to be a sad ending to Force P's strike operation. It was evident that after the losses they had suffered the aircrew were in no shape to carry out further operations until they had been rested. The force returned to Seidisfjord on 5 August, where CS 1 returned to *Devonshire*. They arrived back in Scapa Flow on 7 August.

The object of EF had been to make a gesture in support of the Soviet Union and create a diversion on the enemy's northern flank. At the time it was believed that it had done so and achieved some tangible effect on enemy dispositions but the study of German records showed that this had not been the case. This had been the first long-range carrier strike operation of its kind by any navy and it brought out lessons that proved to be of great value. The need for adequate fighter protection has already been mentioned but it had also become clear that in 'blind' attacks with no recent air reconnaissance, bombs were likely to be more versatile weapons than torpedoes. Two factors that would later become important in Mediterranean and Far Eastern carrier operations also came to light but under wartime conditions they proved difficult to eradicate. The first was that the employment of raw squadrons with insufficient time to work up or rehearse was likely to prejudice the successful outcome of an operation from the outset. Secondly, if casualties and heavy losses had an adverse effect on aircrew morale, they could not be expected to function efficiently until replacements had been absorbed and a new work-up completed.

The first north Russian convoy

The first group of ships loaded with war material for the Soviet Union were gathered at Reykjavik and they sailed in convoy for Archangel on 21 August. The convoy comprised seven ships and was designated Operation Dervish. Concurrent with it was Operation Strength in which forty-eight Hurricanes and their associated RAF personnel were to be transported to Russia; half of them in *Argus* partially dismantled and the remainder in crates spread throughout ships of the convoy.[32] For her own defence *Argus* had two Martlets of 802 NAS embarked and she was escorted by *Shropshire* and the destroyers *Matabele*, *Punjabi* and *Somali*. Both operations were covered by the Home Fleet's Force M commanded by Rear Admiral Wake-Walker, CS 1. This comprised *Devonshire* as flagship with *Suffolk*, *Victorious* and the destroyers *Eclipse*, *Escapade* and *Inglefield*.[33] Designated as Operation EG, Force M left Scapa Flow on 23 August and joined the convoy on 26 August to the west of Bear Island. The escorts were refuelled at sea from the convoy oiler RFA *Alderdale*, which then detached to wait for their return in Bell Sound, Spitsbergen. The various forces continued to Archangel, passing north of Bear Island. On 30 August Force M parted from the convoy off the White Sea and moved to cover *Argus*. No enemy aircraft had been encountered up to

A partial view of *Victorious* in Seidisfjord prior to Operation Dervish showing Albacores of 817 and 832 NAS with Fulmars of 809 NAS ranged aft. The ship's paintwork is in remarkably good condition and she has a 35ft fast motor boat at the port boom. (*Author's collection*)

that time and the ships of the convoy arrived at their destination safely without incident.

After calculating that it would be two days before the *Argus* group came up with Force M, CS 1 decided to carry out a strike with *Victorious*' aircraft against enemy shipping in the Norwegian Leads north of Tromsø. Naval Intelligence believed that convoys were leaving that port for Kirkenes every three days and so Force M refuelled from *Alderdale* in Spitsbergen and CS 1 transferred his flag to *Victorious*, sailing on 2 September. At 0030 on 3 September two striking forces were flown off. The first comprised six Albacores of 817 NAS armed with torpedoes and the second six Albacores of 832 NAS, each armed with six 250lb SAP and eight 40lb GP bombs. They were briefed to attack shipping and oil tanks in Hammerfest but, because enemy fighters were known to be based at nearby Banak, CS 1 gave instructions that they were to abort if there was no cloud cover. One of the strike forces located a small enemy convoy in Svaerholthavet but the sky cleared near the coast and its leader decided to follow instructions and returned to *Victorious* without attacking. The other strike force found its designated search area to be empty and it too returned to the carrier. This ill-considered strike operation achieved nothing but alert the enemy of the carrier's presence and Force M was shadowed continuously for the next two days. Fulmars attempted several interceptions but only succeeded in shooting down a single Do 18.

The Russian Convoy Area

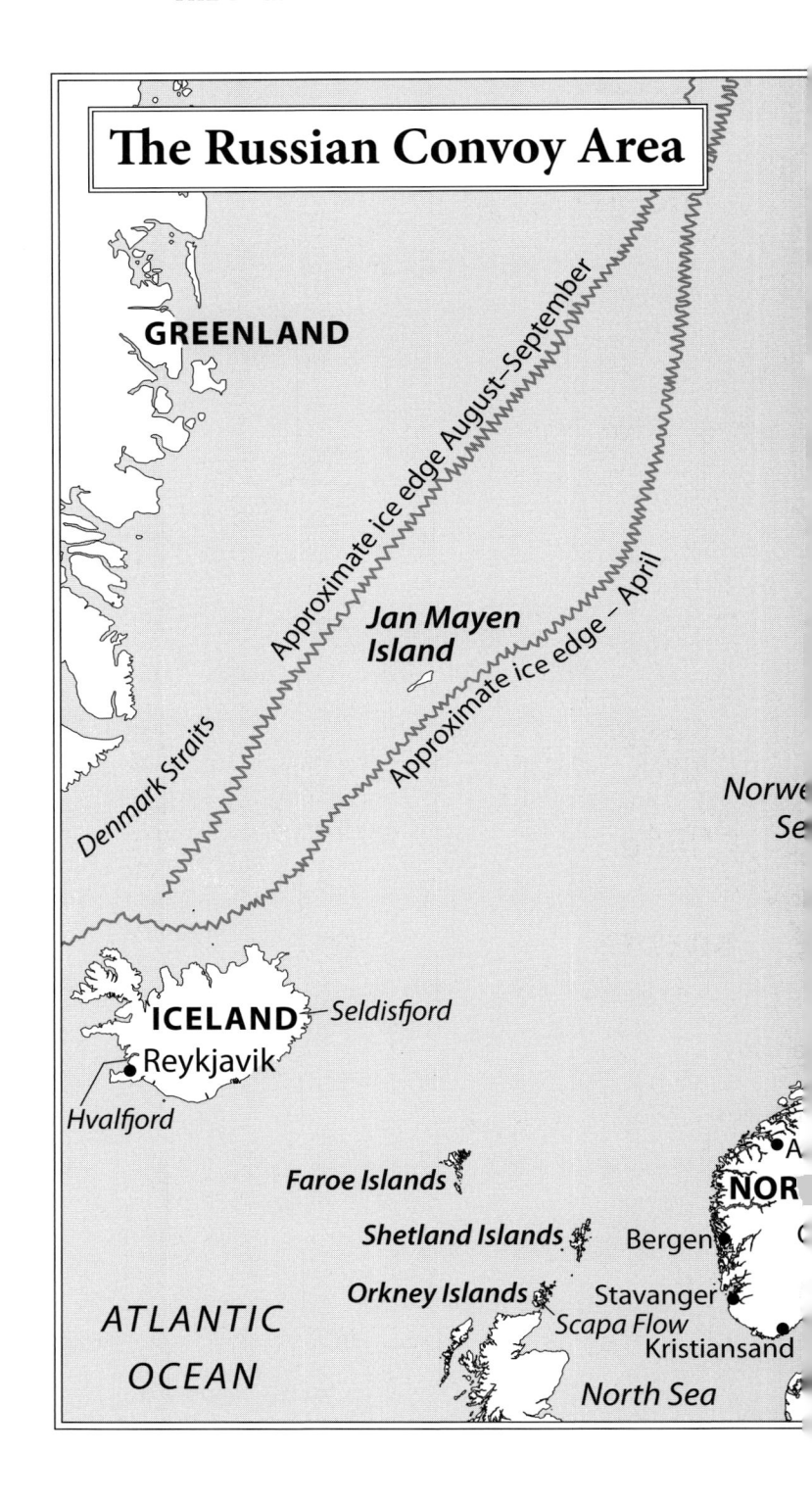

GREENLAND

Approximate ice edge August–September

Jan Mayen Island

Approximate ice edge – April

Denmark Straits

Norwegian Sea

ICELAND — Seldisfjord
Reykjavik
Hvalfjord

Faroe Islands
Shetland Islands — Bergen
Orkney Islands — Stavanger
Scapa Flow
Kristiansand

ATLANTIC OCEAN

NOR

North Sea

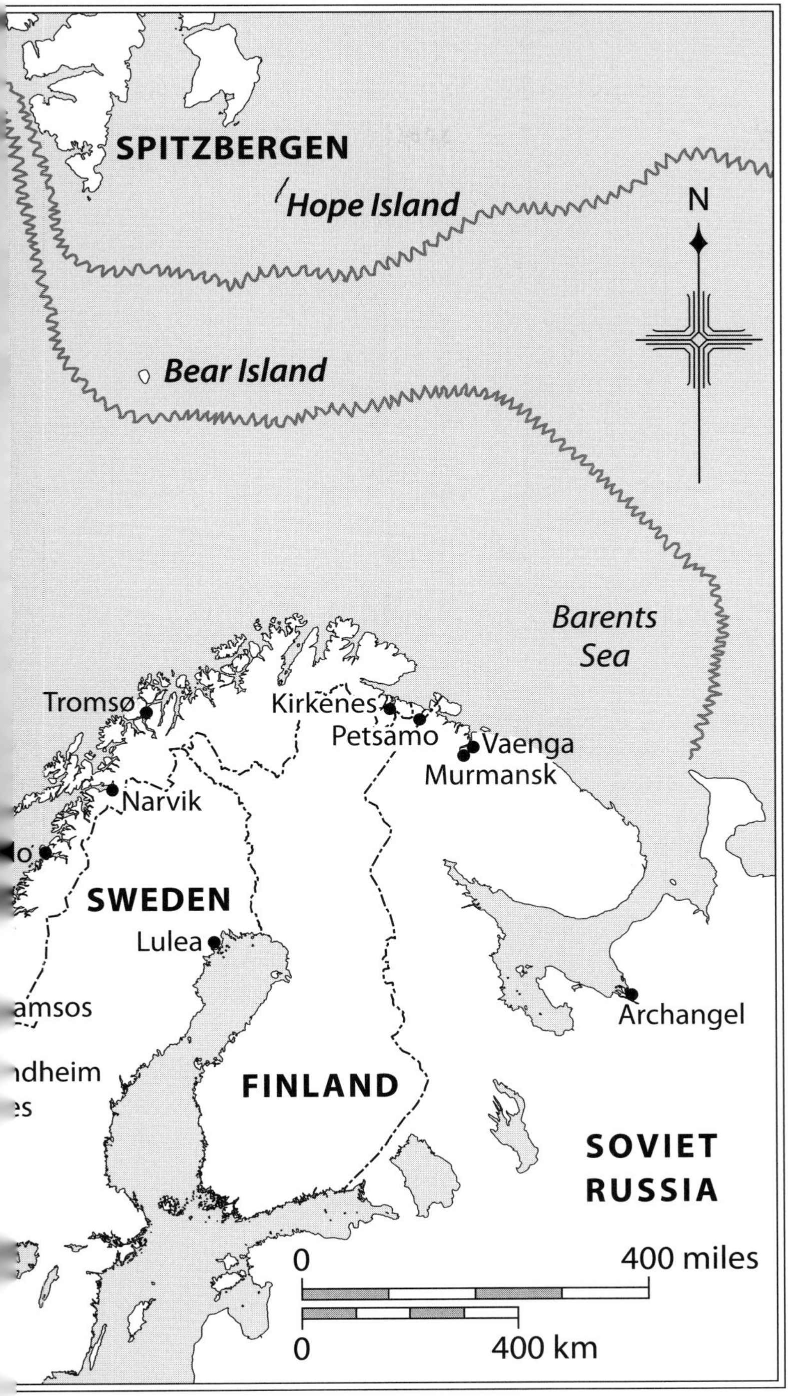

SPITZBERGEN
Hope Island
N
Bear Island
Barents Sea
Tromsø
Kirkenes
Petsamo
Vaenga
Murmansk
Narvik
SWEDEN
Lulea
Archangel
amsos
dheim
FINLAND
SOVIET RUSSIA
0
400 miles
0
400 km

A Fulmar of 809 NAS about to fly off *Victorious*. Note the sign on the island, Visible just forward of the cockpit, which states 'W/T SILENCE – BEACON RUNNING', which informs aircrew that although communications are not permitted, the ship's Type 72 aircraft homing beacon is operating for their recovery. The application of individual artwork to Fleet Air Arm aircraft was unusual in 1941 but, as Donald Duck shows, aircrew in 809 NAS put individual markings on their aircraft to give them personality. (*Author's collection*)

Argus was met on 4 September and the combined force moved north of Hope Island, where it was thought that fog might force shadowers to lose contact and this proved to be the case. The Germans seemed to be content merely to track Force M, which was more than 400nm from the shadowers' base, and made no attempt to attack it. On 6 September the two Martlets of 802 NAS transferred to *Victorious* and on the morning of 7 September a short period of good weather allowed *Argus* to fly off her twenty-four assembled Hurricanes in four groups to Vaenga airfield near Murmansk, where they all arrived safely. The flying off position was carefully chosen to be reasonably free from the risk of enemy interference but was 100 miles from the nearest friendly territory and 200 miles from Vaenga. An RAF advance party received the Hurricanes, which were then turned over to the Red Air Force. *Argus* and her escorts then returned to Scapa Flow via Seidisfjord, arriving on 14 September.

Meanwhile, Force M returned to Spitsbergen, where its ships were refuelled before carrying out the second planned element of Operation EG, strikes against shipping and military targets in the Bodø area. At 0100 on 12 September seven Albacores of 817 NAS armed with torpedoes and five Albacores of 832 NAS, each armed with six 250lb

SAP and eight 40lb GP bombs, were flown off from a position 40 miles west of the Lofoten Islands. They were briefed to attack shipping in Vest Fjord and both a power station and aluminium works near Glom Fjord 30 miles to the south. This strike succeeded in sinking a medium-sized merchant ship in Vest Fjord. A quay and a smaller ship in Bodø were also destroyed. In Glom Fjord fires were started by hits on the aluminium works and a German direction-finding station on Rost Island. When they were examined, German records showed that the latter target had been destroyed. Unfortunately, two of 817 NAS' torpedoes missed other worthwhile ship targets. There was no air opposition and Force M withdrew to the west but at 0930 a single He 111 appeared. It was shot down after a 50-mile chase by two CAP Martlets flown by Lieutenant J W Sleigh RN and Sub Lieutenant (A) H E Williams RNVR. Shadowing duties were taken up by two BV 138 flying boats, which were attacked by Fulmar CAP aircraft but with no apparent result even after they had fired out all their ammunition. The continuous shadowing led CS 1 to decide against mounting a second strike the following night and the force returned to Scapa Flow, arriving on 13 September. *Victorious*' log shows that Force M had covered 8,000nm during Operation EG. After Dervish PQ/QP convoys to and from north Russia ran at roughly three-week intervals between Hvalfjord or Reykjavik in Iceland and Archangel or Murmansk. They usually had a close escort of a cruiser and two or three destroyers together with anti-submarine vessels but, apart from the Arctic weather, they proved relatively uneventful. The Germans had not yet appreciated that their campaign against the Soviet Union would be prolonged and nor had they taken into account the scale of Allied logistic support for the Soviets.

Further Arctic strike operations

Admiral Tovey decided to carry out a second air strike against Norwegian targets in a new operation designated Operation EJ. *Victorious* was now the only Home Fleet carrier in northern waters as *Furious* was ferrying RAF Hurricanes to Malta. Much of *Furious*' war had involved fast steaming over large distances and her machinery, besides being damaged during the Norwegian campaign, had begun to show signs of strain. After the ferrying operation she proceeded to the USN's Philadelphia Navy Yard, where she was refitted between October 1941 and April 1942 following an agreement between the British and US governments.[34] *Victorious* played the leading part in EJ, supported by *King George V*, *Penelope* and escorting destroyers. The aim was to attack enemy shipping in the coastal route between Glom Fjord and Vest Fjord in the vicinity of Bodø and *Victorious* joined *King George V* off Seidisfjord on the evening

A Fulmar flying off *Victorious* in Scapa Flow with the battleship *King George V* moored astern. The arrester wires and after crash barrier have been unrigged. (*Author's collection*)

of 6 October. The force then moved to a position west of the Lofoten Islands at dawn on 9 October. Five Albacores out of a range of thirteen from both 817 and 832 NAS were damaged in a heavy squall encountered just before they were due to fly off but the remaining eight took off safely, three armed with torpedoes and the remainder with six 250lb GP bombs each. They were briefed to attack any shipping they found but adverse weather forced five to return to *Victorious*, which was, by then, pitching badly. One Albacore was severely damaged attempting to land on with its torpedo still in place but its crew were unhurt. The other three found a medium-sized merchant ship in Glom Fjord, which they hit with two bombs and left on fire. Overhead cable pylons on Grond Island were hit and damaged. A further ship found in Bodø was attacked but missed. There was some light anti-aircraft fire but no other opposition and all these aircraft returned safely.

Later during the forenoon, a second strike force, this time of eight Albacores, was flown off, all of which were armed with bombs. They found a small convoy comprising two large merchant ships escorted by two 'flak' ships and this was attacked by 817 NAS aircraft 10 miles north of Bodø. One ship was sunk, with its crew being seen to take to their lifeboats. These attacks were all made with a combination of low-level and low dive-bombing and all aircraft returned safely to the carrier. Two

A Fulmar from 761 NAS, part of the Naval Fighter School at RNAS Yeovilton in 1941. The pilot is flying without an observer and the holes in the patches over gun muzzles indicate that they have been fired recently. (*Author's collection*)

crashed on landing, however, one of which had been damaged by antiaircraft fire and had a wounded TAG. During this whole day's flying no enemy aircraft were seen, confirming intelligence reports that German air forces in Norway had been weakened by the heavy fighting against the USSR. After this strike the task force withdrew and arrived back in Scapa Flow late on 10 October.

Operation EJ was the last strike operation against the Norwegian littoral by *Victorious* during 1941 and in the last weeks of the year she operated between Scapa Flow and Hvalfjord to counter possible moves by German cruisers thought to be trying to break into the Atlantic. Her first year in service had proved difficult for both the ship and her squadrons, for much of the time as the Home Fleet's only operational carrier. She had frequently operated in bad weather to carry out 'tip and run' strikes from which there had been little glory and disproportionate losses. From now on Fleet Air Arm aircraft in the European theatre continued to counter any movement by enemy warships as part of a concentrated task force within the Home Fleet, participate in the provision of heavy cover and the immediate escort for convoys to north Russia and to operate disembarked from a number of naval air stations or other airfields whenever necessary.

6

1942

After their sorties against the Atlantic convoys in 1941 the German battlecruisers *Scharnhorst* and *Gneisenau*, together with the heavy cruiser *Prinz Eugen*, remained in Brest, where they posed a considerable threat that was difficult for the Home Fleet to contain.[1] Their presence led to the WS-series troop convoys carrying reinforcements to the Middle East, some of them carrying tens of thousands of men destined for the Eighth Army, having to be heavily escorted and routed further out into the Atlantic than would otherwise have been necessary. The Admiralty requested Bomber Command to attack these ships and damage had been caused to all three during 1941 that prevented their movement.[2] This powerful enemy task force in Brest formed the southern arm of a potential pincer attack on the Atlantic convoys, the northern arm comprising the new battleship *Tirpitz*, which arrived in northern Norway on 23 January. Had the Brest ships not been damaged by bombing, the Home Fleet would have been forced to counter these two enemy battle groups in the Atlantic based more than 1,000 miles apart. Fighting on the Russian front had not been concluded as quickly as the German high command anticipated, causing increasing numbers of aircraft to be transferred from France to the east, and Goering persuaded Hitler that none could be spared to defend the ships if they remained in Brest or La Pallice. Camouflage netting was stretched over them and smokescreens were used as cover when approaching air raids were detected. Hitler had convinced himself that the British intended to invade northern Norway and, rather than see the ships remain at Brest where they might suffer continuing damage from air attacks, Admiral Raeder was given two choices: the heavy ships in Brest must be redeployed either to Germany or northern Norway. If neither were possible, they must be dismantled and their guns used to defend the Norwegian coast. Raeder decided in early January to bring the ships back to Germany and Admiral Ciliax, commander of the Atlantic task force, was put in charge of planning a break-out. A conference between the naval and air staffs with Hitler present was held on 12 January, at which it was decided that

RAF Halifax bombers over Brest dockyard. *Scharnhorst* and *Gneisenau* are in dry docks to the left of the picture, their shape partially obscured by netting. (*Author's collection*)

a dash through the English Channel was preferable to the longer route through the Iceland–Faroes gap, which would take the force closer to the Home Fleet's main base at Scapa Flow.

The lack of recent operational training by all three German ships at Brest led to valid concerns about their fighting efficiency and it is arguable that this had been another reason for choosing the shorter route. Interception by carrier-borne aircraft and battleships north of the Faroes if the alternative scheme had been adopted would have put the squadron at a considerable disadvantage. The Ciliax plan was approved personally by Hitler and included extensive cover by Luftwaffe fighters and surface craft including destroyers, flak ships and E-boats as it passed through the narrows off Dover. By early February elements of the German plan had already been put into place, with increased minesweeping activity at night along the coasts of France, Belgium and Holland. Destroyers were deployed to Brest and tugs were placed in French, Belgian and Dutch harbours to assist any ships that were damaged. British radar sites were jammed daily by gradually increasing amounts so that operators would not see anything unusual when full-scale jamming eventually attempted to mask the passage of the German ships.

The Admiralty was convinced by February that a break-out by the German Brest Squadron was imminent and an appreciation was issued to naval and RAF commands. The Air Ministry had already given operations to counter a break-out through the Channel the code word Fuller. Countermeasures were to be brought into action swiftly with the order Executive Fuller and, at least in theory, nothing further was needed to set them in motion. However, the countermeasures involved aircraft of Fighter, Bomber and Coastal Commands and each of them produced their own unique set of orders. All were classified at the highest level and their substance was not briefed downwards to officers whose everyday experience did not include naval operations. The Admiralty attached its own orders to the Fuller directive but made it clear from the outset that it expected RAF aircraft to be the primary means of attack if the dash happened, although light surface forces including destroyers and MTBs were to carry out torpedo attacks as the enemy passed through the Dover Straits. It was considered unlikely that the German warships would attempt to pass through the Straits in daylight but if they did so, the planning staffs believed that heavy and accurate bomber attacks could be delivered under cover provided by Fighter Command. On 3 February the Admiralty instructed the Vice admiral Dover, Vice Admiral Sir Bertram Ramsay, to keep 11 Group Fighter Command and 16 Group Coastal Command fully informed about attacks to be carried out by surface forces under his control so that they could be co-ordinated with air attacks and fighter cover provided for them. Various RAF units were ordered to stand by for Fuller but none were actually redeployed. All of them remained under the remote control of their commands. For example, the Air Ministry directive included 300 aircraft of Bomber Command that were to be set aside for what it described as 'the maximum practical effort' to be held at two hours' notice. This prevented them from taking part in their normal raids over Germany, however, and on 7 February the C-in-C Bomber Command asked for them to be released. The Air Ministry asked the Admiralty for its opinion and 1 SL stated unambiguously that the break-out was believed to be imminent and that the destruction of the German ships was more likely to affect the course of the war than air raids on Germany. This assessment was passed to Bomber Command by the Air Ministry but despite this, Air Vice Marshal Jack Baldwin, its C-in-C, decided on his own initiative to withdraw 200 of the 300 bombers from their Fuller commitment and to place the remainder on their normal standby notice. The Air Ministry, Admiralty, Fighter and Coastal Commands were not informed of this fundamental change and on 12 February, when Fuller was activated at very short notice, Bomber Command aircraft took more than three hours to respond, not the two directed by the Air Ministry. This meant that their attacks were made in the late afternoon when the light was fading, conditions made even worse by the aircrews' lack of any training in attacks against fast-moving warships. It is hardly surprising after such a major failure that Baldwin was replaced by Sir Arthur Harris on 22 February after only spending forty-five days as C-in-C Bomber Command.

A minelaying programme was ordered by Admiral Ramsay in the waters through which the Germans would be likely to pass, including five fields of magnetic mines off the Frisian Islands laid by aircraft of Bomber Command at the end of January that were not known to the Germans. These inflicted damage on both battlecruisers. *Plover* also laid three fields in the last week of January and *Welshman* laid a series of four fields north off Cape Barfleur on the night of 7/8 February. These were discovered by the enemy but only just swept in time for the German ships to pass. Aware that not every mine might have been neutralised, however, Ciliax ordered the squadron to slow as it passed through the dangerous area despite being under continuous air attack. The original British plan had included torpedo attacks on the enemy ships by RAF Beauforts but Admiral Ramsay was not convinced that their pilots had the skill to hit fast warships at night. To remedy this potential shortcoming, he asked the Admiralty for a squadron of RN torpedo bombers to be placed under his direct orders.[3] It was decided that 825 NAS, commanded by Lieutenant Commander (A) Eugene Esmonde DSO RN, which was disembarked at RNAS Lee-on-Solent, was suitably experienced and it was allocated to the task. It had been embarked in *Ark Royal* when it sank in November 1941, lost all its aircraft and been temporarily disbanded. In January it had re-formed at Lee with six Swordfish and sufficient crews with enough experience to carry out a night torpedo attack under the testing operational conditions likely to be found in the Channel. There were other Swordfish and crews at Lee but they were not considered be sufficiently worked up to have a chance of carrying out an attack with any great chance of success.[4] It was explained to Esmonde that the minefields laid in the Channel would force the enemy warships to pass through the Straits of Dover within two hours of high water and the Admiralty appreciation was that they would probably do so before daylight. It was considered most likely, therefore, that 825 NAS would attack in darkness or very early dawn, minimising the threat from enemy fighters and making an attack by such a small number of aircraft a justifiable risk. Under these circumstances Esmonde and his squadron deployed to RAF Manston in Kent, where they were to be available at the shortest notice for Fuller, arriving on 4 February. Admiral Ramsay's plan was to carry out a combined sea and air torpedo attack with the Dover MTBs and Swordfish in the Straits of Dover either off Calais or Cap Blanc Nez depending on the amount of warning received. Their objective was to stop or slow the enemy in an area where they would be within range of shore batteries and where radar

Swordfish of 822 NAS being loaded with torpedoes at RNAS Hatston while aircrew in their flying kit look on. The procedure followed at Manston by 825 NAS would have been exactly the same. (*Philip Jarrett collection*)

could direct further strike forces on to them. Further attacks were to be made by MTBs from Ramsgate to force the enemy into the minefield laid by *Plover* and by destroyers from Harwich from a position north-east of the West Hinder Light Vessel in waters clear of British minefields. From 4 February the naval forces, including 825 NAS, assumed immediate readiness from 0400 every morning until a time based on the time of high water at Dover. On 12 February this was at 0700 and from then onwards they reverted to four hours' notice to allow maintenance and training flights to be carried out.

The plan that failed to give warning

The RAF accepted the most complex element of Fuller but it was complicated by the lack of an operational staff within the Air Ministry and the service's disparate command structure. Fighter, Bomber and Coastal Commands were effectively separate air forces that made little attempt to co-ordinate their normal daily activities. Only the most senior officers in each command knew what Fuller was and since they had not briefed downwards, the speed with which events unfolded when the German squadron was located meant that most RAF aircrew took off with no knowledge of what they were supposed to be doing or why. The failure to concentrate assets before the event, especially in the case of the torpedo-armed Beaufort squadrons, led to unco-ordinated attacks being carried out piecemeal by badly briefed crews.

The possibility that the Germans might actually sail at night for a daylight passage through the Straits of Dover had been considered and, to give adequate warning if it happened, Coastal Command ordered three different reconnaissance patrols to be carried out throughout the hours of darkness in the western and central Channel areas. The first, known as 'Stopper', was off the entrance to Brest; a central one known as 'Line SE' between Ushant and the Îsle-de-Bréhat and an eastern one known as 'Habo' between Le Havre and Boulogne. All were flown by Lockheed Hudsons fitted with ASV radar but the aircrew were not told why they were carrying them out and probably regarded them as routine. The German task force sailed from Brest at 1930 on 11 February and every British plan put in place to detect German movements on that critical night went wrong. The first Stopper patrol aircraft on 11 February suffered an ASV radar failure. It was switched off while the aircraft evaded a German night fighter and then switched on again at full power rather than low power as laid down in the operating manual. The crew wasted forty minutes trying to fix it before returning to RAF St Eval for a replacement aircraft that, when manned, failed to start. A second aircraft with a serviceable ASV was on task from 2238 but a gap had been left during which the enemy squadron had sailed. This critical gap in surveillance was not reported to any RAF Command, the Admiralty or Admiral Ramsay. The first Line SE aircraft arrived on task from St Eval at 1940 but it too suffered an ASV radar failure. The crew spent ninety minutes trying to trace the fault but at 2113 they reported the failure and were ordered to return. No replacement aircraft was deployed and so the enemy passed through the Line SE area unreported between 0100 and 0400 on 12 February. Precious hours in which the Fuller plan should have been put into execution had been lost and still the gaps were not reported. Aircraft for the 'Habo' patrol line were flown from RAF Thorney Island and the first had a serviceable ASV but detected nothing. The second also had a serviceable radar but after it had flown only two circuits it was ordered to return by its operating authority because of fears that thick mist in the airfield's vicinity might turn into fog and make the aircraft's recovery difficult. Again one can only presume that neither the sortie's controller nor the aircrew in question had any idea of the importance of what they were doing and the consequence of this incredible decision was that the aircraft came off task at 0615, an hour before its briefed departure time. The German squadron actually moved into its area of coverage before it was due off task but yet again this gap was not reported. These three failures corresponded almost exactly with the actual times of passage of the enemy ships and, worse still, the lack of any report about the gaps in coverage meant that the naval headquarters at Dover and all the other agencies concerned with the implementation of Fuller were left in the belief that the patrols had been flown successfully and the enemy was still in Brest. During this period the naval forces under Admiral Ramsay's direct command were normally ordered to assume immediate readiness at 0400 and then stood down to four hours' notice at 0700. Had the admiral been aware that the enemy force was at sea and the timing of its movement, he might well have continued immediate readiness beyond 0700 in order to attack at the earliest opportunity. As it was, the naval forces came to immediate readiness as usual at 0400; Eugene Esmonde's crews manned their aircraft and strapped themselves into their cockpits. MTB crews were ready to sail and six destroyers at Harwich had steam up ready to sail within minutes. At 0700, with no knowledge that the night patrols had failed, Admiral Ramsay's staff gave them the order to stand down. The Germans had not succeeded in proceeding thus far without being detected because of their own careful planning; they had been enabled to do so by a series of British failures.[5]

Plots from radar stations manned by the RAF across the south-east coast of the UK fed their information into the Fighter Command filter room at Stanmore. By 0825 one of these plots was actually tracking the German warships' air escort as they made their way up-Channel but it was assessed by the senior controller as enemy aircraft escorting a coastal convoy. No one thought to ask what kind of coastal convoy would be worthy of such a large air escort and no one seemed to have been briefed about Fuller. A number of stations reported interference on their radar screens but these were thought to be caused by atmospherics; there had, after all, been similar degradation that had got worse over the previous days. Radar jamming would,

Eugene Esmonde photographed next to an 825 NAS Swordfish when he was serving in *Ark Royal*. (*Author's collection*)

logically, have been a significant element of any German break-out plan but when it happened no one in Fighter Command recognised it for what it was and, again, no report was passed up the chain of command. A backstop had been built into the surveillance structure as insurance against the German squadron slipping through the ASV radar patrols undetected. Every day Fighter Command sent out a fighter reconnaissance to carry out a visual search of the Channel between the mouth of the Somme and Ostend. This had been routine for some months but Fuller gave it an added significance; they were known as 'Jim Crow' patrols and if they saw anything an anti-shipping strike was to be organised. Admiral Ramsay was only informed if it was thought that the vessels detected might be suitable for attack by MTBs. The fatal flaw in the 'Jim Crow' procedure was that the pilots were briefed, in accordance with 11 Group instructions, not to make radio transmissions except in an emergency. However, there was no explanation of what constituted an emergency and Fuller was not mentioned. On that fateful morning what greater emergency could there have been in the Channel than the location of the German squadron on which the Fuller plans had been so carefully made? At 0845 two 'Jim Crow' Spitfires took off from RAF Hawkinge and when they returned they mentioned that they had seen a considerable number of E-boat movements. These were reinforcements that had sailed to join the German squadron as it made the transit of the Straits of Dover but they were not recognised for what they were. By 0925 the filter room at Stanmore was receiving a growing number of reports about what it still assessed to be a coastal convoy escorted by aircraft, despite the fact that it was moving up Channel in excess of 20 knots. Fighter Command decided that a shipping strike might be necessary and ordered a second 'Jim Crow' patrol to investigate and this took off at 1020 from Hawkinge flown by Squadron Leader Oxspring and Sergeant Beaumont. Meanwhile, a telephone conference was held between Admiral Ramsay, the Admiralty and the three RAF Commands. They decided that there was little chance of the Germans trying to break through the Dover Straits in daylight and the next full alert was set for 0400 on 13 February. A radar station at Beachy Head was tracking the enemy ships off Boulogne by this stage and tried to telephone Dover on both scrambler and normal telephones but failed to get through. Surprisingly, no one at 11 Group or Fighter Command had thought of passing information about the orbiting aircraft and their supposed high-speed convoy to the Admiralty war room. At 1033 a third 'Jim Crow' Spitfire sortie took off, flown by Group Captain Beamish, Senior Air Staff Officer to Air Vice Marshal Leigh-Mallory of 11 Group with Wing Commander Boyd as his wing man. Beamish had been briefed about Fuller but was apparently only interested in air combat and when the pair saw two enemy fighters off Boulogne they engaged them, losing height rapidly in a turning fight over the Channel. They came down right over the German squadron and could have reported them immediately to initiate Fuller but, hide-bound by the Fighter Command rule about radio silence, they flew back to their base before reporting what they had seen.

At 1040 the Beachy Head radar station managed to telephone its plot information to Portsmouth, from where it was relayed to Dover. Wing Commander Constable-Roberts, the Air Liaison Officer on Admiral Ramsay's staff, was informed immediately and, to his credit, he was the first man to recognise what was happening and try to instil a sense of urgency. He telephoned 11 Group to be told that the filter room had been watching this plot for some time and that it was all right. He asked for a further reconnaissance but was told that Oxspring and Beaumont would return shortly having completed their sortie without breaking radio silence. During their debrief at Hawkinge after 1050 these pilots described seeing 'about thirty or forty enemy ships escorted by five destroyers or E-boats'. Sergeant Beaumont added that he had seen a ship with a tripod mast but when shown a book of silhouettes he failed to pick out *Scharnhorst*, *Gneisenau* or *Prinz Eugen*. Curiously, his identification was taken as final and when the report was passed to Fighter Command there was no suggestion of executing Fuller, only of organising a shipping strike, known within the Command as a 'Roadstead' operation, against an enemy convoy that appeared to be larger than usual. News that the Command was preparing a Roadstead eventually reached Admiral Ramsay's staff at 1105 but there was no mention of big warships or even one with a tripod mast. Constable-Roberts became even more suspicious and, although Admiral Ramsay was sceptical about the possibility of the enemy risking a passage of the Straits in daylight and was inclined to wait for further evidence, his air liaison officer persuaded him approve a telephone call to Manston in which he warned Esmonde 'to get his chaps ready'.[6] Esmonde's immediate response was to ask if he should have his torpedoes set to run deep and Constable-Roberts advised him to do so as there would be no time when he gave the word to go.

At 1109, thirty minutes after he had identified the German battlecruisers, Group Captain Beamish landed and reported what had seen. Although Beamish and his wing man had not specifically been part of the Fuller search plan, both were senior officers who should have realised the importance of what they had seen and radioed their information before flying back. They had actually been in combat with enemy fighters so what on earth was the point of trying to hide their presence over the Channel with radio silence? At 1125 confirmation that the German ships were about to pass through the Straits of Dover was finally telephoned to Dover by the Admiralty war room. Constable-Roberts immediately rang 11 Group to ask for fighters to protect 825 NAS in what was now going to be a daylight torpedo attack against considerable odds rather than the night strike envisaged in the Fuller plan. Simultaneously, Beamish rang his friend Wing Commander T Gleave RAF, the commanding officer of Manston, to tell him what he had seen. Gleave then made his way to 825 NAS' dispersal. After fourteen hours at sea the German ships had finally been detected and frantic efforts were now being made to attack them.

At 1140 the duty controller at 11 Group headquarters telephoned Constable-Roberts to inform him that five fighter squadrons had been ordered to provide close escort for 825 NAS. A further three were to strafe enemy escort ships in advance of an attack by MTBs. Five minutes later Admiral Ramsay ordered Captain Pizey, Captain (D) of the Harwich Flotilla, to attack the enemy in accordance with Fuller orders. Fortunately, these destroyers had remained at sea after 0700 and were carrying out an anti-submarine exercise, which meant that they were immediately available. Unfortunately, the twenty-eight Beaufort torpedo-bombers of 16 Group Coastal Command were less well placed as they were strung out between their normal base at Leuchars in Fife and airfields in southern England, where they were finally being redeployed for a potential night attack against the German squadron. RAF Coltishall, where the first aircraft landed, did not have torpedo support facilities. The senior air staff officer of 16 Group telephoned Constable-Roberts to request that 825 NAS' attack should be delayed to allow a co-ordinated strike with the Beauforts when they were ready but with remarkable coolness, Constable-Roberts informed him that this was not possible.[7] It was important to attack the enemy as soon as possible, not to add further delay. The enemy was already through the Dover Straits and heading away from Manston at high speed; fully loaded the Swordfish could only fly at 90 knots and a prolonged tail chase under constant attack from enemy fighters was hardly the best option. Also, the twin-engined, monoplane Beauforts were much faster than Swordfish, making a combined attack difficult to co-ordinate between squadrons that had never worked together or even briefed together that morning. The difference in speed also meant that separate escorts would have to be provided for the slower Swordfish and the faster Beauforts over considerable distances from their different airfields. The shallow water around the sandbanks north-east of Calais were also a factor and it was important for 825 NAS to attack while it still had the depth of water to do so.

The first British units to go into action were the MTBs based at Dover, which were commanded by Lieutenant Commander E N Pumphrey RN. Like all the other units in the Fuller plan, they had been stood down at

0700 but at 1130 they were informed by a telephone call from Admiral Ramsay's chief of staff that the Germans were off Boulogne. Pumphrey's own boat was in dry dock but by 1155 he was leading his small force to sea in *MTB 221*.[8] At 1223 he signalled that the enemy was in sight 5 miles from his own accurately reported position to the south-east heading just north of east at high speed. The information was passed quickly to the Ramsgate MTB squadron and Manston. At about the same time the Dover coastal gun batteries opened fire but the enemy was already drawing out of their range.

At 1210 the 11 Group controller telephoned Constable-Roberts and asked him to confirm that Dover Command considered the fighter escort to be provided for the Swordfish was adequate. Constable-Roberts told him to ring Manston and ask Esmonde directly; he did so at once and, given the assurance that there would be five squadrons of fighters, Esmonde decided to attack at once. Between them they agreed that three squadrons of Spitfires from RAF Biggin Hill would act as top cover while two others from Hornchurch would stay close to the Swordfish and try to suppress enemy anti-aircraft fire. The time fixed for the fighters to rendezvous with the Swordfish over Manston was 1225. The Germans had already passed through the narrowest part of the Straits and were steaming away from Manston at 28 knots.

The gallant sortie

Like other units in the Dover Command, 825 NAS stood down at 0700. Sub Lieutenant (A) B W Rose RNVR, with his observer Sub Lieutenant (A) E F Lee RNVR and TAG Leading Airman A L Johnson, took off in Swordfish W5983 at 1000 for a torpedo attack training session in Deal Bay. Esmonde had returned late the night before from an investiture at Buckingham Palace in which he had received the DSO for leading his squadron in its attack on *Bismarck*. After the early morning stand-to he returned to the wooden hut allocated to 825 NAS as a combined maintenance control office and crew room to check the board on which aircraft and their crews for the day were chalked up. It was a bitterly cold morning with powdery snow blowing across the airfield and limited visibility under a low cloud base. Unlike RAF senior officers, Esmonde had fully briefed his men on the part 825 NAS was to play in Fuller and shortly after their arrival at Manston he told them that the passage of the German ships through the Dover Straits was no longer theory but practically certain. He explained his own belief that their attack was most likely to be carried out at night but that whenever the order to take-off was given he expected them to carry out their mission without need of further orders. He then passed round slips of paper on which the names of the target ships and his plan of attack were written. His plan was based on the Fuller appreciation that the Germans would attempt the passage at night and that air patrols would give several hours' warning. His six aircraft were to remain at low level in a crescent shape and attack the enemy ships from ahead. As they approached their drop positions, the two flights of three were to split with one attacking the German heavy ships from their port and the other their starboard bow, dropping their torpedoes at 1,000yd. If the enemy ships held their course they would have to pass through a 'fan' of torpedoes; if they altered to port or starboard they would present their broadsides to the tracks of one flight's torpedoes. After take-off the flights were initially to form into line astern before reaching the attacking position. Early plans envisaged Hurricanes from Manston dropping flares to illuminate targets for the Swordfish, although this difficult tactic was never practised. Esmonde's plan exactly met the role intended for his squadron but, regardless of whatever type of attack 825 NAS might have to carry out at short notice, his careful briefing meant that his men knew exactly what was required from them in any circumstance. Once they had digested their contents, the aircrew burnt their briefing papers. Such was the respect they had for him there were no questions and it is clear that they would have followed him, whatever the odds against them, without a moment's hesitation. There were seven pilots but only six Swordfish and it is a measure of the aircrew's dedication that the two most junior pilots both wanted to fly with Esmonde and tossed a coin to see who would do so. Sub Lieutenant (A) P Bligh RNVR 'won' the toss and Sub Lieutenant (A) Bennet RNVR stayed on the ground at Manston. After breakfast some aircrew stayed in their accommodation but Esmonde checked over his aircraft torpedoes with their maintenance ratings. They had all worked tirelessly, night and day, to ensure that the weapons were always ready, another example of the determination inspired by Esmonde's leadership.

Shortly before 1130 a messenger arrived at 825 NAS' office in an RAF vehicle to tell Esmonde that he was urgently wanted by Dover Headquarters on a telephone in the operations room. Minutes later he spoke to Constable-Roberts, who briefed him on the events of the past few minutes and told him to stand his squadron to as quickly as possible. Rose was told to get back to the airfield so that the aircraft could be made ready. Within minutes Constable-Roberts confirmed that it was the Brest squadron, that it had already reached the narrows and that there was now no chance of an attack from ahead. Esmonde was already faced with a stern-chase under air space dominated by enemy fighters. He remained by the telephone and was called next by the 11 Group controller, who confirmed that the Biggin Hill wing of three Spitfire squadrons was to fly top cover for him with the Hornchurch wing of two squadrons suppressing anti-aircraft fire. Was that all right? Esmonde replied that this sounded fine but asked for them to keep a close watch on his six Swordfish as the Luftwaffe would be up in strength. The controller said that orders had already gone out and both wings had been ordered to rendezvous with them over Manston; when was Esmonde planning to take off? After glancing at his watch Esmonde asked for them to join him over Manston at 1225 'and for the love of heaven get them here on time'. Constable-Roberts rang back to ask if an escort had been arranged and was given the details. Then Constable-Roberts said that Admiral Ramsay wanted to know how he felt about attacking in daylight, 'he wants it to be your decision'. Esmonde replied that his squadron was going to attack but 'that they were not heroes and that the admiral should not expect miracles'.

By then Esmonde's aircrew had joined him in the operations room. Survivors remembered him speaking to them quickly and with authority in his voice to say:

> The balloon's gone up and I want to say how sorry I am that you were not warned that a day attack might be possible. I accept responsibility for that; it was my job to see that you were ready. In a few minutes we will be going in. Forget all you have been told of the night attack plan. We will attack in sub-flights in line astern, height fifty feet. Object to hit and thereby slow down any one or all of the big ships. Lieutenant Thompson is to lead the second flight and follow behind me. Keep 1,000yd between us, that way we will divide their flak fire and with any luck we can draw some of it away from you. We will have plenty of fighter cover ...

As he finished, the telephone rang again. It was Constable-Roberts to brief that the enemy ships were 10 miles north-east of the Straits steaming at 21 knots and to tell him that Admiral Ramsay said it was alright to go if Esmonde was satisfied with the fighter escort. Esmonde confirmed that he was satisfied but as he was leaving the operations room, the telephone rang again. It was 11 Group to say that some of the fighters might be a little late at the rendezvous. Esmonde asked how late and was told 'a few minutes'. In reply, he said that he was taking off at 1225 and would orbit near the coast. 'Tell your chaps not to be later than two minutes, will that do?' The controller confirmed that that would be fine and Esmonde hurried off to man his aircraft. His observer and TAG were already in the aircraft and the fitter had started the engine so that its oil temperature was already within the normal operating range. As he climbed into the cockpit a runner arrived from the control room who shouted a message from Dover into his ear that the enemy's speed was now estimated at 27 knots.

825 NAS aircraft and crews on 12 February 1941

First sub-flight

H	W5984	Lieutenant Commander (A) E Esmonde DSO RN	Pilot
		Lieutenant W H Williams RN	Observer
		Leading Airman W J Clinton	TAG
L	W5907	Sub Lieutenant (A) C M Kingsmill RNVR	Pilot
		Sub Lieutenant (A) R McC Samples RNVR	Observer
		Leading Airman D A Bunce	TAG
G	W5983	Sub Lieutenant (A) B W Rose RNVR	Pilot
		Sub Lieutenant (A) E F Lee RNVR	Observer
		Leading Airman A L Johnson DSM	TAG

Second sub-flight

F	W4523	Lieutenant (A) J C Thompson RN	Pilot
		Sub Lieutenant (A) R L Parkinson RN	Observer
		Leading Airman E Tapping	TAG
K	W5985	Sub Lieutenant (A) C R Wood RN	Pilot
		Sub Lieutenant (A) E H Fuller-Wright RNVR	Observer
		Leading Airman H T A Wheeler	TAG
M	W5978	Sub Lieutenant (A) P Bligh RNVR	Pilot
		Sub Lieutenant (A) W Beynon RNVR	Observer
		Leading Airman W G Smith	TAG

The crew board for 825 NAS' gallant sortie photographed outside the squadron building on 12 February 1942. (*Author's collection*)

The Swordfish flown by 825 NAS on that day have often been referred to by historians who should know better as a handful of 'ancient biplanes'. In fact, with the sole exception of W4523, they were all brand new and had been delivered to the RN at Lee-on-Solent in December 1941. W4523 had been delivered in July 1941. They had actually been allocated to the squadron on 1 January 1942.[9] In February 1942 Manston was still a grass airfield and Esmonde led his aircraft to the eastern end of it, turned into wind and began to take off at 1225. There was no sign of any Spitfires overhead and Wing Commander Gleave stood watching the aircraft depart, noting that Esmonde's sub-flight went into line astern formation as briefed but Thompson's second sub-flight took up a vic formation. When interviewed by Terence Robertson more than a decade later, Gleave told him that he regarded the Swordfish crews at that moment 'as courage personified'. Esmonde led his aircraft west as they formed up and then turned back over the airfield at 1,500ft expecting to meet his escort. Over the coast, near Ramsgate slightly east of the airfield, he began his single orbit looking out for the Spitfires that had still not arrived. Esmonde had hoped to attack at 1245 at about the same time as the MTBs but the enemy was steaming away from him at a rate of nearly a nautical mile every two minutes. This was the supreme moment; 825 NAS had been deployed to carry out a night attack unopposed by enemy fighters. Now things were very different but Esmonde's sense of duty led him on and his devoted aircrew followed him. At 1230 he decided that he could wait no longer and turned towards the enemy task force but two minutes later he was joined by the ten Spitfires of 72 squadron led by Squadron Leader B Kingcombe RAF. Alone among his badly briefed contemporaries, Kingcombe had realised that an escort from 11 Group on this scale must involve more than the briefed 'skirmish' between naval units off Calais mentioned at his briefing and that his presence with the Swordfish might be of critical importance. He led his aircraft at maximum engine boost[10] and they tried, desperately, to defend the six Swordfish from the outset. The other two Biggin Hill squadrons used maximum continuous power and arrived over Ramsgate some minutes later; they found no Swordfish and headed east but became engaged in a series of combats with German fighters. The two Hornchurch squadrons arrived over Manston at 1245, found nothing and headed for Calais where they might, or might not, have shot down two enemy aircraft. Hurricanes from Manston took off at 1240 having been hastily briefed to catch up with the Swordfish and escort them. They had been a last-minute addition to the plan, had no clear idea of what they were trying to achieve and made no significant contribution to the battle.

Esmonde led his squadron at low level with the 72 Squadron Spitfires weaving above them trying to remain close despite their disparity in speed. Ten miles east of Ramsgate they encountered thickening overcast conditions with a visibility of only 4 miles as the first Luftwaffe fighters attacked them. These were driven off by the Spitfires at first but 72 Squadron was outnumbered and enemy fighters soon broke through to engage the Swordfish, all six of which turned hard to evade them, reducing their speed of advance towards the enemy force. A number of rounds shot through the fabric-covered Swordfish airframes but failed to hit anything vital. One enemy fighter group, estimated at twenty Bf 109s, attacked from port opposed by only three Spitfires. Some broke through and Esmonde and Rose broke hard away from each other to present difficult targets. Survivors spoke later of seeing strips of ripped fabric streaming from their damaged wings. At 1250 they saw the enemy force ahead; E-boats on the outer screen laying smoke with destroyers beyond them and the heavy ships shrouded in smoke from their own anti-aircraft fire. Esmonde selected *Scharnhorst* as his target and was seen to fly towards it, followed resolutely by the rest of his sub-flight. Enemy fighters continued to attack them with one approaching from astern and one from either beam simultaneously to present TAGs with multiple targets for their defensive fire. The Spitfires lost contact in a number of individual combats and the remainder of the planned escort, having lacked Kingcombe's foresight, had headed too far to the south to intervene effectively. As the Swordfish passed over the outer screen, Thompson's sub-flight was seen to maintain its position astern, still in its vic formation. Lee in Swordfish 'G' had been looking ahead past Rose's shoulder at their targets through the smokescreen and mist when he realised that Johnson, their TAG, was no longer firing. He looked back and saw that he was dead, slumped over his Lewis gun. He could not move the body to get at the gun but instead stood up and called to Rose as each enemy fighter reached a firing position on their beam so that he could turn into the attack and confuse the enemy pilot's aim. Flight Lieutenant Crombie in his Spitfire flew close to Esmonde's Swordfish 'H' at this stage and saw Leading Airman Clinton sitting astride the fuselage just aft of his cockpit beating at flames with his hands. After extinguishing them he returned to his gun. There were big holes in 'H' by this stage and heavy shells were being fired into the sea ahead of it to create splashes; the aircraft flew through the spray from them towards its target but had not yet received a fatal hit. A cannon shell hit 'G' and exploded between Rose and Kingsmill, wounding Rose in the back. He slumped forward and the aircraft's nose dropped but Lee shouted at him and he regained control. Their target was less than 2,000yd ahead and Lee could see 'H' ahead of him as a heavy shell hit and shot away its port lower wing. He could see Esmonde's jerky movements as he regained control and appreciated that he was aiming at *Scharnhorst*. Both Williams and Clinton appeared to be slumped, dead, in the rear cockpit. Lee shouted at Rose to aim at *Gneisenau* and as they opened away from 'H' he saw a burst of tracer hit its cockpit. Lee saw Esmonde drop his torpedo and then crash into the sea as it ran towards its target. Unfortunately it did not hit its target.

Rose retained control long enough to release his own torpedo 1,000yd from what Lee now recognised as *Prinz Eugen* but this also missed. A shell hit their main fuel tank and avgas poured out along the fuselage sides. Rose switched to the reserve tank, which held 15 gallons, shouting to Lee for directions away from the screen. Lee remembered seeing Kingsmill's 'L' flying over the destroyer screen surrounded by tracer from ships and fighters. A mile from the heavy ships 'L's engine and port upper wing caught fire and Kingsmill released his torpedo towards *Prinz Eugen* while he still had control of the aircraft. He then turned away and Lee saw 'L' heading towards the rear of the enemy force. As Kingsmill passed the aftermost E-boat his engine died and he ditched; all three crew members managed to get clear but their dinghy had been burnt in the upper wing and they had only their lifejackets to keep them afloat. Fortunately an MTB that was withdrawing from the scene of action saw them come down and rescued them. Swordfish 'G' was also in a desperate position. Its engine coughed as they passed over the outer screen and Rose managed to carry out a perfect 'dead-stick' ditching in the choppy sea. Lee managed to deploy the yellow dinghy from the upper wing and then saw that Rose was slumped semi-conscious in his cockpit. He tied the dinghy to the side of the aircraft and then tried to extricate Johnson's body from the rear cockpit but could not manage to do so. On seeing Rose stir, however, he moved forward, unstrapped him and hauled him into the dinghy. He just managed to untie the dinghy lanyard as 'G' rolled on to its side, crumpled and sank, taking Johnson's body with it. As they took stock, Rose found his left arm to be useless but he insisted on using his right to help Lee bail water out of the dinghy. Lee saw Thompson's vic of three Swordfish begin their attack, fired at by enemy fighters that had lowered their flaps and undercarriages to reduce their speed as they made firing passes at the slow Swordfish. For a brief instant, Lee saw the fighters draw off as they passed the outer screen and then Thompson's flight seemed to vanish into the splashes thrown up ahead of them by heavy shells. They were never seen again; all three Swordfish of Thompson's sub-flight were shot down and there were no survivors from the nine young men who manned them. Esmonde's 825 NAS had done all it could against overwhelming odds; all six Swordfish had been lost with thirteen out of the eighteen aircrew.

Lee and Rose were fired on by E-boats and Lee used his own body to shield Rose as they lay in the bottom of their dinghy. It was bitterly cold

Scharnhorst photographed from *Prinz Eugen* giving an idea of the speed at which the German ships were moving after they passed Dover. (*Author's collection*)

and the weather continued to deteriorate; Lee tried desperately to prevent Rose from slipping into unconsciousness. After more than an hour he fired a red flare in the hope that someone was searching for them and it was seen at 1500 by an MTB. After all his exertions, Lee collapsed as it drew near them and a sailor jumped into the sea to help lift them on to the deck. Minutes later he and Rose were wrapped in blankets, placed on bunks and given rum to drink. When they returned to Dover, they were warmed in a heated shed in the docks and then Rose was taken to hospital to join Kingsmill, Samples and Bunce. As the only one of the five survivors able to stand, Lee was taken to Dover Castle to report to Admiral Ramsay. The results could not yet be known but the fact that 825 NAS had carried out its attack against such appalling odds despite the majority of the escort fighters failing to arrive in time moved the Admiral deeply. After speaking to Lee he signalled the Admiralty that in his opinion:

> The gallant sortie of these six Swordfish constitutes one of the finest exhibitions of self-sacrifice and devotion to duty that the war has yet witnessed.

That evening Lee was driven back to Manston, where he found the fitters, riggers and ordnance ratings still waiting at the squadron dispersal in the hope that someone would return. He told them what had happened, allowing them all to share his pride in being a part of Esmonde's squadron.

The wider picture

The strike by 825 NAS was one part of a wider plan to cripple or slow the advance of the German ships and the naval units had reacted with commendable speed when the enemy was eventually detected. The MTBs from Dover and Ramsgate had attacked first, followed shortly by the Swordfish and then the six destroyers from Harwich. *Campbell*, *Vivacious* and *Worcester* were part of the 21st Destroyer Flotilla and *Mackay*, *Whitshed* and *Walpole* part of the 16th Destroyer Flotilla. All six dated from 1917–18 but retained the torpedo armament and speed required for a fleet action and they operated together as a single tactical unit under the command of Captain C T M Pizey RN, Captain D21. The original plan had been to intercept the enemy near the West Hinder Buoy off the Belgian coast in concert with attacking aircraft, having passed south of the East Coast mine barrier, but as Pizey received news of the enemy's position, course and speed from Dover he realised from his tactical plot that the enemy was advancing at 27 knots. This meant that he would have to attack without support further east than he would have wished and even then he would have to cross directly over a mine barrier. Like Esmonde and Lieutenant Commander Pumphrey who commanded the MTBs, Pizey was certainly aware of the risk to his force but determined that it was vital to carry out his part of the plan and attack as soon as possible. Failure to do so might have made the attacks carried out by other naval elements even more difficult and dangerous and at 1318 he signalled his destroyers to turn on to east at 28 knots and cross the barrier, hoping to make contact with the enemy off the River Maas at about 1530.[11] They were attacked by RAF bombers spasmodically but none dropped their weapons near enough to damage them, although *Walpole* had to drop out when her engine bearings began to run hot. Operational command was transferred from Dover to the Nore Command at 1411 when Pizey's ships moved into the new command area as they moved east.

At 1571 *Campbell*'s Type 271 radar detected two large contacts to the south-east at 9½ miles; these were *Gneisenau* and *Prinz Eugen*. *Scharnhorst* had stopped after detonating a mine but had got under way again and was beginning to catch up with the others from astern. A surprising feature of the battle at this stage was that most German aircraft took Pizey's destroyers to be German and fired red recognition signals to identify themselves. RAF aircraft, on the other hand, continued to bomb and strafe the British destroyers relentlessly, fortunately without hitting them. Pizey saw the enemy force at 1542 and the destroyers closed at high speed to within torpedo-firing range. Unfortunately none of the weapons launched in this determined attack hit their target but *Prinz Eugen* was seen to turn hard through 180 degrees to avoid one. *Mackay* had to take violent avoiding action of her own to avoid a torpedo attack on her by RAF Beauforts. Four of the British destroyers escaped serious damage but *Worcester* was badly hit and stopped in the water. She lost all power and her captain, Lieutenant Commander E C Coates RN, gave a verbal shout to 'prepare to abandon ship'. Unfortunately, this was misinterpreted as it passed through those on deck as 'abandon ship'; life rafts and Carley floats were launched and many of the wounded were placed in them before the order was countermanded. *Campbell* and *Vivacious* saw her distress and stopped alongside to rescue the men in the water, a task made more difficult by the worsening sea conditions. At 1615, while thus employed, *Campbell* had to go full astern to avoid a torpedo attack by Beauforts and the wash from her propellers capsized some of the rafts and tipped their occupants into the bitterly cold sea. An hour later the work of rescue was completed but twenty-three of her ship's company were dead or missing and eighteen were wounded. Four died later from their wounds. *Worcester* was eventually able to return to Harwich under her own steam, albeit slowly. The others returned at high speed to reload their torpedo tubes in case there should be a chance to attack enemy ships that had been damaged and stopped.

    Attacks by the RAF, a service that had claimed for more than two decades that its aircraft had rendered all the older forms of warfare obsolete, were bitterly disappointing. The twenty-eight torpedo-armed Beauforts of Coastal Command were caught unprepared, attacked in small numbers separated by time and, as we have seen, even attacked British destroyers rescuing survivors after their own torpedo attack. Bomber Command's attacks on the day were totally ineffective. A total of 242 aircraft were launched in three different waves made up of Halifax, Hampden, Manchester, Stirling and Wellington bombers, all of which failed to hit the enemy and some of them attacked British destroyers by mistake. The Fuller plan had called for the bombers to be armed with 500lb SAP bombs but these would need to be dropped from high level to be effective and they were replaced at the last moment with 500lb HE bombs, adding to the delay before they took off to attack between 1445 and 1700. The low cloud base at 1,500ft meant that they had to bomb from below that height, something they had never been trained to do, and the poor visibility made it difficult to find and identify the enemy. Records show that out of the 242, only thirty-nine RAF bombers actually found the enemy warships and dropped bombs near them; none of these had any effect. By nightfall Fighter Command had committed 398 Spitfires, Hurricanes and Whirlwinds but their effectiveness in the one aspect of Fuller that mattered, clearing the way for the strike aircraft, MTBs and destroyers to get to grips with the enemy was marginal.

Recognition of the Gallant Sortie

In the *London Gazette* of 3 March 1942,[12] the Admiralty listed the awards for bravery that had been made to the members of 825 NAS. At the head of the list was Eugene Esmonde, who was posthumously awarded the Victoria Cross for his valour and resolution in action against the enemy. The citation read:

> On the morning of Thursday 12 February 1942, Lieutenant Commander Esmonde, in command of a Squadron of the Fleet Air Arm, was told that the German battlecruisers Scharnhorst and Gneisenau and the cruiser Prinz Eugen, strongly escorted by some thirty surface craft, were entering the Straits of Dover, and that his Squadron must attack before they reached the sand-banks north-east of Calais.

The funeral of Lieutenant Commander (A) Eugene Esmonde VC DSO RN at the Woodlands Cemetery, Gillingham, Kent, on 30 April 1942. (*Author's collection*)

Lieutenant Commander Esmonde knew well that his enterprise was desperate. Soon after noon he and his squadron of six Swordfish set course for the enemy and, after ten minutes' flight were attacked by a strong force of enemy fighters. Touch was lost with his fighter escort; and in the action which followed all his aircraft were damaged. He flew on, cool and resolute, serenely challenging hopeless odds, to encounter the deadly fire of the battlecruisers and their escort, which shattered the port wing of his aircraft. Undismayed, he led his squadron on, straight through this inferno of fire, in steady flight towards their target. Almost at once he was shot down but his squadron went on to launch a gallant attack in which at least one torpedo is believed to have struck the German battlecruisers and from which not one of the six aircraft returned.

His high courage and splendid resolution will live in the traditions of the Royal Navy and remain for many generations a fine and stirring memory.

We now know, of course, that none of the torpedoes hit but that is hardly the point; Esmonde justly deserved the recognition he was given. Of interest, the recommendation for the award of the VC did not come from a naval source but from Wing Commander Gleave at Manston. After Sub Lieutenant Lee had given him his report, Gleave wrote to Air Marshal Leigh-Mallory, the AOC of 11 Group, asking him to forward his letter 'at his discretion to the proper naval authorities'. In it he wrote:

> I respectfully submit that it would not be presumptuous on my part to express an opinion on the manner in which Lieutenant Commander Esmonde and the crews under his command carried out their duties on this occasion.
>
> I discussed the operation with Lieutenant Commander Esmonde prior to the squadron taking-off at 12.30. His pilots and crews present at this meeting displayed signs of great enthusiasm and keenness for the job they were about to undertake and it was no doubt due to Lieutenant Commander Esmonde's leadership that such fine spirit prevailed.
>
> Nothing more was heard of the squadron until the five survivors were brought ashore. The German battleships (sic) were undoubtedly protected by a terrific barrage of flak and covered by one of the biggest fighter screens ever seen. Against this, the determination and gallantry shown by Lieutenant Commander Esmonde and his pilots and crews is beyond any normal praise.
>
> I am of the opinion that Lieutenant Commander Esmonde is well worthy of the posthumous award of the Victoria Cross.

The same *London Gazette* announced that Sub Lieutenants Rose, Lee, Kingsmill and Samples had been made companions of the Distinguished Service Order and that Leading Airman Bunce[13] had been awarded the Conspicuous Gallantry Medal. Rose's citation read that:

> ... his aircraft was hit early in the action but though in great pain from a wound in his back, he held on his course. Another hit burst his petrol tank and his engine began to fail, but with unshaken resolve he flew on and came within 2,000yd of the enemy before he dropped his torpedo which was seen running well towards the target. Then he flew back across the fire of the enemy escort and his aircraft, now on fire, came down into the sea just beyond.

Lee's citation stated that:

> ... before the Swordfish had reached the enemy escort vessels their air gunner was killed. Sub Lieutenant Lee stood up in the cockpit and directed the pilot so that he could evade the attacking enemy fighters. He went on doing this until the aircraft came down in flames. Then, although under fierce fire from the enemy, he got his wounded pilot, who was very much heavier than he, into his dinghy and returned to the aircraft but found it sinking. For an hour and a half he stayed in the flooded dinghy, tending and encouraging his wounded pilot and never losing heart until both were rescued.

Kingsmill and Samples had a joint citation, which read that their

> ... Swordfish was badly hit early in the action by cannon shells from an enemy fighter. Both were wounded, but with part of the aircraft shot away and the engine and the upper wing in flames, they flew on undaunted until they had taken aim and fired their torpedo. They then turned and tried to come down near some ships but these opened fire so they flew on until their engine stopped and their aircraft came down into the sea. Soon afterwards they were picked up, still cheerful and dauntless, by one of HM vessels.

Bunce's citation noted that:

> ... with his machine on fire and the engine failing, he stayed steadfast at his gun, engaging the enemy fighters which beset his aircraft. He is believed to have shot one of them down. Throughout the action his coolness was unshaken.

Leading Airman Johnson, Rose and Lee's TAG, was awarded a Mention in Despatches for 'showing the same dauntless spirit' as his pilot and observer before being killed early in the action. The two men who flew with Esmonde, Lieutenant Williams and Leading Airman Clinton, were described as sharing his fate in this gallant action and showing the same high courage. They were both awarded a Mention in Despatches, the highest award short of a Victoria Cross that could be made posthumously at the time. The same posthumous recognition was made to the nine men of the second sub-flight. Their combined citation read:

> The last that was seen of this gallant band, who were astern of the leading flight, is that they were flying steadily towards the battlecruisers, led by Lieutenant Thompson. Their aircraft shattered, undeterred by an inferno of fire, they carried out their orders which were to attack the target. Not one came back. Theirs was the courage which is beyond praise.

Analysis of the Channel Dash

Neither *Scharnhorst* nor *Gneisenau* reached their destination unscathed, however, as both detonated mines laid a few days earlier by Bomber Command at the request of the Admiralty. In fact, mines had proved to be the Command's most effective weapons, although its senior officers would hardly care to admit it. *The Times* of London summed up the public reaction with the headline 'Vice Admiral Ciliax has succeeded where the Duke of Medina Sidonia[14] failed', a headline that was not entirely accurate since the English fleet had prevented the Spanish Armada from embarking an invasion force at the Battle of Gravelines, it had not actually prevented it from sailing through the Straits of Dover. Churchill reacted to the public disquiet by ordering a judicial enquiry under Mr Justice Bucknill, an English judge and privy councillor specialising in maritime law. Its other members were Admiral Sir Hugh Binney and Air Marshal Sir Edgar Ludlow-Hewitt. It sat for twelve days and produced its report on 2 March. It was presented to Parliament on 18 March by Clement Attlee, the Deputy Prime Minister, but not made public until 1946. Overall, the report was not as critical as it might have been and Attlee was able to inform Members of Parliament that it had not revealed 'any serious deficiencies in either foresight, co-operation or organisation between the Services concerned and their respective Commands'. The part that concerns us most is contained in sections 118(a) and (b).[15] In these it was stated that:

Two questions arise as to the use of the Swordfish:

(a) Coastal Command, on hearing of the approach of the German ships, asked the naval authorities at Dover to co-ordinate the Swordfish attack with an attack by Beaufort torpedo bombers. The Vice Admiral Dover decided to operate these forces as early as possible and independently of the Beauforts, and informed Coastal Command that the aircraft would be leaving Manston at 1230, but it was impossible for Coastal Command to co-ordinate an attack with Beauforts so early. Having regard to the short time available and the necessity of trying to disable one of the big ships and thereby slow up the enemy squadron, the Board think that the decision to send the Swordfish to the attack alone was right.

(b) The five fighter squadrons detailed to provide protection for the Swordfish unfortunately did not all arrive in time. We have considered this question and we have come to the conclusion that, in view of the short notice and other circumstances [set out in paragraph 36] those responsible for getting the five squadrons to the rendezvous in time did their best to do so. The only other question that arose on this point was whether Lieutenant Commander Esmonde, who was leading the Swordfish, was told that his escort would be late. The evidence given before us was that he was told that part of his escort would be late and that he replied that he would leave at 1225 whatever happened and that he could not possibly leave later than that. In the event he left with one squadron of Spitfires as escort. Here again, having regard to the necessity for the Swordfish to deliver their attack as soon as possible, the Board think this decision of Lieutenant Commander Esmonde was right.

The report 'ventured to express' the view that against fast, heavily armoured ships the most effective air weapon available at present was undoubtedly the torpedo-bomber and that 'the need for the development of a powerful and highly trained striking force of torpedo bombers seems to be one which calls for urgent consideration'. One of the report's most surprising omissions was the lack of any criticism of the failure of the 'Jim Crow' patrol pilots to break radio silence and report their sightings, especially since detailed research had revealed that the original Fighter Command order only required R/T silence on the outbound leg and gave discretionary permission to break it in an emergency. More surprising still was the acceptance of Group Captain Beamish's silence, since he had actually recognised the ships in question and should, surely, have considered that fact as justifying the breaking of R/T silence. A new fighter Command order was issued that made it mandatory to report, immediately, the sighting of an enemy warship of destroyer size or larger.

There was no mention in the report about the lack of intervention by heavy ships of the Home Fleet. At the time the only fully worked up battleship immediately available was *King George V* at Scapa Flow, with *Rodney* undergoing repairs at Rosyth. The new battleship *Duke of York* commissioned in November 1941 was not yet considered fully worked up. *Renown* was in the Clyde, about to sail as the heavy escort for a WS convoy to the Middle East. There was considerable public comment that part of the Home Fleet should have been moved south, perhaps to the Humber Estuary, when the German move was thought to be imminent. Had this been done, and the ships kept at immediate notice, it would have been possible for them to intercept the enemy squadron in the winter darkness off Heligoland with the prospect of a night action. To do so, however, would have forced the Home Fleet to abandon one or both of the principal commitments with which it was charged. These were the heavy escort of the WS troop convoys and the denial to the *Tirpitz* of a clear route into the main Atlantic convoy routes from the north. To bring a battle squadron powerful enough to overwhelm the German battlecruisers south to the Humber to await developments would have meant abandoning both priorities. It was for these very reasons that both the Admiralty and Air Ministry had accepted from the outset that Fuller must be primarily an air operation with the RN contributing light forces, including 825 NAS, intended to slow the enemy and ease the bombers' task. The British had suffered from overreliance on their own appreciation that the enemy would probably, although not certainly, pass through the Channel in the hours of darkness. After the failure of the night radar reconnaissance patrols and the morning 'Jim Crow' patrols to find or report the enemy, few of the British units allocated to Fuller had proved to be able to act effectively after the surprise of the enemy's late detection. Captain Pizey's destroyers, Lieutenant Commander Pumphrey's MTBs and Lieutenant Commander Esmonde's Swordfish had all reacted at once in the moment of crisis and done everything that had been expected of them, to their ever-lasting credit.

Although the Channel Dash was a tactical victory for the German squadron, their repositioning proved to be a strategic defeat. After passing through the Kiel Canal on 13 February, *Gneisenau* was dry-docked in Kiel for the mine damage she had suffered to be repaired. Bomber Command attacked her there on 25, 26 and 27 February, breaking her back and causing extensive damage to her forecastle, as a result of which she was towed to Gdynia and grounded for use as a harbour defence blockship. *Prinz Eugen* sailed with *Admiral Scheer* for northern Norway on 21 February but was torpedoed by the British submarine *Trident* and had to return to Kiel for repairs. Further attempts to deploy north were cancelled when she was detected by air reconnaissance and she spent the remainder of the war in the Baltic. Repairs to *Scharnhorst* took nearly a year but then she did eventually reach Altafjord in north Norway in February 1943.

Victorious *in operations off Norway*

Victorious remained with the Home Fleet in Scapa Flow as a counter to *Tirpitz* and *Lützow*, which were both now based in northern Norway. Operations as part of the Fleet's heavy squadron meant that *Victorious* had not carried out any strike operations[16] in the Norwegian littoral until February, when she sailed with *King George V*, *Berwick* and seven destroyers to carry out an air attack on shipping in the Tromsø area. However, on 21 February a Coastal Command aircraft reported *Scheer* and *Prinz Eugen* off Jutland heading north. The C-in-C therefore cancelled the Tromsø plan and headed south. *Victorious* was ordered to prepare for a night sweep by torpedo-armed Albacores down the coast to intercept the German ships. However, on realising that they had been detected, the two enemy ships turned back and anchored in Grimstad Fjord south of Bergen at dawn on 22 February. On learning this the C-in-C turned to head for Iceland until 1700, when he received a signal from the Admiralty telling him that the German ships were expected to resume their passage north. He therefore detached *Victorious*, *Berwick* and four destroyers with instructions to proceed at 27 knots to reach a flying off position 100nm off Stadtlandet by 0100 on 23 February, from where they were to locate and attack the enemy. The task force was to rendezvous north-west of the Shetland Islands later in the day but the Albacores were to make their way to the RAF airfield at Sumburgh at the end of their sortie. Before *Victorious* could arrive at the flying off position, however, the barometer fell rapidly and she passed through a front but her senior meteorological officer forecast much better weather off the Norwegian coast. Snow showers with visibility less than a cable delayed the flying off but at 0100 on 23 February ten Albacores of 832 NAS armed with torpedoes took off led by Lieutenant Commander A J P Plugge RN, its commanding officer. They were briefed to fly at the lowest height consistent with ASV radar efficiency to the coast west of Stadtlandet and, having made landfall, they were to carry out a sweep to the south parallel to but 10 miles off the coast until they reached the prudent limit of the aircraft's endurance. Any enemy ships encountered were to be attacked. Aircraft that lost formation in poor visibility were to continue independently. In fact Albacore 4C, the last to take off, flew straight into a snowstorm and had to fly independently from the outset. It was flown by Sub Lieutenant (A) J D Landles RNVR with his observer Sub Lieutenant (A) D J R Harvey RNVR and TAG Leading Airman T Armstrong RN. Three-quarters of an hour later a second range comprising seven Albacores of 817 NAS led by its commanding officer, Lieutenant Commander D Sanderson RN, was flown off. Their briefing was the same as that as that for 832 NAS except that they were to fly 20 to 30 miles off the coast. Two of their aircraft were fitted with ASV radar.

As the formations approached the coast at between 500 and 800ft the weather deteriorated with cloud down to 250ft, heavy snowstorms and very poor visibility. At 0200 the ASV-fitted aircraft in 832 NAS gained three contacts at 8 miles, 18 miles off the coast. Course was altered to close them but nothing was seen in the bad meteorological conditions and after reaching the Utvoer Light, the aircraft set heading for Sumburgh. Some aircraft jettisoned their torpedoes to conserve fuel and all of them became separated in the appalling weather. When it was about 30 miles from the Shetland Islands, Plugge's aircraft fired a flare, apparently prior

Albacores being ranged on a fleet carrier's flight deck. (*Author's collection*)

to ditching because it was never seen again. He had been one of the most experienced observers in the Fleet Air Arm.

The operation ended with fourteen of the seventeen Albacores landing at Sumburgh between 0445 and 0600. Apart from Plugge's loss, two aircraft of 817 NAS had disappeared from their formation while it was in cloud off the Norwegian coast and were thought to have collided. Some had as little as 20 gallons of fuel remaining and the only offensive action carried out had been by an aircraft of 817 NAS, which had emerged from cloud at 200ft close to Sando Light and seen a small craft thought to be an E-boat. The result of its torpedo attack was not seen. The German ships did not reach their destination unscathed, however. As mentioned above, *Prinz Eugen* was torpedoed by *Trident* and had her stern and rudder blown away. Repairs took nine months. The commanding officer of *Victorious* complained in his report about the lack of up-to-date weather forecasts for the Norwegian coast supplied by the Admiralty in its fleet synoptic messages, especially in view of the fact that RAF aircraft had been operating in the area. He ended by writing that '... had I known the conditions over the Norwegian coast I would never have flown off the striking force. Long odds must be taken in war and losses accepted but I submit that the Service cannot afford to squander its slender capital of trained Fleet Air Arm personnel when information is available that there is no chance of success.'

Strenuous action was taken afterwards to improve the weather forecasting available to the Home Fleet during its air operations by more frequent reporting of weather by RAF aircraft on patrol and its inclusion in fleet messages. With regard to intelligence prior to this and previous operations, the commanding officer of *Victorious* said that 'one of the chief lessons in this war has been that, if an air attack is not to be a costly "blow in the air", recent and accurate reconnaissance is essential. In no operation except that which resulted in the sinking of the *Bismarck* do I feel that I have received the quantity and quality of information necessary to success.'

In the light of post-war naval staff analysis of 1941–42 Norwegian littoral operations by *Victorious*' squadrons it is difficult not to share this view. Lack of recent intelligence from air reconnaissance had been the main problem and, while these might have compromised the element of surprise to some extent, that surprise was valueless if aircraft were wasted in attacks on places where there were no targets.

On 7 March a Home Fleet task force comprising *Victorious, King George V, Duke of York, Renown, Berwick* and nine destroyers was covering convoys PQ 12/QP 8 to and from Russia when the Admiralty signalled a warning that *Tirpitz* had sailed from Trondheim. *Victorious* formed part of the covering force to ensure what the Admiralty described

DISCOVER MORE ABOUT MARITIME AND NAVAL HISTORY

Seaforth PUBLISHING is probably the country's leading maritime book publisher, producing the very best reference books, narrative histories, ship monographs and modelling books, all reflecting the latest research and designed and printed to the highest standards.

Keep up to date with our new releases by completing and returning the form below (no stamp required if posting in the UK).

Alternatively, please enter your details online at **www.seaforthpublishing.com**

All those subscribing to our mailing list via our website will receive a free e-book, *HMS Victory, First Rate 1765*. Please enter code number ACC2 when subscribing to receive your free e-book.

Mr/Mrs/Ms ....

Address..............

Postcode.............. Email address..............

Website: www.seaforthpublishing.com – Email: enquiries@seaforthpublishing.com
Telephone: 01226 734555

Freepost Plus RTKE-RGRJ-KTTX
Pen & Sword Books Ltd
47 Church Street
BARNSLEY
S70 2AS

as 'the presence of the fighter protection provided by her aircraft ... although the enemy's air strength in Norway was still small'.[17] *Tirpitz* failed to make contact with either convoy despite Luftwaffe air searches but one of her screening destroyers did find and sink a straggler from QP 8. The two convoys actually passed through each other in heavy snow approximately 200 miles south-west of Bear Island when *Tirpitz* was only 70 miles south-south-west of them. At 1720 the cruiser *Kenya* catapulted a Walrus briefed to search between 210 and 270 degrees ahead of QP 8 to a depth of 45 miles. It reported on its return that the sector was clear but a later study of German records revealed that *Tirpitz* had been only 60 miles from the convoy bearing 290 degrees when the Walrus was launched. It must, therefore, have failed to gain contact by a very narrow margin. Earlier in the day the C-in-C had ordered *Victorious* to carry out an air search to the south of the two convoys out to 120 miles but 'by great misfortune' severe icing conditions in the vicinity of the carrier were encountered all day and any air reconnaissance proved impossible.[18]

A straggler, the Russian *Ijora*, was attacked but managed to transmit an accurate distress signal before sinking and it was thought in the flagship, *King George V*, that this might be *Tirpitz*. D/F bearings showed a German ship moving rapidly south from the position in which *Ijora* was sunk and destroyers were ordered south-east to intercept it. The bulk of the task force remained in the area of Bear Island. By midnight on 7/8 March the C-in-C had heard nothing from these destroyers and turned south to be within air striking distance should they find anything. At 0400 on 8 March he turned towards Iceland at 24 knots thinking that *Tirpitz* had eluded him. By then she was actually 250 miles to his north-east and both convoys eventually reached their destinations without further mishap. At about 1800, *Tirpitz* gave up searching for the convoys and turned south for the Norwegian coast but Admiral Tovey thought that she might still pose a threat and turned his task force north-east to search for her. However, information from the Admiralty war room made it clear that *Tirpitz* was heading for Trondheim and so at 0243 on 9 March he altered course again to close the Lofoten Islands at 26 knots. However, the distance travelled to the west on 8 March meant that the enemy could not be intercepted unless an air strike could slow *Tirpitz*.

At dawn, which was at 0645, on 9 March *Victorious* flew off six Albacores briefed to search for *Tirpitz* on tracks between 105 and 155 degrees out to 150 miles. Weather conditions included almost complete cloud cover at 2,000ft; icing conditions down to sea level and a 25-knot wind from the east-north-east. Visibility varied between practically nothing in snowstorms and extreme clarity outside them. Recent changes had diluted the number of experienced aircrew in both the carrier's squadrons; none of the pilots or observers had much previous experience of shadowing but they achieved their briefed task well. At 0802 Duty 'F' flown by Sub Lieutenant (A) W H G Brown RNVR with his observer Sub Lieutenant (A) T T Miller RN and TAG Leading Airman Lindley identified a suspicious vessel as *Tirpitz* 80 miles from the fleet. Two minutes later they transmitted their first sighting report but gave an inaccurate bearing; fortunately Sub Lieutenant Miller realised his error and corrected the bearing fifteen minutes later.

At 0735 *Victorious* flew off a strike comprising twelve Albacores armed with torpedoes from both 817 and 832 NAS led by Lieutenant Commander W J Lucas RN. He had only just taken over command of 832 NAS after the death of Lieutenant Commander Plugge; this was the first time he had flown with it and had not practised torpedo attack tactics since 1937. The strike aircraft made good a track of 135 degrees at 500ft initially but were briefed to act on any updated contact reports from the shadowing aircraft. Duty 'F's reports were taken in by the strike leader, who altered course to intercept, and further reports were received from Duty 'C', which had also made contact. At 0810 *Tirpitz* saw these two shadowing aircraft and then a third and at 0830 she launched a single Arado seaplane out of the three she had embarked 'as a defence measure against submarine and aerial attack'.[19] It attacked two shadowing Albacores inconclusively before the strike force arrived. The third shadowing Albacore was attacked by what the pilot thought was a Ju 87 and his observer, Sub Lieutenant (A) G Dunworth RNVR, was badly wounded by cannon fire but continued to navigate the aircraft until its successful return to the carrier, earning a DSC for his gallant effort. At 0834 *Tirpitz* altered course to 080 degrees and increased speed to 29 knots. Duty 'F' reports on her new course and speed were picked up by Lieutenant Commander Lucas, who made two track alterations to intercept before sighting *Tirpitz* 25nm away at 0842.

Once contact was gained, Lucas led his strike force up into the cloud, levelling out at 3,500ft. Two ASV radar contacts were held, the enemy battleship and an escorting destroyer at 16 miles, but at that height the wind was much stronger than it had been at 500ft and the closing speed on a target steaming at nearly 30 knots into a 30-knot wind was only 30 knots. Lucas' original intention had been to gain the classic position ahead of the target, unseen if possible, before diving to attack at 0850 but he changed his mind and ordered his sub-flights to act independently. This was probably to simplify the problem of cloud flying in icing conditions since there can be no other rational explanation for his decision. As the strike force got directly overhead *Tirpitz*, however, there was an unexpected gap in the cloud cover and the Albacores were seen, although their presence had probably already been detected by radar. The enemy did not open fire at once, however, leading Lucas to deduce that *Tirpitz* was not at action stations and he thought this offered a brief opportunity for a surprise attack. At 0917 he signalled 'dive to attack' before reaching the ideal position ahead and up wind of *Tirpitz* but this proved to be a critical mistake because she opened fire at that moment. Thus the advantage of a high relative speed on the final approach from the bow was lost and by the time the second and following sub-flights had reached sea level *Tirpitz* was already taking effective avoiding action. She was further helped by the length of time it took the sub-flights, which were down wind of the leader, to get into positions from which they could drop their torpedoes with any chance of success. Evidence provided by the one torpedo-aiming camera that produced a photograph after the action showed that this aircraft had been at a range double that intended by the pilot when he dropped his torpedo and it was thought at the time that other pilots might have made the same error. However, German records revealed that this underestimation of *Tirpitz*'s range was not a common factor. Entries in the battleship's log actually described the attack as being pressed home with determination and aircraft dropping their torpedoes at ranges estimated between 400 and 1,200yd, with one torpedo passing only 10yd from her stern. In spite of the opinion expressed by most Albacore pilots that the enemy's anti-aircraft fire was ineffective and ragged, two Albacores were shot down by close-range weapons and must, therefore, have been inside the ideal torpedo-dropping range. Sub Lieutenants (A) RC

Albacores photographed from *Tirpitz* as they attacked her on 9 March 1942. The wake in the middle distance is from the destroyer *Friedrich Ihn*. (*Author's collection*)

Jones, L Brown and D J Shephard RNVR together with leading Airmen S G Hollowood and CF Sivewright, all of 832 NAS were reported as killed in action by the Admiralty.

All the torpedoes had been set to run at 40 knots at a depth of 25ft with impact pistols because the non-contact setting was believed to have caused a number of premature detonations recently in swell or rough seas. These settings meant that the most that could be expected from any hit, assuming the absence of a lucky hit on rudders or shafting, like the one that had crippled *Bismarck*, would have been some reduction in speed. This might just have given time for the Home Fleet to close within gunnery range before *Tirpitz* reached the shelter of the fjords, about 60 miles distant at the time of the attack, but there were no hits and once again it had been demonstrated that an airborne torpedo attack on a fast capital ship with freedom to manoeuvre was a specialised task that required constant training. Twelve Albacores hardly constituted a large enough strike force to command success and after the last Albacore was recovered on *Victorious* at 1045, Admiral Tovey decided that further shadowing was pointless and he turned his force towards Scapa Flow. Soon afterwards a BV 138 shadower was detected and three Fulmars were flown off to intercept it. After several attacks from beam, quarter and astern it was driven off with an engine on fire but German records made no mention of its failure to return to base. Other enemy aircraft continued to shadow and in the late afternoon three Ju 88s were seen, two of which were driven off by fighters and gunfire but the third carried out a bombing attack on *Victorious*, fortunately without scoring any hits.

There was disappointment at the strike force's lack of success, the conditions for which could hardly have been more favourable. The commanding officer of *Victorious* wrote that 'the gravity of the failure to take full advantage of this opportunity, which may never recur, and its far-reaching implications are fully realised. No one is more disappointed than the crews of the aircraft who took part in the attack; it was the chance they had dreamed of and prayed for.' There was never to be another opportunity for an attack on *Tirpitz* at sea by carrier-borne aircraft but the narrowness of her escape did have a considerable impact on the German naval staff when they considered future operations. Vice Admiral Weichold wrote[20] that:

> The Tirpitz operation [against PQ 12/QP 8] had not resulted in any direct success. Only sheer good fortune had saved the ship from damage by enemy ships, torpedo-bombers and submarines. But the operation clearly revealed the weakness of the German Navy's position in the north. Admiral Ciliax pointed out that operations

by single ships without adequate air cover in an area patrolled by the British Fleet offered slight prospects and were not worth a great risk. Grand Admiral Raeder stressed the risk involved in such operations in view of the lack of aircraft carriers and the weakness of the Luftwaffe. He queried whether the use of capital ships in this way was consistent with their main task of defence against invasion.

The Tirpitz episode impressed on the Germans very forcibly the need for an aircraft carrier of their own. Hitler therefore again gave orders for the immediate completion of Graf Zeppelin and the construction of the requisite carrier aircraft. These could not, however, be ready before the autumn of 1944 owing to labour shortages. As a further reinforcement Hitler ordered that the cruiser Seydlitz and the liner Potsdam should be converted into auxiliary carriers.

The lessons drawn from the failure of this torpedo attack were taken very seriously by NAD. Larger and faster ships were made available to act as targets in the Firth of Forth for TBR pilots to carry out attack drills with practice torpedoes and these helped to ensure that pilots, especially those new pilots coming through the TBR pipeline at RNAS Crail, were able to estimate target range accurately. Efforts were also made to design and build a torpedo attack trainer, TAT, effectively the first synthetic pilot training simulator, at Crail. It was the first device of its kind and

A practice torpedo attack on the target ship *Glenavon* in the Firth of Forth by a Barracuda from RNAS Crail. The splash from the torpedo is on the right and it is running accurately towards its target. Every aircraft photographed its target during practice attacks so that range and inclination could be assessed accurately. Attacks were also photographed by an instructor overhead to assist in debriefs. Unfortunately, I am not aware that any of these photographs survived. May Island is visible on the horizon. (*Author's collection*)

was designed to meet an Admiralty specification by 'Fitups',[21] a firm of theatrical scenery and lighting manufacturers based in London and Manchester. It consisted of a solid, circular screen known as a cyclorama, 44ft in diameter and 23ft high and curved inwards at the top and bottom. A small aeroplane-shaped training device, based on the Link Trainer, was placed in the centre and control inputs from its cockpit moved it like a real aircraft in pitch, yaw and roll, although it remained fixed to the floor. Clever lighting effects helped to give the pilot a feeling of speed, height and movement while he carried out a torpedo attack profile. A 10-degree segment of the cyclorama was open to allow access and to provide space for the control position, to the rear of the little aircraft. This contained the instructor's position, which had lighting controls and a glass-topped table with two recorders that traced the courses of the attack aircraft and the target. The building's inside walls were painted black, helping the lighting to simulate effects inside the cyclorama, including both fleecy and stormy clouds, sunny day, stormy day, moonlight, dark night, sunset, rain, sleet and many others all controlled through a motor-driven dimmer bank operated by push-button selector control. Special lanterns also shone on to the cyclorama floor to give the impression of forward motion over the sea, turning and diving. The lighting was fixed in a gantry suspended over the 'aircraft', which also contained an epidiascope that projected the image of the target ship. This image could be varied in size and inclination according to the position of the attack aircraft set up by the pilot in the simulator. Accurately made brass models of German and Japanese warships were used for this purpose, each scaled at 100ft to 1in.

The simulator cockpit contained the same torpedo sight controls as aircraft, Albacores at first, then Barracudas, and the pilot had to set target speed and inclination. When he simulated torpedo release by pressing a button on the throttle, the target was frozen and the instructor at the control console worked out the distance the weapon would have to travel and a line of sight was switched on the cyclorama to indicate its course. The target was then restarted and allowed to travel for the exact period required for the weapon to reach the ship's course to show a hit or miss. The TAT was a great success and Fitups was contracted to produce further simulators at RN Air Stations including Machrihanish, Arbroath and Fearn to provide operational refresher training for front-line TBR crews. Modified versions were produced to simulate torpedo attacks by destroyers,[22] submarines and MTBs, and the concept was exported to the USN under Lend-Lease arrangements.

Inside the Torpedo Attack Trainer at RNAS Crail. (*Author's collection*)

Naval Air Squadrons operating ashore

During the second half of 1942 several front-line TBR squadrons operated temporarily ashore under the control of RAF Coastal or Fighter Commands for varying periods.[23] The six NAS attached to Coastal Command were each equipped with six Swordfish intended for use in the anti-submarine role embarked in new escort carriers, CVE, as they came into service. They operated at various times from the RAF airfields at Bircham Newton, Docking, Thorney Island and Langham. They were:

819 NAS	July to October
811 NAS	August to December
812 NAS	September, October
816 NAS	September to December
825 NAS	From mid-December
836 NAS	From 29 December

Of these, 819 NAS went on eventually to embark in *Archer*, 811 NAS embarked in *Biter*, 816 NAS embarked in *Dasher* and 812 NAS was temporarily disbanded. After some time at various naval air stations, 825 NAS embarked in *Furious* and 836 NAS became the headquarters unit that provided detached flights to MAC ships employed on the Atlantic convoy routes.

Three naval air squadrons were attached to Fighter Command and operated from Manston and Tangmere. They were:

841 NAS	with four Albacores	From September
832B NAS	with three Albacores	October to December
823 NAS	with three Albacores	From October

The units attached to Coastal Command flew variously in night torpedo or bombing attacks on enemy shipping, night minelaying and night anti-shipping/E-boat armed search and patrol in the English Channel. Those attached to Fighter Command were equipped with ASV radar and had VHF voice radio for direct communication with the headquarters ashore. They had capabilities and skills that were not available within the RAF and were used for the development of night armed search and patrol tactics under shore radar control in a series of attacks on enemy shipping in the Channel area. The difficulties of location, attack and the observation of results in conditions of poor visibility, however, meant that for every sortie in which the enemy was encountered, there were many that found no targets and were uneventful. Overall, the results might have appeared meagre when compared with the number of aircraft employed but they maintained an offensive posture that forced the enemy to maintain a disproportionately large convoy escort organisation in the Channel. The majority of squadrons returned to their naval duties in late 1942 but 841 NAS remained a core element of Fighter Command's Channel operations until November 1943 and its aircrew became the acknowledged experts in their field. The squadron had been commissioned at RNAS Lee-on-Solent on 1 July specifically for use in Fighter Command operations intended to limit the amount of enemy minelaying in the Straits of Dover. Initially the unit had two Albacores, increased to four a few weeks later, and it underwent weapon training at RNAS Machrihanish for a month and then deployed to RAF Middle Wallop, where its aircraft were fitted with VHF radios. It arrived at Manston on 23 August to commence operations[24] and on nights when enemy minelaying was considered possible the aircraft were kept at five minutes' readiness. They were scrambled when vessels were detected on radar outside Calais, Boulogne or Dieppe and then vectored on to them. Initially, attacks used a glide bombing technique with a stick of twelve 100lb A/S bombs usually set at 35ft intervals. A system of air patrols was adopted later, intended to intercept the enemy boats off their own coasts. The success of 841 NAS in reducing enemy activity in the Straits of Dover led to increased tasking to include attacks on all enemy shipping passing along the French Channel coast.

Further cover for Russian convoys

A Home Fleet task force provided distant cover for convoys PQ 15/QP 11 in early May but carrier aircraft played no active part in their defence. The force was notable for the inclusion of the US battleship *Washington*, on loan to the Home Fleet, which joined the British battleships *King George V* and *Duke of York* with *Victorious* to make up the most powerful covering force yet deployed. The American squadron, designated Task Force 39 by the USN, also included the carrier *Wasp* but after her arrival in Scapa Flow she was used to ferry Spitfires to Malta. PQ 15 was the first Russian convoy to include a CAM ship, *Empire Morn*. Fifteen of the twenty-six merchant ships were American, the largest percentage yet.[25] *Victorious* also formed part of the covering force for PQ 16, which sailed from Reykjavik on 21 May but again her aircraft did not become directly involved. She had been at sea covering the intended return of the damaged cruiser *Trinidad* from Murmansk. Further damage had led to the cruiser having to be sunk by a British torpedo after she was abandoned, however. Prior to this operation *Victorious* had demonstrated her versatility by carrying out deck landing trials under Admiralty direction in Scapa Flow. These helped in the much-delayed development of the Fairey Barracuda TBR aircraft and the Supermarine Seafire fighter. Both had their problems; the former had to be re-engined after the cancellation of its Rolls-Royce Exe engine by the MAP and its entry into service was three years later than intended. The Seafire was not an easy aircraft to deck land and required a tight curved approach to allow the pilot to keep the batsman in sight on finals. It also suffered from a weak undercarriage and was prone to wrinkling of the stressed skin rear fuselage if the landing was not well executed. Given the political opposition that had cursed the procurement

A Fulmar being manhandled clear of the hardstanding at RNAS Hatston as aircraft from USS *Wasp* are prepared for an inspection by senior Home Fleet officers in 1942. (Author's collection)

Captain H StJ Fancourt RN, Captain of HMS *Sparrowhawk*, RNAS Hatston, landing on USS *Wasp* in 1942. This is believed to be the first time that a British naval aircraft had ever landed on an American aircraft carrier. (*Author's collection*)

of naval fighters, however, it was the best that could be produced quickly in the UK. Fortunately for the RN, USN fighters were becoming available in larger numbers to fill the gap.

The role of *Victorious*' aircraft was the provision of anti-submarine patrols around the task force itself and the maintenance of CAP fighters

Barracuda flying trials being carried out on *Victorious* in Scapa Flow. This aircraft is being flown off in a strong wind from port to starboard across the flight deck to establish safe limits; note the steam jet at the bow. The pilot has applied full starboard rudder to counter the 'weathercock' effect of the wind. Personnel on deck include civilians from the Royal Aircraft Establishment as well as naval officers. (*Author's collection*)

to drive off shadowers but records show no examples of them achieving success against either U-boats or enemy aircraft during this period. The Soviet authorities had promised to attack German airfields in north Norway with a force of 200 Red Army bombers as PQ 16 and QP 12 passed but Admiral Tovey noted in his report that 'this undertaking went the way of all Russian promises and air raids were limited to one attack by twenty aircraft after the German air attacks on the convoys had been completed'.[26] Enemy air attacks on PQ 16 were the largest yet attempted; beginning on 25 May and continuing for four days. It was estimated that thirty-four torpedo aircraft and 208 bombers attacked but the C-in-C reported that the bombers only pressed home their attacks on one day and the torpedo aircraft were 'cautious in the extreme and generally ineffective'. They sank six ships out of thirty-five, however, and another was sunk by a U-boat. Several U-boats were believed to have been damaged by the escorts, which drove off a number of attempted attacks. It was also believed that four enemy aircraft had certainly been shot down and another sixteen probably so. German records studied after the war showed that Luftflotte V had lost eight Ju 88 bombers. One of the enemy aircraft definitely accounted for was shot down by the Hurricane from the CAM ship *Empire Lawrence*, which was launched on 25 May although, interestingly, its pilot, Flying Officer Hay RAF, identified it as a He 111.

Victorious formed part of the Home Fleet distant cover for PQ 17 and QP 13 from 2 July. The former was the convoy ordered to scatter by 1SL because he feared that *Tirpitz* was in its vicinity and, in consequence, it suffered the most serious losses yet suffered by any convoy on this route. Lacking escorts, ten merchant ships were sunk by U-boats and a further thirteen by aircraft out of the thirty-six that had started. *Victorious* never came within range of the German aircraft attacking the convoy and played no part in its defence. This convoy contained the CAM ship *Empire Tide* but its Hurricane was not launched. On 4 August *Victorious* was detached from the Home Fleet for the Pedestal relief convoy that fought through to Malta, and in November she formed part of the covering force for Operation Torch, the Allied landings in North Africa. There was, therefore, no fleet carrier available to form part of the covering force for the remaining Russian convoys in 1942.

This lack was partially resolved by allocating the CVE *Avenger* to the escort for the next convoys in sequence, PQ 18 and QP 14. She was the second CVE converted in the USA for service in the RN under Lend-Lease arrangements, converted from the mercantile *Rio Hudson*. She had been completed and commissioned into the RN at Staten Island, New York, on 2 March and arrived in a Clyde shipyard to have her flight deck

Victorious with Albacores ranged on deck. (*Author's collection*)

lengthened in May. On 16 July she was allocated to the Home Fleet and worked up with 825 NAS embarked with three Swordfish and both 802 and 883 NAS embarked with a total of twelve Sea Hurricanes. Six spare Sea Hurricanes with their wings removed were slung from the hangar deck-head for use as replacements when necessary. The original intention had been to sail PQ 18 on 16 July in accordance with the regular convoy schedule but, because *Victorious* and other ships from the Home Fleet had been deployed to the Mediterranean, its sailing was postponed until September and this gave more time for *Avenger* to prepare.

The postponement also gave time for Coastal Command to deploy aircraft to north Russia. These included four photographic reconnaissance Spitfires to Vaenga intended to locate German warships in the north Norwegian fjords; two squadrons of Hampdens to Vaenga for use as torpedo bombers against enemy heavy ships if they sailed and Catalina flying boats to Lakes Lakhta and Grasnaya for reconnaissance and anti-submarine patrols. The USN cruiser *Tuscaloosa* took RAF ground crew, stores and torpedoes to Vaenga, arriving on 23 August. Thirty-two Hampdens took off for Vaenga from Sumburgh on 4 September but only twenty-three reached their destination. Of the remaining nine, six crashed in Sweden or Norway and, although the remaining three reached north Russia, one entered a prohibited zone and was shot down by Soviet fighters and two crashed. The Catalinas made sixteen trips ferrying ground personnel and equipment that could not be carried in *Tuscaloosa* prior to taking up their intended tasking. The Spitfires arrived safely and their flight over considerable tracts of land held by the enemy was a significant achievement.

PQ 18 left the UK on 2 September after elaborate deception plans including 'feint' sailings intended to confuse the enemy. By then Luftflotte V was equipped with ninety-two torpedo aircraft; 103 long-range bombers and ten long-range reconnaissance aircraft. It also had thirty dive bombers and fifty fighters but these lacked the range to attack the convoys that passed close to the edge of the pack ice to the north, as far away as possible from the German air base at Banak. As an added security measure, the convoy sailed from Loch Ewe and passed to the west of Iceland. German air reconnaissance was thorough, however, and it was sighted north of Iceland and then shadowed throughout much of its passage except during two days of bad weather. The Home Fleet element of this convoy was designated Operation EV and *Avenger* was commanded by Commander A P Colthurst RN, a very experienced Fleet Air Arm pilot who had qualified from Number 2 pilots' Course in 1925. She did not sail with the close escort but proceeded from Scapa Flow to Seidisfjord in Iceland under the cover of bad weather. From there she sailed on the evening of 8 September in company with the cruiser *Scylla*, which flew the flag of Rear Admiral Destroyers, Rear Admiral R Burnett, and the destroyers *Wheatland* and *Wilton*.[27] Soon after gaining the open sea she had to stop when 'water, sludge and sand' were detected in her diesel fuel. After an anxious two hours, the problem was resolved and there was no recurrence. She joined the convoy on the evening of 9 September, taking up alternative positions at the rear of columns two or nine, which gave her the freedom to manoeuvre whenever flying operations required it.

From 10 September *Avenger*'s aircraft augmented British and American patrol aircraft from Iceland around the convoy. A Swordfish was flown off on anti-submarine patrol during the morning but had to return after less than an hour because of poor visibility in snow squalls and fog. It was slightly damaged landing on but was repaired within three hours. Aircraft from Iceland continued to patrol until 11 September, which was fortunate because patches of fog continued to prevent *Avenger* from flying until the afternoon of 12 September. She usually took up a position on the side of the convoy that allowed her to turn on to the designated flying course inside the screen with sufficient space to launch and recover aircraft as necessary. This ensured that she had the best anti-submarine protection from the screen and the maximum gun support from destroyers when they closed in during air attacks.

The visibility improved at noon on 12 September and a Bv 138 was seen to be shadowing the convoy. Radar and radio silence had been maintained

Avenger with Swordfish and Sea Hurricanes ranged aft. Note that she did not have an island structure; the ship was conned from a compass platform by the Type 79 radar housing and the small mast on the starboard side. (*Author's collection*)

until then but it was relaxed to allow *Avenger* to fly off two sections of Sea Hurricanes; unfortunately the shadower managed to escape into cloud. Visibility deteriorated again but improved in the dog watches sufficiently to allow a Swordfish to be flown off on an anti-submarine patrol around the convoy. By the time it was recovered at 2050 its crew had sighted two U-boats on the surface and directed destroyers toward them. On both sightings the boats had been too far away to allow the aircraft to carry out a depth charge attack before they dived but by forcing them down the aircraft had limited their freedom to get into an attacking position on the surface, where they had higher speed than when dived. These were the first of sixteen sightings made by *Avenger*'s Swordfish during EV and in nearly every case visibility had become so good, and cloud cover so rare, that there were few opportunities for depth charge attacks by the aircraft. The re-enforcement of radio silence made it difficult to direct surface escorts towards the U-boats as they dived but the three Swordfish kept them submerged and they shared in at least one of the three kills made by the escorts. However, Commander Colthurst noted in his report that the operation of Swordfish on anti-submarine patrols had had limitations.[28] *Avenger* only had a maximum speed of 16 knots and a flight deck 440ft long, which meant that Swordfish could not take off with a full load of depth charges or a torpedo unless there was significant natural wind. On the other hand, there had been no difficulty flying off and recovering the Sea Hurricanes. Later CVE classes had slightly longer flight decks and about 2 knots extra speed, which helped, but the problem of operating Swordfish at their maximum weight was not solved until the introduction of rocket-assisted take-off gear, RATOG, in 1944.

On Sunday, 13 September radar and radio silence were relaxed and anti-submarine patrols were flown off from 0345. The first aircraft sighted and attacked a U-boat but saw no visible result. At about 0900 two merchant ships, one Russian and one American, were hit and sunk by torpedoes from a U-boat that fired from beyond the escorts' sonar range. A Sea Hurricane CAP was maintained and directed towards a Bv 138 shadower during the morning but it escaped into cloud. Until this point the bad weather and a lack of shadowing reports had prevented the enemy from locating the convoy with sufficient accuracy to launch an air attack. Admiral Tovey commented in his covering letter to the convoy's operational reports that a heavy air attack on this day was anticipated but until it began 'the escorts had not gained the benefits of experience'. Admiral Burnett and his destroyers had detached to refuel in Spitsbergen on that day but at 1500, shortly after they re-joined, a group of enemy aircraft was detected on radar closing the convoy from 62 miles away to the south. The CAP had been vectored to intercept groups of up to five shadowers during the morning and a Swordfish reported seeing a Bv 138 drop objects into the sea ahead of the convoy, which altered course to avoid them. At about this time numerous U-boats on the surface were seen and attacked by both Swordfish and some of the Sea Hurricanes as they chased shadowers. One Bv 138 drove off a Swordfish as it tried to attack a U-boat and then remained over it to protect it against further attack.

Shortly after 1500 six Ju 88s bombed the convoy but failed to hit anything. Their attack, through patchy cloud with a base at 1,500ft, was a rather haphazard effort but it drew the CAP fighters out of position before a big attack by torpedo aircraft at 1530. A force estimated at fifty He 111 and Ju 88 torpedo bombers flew towards the convoy at low level in line abreast about 150yd apart. Most aircraft were armed with two torpedoes. The attack was pressed home in the face of an intense gun barrage and the ninety-six torpedoes dropped hit eight ships, which subsequently sank. Five enemy aircraft were shot down but at 1615 nine He 115s carried out a further torpedo attack. This was less successful as the barrage from the destroyers forced them to drop at extreme range and there were no hits. Two of these aircraft were also shot down. In both attacks the CAP had been unable to intervene as the aircraft had been directed away to intercept shadowers, a sign of the fighter direction team's inexperience. The only aircrew casualty on this day was Lieutenant E W T Taylour DSC RN,[29] the commanding officer of 802 NAS, who was shot down in flames and killed while attacking a Bv 138. At 2040 there was a further attack, this time by twelve He 111 torpedo bombers, which approached in small groups from ahead of the convoy for about three-quarters of an hour. They were met by a fierce gun barrage and this time by the CAP Sea Hurricanes. There was no damage to the convoy's ships and six of the enemy aircraft were seen to crash. *Avenger* had flown eighteen fighter sorties on 13 September but only succeeded in damaging a single Bv 138. Commander Colthurst was far from satisfied with this result and wrote in his combat report that:

> At the end of this unfortunate day I realised that my operation of the ship and her fighters had been very wrong. At the start of it I had not realised the heavy scale of the attack to which the convoy would be subjected, nor the duration of the attack.
>
> I had not appreciated the hopelessness of sending even four Sea Hurricanes to attack the heavily armed shadowers. We had not learnt to differentiate between small groups of shadowers and striking forces on the RDF [radar] screen. I then decided that with the small number of obsolete fighters at our disposal, and with their slow operation in an auxiliary carrier [CVE], we must use them only to try and break up large attacking formations rather than to destroy individuals. Further that we must endeavour to maintain a continual cycle of sections taking off, landing-on to rearm and refuel, and taking off again. The achievement of this would avoid congestion in the carrier and ensure that there were always some fighter sections ready to counter-attack striking forces.

His new tactics worked well a day later. Monday, 14 September started badly when the tanker *Atheltemplar* was torpedoed by a U-boat that had come up astern of the convoy. It was stopped in the water and had to be sunk by one of the escort. *Avenger* began Swordfish patrols at 0415, with both the first and second aircraft sighting a U-boat. Contact with the first was lost but it proved possible to track the second, which remained at periscope depth, and its position was passed by W/T on 2410kc/s to Admiral Burnett, who detached *Onslow* to prosecute it. The subsequent attack sank it and German records revealed that it had been *U-589*. There were a number of short combats during the forenoon between patrolling Swordfish and enemy shadowers but none were conclusive.

Commander Colthurst and his direction officers kept resolutely to their new tactics and no CAP fighters were sent off after shadowers, even though there were nine around the convoy at one point. At 1230 groups of enemy aircraft, assessed as about twenty-two Ju 88s and He 111s, were detected on radar approaching the convoy at low level from ahead. *Avenger* flew off three sections totalling nine Sea Hurricanes to attack them and five minutes later a combined bombing and torpedo attack began. One group of torpedo aircraft made a dead set at *Avenger* but the fighters turned some of them away and forced the remainder to drop their weapons outside their maximum effective range. The barrage deterred many of the bombers and Admiral Burnett said in his own report that 'it was a fine sight to see *Avenger* peeling off Sea Hurricanes while streaking across the front of the convoy from starboard to port inside the screen with her destroyer escort blazing away with any gun which would bear and then being chased by torpedo bombers as she steamed down on an opposite course to the convoy to take cover ... altogether a most gratifying action'. A few minutes later there was a further bombing attack with twenty Ju 88s closing from astern through gaps in the cloud. They attacked individual destroyers and *Avenger* was shallow dive-bombed but missed by 50yd. While this attack continued for over an hour, *Avenger* landed on sections of fighters to be refuelled and rearmed before being flown off again as quickly as possible. One of the bombers was seen to crash into the sea.

Almost as soon as the last bomb fell, a further force of about twenty-five He 111 torpedo bombers was detected ahead of the convoy. They split up with groups passing down either side of *Scylla* and in the ensuing action one torpedo hit an ammunition ship, which blew up spectacularly,

A Sea Hurricane taking off from *Avenger* with another ranged astern. Flag 'F' is close up on the starboard yard arm. (*Author's collection*)

damaging the next ship astern and destroying a He 111 that was caught in the blast. Three Sea Hurricane pilots continued to chase the enemy aircraft into the barrage being put up by the convoy and its escort and were, unfortunately, shot down by it. All three pilots survived, however, rescued by the destroyers *Faulkner*, *Wheatland* and *Tartar*. Commander Colthurst remarked that all his pilots now realised that they had nothing to fear if they were forced to abandon their aircraft. Admiral Burnett added that, 'I shall never forget the reckless gallantry of the Fleet Air Arm pilots in their determination to get in amongst the enemy despite the solid mass of our fire.' A minute or two after the third pilot had been rescued, a large number of Ju 88s began a medium-level bombing attack, mostly directed against *Avenger*, *Scylla* and the escort. None were hit but near misses started a small electrical fire in the carrier's catapult room that was soon extinguished by the damage control party.

By 1530 the radar screen was clear and remained so for the remainder of the day. Commander Colthurst estimated that his ship had been the target for seventeen torpedoes and his pilots had claimed five enemy aircraft certainly destroyed, four probables and fourteen damaged, while further analysis showed that a total of twenty-four had been seen to crash in and around the convoy and its escorts. Between 1240 and 1520 there had been sixteen fighter sorties against attacks by nearly 100 enemy aircraft. It is an interesting reflection on British war policy that the embarked Sea Hurricanes were of the original version with eight 0.303in Browning machine guns and several were not even new but refurbished RAF airframes. In their holds several merchant ships were carrying brand new Mark IIC Hurricanes with 20mm cannon armament intended for the Soviet Union, which could have mounted a more effective defence of the convoy if built as Sea Hurricanes for the RN[30] and actually enabled a greater quantity of war material to reach the Soviet Union, including older Hurricanes not needed for convoy defence.

At 0300 on Tuesday, 15 September, the first Swordfish was flown off on an anti-submarine patrol but had to be recovered when it reported fog ahead of the convoy. This cleared by 0440 and another Swordfish was flown off. Almost immediately its crew saw a U-boat on the surface 15 miles from the convoy's port bow. Unfortunately this aircraft had no depth charges as the wind over the deck when it took off was only 15 knots. There was occasional fog after that but it did not stop the Swordfish flying and a later aircraft was attacked by a Ju 88 shadower but managed to evade it. At 1220 a large group of enemy aircraft was detected on radar closing the convoy. *Avenger* flew off ten Sea Hurricanes against this force, estimated at about seventy, but the enemy made skilful use of cloud to evade both interception and the gun barrage. Haphazard and sporadic bombing went on for three hours, with the enemy aircraft occasionally dipping below cloud to make attacks. Frequent enemy radio transmissions helped the defenders to judge where their next attack would come and have guns trained ready. By 1645 the radar screens were clear again and it was felt that the enemy aircraft had shown little inclination to fight, possibly because many of their best pilots had been lost in the earlier attacks. A careful analysis by Admiral Burnett's staff calculated that forty-one enemy aircraft had been shot down. German sources examined by the Admiralty after 1945 found that this figure had been exactly right. Out of 337 sorties flown by Luftflotte V, of which 102 were by torpedo-carrying aircraft, against PQ 18, thirty-three torpedo bombers, six Ju 88 bombers and two long-range reconnaissance aircraft had been lost. Between 1220 and 1640 on 15 September *Avenger* had flown twenty-one fighter sorties in a cycle of take-offs and landings at roughly twenty-five-minute intervals. This gave four sections constantly available with adequate ammunition and fuel, except during the short periods when two newly fuelled sections were being flown off and two waited to land on.

In the early morning of 16 September the RAF Catalinas based in north Russia took over the anti-submarine patrol task and *Avenger* used her flight deck exclusively for fighters. Several shadowers appeared during the morning watch but left during the forenoon when the weather deteriorated and no other enemy aircraft were detected on that day. This gave *Avenger* time to assemble her reserve Sea Hurricanes and repair others that had been damaged before she left PQ 18 and joined QP 14 as planned. Meanwhile, PQ 18 continued towards its destination with a reduced escort. There were no further air attacks until 18 September, when nine He 115 torpedo aircraft were detected as they began their attack. The CAM ship *Empire Morn* catapulted its Hurricane flown by Flying Officer A H Barr RAF. He narrowly avoided one of the convoy's kite balloons seconds after becoming airborne and was fired at by several American merchant ships but went on to shoot down one He 115 despite stoppages in two of his port guns that limited him to firing only about 2,000 rounds. After destroying his first victim, he proceeded to drive off other enemy aircraft by making dummy attacks on them, text-book tactics for a CAM ship fighter. After a radio discussion with his fighter direction officer in *Empire Morn*, Barr elected to fly 240 miles to Archangel, where he landed safely at Keg Ostrov airfield with only 5 gallons of fuel remaining. Only one ship in PQ 18 had been sunk by the final batch of air attacks, making a total of thirteen lost out of the forty that set out. When the ships were finally moored alongside jetties in Archangel they presented an excellent target but, surprisingly, German air attacks were concentrated on the town and not these ships or their valuable cargoes.

QP 14 comprised fifteen merchant ships and it was met by Admiral Burnett's task force at 0500 on 17 September. *Avenger* took up a station as the second ship of the centre column and was tasked to fly off a Swordfish to search for straggling merchant ships and some of the close escort that had not yet joined in thick weather. The aircraft reported severe icing conditions from sea level upwards. The carrier had managed to keep all three Swordfish serviceable and had thirteen serviceable Sea Hurricanes, five of which were newly assembled from the spares carried between the deep beams in the hangar deck head. Normal anti-submarine patrols were flown from the afternoon of 17 September and four Sea Hurricanes were kept ranged and warmed up on deck but neither U-boats nor enemy shadowing aircraft were encountered. Patrols were repeated on 18 September but icing was found to be so bad that they had to be discontinued until later in the day when the weather improved. Better weather brought out the shadowers again but Commander Colthurst was not tempted to launch fighters against them and they were conserved to oppose the expected mass air attack, but it never came. On rounding South Cape, Spitsbergen, the convoy steered up the coast so as to increase its distance from enemy air bases and this route deviation proved successful. An entry in Luftflotte V's war diary found after the war revealed that the convoy had been sighted on 20 September but an attack had been impossible because it was out of range. There was no other air activity and *Avenger* was detached to return to Scapa Flow via Seidisfjord with her destroyers at 1845 on 20 September, arriving on 24 September. The experience gained in EV with *Avenger* and her small air group had emphasised the need for a second CVE to accompany Arctic convoys so that sufficient anti-submarine aircraft could be embarked in addition to fighters.

In the defence of these two convoys, the three Swordfish of 825 NAS had flown twenty-nine anti-submarine sorties and three others totalling eighty and a half flying hours. They had sighted sixteen U-boats over a seven-day period at an average distance estimated at 6 to 8 miles and carried out six depth charge attacks, one of which was considered promising. Its Swordfish made thirty-two deck landings and damage comprised two tail oleos that were repaired within three hours and one rear fuselage section that was broken on landing but repaired. The Sea Hurricanes of 802 and 883 NAS carried out fifty-nine fighter sorties totalling seventy and a quarter flying hours, during which they were involved in thirty-one combats. Four aircraft were lost but three of their pilots were rescued. They carried out fifty-five deck landings, during which two tail oleos were damaged but quickly repaired. Five aircraft suffered damage due to enemy action but all were repaired on board within four hours. The fighters were credited with shooting down five enemy aircraft with another three probables. Eighteen enemy aircraft were assessed as damaged.

After examining all the reports on EV, the Director of NAD, DNAD, minuted[31] that:

> ... it is quite clear that the day of the 0.303 [in machine-gun] fighter in European waters is done. For months past efforts have been directed to obtaining Hurricane IIC (20mm cannon) aircraft with which to equip escort carriers. It is hoped that these aircraft will be available to protect the future PQ convoys, if not, Martlets with 0.5in guns must be used in lieu. Fighters armed with 0.303 guns will not be used again on these operations.

It is a sad reflection on the Air Ministry policy forced on the Admiralty for use in the Fleet Air Arm that these inadequate weapons were still in use at this advanced stage of the war and fitted in fighters that were themselves inadequate when compared with those of the US Navy. On the credit side, however, German records later revealed that Luftflotte V had suffered an unsustainable loss rate of 20 per cent during its operations against PQ 18. Subsequent torpedo attacks were made in smaller numbers and the participating aircrew never displayed the same degree of skill. U-boats became the main threat to the Arctic convoys.

A pall of smoke marking the end of an ammunition ship that had been torpedoed in a Russian convoy. (*Author's collection*)

Expanding on the work of 825 NAS, DNAD commented on the different tactics required by aircraft in forcing U-boats to dive compared with those required to attack them. In the former, the aircraft required good visibility so that the U-boat would see it, dive and probably lose the chance to gain a torpedo-firing position. In the latter case the aircraft needed minimal visibility and low cloud to avoid being seen until the last moment so that it could drop its depth charges before the submarine had time to dive. DNAD believed that the first case probably provided more benefit to a convoy as it allowed the aircraft to cover a wider area and was particularly applicable when there were few aircraft available. In the second case the chances of kills were greater but the aircraft's more limited range of visibility might result in undetected U-boats getting into attacking positions.

The Director of Anti-Submarine Warfare, DASW, felt that whenever possible carrier-borne aircraft should be armed with depth charges set to detonate at 25ft, surprise attacks were always to be attempted and the aircraft flown accordingly. For safety reasons, *Avenger*'s Swordfish had been restricted to 50ft settings, which meant that on at least one occasion the aircraft had to wait for the U-boat to dive. DASW added that if the large number of Home Fleet destroyers covering the convoy been given greater freedom of action to work with *Avenger*'s aircraft, they could have taken a more offensive role and killed more U-boats. However, this theory discounted the severe air threat against which the fire power of these destroyers was so effective.

Other than *Victorious*, few RN carriers had spent time with the Home Fleet during 1942. *Furious* had been refitted in Philadelphia Navy Yard between October 1941 and April 1942 and on her return she was allocated to the Home Fleet but spent time in a Clyde shipyard, where new British equipment including search and fire-control radars was fitted. This work was completed in July but almost immediately she deployed to the Mediterranean to ferry RAF Spitfires to Malta and then to Operation Torch. She did not return to the Home Fleet until 1943.

7

1943

A new numbering sequence was introduced after PQ 18 that designated east-bound convoys as JW and west-bound convoys as RA. No CVEs were available to join the escort until JW 53 in February 1943 because of commitments outside the Home Fleet area that included Operation Torch and the defence of Atlantic convoys by Western Approaches Command. *Dasher* was the first to join the Home Fleet, having served with the Eastern Naval Task force during Operation Torch. She had subsequently been refitted in Liverpool with an air defence operations room in December 1942 and she arrived in Scapa Flow on 1 February 1943. During her work-up she embarked 891 NAS with nine Sea Hurricanes and 816 NAS with six Swordfish and sailed with this air group to join the escort of JW 53 on

Dasher flying off a Sea Hurricane. She incorporated improvements over earlier CVEs including a small box-shaped island structure. (*Author's collection*)

15 February. Unfortunately, on 17 February she suffered severe structural damage during a storm off Iceland and had to proceed to Dundee for repairs. The convoy was subsequently attacked by up to thirty enemy aircraft but all twenty-two of its ships arrived safely at their destination. After repairs, *Dasher* carried out a further work-up in the Clyde from 24 March with the same air group but on 27 March she suffered a massive internal explosion while she was at anchor off Little Cumbrae island.[1] The subsequent board of enquiry assessed that it was the result of an accidental avgas explosion and fire, probably caused by someone smoking near a leaking avgas pump, and the Admiralty decided that all American-built CVEs in RN service must be modified to full RN avgas stowage standards as a matter of urgency.[2] The loss of *Dasher* exacerbated the Home Fleet's shortage of carriers and it is symptomatic of the Admiralty's desire to strike at the enemy as soon as possible that consideration had been given to embarking an all-Swordfish air group in *Dasher*, before her loss, to attack *Tirpitz* in Alta Fjord with torpedoes. Such a complex operation would probably have been carried out at night and would have required considerable training. Even then, the mountainous geography and the strength of the defences meant that an attack by Swordfish would have been at best difficult and at worst suicidal. The tentative plan was dropped after *Dasher*'s loss.[3]

Formidable joined the heavy cover for RA 54A together with *Anson* and *Jamaica*. She had been attached to the Home Fleet for a short period with an air group comprising 820 NAS with Albacores, 888 and 893 NAS with Martlets and 885 NAS with Seafires. RA 54A comprised ships that had spent the summer of 1943 in Archangel and it sailed from the Kola Inlet on 1 November but soon encountered thick fog that caused delay, although it did hide it from enemy reconnaissance. It arrived in Loch Ewe on 14 November without being attacked and the carrier's aircraft saw no action.[4]

By this stage of the war the Home Fleet's principal tasks were the containment of *Tirpitz* and other German warships in north Norway as well as providing heavy cover for the Arctic convoys. The Admiralty wanted to recommence strike operations against enemy shipping in the Norwegian littoral but the shortage of carriers available to the Home Fleet prevented it from doing so for some months. *Furious* became available but her relatively small aircraft complement and limited endurance precluded her taking part in sustained operations. The majority of the fleet carriers were committed to the Mediterranean, Indian Ocean and the Pacific, and the Admiralty had agreed that *Victorious*, for so long at the centre of Home Fleet operations, would be lent to the US Pacific Fleet, which only had one operational carrier at this time. She had sailed for the

Formidable with Sea Hurricanes on deck. The spray being blown off wave crests gives an indication of wind strength and she has her flight deck wind breaks raised to protect aircraft and men working on deck. (*Author's collection*)

USA on 20 December 1942 and did not return to the UK until September 1943, after which she carried out a refit that lasted into 1944. Western Approaches Command and support groups for amphibious operations in the Mediterranean were given greater priority for CVEs than the Arctic convoys and were not available to escort JW/RA convoys until 1944. Such fleet carriers as were available joined covering forces, *Formidable* relieving *Furious* in October for two of these.

There were, however, three offensive operations carried out by fleet carriers during 1943. Two were in July, designated as Operations Camera and Governor by the Home Fleet. Both had the aim of drawing enemy attention away from the Allied landings in Sicily. *Furious* carried out the first, which was a sweep off the Norwegian coast, followed by *Illustrious* and *Unicorn* operating together in the second. During Governor, Martlets of 881 NAS embarked in *Unicorn* intercepted and shot down five Bv 138 shadowing aircraft. The successful pilots were Lieutenant Commander R A Bird RN, the commanding officer, together with Sub Lieutenant (A) A F Womack RNVR and Sub Lieutenant (A) J A Pullin RNVR. The Admiralty's operational intelligence centre assessed that the Germans might have taken anti-invasion measures in south Norway for a few hours but the effect of these operations was only transitory. However,

Flight decks are used for many things other than flying. *Formidable* is seen here embarking ammunition; each of the tubular containers gives protection for a single fixed 4.5in round as they are brought on board. They were taken out when they were stowed in the ship's magazines. (*Author's collection*)

they proved that a carrier task force could operate with impunity off the coast of Norway despite having been located and this was a good augury for the future. The tempo of the Home Fleet's anti-shipping campaign gathered momentum from this point as more CVEs were made available from American production and the Allies gained the upper hand in the Battle of the Atlantic.

Unicorn operating as a light fleet carrier with the Home Fleet during 1943. The aircraft ranged aft is a Swordfish. Note the aircraft-ferrying lighter stowed under the flight deck overhang right aft. (*Author's collection*)

USS *Ranger* photographed shortly after her completion. (*Author's collection*)

The only strike operation mounted by the USN in northern European waters during the entire war was designated as Operation Leader by the Home Fleet and it can fairly be described as the first in a long series of better-organised strikes against German shipping in the Norwegian littoral. The USS *Ranger* was lent to the Home Fleet for a short while in the autumn to replace *Illustrious*, which had deployed to the Mediterranean to replace the damaged *Indomitable*. *Ranger*, with Air Group 41 embarked, formed part of the combined USN/RN Task Group 121 that carried out a most successful attack on Bodø and the leads south of it on 4 October. A number of enemy vessels were found in and around the harbour, showing that the Germans had become complacent after suffering no attacks from the sea in recent months. Inter-Allied co-operation was excellent and the weather was perfect except that a lack of natural wind before the first strike was flown off, and *Ranger*'s lack of speed to provide an adequate wind over the deck, led to a delay of eighteen minutes. The foremost six Dauntless dive bombers in the range had to have their 1,000lb bombs replaced by 500lb bombs to enable them to take off at maximum weight from the deck run and wind available. The bomb change was quicker than resetting the whole range. Leader consisted of two early morning strikes thirty minutes apart; the first by twenty Dauntlesses escorted by eight Wildcats and the second by ten Avengers with six Wildcats as escort. The escorting fighters were also briefed to strafe anti-aircraft gun positions as the bombers made their attacks. The fourteen Dauntlesses at the back of the range had longer deck runs and retained their 1,000lb bombs, and the Avengers each carried four 500lb bombs. The air group commander had considered arming a proportion of the Avengers with torpedoes but rejected the idea because the narrowness of the leads made manoeuvring for attack positions difficult. The possibility that land targets could be attacked with bombs if no ships were found was another factor but, as events turned out, they found several enemy ships under way in the centre of the shipping channel that could have been torpedoed. Sixty per cent of the USN pilots were taking part in their first combat operation and they attacked using a skip-bombing technique at masthead height. At their debriefing, the aircrew estimated that forty-one 500lb bombs and fourteen 1,000lb bombs had been dropped, including two that failed to detonate. Three aircraft were shot down by anti-aircraft fire and several others were damaged severely but there had been no opposition from enemy fighters. German records confirmed that five ships had been sunk or beached and destroyed by fire with a further five damaged. The fighter escort had been minimal by later standards but *Ranger* also had to provide a substantial CAP over the task force in the absence of another carrier. The CAP added to the day's success by shooting down two shadowers, which German records confirmed as destroyed. Unfortunately *Ranger* was withdrawn from the Home Fleet before any further strike operations could be carried out and she returned to the USA in December for use as a training carrier. The lack of open-ocean reconnaissance capability caused by the lack of sufficient carriers was, in part, made up by flights of aircraft embarked in armed merchant cruisers. These included American Chance Vought Kingfishers, supplied under Lend-Lease arrangements.[5] They cannot be said to have achieved anything outstanding but proved to be a valuable means of searching vast areas of sea for enemy raiders, supply ships or blockade runners, where even negative reports had intelligence value.

Improved types of fighter enter service

The Martlet Mark VI was designed specifically for operation from CVEs; it was the equivalent of the USN FM-1 built by the Eastern Aircraft Division of General Motors and unlike the early Martlets, which were purchased from the USA, these were provided under Lend-Lease arrangements. The RN received a total of 312 Mark V/VI Martlets, which were renamed as Wildcats on 1 January 1944 to conform with the USN. For the sake of simplicity, the name Wildcat is used from now onwards. By early 1943 Grumman had tapered off Wildcat production in order to free space to manufacture its latest fighter, the Hellcat, in the largest possible numbers.

The Hellcat was a robust fighter with a maximum level speed of 350 knots and a radius of action in excess of 600nm when fitted with a 125-gallon external tank.[6] Its armament of six wing-mounted 0.5in machine guns, three in each wing firing outside the propeller arc, was the same as the Wildcat VI but it carried more rounds per gun. Early in 1943

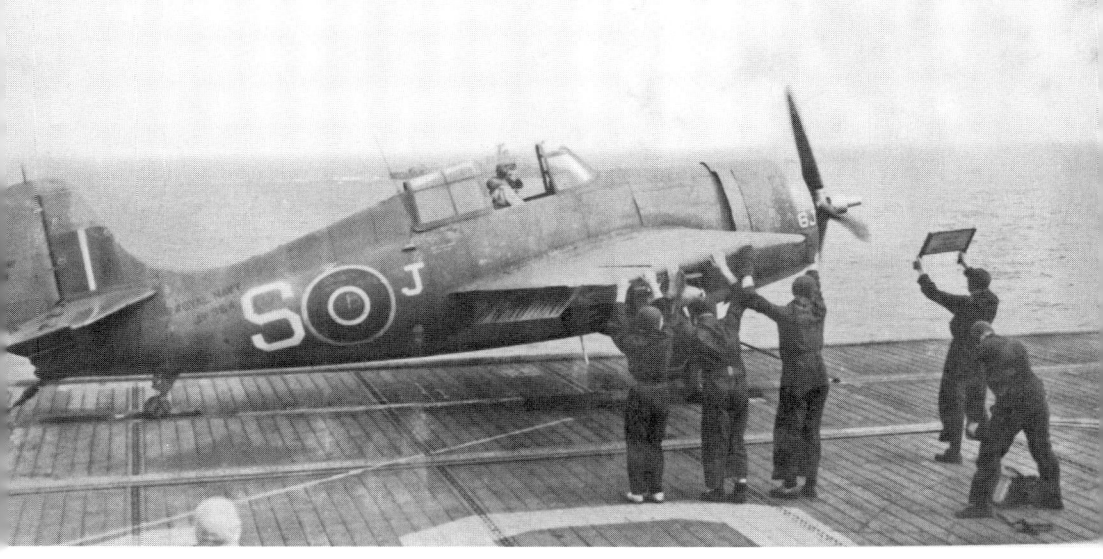

A Wildcat of 882 NAS about to be catapulted from *Searcher*. The strop is tensioned, handlers are steadying the wingtips against rocking as the ship turns into wind and another handler is holding up the pilot's check board, which reads 'BRAKES OFF – FLAPS AT TAKE-OFF SETTING'. Note the CVE's unpainted wooden flight deck. (*Philip Jarrett collection*)

Hellcats were made available to the RN under Lend-Lease arrangements, although its popularity with the USN limited the numbers supplied at first. Eventually the RN received 1,182 Hellcats, of which 252 were of the original Mark I variant equivalent to the USN F6F-3 and the remaining 930 were of the improved Mark II equivalent to the USN F6F-5. They were originally known as Gannets in RN service but this name never proved popular and pilots referred to the type by its USN name, which was adopted officially by the Admiralty on 1 January 1944. The first Fleet Air Arm unit to be equipped with Hellcats was 800 NAS on 1 July.

Another new American fighter that entered Fleet Air Arm service during 1943 was the Chance Vought Corsair, designated the F4U by the USN. This had not performed well in its initial deck landing trials and had been limited to service ashore with the US Marine Corps at first but this adverse opinion meant that more were made available to the RN under Lend-Lease. The first Fleet Air Arm squadron, 1830 NAS, formed at USNAS Quonset Point on 1 June. The first aircraft were to Mark I standard equivalent to the USN F4U-4 but the majority of British aircraft were to the Mark II standard equivalent to the USN F4U-5. As originally delivered, the Corsair had a folded height of 16ft 9in, just too high for the 16ft hangar height in the first three *Illustrious*-class fleet carriers but well within the 17ft 6in of American-built CVEs and the future light fleet carriers. The solution was to square off the wingtips to create a folded height of 15ft 9in when the aircraft arrived in the UK, where they were modified at RN air yards with British radios and other RN equipment. In fact the modified wingtips improved aircraft handling at low speed and improved the rate of roll, both positive features. The long nose of the Corsair meant that, like the Seafire, pilots had to carry out a tight, steeply banked curving approach on finals to keep the batsman in sight. By comparison with earlier British fighters, the Corsair was a big aircraft with its 2,000hp Pratt and Whitney Double Wasp turning a three-bladed propeller, which had a disc diameter of 17ft 6in. The sheer size of the propeller led to the 'bent-wing' design to keep the undercarriage legs within reasonable size. A total of 2,012 Corsairs were delivered to the Fleet Air Arm in Marks I to IV; the Mark III version being built by Brewster and the Mark IV by Goodyear. The Mark II had a maximum level speed of 365 knots and a radius of action approaching 600nm with overload tanks. The Corsair had six wing-mounted 0.5in front guns but the Mark II and Mark IV had provision to carry two 1,000lb bombs in the strike role.[7]

New Fleet Air Arm Corsair squadrons formed at USN air stations at the rate of one a month for the remainder of the war, each manned by a small group of experienced pilots augmented by others straight from training in the USA or Canada. The sheer size of the Corsair and its reputation as

Early production Fleet Air Arm Corsairs flying in formation during 1943. (*Author's collection*)

a difficult aircraft to deck land made even experienced pilots treat it with respect, although one confided to me that he had made a will shortly after seeing one for the first time. There is a delightful quotation in the Naval Staff History,[8] presumably factually correct, which captures the Corsair's reputation exactly:

> Before long Corsairs were also being landed on successfully by Fleet Air Arm pilots in escort carriers, albeit not without some very anxious moments and lurid incidents. As a tribute to the strength of this aircraft … it is recorded that during an initial deck landing on the escort carrier Rajah in 1944 a Corsair pilot came on so fast that he missed all the arrester wires, cut through both barriers and was then, still airborne, sent back to the local airfield, not without some misgivings as to his eventual arrival. On successfully reaching it, however, his aircraft was found, barring the necessity for refuelling, to be completely serviceable.

The Fairey Firefly was conceived as a fast two-seater fighter/reconnaissance aircraft similar in concept to the pre-war Hawker Osprey. Powered by a 1,990hp Rolls-Royce Griffon XII engine, it had a maximum level speed of 280 knots, roughly comparable with a Wildcat Mark VI. It was armed with four 20mm cannon with underwing hard points capable of carrying eight 60lb rocket projectiles or two 1,000lb bombs, which gave it an impressive strike capability. Its radius of action with external tanks was up to 300 miles. From the outset it was seen as a potential night fighter but its development was slowed by the MAP, which gave greater priority to RAF fighters, and the first prototype did not fly until December 1941. Three further prototypes flew in 1942 but the first operational squadron could not be formed until October 1943 when 1770 NAS was commissioned at RNAS Yeovilton.

Priority for the Seafire during 1943 was given to squadrons operating in the Mediterranean, especially those allocated to cover the Salerno landings. By April there were 120 in front-line squadrons but the losses at Salerno reduced that number to ninety-eight by October. By then the Mark III, fitted with folding wings and a strengthened undercarriage, was in production with contracts for a total of 1,220 aircraft of this mark being built by the parent company Supermarine together with Cunliffe-Owen and Westland. The Seafire III had a maximum level speed of 310 knots but, apart from its weak deck-landing characteristics, its 'Achilles Heel' was its limited endurance and radius of action. Even with a 30-gallon overload fuel tank under the fuselage its radius of action was less than 200 miles. Despite its limitations, it was a useful multi-role

A Firefly Mark I showing off its beautiful lines in flight. The type proved very successful and remained in front-line service with the Fleet Air Arm for more than a decade. (*Author's collection*)

aircraft capable of carrying one 500lb or two 250lb bombs instead of the overload tank. Cunliffe-Owen built aircraft were fitted with two F.24 cameras for use in the reconnaissance role; one vertical and one oblique. Standard armament was two 20mm and four 0.303in front guns all firing clear of the propeller arc.

An early production Seafire Mark II catching number 1 wire on *Victorious*. Note the batsman in his Irvine jacket giving the 'cut' signal with his bats. (*Author's collection*)

The delayed torpedo bomber

The Admiralty had considered the Fairey Albacore to be a stopgap Swordfish replacement from the outset and before it had even flown a specification was issued in October 1937 for a more advanced monoplane torpedo/dive bomber/reconnaissance aircraft. Seventeen firms offered design solutions but the Air Ministry advised the Admiralty to order the Fairey Type 100 'off the drawing board' in September 1938 without any competition.[9] It was given the name Barracuda and proved to be a complex and sophisticated aircraft that required considerable development before it could enter service. It featured a high wing position to give the observer windows below it on either side of the fuselage, which gave unobstructed views downwards and from right ahead to right astern; it had a retractable main undercarriage and, in line with the Air Ministry's recommendation, it was designed to be powered by the Rolls-Royce Exe sleeve-valve, high-pressure-air-cooled, in-line 'X' configuration engine, which was, itself, still under development. This was a lightweight, high-power unit specifically intended for naval aircraft. It had four banks of six cylinders in an 'X' configuration, each bank set at 90 degrees from the next[10] but weighed less than the contemporary Rolls-Royce Merlin. Being air cooled, it did not need the added weight and complexity of a radiator or its associated coolant liquid and pipework. A development Exe was fitted in a Fairey Battle test bed in November 1938, which continued to fly until 1943 with the engine giving no trouble at all, although it did initially suffer from high oil consumption, later cured. It consistently demonstrated higher speeds than standard Merlin-engined Battles and the Exe would undoubtedly have been the ideal power plant for the Barracuda.

It was not to be, however. In September 1939 Rolls-Royce recommended that work on the Exe should be discontinued and this was accepted by the Air Ministry without, apparently, the Admiralty having any say in the matter. For some reason the firm only considered a small production run for the Barracuda and its engine, although why this was so is far from clear. By 1943 the RN had 2,843 Barracudas on order from an industrial group that included Blackburn, Boulton Paul and, to a limited extent, Westland as sub-contractors in addition to Fairey. Although 273 of these were cancelled in 1945, the Barracuda was built in larger numbers than any other aircraft for the RN before or since. Development had to be delayed by two years to replace the Exe with liquid-cooled Merlin engines. Replacement of the obsolescent Swordfish and Albacore should have been one of British industry's most important targets but the tragedy that stemmed from the muddled Air Ministry and MAP thinking in 1939–40 is that the Barracuda proved to be under-powered and entered service years later than the Admiralty had wanted. The equally advanced Rolls-Royce

An early production Barracuda Mark II, BV733, showing the type's complicated wing-fold arrangements. The torpedo is a drill round. This aircraft was demonstrated to the USN by the British Admiralty Delegation in the USA at Floyd Bennet Field, New York, in December 1943 and was evaluated by the USN at NAS Patuxent River in 1944. (*Author's collection*)

Vulture engine intended for the Avro Manchester heavy bomber[11] was not terminated.

After the cancellation of Exe development, the Merlin VIII was substituted and Fairey had to rework the whole design to accommodate it from October 1939. Increased weight and the radiator assembly fitted under the nose added significantly to drag and work on the first prototype was halted in the summer of 1940 when the MAP made the production of fighters for the RAF its priority. The first prototype eventually flew from Fairey's Great West Aerodrome[12] on 7 December 1940; by then the Merlin VIII had been replaced by the more powerful Merlin 30, which was also used in the Fairey Fulmar. Even with this engine the basic Barracuda performed well, with the prototype, P1767, reaching 235 knots in level flight with no equipment or external weapon load. However, significant changes had to be made as development slowly gained momentum from 1941 and it would be fair to say that the Barracuda missed its intended generation. Had it entered service with the Exe engine in 1941 as the Admiralty wanted, it could well have been a 'game-changer' and I leave to the reader's imagination what could have been achieved by Barracuda squadrons rather than Swordfish and Albacores in strike operations from 1941 onwards. New equipment including ASV IIN radar with its Yagi arrays on the upper, outer wings and a comprehensive communications fit added to weight and reduced performance. The final radio fit was an ARI 5206 HF W/T set and an SCR 522 VHF voice radio set, and there was a twin Vickers gas-operated machine gun in the after cockpit for the TAG aimed, from 1944, using a gyro gunsight.

The Barracuda's intended primary weapon was the 18in Mark XIIB torpedo, to be dropped at 200 knots after a steep diving approach to low level. The pilot aimed using the sophisticated Type F Torpedo Director, which used an analogue computer to allow him to aim at the centre of the target during the last half mile run-in low over the water. The computer adjusted the torpedo's course gyro to give the optimum aim-off track to intercept the target. Target heading and estimated speed had to be set manually. The torpedo's brief flight in air was stabilised by a wooden monoplane air tail that broke off on water entry at about 175 knots, having prevented roll, corrected the pitch angle and ensured that the critical angle of entry was achieved. The torpedo was carried on centreline crutches under the fuselage and modifications to strengthen the airframe were carried out in 1943 to allow an American 1,600lb armour-piercing bomb to be carried under the fuselage. Other alternative loads included up to six 250lb bombs under the wings or three 500lb, although the latter had to be carried asymmetrically with two under one wing and one under the other. The latter configuration was considered marginal, especially

An air engineering officer of 787 NAS, the Naval Air Fighting Development Unit, demonstrating the twin Vickers machine gun installation in a Barracuda. The ammunition drums are not fitted. Note the dinghy lanyard wire held in place over the white diagonal stripe by patches of doped fabric. (*Author's collection*)

in hot conditions, and was seldom used. Trials with two 500lb and two 250lb were carried out but their drag reduced the practical radius of action so much that this configuration was not used operationally. Depth charges were carried on anti-submarine sorties, with either three 450lb Mark VII or four 250lb Mark VIII being carried.

The first squadron re-equipped with Barracudas was 827 NAS. Its personnel underwent courses organised by Fairey and received its first aircraft at RNAS Stretton on 15 December 1943. By then the USN Grumman Avenger was already coming into RN service under Lend-Lease arrangements; it had first been procured by the USN under a 1940 contract and was a generation later than the Barracuda, making a straight comparison between the two unfair. The Barracuda Mark I, identified by its three-bladed propeller and its Merlin 30, gave only just sufficient power for it to operate safely. In 1942, therefore, a further delay had been accepted to replace the engine in a Mark II version with the Merlin 32, which gave 1,640hp on take-off, 33 per cent more than the Merlin 30. Four-bladed propellers were fitted to make use of the extra thrust and the Mark II's performance, if not startling, was at least improved. The first squadron's conversion to the Barracuda was unfortunately marked by a number of accidents, some fatal, which gave the aircraft a notorious reputation that it never, entirely, overcame. It did have inherent design faults but they were not the basic cause of every accident. The early pilots were all experienced but that experience had been gained in biplanes with their low wing loading and their monoplane conversion had been limited and insufficiently well supervised. High-speed stalls were an unknown phenomenon in the Albacore and coarse applications of rudder in a banked turn did not result into a flick into a spin. Spin recovery in a Barracuda was not difficult but considerable height could be lost in carrying it out. Dive brakes also introduced handling eccentricities. Retraction of the dive brakes was followed by a strong nose-down change of trim some seconds after the pilot had made the selection. During a torpedo attack he thus had to re-trim as he levelled the aircraft below 500ft at about 200 knots while tracking the target through his sight and maintaining formation on his leader. Engine-bay fires were another early problem; the original exhaust system used collector pipes on either side of the fuselage, which gathered exhaust gases from the cylinder banks and led them down through channels at an angle of 75 degrees in the fuselage sides to discharge outboard and aft. Their purpose was to remove bursts of flame from the pilot's line of sight but, while they did this, they overheated the areas behind the channels in which there were both hydraulic and fuel pipes. This excess heat often resulted in fires and on 16 May 1943 all Barracudas were grounded and both collectors and downpipes replaced by conventional exhaust stubs, one for each cylinder. This modification removed the fire risk and reduced weight. Despite these negative points, the pilot's cockpit was comfortable and gave a better than average view for deck landing. The observer's cockpit was roomy with ample space for chart boards, code books and other bulky items of kit and the ASV screen and controls were well-positioned. The TAG had a rotating seat that faced forward to operate the W/T set and aft to maintain a lookout and use the guns. Above all else though, it should be remembered that the Barracuda had the most advanced torpedo-aiming system, centred on an analogue computer, fitted to any strike aircraft of this era.

Night operations by 841 NAS based ashore

On 29 November 841 NAS completed an outstandingly successful period of operations and turned over its Fairey Albacores to 415 Squadron RCAF, which continued the same task under the direction of Coastal Command. It had been joined from time to time by Swordfish squadrons waiting to join their CVEs but, for a brief spell, shore-based operations by naval air squadrons off the south and east coasts of England ceased. The effect of 841 NAS' activities on the enemy had been a noticeable decline in enemy minelaying and other offensive activities. During its time ashore 841 NAS had grown to sixteen aircraft with a commensurate increase in its scheme of complement. In addition to its offensive sorties against enemy vessels sailing in convoy or singly along the northern coast of France, 841 NAS flew defensive patrols over British convoys and intercepted enemy E-boats detected on radar. Based at RAF Manston, its first task had been to oppose German attempts to lay a minefield in the Straits of Dover intended to interfere with British operations across the narrows.[13] German merchant ship movements up and down the French coast generally took place when the enemy considered the weather too bad for British light forces to operate. Advance warning of their sailing was gathered from photographic reconnaissance, SIGINT or other intelligence sources, which triggered patrols by two aircraft and these patrolled to the north and south of the harbour in question. When the first aircraft located the enemy it attacked as soon as possible, dropping a flame float while in the dive to mark the target for the second aircraft. While they did so a larger strike force was scrambled from immediate notice. RAF radar interception controllers had difficulty controlling more than four aircraft working as separate units and so the strike force flew in formation. The leader used a pre-arranged code word to indicate that he was commencing his attack and then dropped six 250lb bombs with fuses set at 0.025 second delay from a 50-degree dive in a stick 175ft long. One minute after the leader's code word the second aircraft attacked, followed at one-minute intervals by the rest. After the attack each aircraft returned to Manston at pre-arranged heights to avoid confliction in the dark and was refuelled and rearmed after landing.

On some occasions 841 NAS Albacores worked with MTBs but because of the limited stretches of water in which the latter could launch their torpedoes effectively, the time allowed for Albacore attacks was limited to fifteen minutes on these occasions. In that time the squadron had to carry out its own ASV search and bomb the target but this tactic had the advantage of distracting the enemy before the MTBs attacked into the confusion caused by the aircraft. This rigid time limit sometimes meant ordering an aircraft to break off its attack while it was in the dive but combined strikes successfully sank at least one large merchant vessel and no MTBs were ever bombed by friendly aircraft. As a direct result of 841 NAS' operations in the Straits of Dover, enemy minelaying virtually ceased and the enemy E-boat packs shifted to attacks on convoys off the east and south-west coasts of England. This dispersion led to a further increase in the number of Albacores operating under Fighter Command control. A strike force was maintained on alert at Manston but detachments were sent at various times to operate from Coltishall, Tangmere and Exeter.

The low-level RAF radar warning chain off the east coast gave coverage that was less complete than that in the Straits of Dover and 841 NAS Albacore detachments had to be employed on standing patrols to give warning of the approach of enemy vessels. They were briefed with specific areas within which they could attack any E-boats detected and, having done so, they were often able to guide MGBs to intercept the enemy.

An Albacore of 841 NAS in a sandbagged revetment at Manston on quick-reaction alert. It has the standard weapons load for attacks on enemy light craft, twelve 100lb A/S bombs. (*Author's collection*)

The destroyers and MGBs of the Nore Command were all experienced in anti-E-boat warfare and, with the Albacores' assistance, they broke up virtually every enemy attack in their area of operations during 1943. When German E-boat attacks spread into the Portsmouth and Plymouth Command areas a modified air plan was initiated. In these areas the surface plot was better and enemy vessels were often detected as soon as they left their harbours; the Albacores' aim was to attack them as they did so. To achieve this, several patrols were maintained covering the enemy-occupied coast from Dieppe to the Channel Islands and a striking force was maintained at alert to augment the patrolling aircraft. The Germans tried to counter the Albacore operations with night fighters, which sometimes got quite close, and dropped flares to illuminate them. Countermeasures were taken by changing patrol areas and deploying friendly night fighters to operate in the vicinity. As with 826 NAS in North Africa, the Albacores of 841 NAS were ideally suited to this specialised tasking. With an economical cruising speed of 100 knots it gave the crew time to search the surface within ASV radar range carefully and the type had a remarkably quiet engine, especially when diving into an attack. The observer also had plenty of room to stow his kit and operate the radar. Essentially it was an aircraft that could be flown with relative ease in bad weather and on dark nights when faster, single-seat, fighter-bombers would be much less effective. Bad weather always increased the possibility of locating targets; clear moonlight nights seldom brought any shipping movements.

Pilots were all good at instrument flying techniques, including the ability to carry out accurate night dive-bombing attacks after being vectored on to a target by the ground controller initially and then the observer once he gained ASV contact. Bombing attacks needed constant practice and pilots had to take care not to become silhouetted against the moon or caught in a searchlight beam. Observers had to be adept at night navigation and highly skilled in their use of ASV to pick up small radar echoes close inshore and then home their pilot on to them accurately. It was found by experience that a zig-zag sweep near the coast gave the best results, avoiding confusion with coast echoes and giving a good indication of how close the target was to the shoreline. TAGs were not carried and the observer did all the talking on R/T, keeping any transmissions to an absolute minimum because the enemy was known to be able to obtain bearings on radio traffic. Pilots and observers who came to 841 NAS from 'pool' squadrons had the requisite skills and could be used on operations at once but it was found that pilots who arrived from training squadrons had to be 'nursed' for varying periods until they were ready for this specialised work. Observers who joined straight from the Observers' Training School at RNAS Piarco in Trinidad had undergone most of their ASV experience in the open sea on large targets and had to have extra practice before they could distinguish the difference between echoes from a sandbank, other aircraft or a small ship.

Ground controllers could usually direct aircraft to within 2 miles of a target but on a dark night against a slow ship this was not accurate enough and ASV was essential to complete the interception. Twelve miles was about the maximum range at which a group of E-boats could be detected by ASV; flares were carried but rarely used since they might illuminate the attacking aircraft itself or other friendly forces closing in. Experiments were carried out during training sessions to evaluate an ASV-guided level bombing technique from 2,000ft to see if bombing through cloud would be possible. The average miss distance was 200yd and it was considered that dropping a complete stick of bombs using this technique was preferable to bringing the bombs back if no other attack option was available. The run-up to the release point was timed by a stopwatch as the target entered the ASV ground clutter but NAD felt that better results might have been achieved by using the radar's minimum scale throughout the attack. The best height to gain ASV contact was found to be between 2,000 and 3,000ft and this proved ideal for pilots to begin their bombing runs.

Between July and November Albacores of 841 NAS flew 334 sorties. Sixty-six attacks were carried out in which the squadron was credited with sinking two minesweepers and twelve E/R-boats. They also damaged ten minesweepers, eight E/R-boats and a merchant vessel, with possible further damage to a destroyer, four minesweepers and another ten E/R-boats. Peak activity was in September when 102 sorties were flown, during which twenty-three attacks were carried out.

8
1944

During 1943 the Home Fleet's air operations had been limited by the need to deploy carriers to support other fleets including the US Pacific Fleet.[1] Priority for CVEs had gone to Western Approaches Command for the defence of trade and for use as assault carriers. By early 1944, however, the Fleet Air Arm at last had new aircraft coming into service and new ships to carry them, including the delayed fleet carriers *Implacable* and *Indefatigable* and a number of CVEs. Strike operations in the Norwegian littoral could be resumed and more effective carrier escort could be given to the Russian convoys.

A gun camera image of the Bf 109 shot down by Lieutenant (A) D Wilkinson RNVR flying a Seafire IB of 801 NAS off the Norwegian coast during Operation Post-horn on 11 February 1944. (*Author's collection*)

CVE operations escorting convoys to north Russia

On 21 February *Chaser*, commanded by Captain H V P McClintock RN, sailed from Scapa Flow for Operation FX, the support force for convoys JW/RA 57.[2] The force was commanded by Vice Admiral I G Glennie, Vice Admiral (Destroyers) Home Fleet in the cruiser *Black Prince*. With him were the destroyers *Impulsive*, *Matchless*, *Meteor*, *Milne*, *Obedient*, *Offa*, *Onslaught*, *Oribi*, *Savage*, *Serapis*, *Swift*, *Verulam* and *Vigilant*. Both convoys had their own close anti-submarine escort forces composed of destroyers, corvettes and minesweepers.[3] *Chaser* had 816 NAS embarked commanded by Lieutenant Commander (A) F C Nottingham RNVR; a composite unit comprising eleven Swordfish and eleven Wildcats.

The question of night flying was raised at the pre-sailing conference and, after discussion, it was decided that it was not advisable other than in exceptional circumstances because of the danger to the carrier itself since it would need to operate clear of the convoy for night take-offs and recoveries. The force met JW 57 on 22 February and *Chaser* was stationed in the centre column with two ships ahead of her but none astern. With five cables between columns, the CVE always had sufficient sea room in which to turn into the relative wind and operate her aircraft. Once in position she flew off two Swordfish and two Wildcats to fly low around the convoy and show the merchant ships what they looked like, a sensible precaution because gunners in previous convoys had opened fire on anything that flew. CAPs were flown by Beaufighters of Coastal Command until dusk on that day, which was as well because a heavy swell developed that would have prevented *Chaser* from flying. Anti-submarine

Nairana pitching significantly during a Russian convoy operation in the Barents Sea. As the flight deck in the foreground shows, there would be periods of several seconds during which the flight deck would be steady enough for the batsman to control landing but aircraft operations in such conditions were always hazardous. (*Author's collection*)

patrols were flown by Coastal Command Catalinas for an average of five and a half hours a day.[4]

The convoy was detected by a radar-equipped Ju 88 on 23 February and shadowed by an Fw 200 from 24 February. After their reports were intercepted, radio and radar silence were partially relaxed but Swordfish ASV radar silence was maintained until the visibility fell below the estimated visual sighting range against a surfaced U-boat.[5] The weather conditions continued to deteriorate, however, and for most of the outbound and return passages there were snow showers for half the time, which reduced visibility to 300yd or less. There was considerable swell, the wind was estimated at 38 knots and for most of the time there was complete cloud cover at 200ft. Despite these conditions, *Chaser* maintained two Swordfish on patrol from 25 February. By then, however, a number of U-boats had located the convoy and one of them torpedoed and sank the destroyer *Mahratta*, one of the close escorts. Swordfish patrols continued throughout 26 February despite severe icing in the snowstorms and they sighted three U-boats. German records later revealed that there had actually been fourteen U-boats close to JW 57 but they also suffered from the awful conditions and many had their anti-aircraft guns frozen, preventing them from shooting at attacking aircraft. This limitation forced the Captain, U-boats, Norway, to order his boats to attack only at night and to use the daylight hours to try to gain bearing ahead of the convoy while keeping well clear of it. Interestingly, his diary revealed frustration with the Luftwaffe's shadowing aircraft, which had radio and radar problems that prevented some from making reports until after they had landed, sometimes six hours after contact was made. Early reports had misidentified *Chaser* as a fleet carrier and convoy positions were insufficiently accurate to enable U-boats to be concentrated with any degree of confidence on several days. Fighters were only flown off when, in Captain McClintock's words, shadowing aircraft 'became too inquisitive' as there was considerable motion on the ship and the flight deck was often congested with Swordfish that had been damaged landing on. It says something that Swordfish, that most docile of deck landing aircraft, suffered so much damage in their recoveries, one of them so badly that it was beyond repair and had to be jettisoned over the side. Icing caused two others to return with high engine oil temperatures but they had to be flown again, despite the risk of their engines seizing, in order to maintain anti-submarine patrols.

By 27 February the U-boats appeared to have been kept at bay, justifying the risk taken in continuing aircraft operations. During this day another U-boat was sighted and fighters damaged a Ju 88 shadower. Captain McClintock wrote in his report that 'steam heating pipes were bursting all over the ship and one of these caused the main R/T set to be out of action'. He described the ship's 'Arcticisation'[6] as most unsatisfactory, with guns frozen into position by the lack of heaters. The awful conditions on the flight deck can only be imagined and it is enormously to the credit of the aircraft handlers that they managed to range and strike down aircraft. By noon only six Swordfish and eight Wildcats remained serviceable. On 28 February the weather improved but the wind dropped, which, taken with the ship's low speed, meant there was insufficient wind over the deck for a fully loaded Swordfish to take off and the high speed of Wildcat landings, relative to the deck, damaged their arrester hooks. Patrols continued, however, resulting in another U-boat sighting, and a section of fighters drove off a shadower. Soon afterwards Russian fighters requested by VA (D) arrived overhead to protect the convoy until it arrived in the Kola Inlet. *Chaser* anchored in Vaenga Bay and spent three days repairing aircraft, with the result that she had nine serviceable Swordfish when she sailed to support RA 57 on the evening of 2 March.

By then the weather was as bad as it could be, with low visibility and continuous snowstorms that made flying impossible. However, on 4 March it moderated. Swordfish 'B' was patrolling 27 miles from the convoy south-east of Bear Island when the crew saw a U-boat and attacked it. An accurate salvo of eight 3in rockets with 25lb solid anti-submarine warheads hit and destroyed the boat, and as it wallowed on the surface it was hit again by gunfire from *Onslaught* as it sank. The Swordfish was flown by Sub Lieutenant (A) P J Beresford RNVR with Sub lieutenant (A) D F Laing RNVR as his observer and Leading Airman J Beech as TAG; their attack emphasised the deadly effectiveness of the rocket as an anti-submarine weapon when boats were caught on the surface. Beresford and Laing were awarded the DSC and Beech the DSM.[7] The boat was identified as *U-472* and its loss was confirmed in German records. The same aircraft and crew attacked and damaged another U-boat later but an attack on a third produced no visible result. In each case surface escorts were homed on to the boat's position by the observer using VHF voice radio. The fighters flew three sorties against shadowers but their guns froze and prevented them from engaging.

On Sunday, 5 March only four Swordfish remained fit for flight but patrols continued and Swordfish 'F' sighted and attacked a U-boat north-west of Hammerfest with a skilfully aimed salvo of eight rockets, four of which were seen to hit. This aircraft was flown by Sub Lieutenant (A) J F Mason RNVR with Sub Lieutenant (A) D Street RNVR as his observer and Leading Airman D Franklin as TAG. Again the two officers were awarded the DSC and their TAG the DSM. The boat was identified in German records as *U-366*. Two other U-boats were targeted but no hits

Searcher with Wildcats of 882 and 898 NAS parked forward. (*Philip Jarrett collection*)

were obtained because they dived quickly as the attacks began. In all these attacks visual sighting had been achieved at ranges varying from 3 to 12 miles, the two lethal attacks being obtained at ranges estimated at 8 and 5 miles respectively and through careful stalking using cloud cover. Wildcat sorties continued but suffered further gun jams that prevented positive results. Describing their deck landings in these conditions, Captain McClintock wrote that 'the Wildcats continued to take the most almighty clouts and come up smiling. You apparently cannot ask too much of an American undercarriage beneath a good pilot.'

The forenoon of 6 March brought milder weather with light winds and good visibility and there were nine sightings of U-boats by patrolling Swordfish. The crew of Swordfish 'X', Sub Lieutenant (A) J F Mason RNVR with his observer Sub Lieutenant (A) D Street and TAG Leading Airman D Franklin, detected a U-boat 12 miles from the convoy to the north-west of Narvik and attacked it with a six-rocket salvo, which sank it. The survivors were picked up by *Boadicea*. German records revealed that this U-boat was *U-973*. Mason and Street were awarded DSCs and Franklin a DSM. Following on the other sightings, three U-boats were thought at the time to have been damaged, two were not attacked and three other attacks brought no obvious results. The visibility reduced quickly after noon and fog prevented further flying until two hours before dark, when anti-submarine patrols were resumed. Swordfish 'X' sighted and attacked another U-boat, which was assessed as damaged; the last enemy contact made by *Chaser*'s aircraft during FX, although they continued to fly on 7 March. The record book officer of 816 NAS wrote that this last effort had been 'just to please the Captain and Navigating Officer who could not resist the temptation to fly on the one day when this was possible without moving out of the CVE's station'. The light winds on that day were certainly a problem and Captain McClintock wrote that 'this was an interesting if exasperating day as at times aircraft took off with loads varying from one depth charge and no TAG to eight R/P'.

Chaser's achievement during FX was two U-boats destroyed and one shared kill plus four or five probably damaged for the expenditure of ninety-four 3in rockets after a total of twenty-one sightings. Post-war Admiralty analysis of German records revealed that *U-703* had been sufficiently damaged by a rocket attack on 6 March to have to return to its base immediately and others had to stop tracking the convoy. In eleven of the attacks U-boats had opened fire on the Swordfish but in each case without effect. The maximum distance from the convoy that a U-boat had been sighted was 34 miles. *Chaser*'s Swordfish had flown eighty-one sorties totalling 170 flying hours and the Wildcats had flown thirty-seven sorties totalling forty-seven and half hours; a combined total of 218 hours escorting the two convoys. Of the seventy-three merchant ships that had sailed under the CVE's protection, only one had been lost together with the destroyer *Mahratta*. It had remained bitterly cold throughout the operation and some of the aircraft crews had to be lifted out of their open cockpits after landing on because they were incapable of moving themselves. When *Chaser* returned to Scapa Flow the C-in-C Home Fleet signalled: 'When I visited you recently I thought *Chaser* would be a ship who could overcome all difficulties and strike hard. Now I know.'

A direct comparison between the conduct of air operations in *Avenger* with convoy PQ 18 and *Chaser* with JW 57 eighteen months later would not be straightforward because the main threat to PQ 18 came from aircraft but JW 57 was threatened mainly by U-boats. Fighter direction techniques had been similar because the Type 79B radar fitted in *Chaser* gave results similar to *Avenger*'s Type 79M. Both gave good results against contacts above 2,000ft but were of little use against low-flying torpedo aircraft and shadowers outside 20 miles. *Chaser*'s later mark of Wildcat proved disappointing in combat, however, partly because they lacked the speed to engage enemy aircraft before they reached cloud cover and partly due to their front guns icing up. It was also noted that the carrier's aircraft direction team found the simultaneous direction of Swordfish and CAP fighters difficult. The Wildcats did, however, usually drive off shadowers even if they did not destroy them. One difference is quite clear, however. In the rough weather experienced by *Chaser* it would have been very difficult if not impossible to operate the Sea Hurricanes with which *Avenger* had been equipped and from this perspective the Wildcat was a distinct improvement. It was the operation of Swordfish in *Chaser* that showed the most significant improvement. *Avenger*'s three Swordfish had been operated somewhat haphazardly[8] and had only carried depth charges when wind allowed. *Chaser*'s Swordfish were routinely fitted with 3in rockets and were directed towards U-boats using a tactical plot in the CVE operations room kept up to date with D/F bearings from escorts fitted with high-frequency direction-finding equipment, HF/DF. By early 1944 HF/DF had proved to be the principal means of localising enemy submarines, capitalising on the frequent transmissions their group tactics demanded. The plot was particularly valuable in allowing aircraft to be sent off in semi-darkness to ward off dawn attacks, like those on 6 March, after U-boats had gained favourable attacking positions during the night. HF/DF fixes had to be treated with caution in high latitudes but deliberate changes in a Swordfish Mark III IFF settings enabled *Chaser*'s Type 242 radar operators to tell when it was over a U-boat if R/T and W/T contact had been lost; a not infrequent occurrence when it was some distance away from the carrier. These IFF signals could be held up to 45 miles from the ship and on one occasion a second Swordfish was directed by *Chaser* to a U-boat that was already being attacked, homing itself to the position by ASV bearings on the first Swordfish's IFF. *Chaser* could also home surface escorts on to contacts using a similar technique. Errors of up to 10 degrees in these northerly latitudes made aircraft compasses unreliable and the carrier's Type 251M and YE homing beacons provided an invaluable means of homing them, especially in poor visibility. The former equipment was also found by observers to help with checking and reporting enemy contact reports when the compass was suspect. *Chaser* concentrated on maintaining an anti-submarine, rather than an air interception, plot and in the circumstances this was undoubtedly correct because U-boats posed the greater threat. This had contributed to the indifferent results obtained by the Wildcats and the Admiralty accepted the need to sail two CVEs with every subsequent Arctic convoy.

Captain McClintock made several recommendations after FX. These included the need to fit fighter-type R/T sets in Swordfish to improve direction officers' ability to home them on to U-boat contacts quickly. He noted that open-cockpit aircraft were unsuited for Arctic conditions but felt that assisted take-off would have enabled Swordfish in eight take-offs out of 119 to get airborne with a more effective weapon load. A fighter with better performance and armament was needed if shadowers were to be destroyed rather than merely driven off. The Admiralty took prompt steps to act on these recommendations. Anti-submarine Swordfish were fitted with TR 1460 radios, a distinct improvement on the obsolescent T 1115/R 1116. It did not prove possible, however, to replace all Swordfish

A Swordfish Mark II armed with 3in rocket projectiles about to take off from a CVE. It is painted in the largely white late-war camouflage for anti-submarine aircraft with dark sea grey/slate grey upper surfaces. (*Author's collection*)

in the short term with the Grumman Avenger TBR aircraft being delivered under Lend-Lease arrangements but there were sufficient for a squadron to be embarked in the CVE *Tracker*. The Wildcat continued to be the standard fighter for these operations since it was well suited to operation from CVEs.

To make sure that every possible lesson had been drawn out of FX, 5SL chaired a meeting in the Admiralty on 13 March with Captain McClintock present[9] at which it was agreed that in future either a fleet carrier or two CVEs were essential if simultaneous fighter and anti-submarine sorties were to be flown and directed. It was also accepted that open-cockpit aircraft led quickly to a drop in aircrew efficiency and that the low speed of the Swordfish allowed many U-boats to submerge before they could be attacked, but there were insufficient new aircraft to replace them yet. Better de-icing equipment in carriers was clearly needed if severe weather was not to render barriers, arrester wire sheaves and other vital flight deck equipment inoperable. The meeting took note that enemy aircraft fitted with radar were able to shadow convoys by day and home U-boats on to them at night from 40 to 50 miles away. On the other hand, U-boats frequently found their guns iced up if they tried to fight back on the surface. More success against dived U-boats might have been achieved if aircraft had been armed with depth charges rather than R/P but a hit with the latter fully achieved the aim of crippling the submarine and, overall, R/Ps were considered the better option. Any future increase in flying intensity would require an increase in the number of spare aircrews embarked.

For the first time the escort for the next two convoys, JW/RA 58, was to include two escort carriers: *Activity* commanded by Captain G Willoughby RN as Senior Officer Escort Carriers, and *Tracker* commanded by Captain

J H Huntley RN. The former was a British-built conversion and the latter was an American-built CVE. Both had served with Western Approaches Command on trade protection duties in 1943 before their transfer to the Home Fleet and were, therefore, experienced in convoy protection work. Captain Willoughby was a pilot who had graduated from Number 3 Course in 1926 and flown Flycatchers. Intelligence reports revealed that *Tirpitz* might have been made seaworthy again after an attack by midget submarines in September 1943. It was, therefore, decided to neutralise her with a concentrated attack by Fleet Air Arm aircraft, designated Operation Tungsten. As a precaution in case *Tirpitz* sailed before Tungsten could take place, a heavy Home Fleet covering force sailed with JW 58, with the C-in-C, now Admiral Sir Bruce Fraser, flying his flag in *Duke of York* with *Anson* and *Victorious*, the latter returned from the US Pacific Fleet and refitted for further service.

JW 58 sailed on 28 March. It comprised forty-eight merchant ships, the largest convoy ever to sail to or from north Russia. *Activity* had 819 NAS embarked, commanded by Lieutenant Commander (A) O A G Oxley RN, with three Swordfish and seven Wildcats. *Tracker* had 846 NAS embarked, commanded by Lieutenant Commander (A) R D Head RN, with twelve Avengers and seven Wildcats. The escort was commanded by Rear Admiral F Dalrymple-Hamilton, CS 10, in *Diadem*. The escort and cover for the two convoys JW 58 and RA 58 was designated as Operation FY by the Home Fleet and in addition to their close escorts, the main body of the escort consisted of, in addition to *Diadem*, *Activity* and *Tracker*, the destroyers *Obedient*, *Offa*, *Onslow*, *Opportune*, *Oribi*, *Orwell*, *Saumarez*, *Serapis*, *Scorpion*, *Venus* and the Norwegian *Stord*. The close escort groups lent by Western Approaches Command comprised the sloops *Starling*, commanded by the redoubtable Captain F J Walker DSO*** RN, *Magpie*, *Wild Goose*, *Wren* and *Whimbrel* and the destroyers *Beagle*, *Boadicea*, *Keppel* and *Walker*. The American cruiser *Milwaukee* was also included as she was to be lent to the Soviet Navy, renamed as *Murmansk*. *Activity* had been detailed for FY at very short notice in place of *Biter* and there had been no time to equip either CVE with Arctic equipment but both had previous experience of convoy protection on the UK to Gibraltar route. Against this, 846 NAS' aircrew had not flown for three weeks and neither squadron had previous experience of Arctic operations. The two CVEs had not worked together before and this was to be the first time Avengers had flown in the far north. They had been fitted with P8M compasses specifically designed for use in high latitudes but there had been no time to swing them before *Tracker* sailed. *Activity*'s three Swordfish were not so equipped but at least the compasses they were fitted with had been swung. The inability to adjust the Avengers' compasses and the unsuitability of those fitted in

An Avenger of 846 NAS. (*Philip Jarrett collection*)

the Swordfish limited their value for patrol work as it was not considered practicable to send them more than 40 miles from the convoy. *Tracker* was the first RN CVE capable of launching Avengers from a catapult and this advantage was of considerable value on days when there was little or no natural wind.

The CVEs were allocated the three rear positions in column seven of the convoy, the column on either side of them being given only two ships each. If the wind direction forced them to move outside these positions, flying operations were to take place as far as was possible inside the screen. If one of the CVEs was forced to move outside the screen, the two nearest escorts were to act as its screen until it re-entered. In the unlikely event of a surface action both CVEs were to proceed to the disengaged side of the convoy and stand by to fly off a strike. CS 10's orders showed the contemporary policy for defending a convoy in Arctic waters:

OPERATION FY – NORTH RUSSIAN CONVOYS JW 58 AND RA 58 ORDERS FOR AIR OPERATIONS BY REAR ADMIRAL 10th CRUISER SQUADRON

HM Ships *Activity* (SO) and *Tracker*, Escort Carriers, will accompany both the convoys.

AIRCRAFT
Aircraft carried are as follows:
Activity – 3 Swordfish; 7 Wildcats
Tracker – 12 Avengers; 7 Wildcats

Swordfish are normally armed with eight rocket projectiles but can carry four 250lb depth charges. Avengers carry four 250lb depth charges. It takes a Swordfish about thirty minutes to be loaded with R/Ps. Swordfish can carry torpedoes but will take two hours to prepare.

2. CRUISING SPEEDS
Swordfish 80 knots; Avengers 150 knots; Wildcats 150 knots.

3. ENDURANCE
Swordfish normally do not patrol for more than two hours owing to aircrew fatigue. Avengers can patrol for three hours. Endurance of fighter CAP is about two hours. Maximum speed of Wildcats is 220 knots.

4. R/T SILENCE
R/T silence has to be broken to operate fighters. Night flying cannot be undertaken during conditions of radar silence. Apart from these exceptions, Reptile patrols[10] at distances ordered can be carried out without breaking W/T silence. Owing the present unreliability of aircraft compasses in high latitude searches at distances greater than 80 nm for Avengers and 50 nm for Swordfish cannot be undertaken. If it is decided that convoy has been located and is being shadowed by hostile aircraft R/T silence will be relaxed by CS 10 and fighters may be flown off. R/T and radar silence may be re-imposed at any time by CS 10.

5. AIRCRAFT ATTACKS ON U-BOATS
An aircraft sighting a U-boat will attack at once indicating position by smoke float, flame float or dust marker according to circumstances.

6. NIGHT FLYING
Aircraft will use flare and fire white Very lights when attacking U-boats at night and will drop flame floats.

When night flying is in progress aircraft will investigate any radar contact. Escorts detached from the convoy must, therefore, be prepared to identify themselves instantly.

Aircraft will not attack a U-boat at night within twelve miles of the convoy.

7. MINES
On sighting a mine which is a danger to the convoy, aircraft will not dive but will circle the position and flash letter 'R' to nearest escort.

CS 10's orders were amplified by Captain Willoughby's orders:

SENIOR OFFICER ESCORT CARRIERS' ORDERS TO AIRCRAFT

Reptile patrols will be carried out as required by CS 10.

AIRCRAFT PROCEDURE WHEN RADIO SILENCE IS IN FORCE
(A) On sighting submarine – Attacks, drops smoke float, fires white Very light, returns to deck flashing letter 'S' as he closes. Carrier signals pilot's report to CS 10 and flies off another aircraft to investigate position and continue patrol. NOTE: Aircraft does NOT break silence.
(B) On sighting less than three enemy aircraft – Reports by visual signals when he can do so without giving away the position of the convoy.
(C) On sighting a formation of three or more enemy aircraft – if not approaching the convoy carry out the same procedure as above. If approaching the convoy – break silence and report.
(D) On sighting enemy surface forces – break silence, report, shadow.
(E) Own aircraft about to crash land in sea – if out of sight of surface craft – break radio silence and report. If in sight of surface craft – fire red Very light.

AIRCRAFT PROCEDURE WHEN RADIO SILENCE IS NOT IN FORCE
(A) On sighting a submarine – report, attack and remain in position. If submarine has not dived carrier will fly off a strike. Aircraft over submarine can direct destroyers to target by ACI homing procedure but requests for this procedure must be made through carrier.
(B) On sighting enemy aircraft whether single or in formation – report.

NOTES
1. There can be no night flying until radio silence is relaxed and a considerable amount of light on the flight deck can be accepted.
2. Cold weather may prevent aircraft being left 'At Ready' on deck – delay must be accepted.
3. Until it is known that submarines are in the vicinity we should err on the cautious side with regard to weather, number of aircraft employed and flying hours.
4. It is undesirable to operate aircraft outside visibility distance unless radio may be used (owing to large compass errors).[11]

The intention was that *Activity* would concentrate on the destruction of enemy shadowers while *Tracker* dealt mainly with anti-submarine patrols and strikes. For the latter, the striking forces were to comprise at least one

Avenger and one Wildcat; the TBR to be armed with depth charges and the fighter to use its front guns for silencing the U-boat's anti-aircraft fire and taking its attention away from the Avenger. Neither type had yet been fitted to be armed with R/Ps, although modifications to do so were being implemented as quickly as possible. This combined attack technique was used by both the RN and USN in defence of Atlantic convoys and had proved successful. Pre-arranged action if either CVE required back-up by the other in her particular role was settled before they sailed.

German records revealed that Captain, U-boats, Norway, had written of his disappointment with the performance of his boats against JW and RA 57 in his war diary entry for 21 March and had given precise instructions for a complicated set-piece attack against JW 58. Aircraft were to commence shadowing two days before the attack, transmitting the convoy's position. Homing signals from the aircraft to U-boats were to start '30 minutes before 0300 and continue until shadowing ceased' and flares were to be dropped by aircraft to silhouette the convoy from its flanks. JW 58 was first reported by a Ju 88 early on 30 March, later augmented by an Fw 200 during the afternoon, but the German plan did not go well. Two Ju 88s and two Fw 200s were shot down by 819 NAS Wildcats and Captain Willoughby's report noted that the attack on one of the Ju 88s 'was evidently pressed well home as the leader returned with a considerable length of the enemy's trailing aerial round his starboard wing'. A fifth shadower, another Fw 200, was destroyed by 846 NAS fighters and a sixth, a Bv 138, was shared by one fighter from each carrier. Against these successes, another Wildcat was damaged and set on fire as it strafed a U-boat but its pilot managed a good enough ditching to allow him to get out of the aircraft and into his dinghy. He remained in it for an hour as an Avenger circled over him to indicate his position and he was rescued by one of the escorts. Sub Lieutenant (A) A E Ballantyne RNVR was less fortunate when, after making a promising attack on a U-boat on 1 April, he flew his Avenger into *Tracker*'s round-down when landing on. It caught fire and fell on to the quarterdeck, where he succeeded in getting out of the cockpit and attempted to walk towards the hangar with his clothing alight. Despite gallant attempts to help him, he died from his extensive burns only minutes later. The observer and TAG were also badly burnt but survived. The fire started by the wrecked aircraft could have been serious but was dealt with quickly by a damage control party and caused little interruption to the flying programme.

Other mishaps included one of 819 NAS' Swordfish landing so heavily on *Activity* that it was not repairable on board. One of 819's Wildcats suffered an engine failure on take-off and it went straight into the water. Visibility was low and there were no escorts close by but *Activity* stopped and used her own whaler to rescue the pilot. Survival in the freezing sea water temperatures was seldom more than fifteen minutes and, although the Admiralty was working on the design of an efficient immersion suit for aircrew, it had not yet completed its development. There were also problems with aircraft armament, although the Wildcat icing problems experienced by *Chaser* had been overcome. By 2 April few shadowers had been encountered in daylight, either near JW 58 or RA 58, and after the war a message from Luftflotte V to the German air staff was discovered that revealed the extent of the Luftwaffe's defeat. A translation read:

> The shadowing of the latest PQ [sic] convoy has shown that the aircraft types available to Luftflotte V for such operations are no longer adequate for the purpose.
> Strong enemy fighter cover has led to heavy losses. Moreover it must be assumed that the enemy aircraft are equipped with radar and pursue our aircraft into cloud when [they are] trying to obtain cover there; alternatively, the enemy aircraft may be guided from the carrier.
> Our losses were one Ju 88 on 30 March, three Fw 200 on 31 March, one Bv 138 on 1 April and one Ju 88 on 2 April.
> In relation to the total forces available to Luftflotte V and the tasks they have to perform such losses cannot be allowed to continue. It has therefore been decided that daylight shadowing of QP [sic] convoy now being assembled in Murmansk harbour will cease after it puts to sea. The arrival of the PQ convoy and the sailing of the QP convoy will be watched by reconnaissance of Murmansk harbour. The air force will not be able in future to give the U-boats the preliminary information necessary for their operation unless aircraft of a type capable of dealing with the enemy defences are provided.[12]

The Avengers of 846 NAS had been modified to carry British depth charges but sometimes had difficulty in releasing them, a problem traced to inaccurate machining of the supporting lugs on the depth charge crutches, a small fault that produced disproportionately serious results. Captain Walker reported that there seemed to be a layer of water beneath which sonar detection of U-boats by surface escorts was impossible. In these conditions, he believed, the only likely method of killing them was by aircraft and this view was borne out on 3 April when combined attacks by aircraft from both squadrons sank *U-288* south-east of Bear Island. They had already damaged *U-355* together with *Beagle* south-west of Bear Island on 1 April. Three other U-boats were assessed as having been damaged by air attacks and forced to return to their base. It was

U-288 on the surface south-east of Bear Island on 3 April 1944 being attacked by Swordfish of 819 NAS from *Activity* armed with depth charges. Wildcats had already carried out strafing attacks to suppress the boat's anti-aircraft guns. (*Author's collection*)

The attack on *U-288* was continued by Avengers of 846 NAS from *Tracker*, also armed with depth charges, and the boat was sunk. (*Author's collection*)

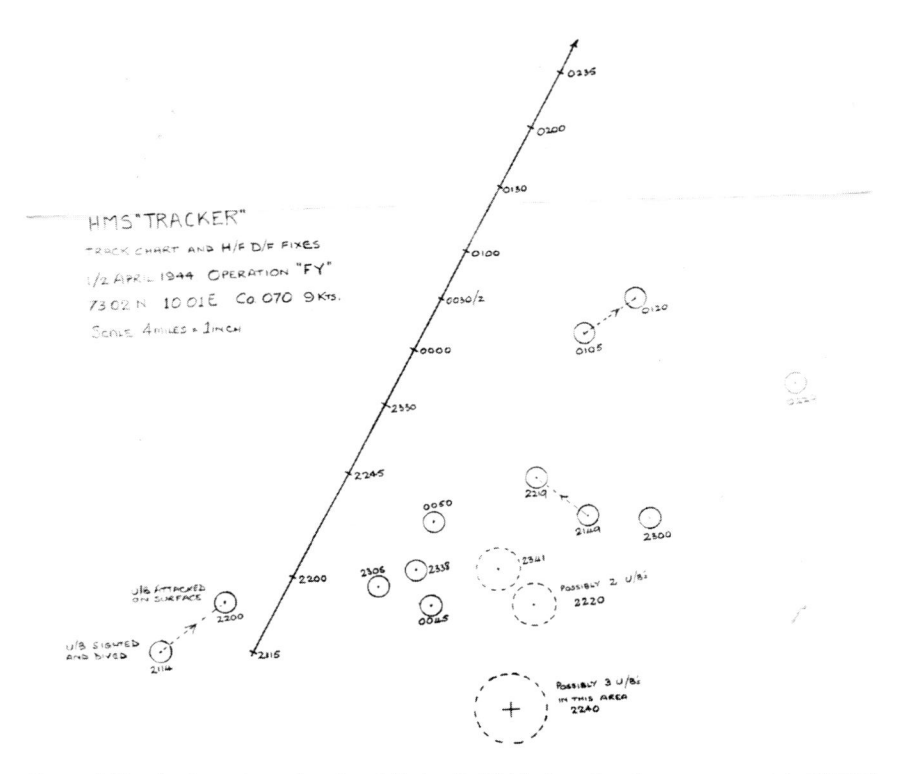

Part of *Tracker*'s action plot for 1/2 April 1944 showing her course with HF/DF fixes on U-boats drawn on during Operation FY. (*Author's collection*)

found, however, that retaining one Avenger and one Wildcat on deck, ready to fly off when a U-boat was detected, allowed insufficient time for them to reach it before it dived. On 2 April, therefore, a new scheme was evaluated in which a Wildcat accompanied the Avenger on patrol and the first occasion on which a U-boat was sighted this team tactic was shown to be worthwhile. A good strafing run by the fighter allowed the Avenger to carry out an attack that left the U-boat at an extreme nose-down attitude and leaking oil with its propellers in the air. On the evening of 4 April, after both carriers had flown anti-submarine patrols without incident despite the lack of natural wind, the two CVEs preceded the convoy into Kola Inlet. The merchant ships had suffered no losses.

RA 58 comprised thirty-six merchant ships with the same escort forces. *Activity*'s 819 NAS had two Swordfish and six Wildcats left serviceable; *Tracker*'s 846 NAS had ten Avengers and four Wildcats. They still suffered from a lack of natural wind and, even with the use of her catapult, *Tracker* had to cancel some Avenger sorties, while *Activity* had to fly unarmed Swordfish, but between them they maintained anti-submarine patrols through the hours of daylight and shadowers were conspicuously absent until it became too dark for the CVEs to operate fighters. *Activity* did not fly off any Wildcats in the whole time she was with this convoy. Some promising attacks on U-boats were made by Avengers that were followed up by the surface escorts but the passage was largely uneventful and the CVEs left the convoy on 11 April, returning to Scapa Flow on 13 April. During FY *Activity*'s aircraft had flown fifty-seven hours and *Tracker*'s 208 hours. The west-bound convoy eventually arrived unscathed, making the total number of merchant ships safely escorted during the round voyage eighty-four. The experience with JW/RA 58 fully justified the use of two CVEs and set the pattern for future Arctic convoy operations. However, they temporarily ended the cycle until August except for one more west-bound convoy of forty-five ships, RA 59, which left on 28 April to bring back ships that had collected in north Russia and to repatriate the USN ship's company of *Milwaukee*. It was also to bring 2,300 Soviet officers and men to the UK to take over the battleship *Royal Sovereign*, which had been lent to the USSR.

Operation Tungsten

The German naval command in north Norway feared that another attack on *Tirpitz* was likely and had asked the Luftwaffe for increased fighter protection over Kaa Fjord, a small inlet at the southern extremity of Alten Fjord, where she now lay.[13] An attack on her by aircraft of the Home Fleet, designated Operation Tungsten, had actually been projected for mid-March but the delayed completion of *Victorious*' post-Pacific refit delayed it. In order to reduce the risk to the forces taking part from U-boats and also to provide a better prospect of surprise, the eventual date chosen was 4 April to coincide with the passage of JW 58. Responsibility for the organisation, planning and execution of Tungsten was given by Admiral Fraser, the C-in-C Home Fleet, to his deputy, Vice Admiral Sir Henry Moore, the Vice Admiral Second Battle Squadron, VA 2BS. He had Captain L D Mackintosh DSC RN as his chief of staff, who had qualified as an observer in the very first RN observers' course in 1921, and he used his considerable air experience to good effect both in planning and executing the operation. It was to be the first time the new Barracuda TBR aircraft had been used in large numbers and dive-bombing was the chosen attack method because the fjord offered insufficient space for a torpedo attack. The Corsairs embarked in *Victorious* and the Hellcats embarked in *Emperor* were also going into action for the first time and both were capable of accompanying the strike force all the way to the target. After years of having to put up with inadequate fighters, many pilots were hoping that there would

Part of the Tungsten task force, *Fencer*, in the foreground with *Furious* and another CVE in the distance. (*Author's collection*)

be German air opposition so that they could overwhelm it with their powerful new American-built fighters.

A full-scale range was created at Loch Eriboll in the remote north-west tip of Scotland to replicate *Tirpitz* as she was moored in Kaa Fjord using a rocky island to simulate the ship. This was used by both bombers and fighters but there was very little time for intensive training, especially for the squadrons that were newly commissioned. A full-scale dress rehearsal using Loch Eriboll was carried out on 28 March with the carriers operating off Scapa Flow. The assault carrier task force under Rear Admiral Escort Carriers, RAEC, Rear Admiral A W LaT Bisset, who had previously commanded *Formidable*, was working up in UK waters to be ready for operations in the Mediterranean and it was decided to add them to the strike force, both to enlarge it and to give them combat experience. The covering force for JW 58, designated Force I, sailed on 30 March comprising the C-in-C in *Duke of York* with VA 2BS in *Anson* and *Victorious* together with a cruiser and six destroyers. Force II, concerned only with Tungsten, was already at sea making for a planned rendezvous position with Force I. Admiral Bisset flew his flag in the new cruiser *Royalist*, which had been completed with improved radar and plotting facilities to act as an assault carrier command ship, and with him were the CVEs *Searcher*, *Emperor*, *Pursuer* and *Fencer*, together with two further cruisers, ten destroyers and two RFA oilers.

Aircraft carriers that took part in Operation Tungsten and their air groups[14]

Victorious	Captain M M Denny CB CBE RN
1834 NAS	Lieutenant Commander (A) P N Charlton DFC RN[15]
1836 NAS	Lieutenant Commander (A) C C Tomkinson RNVR
827 NAS	Lieutenant Commander (A) K H Gibney DSC RN
829 NAS	Lieutenant Commander (A) D W Phillips DSC RN
Furious	Captain G T Philip DSO DSC RN
801 NAS	Lieutenant Commander (A) H F Bromwich RN
880 NAS	Lieutenant Commander (A) W H Martyn DSC RN
830 NAS	Lieutenant Commander (A) R D Kingdon DSC RNVR
831 NAS	Lieutenant Commander (A) D Brooks DSC RNVR
Emperor	Captain T J N Hilken DSO RN
800 NAS	Lieutenant Commander S J Hall DSC RN
804 NAS	Lieutenant Commander (A) S G Orr DSC* RNVR
Pursuer	Captain H R Graham DSO DSC RN
881 NAS	Lieutenant Commander D R B Cosh RCNVR
896 NAS	Lieutenant Commander (A) L A Hordern DSC RNVR
Searcher	Captain G O C Davies RN
882 NAS	Lieutenant Commander (A) J Cooper DSC RNVR
898 NAS	Lieutenant Commander (A) G R Henderson DSC RNVR
Fencer	Captain W W R Bentinck OBE RN
842 NAS	Lieutenant Commander (A) G F S Hodson RNR

Operation Tungsten – aircraft complements

Victorious	
1834 NAS	14 Corsair
1836 NAS	14 Corsair
827 NAS	9 Barracuda
829 NAS	12 Barracuda
Furious	
801 NAS	6 Seafire IB
880 NAS	8 Seafire LIIC
830 NAS	9 Barracuda
831 NAS	9 Barracuda

Emperor
800 NAS   10 Hellcat
804 NAS   10 Hellcat

Pursuer
881 NAS   10 Wildcat
896 NAS   10 Wildcat

Searcher
882 NAS   10 Wildcat
898 NAS   10 Wildcat

Fencer
842 NAS   12 Swordfish & 8 Wildcat

Of these, 1834 and 1836 NAS constituted Number 47 Naval Fighter Wing commanded by Lieutenant Commander (A) F R A Turnbull DSC* RN. Nos 827 NAS and 830 NAS constituted Number 8 TBR Wing commanded by Lieutenant Commander R S Baker-Faulkner DSO DSC RN and 829 NAS with 831 NAS constituted Number 52 TBR Wing commanded by Lieutenant Commander V Rance OBE RN. *Fencer* was an

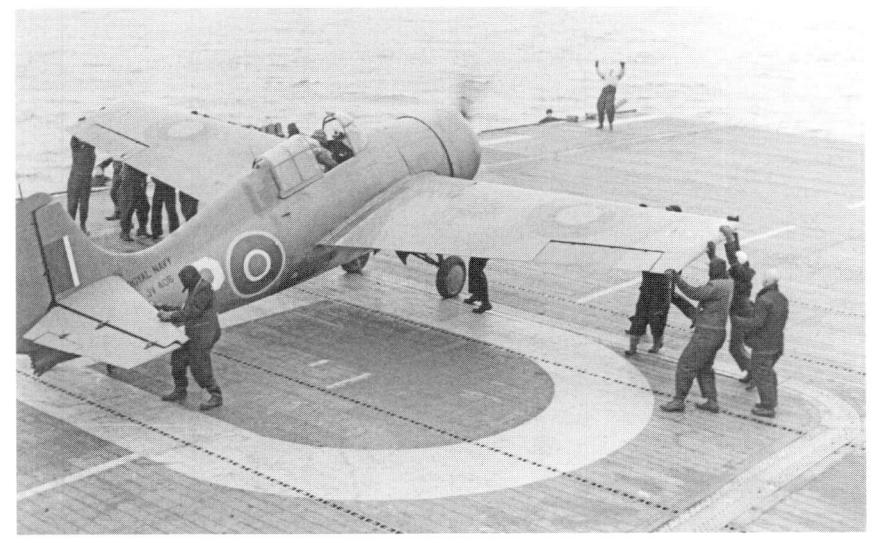

A Wildcat of 881 NAS shortly after landing on *Pursuer*. It has stopped on the forward lift and the marshaller at the bow is giving the 'brakes on' signal. The pilot is reaching down for the wing-fold selector and handlers are at the wingtips ready to steady them as they fold aft. (*Author's collection*)

anti-submarine CVE and had a composite squadron embarked for force protection with the surface escort. The fighter squadrons embarked in *Emperor* and *Pursuer* formed Number 7 Naval Fighter Wing commanded by Lieutenant Commander (A) M F Fell DSO RN.

The TBR wings had carried out their practice strikes on Loch Eriboll as cohesive units but their squadrons were normally embarked in the different fleet carriers. There was some discussion in Admiral Moore's staff during the practice period about whether it was better for each carrier to operate its normal air group or to swap one squadron from each to the other so that wings could attack as a cohesive unit that had trained together. Both methods had merits and objections but Admiral Moore finally decided that the Barracudas should all operate from their own carrier but 'the advantage of operating a complete wing as a unit which has been trained together outweighs the disadvantages'.[16] For Tungsten, therefore, one of 8 TBR Wing's squadrons from each carrier took off for the first strike followed an hour later by one of 52 TBR Wing's squadrons from each carrier. *Victorious* had an air group of forty-six aircraft, ten more than her originally designed complement, and this meant that some would have to be kept in a deck park despite the Arctic conditions. *Furious* had thirty-two aircraft embarked.

By 1 April Admiral Fraser knew that JW 58 was making good progress with very little interference from the enemy. Moreover, it was clear that neither Force I nor Force II had been detected. The weather was perfect and so Admiral Fraser decided to advance the date and time for Tungsten by twenty-four hours; Forces I and II moved into position to carry out his revised orders and met on the afternoon of 2 April 220 miles to the north-west of Alten Fjord. They were then reorganised into two new task groups while the C-in-C in *Duke of York* with its escort continued to cover the convoy before returning to Scapa Flow on 5 April. The CVEs had to proceed at their maximum speed of 17 knots to reach the rendezvous at the revised time but the two RFA tankers, *Blue Ranger* and *Brown Ranger*, were unable to keep up and so they were detached to position QQ, 300 miles north-west of Alten Fjord, escorted by *Javelin* and the Polish *Piorun*, where they stood by to refuel the destroyers if necessary. By 1650 on 2 April the strike force was 220 miles north-west of Alten Fjord and had formed into two new task forces. Force 7 comprised Admiral Moore's flagship *Anson*, with *Victorious*, *Furious*, *Jamaica*, *Belfast* and six destroyers. Force 8 comprised Admiral Bisset's flagship *Royalist* with *Emperor*, *Searcher*, *Fencer*, *Pursuer*, *Sheffield* and six destroyers. Once re-formed, these forces proceeded to the designated flying off position 100 miles nearer Alten Fjord, where they were due at 0415 on 3 April.

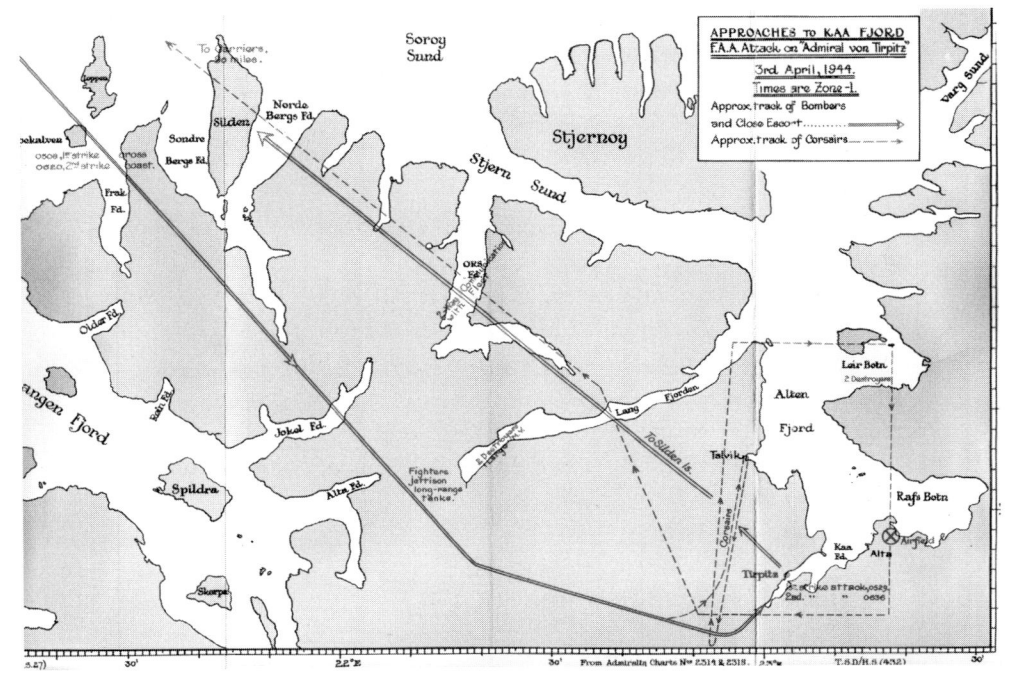

An Admiralty chart showing the route to and from Kaa Fjord used by both strike forces in Operation Tungsten on 3 April 1944. (*Admiralty – Crown Copyright*)

In all the carriers the aircrew had undergone extensive briefing for what was to be the biggest set-piece strike carried out by the Fleet Air Arm to date and the most important since Taranto in November 1940. There were to be two separate strikes on *Tirpitz*, one hour apart with the option of a re-strike if necessary. Each was to comprise twenty-one Barracudas escorted by forty fighters from both fleet carriers and CVEs. *Fencer* and *Furious* were to provide task force anti-submarine patrols and CAP. The Seafires in *Furious* lacked the radius of action to take part in the strike. The first attack was to be by 8 TBR Wing led by Lieutenant Commander Baker-Faulkner and the second by 52 TBR Wing led by Lieutenant Commander Rance. Both these officers had a full briefing in *Victorious* and were then flown across to *Furious* to co-ordinate the other wing's briefing. Of the 163 pilots and observers due to take part in the strike, 148 came from the RNR, RNVR, RNZNVR, RCNVR or the South African Naval Force Reserve, giving a good idea of the Fleet Air Arm's composition in early 1944. Most of them were about to experience their first action. Activity in the carriers was intense during the hours before the strike began. Captain Denny of *Victorious* commented that last-minute maintenance and movements put a great strain on to maintenance personnel and handlers. Armourers sometimes had to chase aircraft through the hangar, up one lift and on to the flight deck because of last-minute, unforeseen servicing requirements and had to load four different types of bomb. As a precaution against icing while aircraft were exposed on deck a film of anti-freeze grease was applied to the leading edges of their wings.

Admiral Moore's staff had put considerable thought into bomb loads during the planning process. *Tirpitz* lay in the narrow confines of Kaa Fjord and torpedoes had been ruled out but different effects were required from bomb hits. The mixture best suited to crippling the battleship and limiting its ability to defend itself would be a combination in each strike force of the following:

(a) 1,600lb armour-piercing Mark 230 fused for 0.08-second delay. Only one of these could be carried under a Barracuda's centreline.
(b) 500lb semi-armour-piercing Mark V with Pistol No. 30 fused for 0.14-second delay with 60ft spacing between bombs.
(c) 500lb medium-capacity Mark II filled with Torpex with Pistol DA No. 42 Mark I fused for instantaneous detonation with 0.07-second interval between bombs.
(d) 600lb anti-submarine bomb Mark I with fuse No. 862 Mark I with 60ft spacing.

The staff calculated that (a) should penetrate the main armoured deck if released at 2,000ft or higher and that (b) should penetrate the 2in weather deck and cause damage between decks. The intention was that (c) should detonate above the deck or on striking the water in the case of a near miss and cause casualties to exposed personnel such as light gun's crews. The bombs listed as (d) were intended to cause underwater damage if they fell within 30ft of the hull, or if they hit it, to cause damage to superstructure, guns and upper deck fittings. The first strike was to be armed with seven 1,600lb bombs, nine 500lb MC. four 600lb A/S and twenty-seven 500lb SAP. The second strike was to have the same types of bomb but with fewer 1,600lb and more 500lb SAP.

By 1800 on 2 April every aircraft was serviceable and had been fully fuelled and armed as required. As a precaution all the aircraft in *Victorious*' deck park were allocated to the second strike and at 0200 on 3 April they had their engines started and warmed through before being struck down into the relatively warm hangar after the first strike aircraft were ranged. At 0130 aircrew were called for a last-minute briefing, with the Army liaison officers embarked in the assault CVEs giving valuable

One of *Victorious*' armourers has chalked 'TIRPITZ ITS YOURS' on a 1,600lb bomb fitted under a Barracuda. Aircraft had to be modified to carry these bombs on the centreline hard point and the attachment method can be seen clearly in this close-up photograph. (Author's collection)

assistance to the air staff officers by briefing on intelligence matters. All the aircraft in the first ranges started without a single failure. There was still no sign of enemy activity and there was growing hope that surprise had been achieved. Captain Denny wrote afterwards that:

> Knowing they were about to attempt an opposed attack of a character that hitherto had not been attempted in the European theatre, they left the carriers' decks in the greatest of heart and brimful of determination and proceeded through the complicated business of forming up and taking departure to the target exactly as if a parade ground movement. That in fact they met no German Air Force opposition subtracts not one iota from the credit that is due to them.

Typical of the precautions taken to prevent the Germans from deducing that a strike was being mounted by the Home Fleet was the maintenance of W/T traffic at Scapa Flow to give the impression that ships were still in harbour. Bogus signals continued to be transmitted from the temporary W/T station set up at Loch Eriboll for bombing practices.

Barracudas from *Victorious* en route to Kaa Fjord. The two aircraft on the left and the three to the right are armed with 1,600lb bombs; the aircraft nearest the camera is armed with two 600lb A/S bombs. (*Author's collection*)

At 0416, one minute after zero-hour, the first of ten escorting Corsair fighters from 1834 NAS flew off *Victorious* led by Lieutenant Commander Turnbull, followed eight minutes later by the twenty-one Barracudas of 8 TBR Wing led by Lieutenant Commander Baker-Faulkner. The remaining fighter escorts from 881, 800 and 882 flew off from *Pursuer*, *Emperor* and *Searcher* almost simultaneously, also led by their commanding officers. The whole strike force then formed up quickly into a shallow vee and set heading. *Furious* and *Fencer* flew off CAP fighters and anti-submarine patrols. Admiral Bisset wrote in his report that 'it was a grand sight with the sun just risen to see this well-balanced striking force ... departing at very low level between the two forces of surface ships and good to know that a similar-sized force would be leaving again in about an hour's time ... it was especially heartening to an ex-carrier captain accustomed for several years to be very short of aircraft, especially fighters, and made one wonder what might have been if the Fleet Air Arm had been adequately supplied with aircraft in the early days of the war.' The careful planning for Tungsten and the skill with which it was carried out can be judged from an analysis of the fleet carriers' flying programmes subsequently carried out by NAD. This table shows how nearly everything went to plan:

Fleet carriers' Tungsten flying programmes

Zero hour	Actual time	*Victorious*	*Furious*
0415–0425	0416–0424	fly off 10 Corsairs	
0425–0435	0424–0430	fly off 12 Barracudas	
0423–0425	0423–0424		fly off 2 Seafires
0425–0435	0424–0428		fly off 9 Barracudas
0435	0436	1st strike departure	
0530	0529	1st strike attack	
0515–0525	0515–0510	fly off 10 Corsairs	
	0520–0533	fly off 11 Barracudas*	
0525–0535	0521–0524		fly off 9 Barracudas
0535	0538	2nd strike departure	
0545–0550	0548–0550		fly off 4 Seafires
0550–0600	0552–0557		recover 2 Seafires
0610	0610	1st strike returned	
0630	0636	2nd strike attack	
0610–0650	0618–0640	recover 1st strike	
0610–0640	0618–0637		recover 1st strike
0635–0640	0709–0710		fly off 4 Seafires
0640–0650	0712–0726		recover 4 Seafires
0710	0715	2nd strike returned	
0710–0750	0720–0755	recover 2nd strike	
0710–0740	0728–0758		recover 2nd strike

* Barracuda 'Q' of 829 NAS crashed into the sea after flying off from *Victorious*. Its crew were all killed.

The flying programme carried out by *Pursuer*, *Emperor* and *Searcher* was less complicated and went largely to plan so that interaction with the fleet carriers went well. They each flew off ten fighters between 0423 and 0435 and then ranged a further ten. The second strike escort was launched between 0525 and 0535. First strike escort and CAP fighters were recovered between 0650 and 0710 and the second strike escort and the last CAP between 0750 and 0810.

The first strike force comprised the following aircrew listed in the order pilot, observer and then TAG:

8 TBR Wing

827 NAS flown off *Victorious*

- K Lieutenant Commander (A) R Baker-Faulkner RN
     Lieutenant G M Micklom RN
     L/Airman A M Kimberley
- A Lieutenant (A) H R Emerson RNZNVR
     Lieutenant Commander (A) K H Gibney RN
     Chief Petty Officer Airman C Topliss
- Q Sub Lieutenant (A) C M Lock RNVR
     Sub Lieutenant (A) J Grieveson RNVR
     Leading Airman D E Wootton
- C Sub Lieutenant (A) J D Herrold RNZVR
     Sub Lieutenant (A) G Alexander RNVR
     Leading Airman H N Hoyte
- M Sub Lieutenant (A) I G Robertson RNVR
     Sub Lieutenant (A) H W Pethick RNVR
     Leading Airman J Coulby
- F Sub Lieutenant (A) D W Collett RNVR
     Lieutenant G C Yorke RN
     Leading Airman T Cartnell
- G Sub Lieutenant (A) E E Green RNVR
     Sub Lieutenant (A) L J Jouning RNVR
     Leading Airman R H Lee
- P Sub Lieutenant (A) J A Gledhill RNVR
     Sub Lieutenant (A) J McCormack RNVR
     Leading Airman N A F Poole
- H Sub Lieutenant (A) J Watson RNVR
     Sub Lieutenant (A) R D Smith RNVR
     Leading Airman R R Williams
- B Lieutenant P G Darling RCNVR
     Sub Lieutenant (A) H E K Gale RNVR
     Leading Airman E Hunter
- R Sub Lieutenant (A) A D Ritchie RNVR
     Sub Lieutenant (A) K A Sellers RNVR
     Leading Airman W Murray
- L Sub Lieutenant (A) J R Brown RNVR
     Sub Lieutenant (A) D L Pullen RNVR
     Leading Airman W H A Reynolds

830 NAS flown off *Furious*
A Lieutenant Commander (A) R D Kingdon RNVR
   Lieutenant (A) J B Armitage RNZNVR
   Chief Petty officer Airman A E Carr
C Sub Lieutenant (A) A E Browse RNVR
   Sub Lieutenant (A) A H Dubbie RNVR
   Leading Airman G F Priestly
B Sub Lieutenant (A) D S Clarabut RNVR
   Sub Lieutenant (A) E D Knight RNVR
   Leading Airman W A Ball
H Sub Lieutenant (A) J A Grant RNVR
   Sub Lieutenant (A) A C P Walling RNVR
   Leading Airman B P Bussey
M Sub Lieutenant (A) T C Bell RNVR
   Sub Lieutenant (A) R N Drennan RNVR
   Leading Airman G J Burns
F Lieutenant (A) J B Robinson RNVR
   Sub Lieutenant (A) R L Eveleigh RNVR
   Petty Officer Airman S W Lock
G Sub Lieutenant (A) D E Rowe RNZNVR
   Sub Lieutenant (A) D A Brown RNZNVR
   Leading Airman A C Wells
K Sub Lieutenant (A) J D Britton RNVR
   Sub Lieutenant (A) J C Fairclough RNVR
   Leading Airman J Whyte
L Sub Lieutenant (A) R G Williams RNZNVR
   Sub Lieutenant (A) R D Burton RNVR
   Leading Airman A H Thomson

Having formed up, the first strike flew south-east only 50ft above the water until 0457, when they began a steady climb to 10,000ft 25 miles from the Norwegian coast. They crossed the coast at 0508 and passed close to the head of Lang Fjord before turning east to follow a snow-covered valley towards Kaa Fjord. As they did so *Tirpitz* was weighing her first anchor and having her torpedo net protection cleared away in preparation for the start of the sea trials that were to follow her repairs. Her forecastle party was still hoisting in the third shackle of the second anchor when personnel on the bridge noticed that the protective smokescreens had been started ashore and a report was received that aircraft were approaching from the north-west. German records revealed that the ship was ordered to action stations at 0528, just as the first aircraft was seen. The smokescreen had not yet obscured her, most of the ship's company were not yet at their

Barracudas of the first strike passing Lang Fjorden. (*Author's collection*)

action stations and a number of watertight doors were open to allow the passage of men through the ship. With seamen closed up at harbour stations, the anti-aircraft armament was only partially manned and some initially lacked ready-use ammunition.

The fighters jettisoned their long-range tanks between Alta and Lang Fjords after sixty-five minutes airborne, after which the Corsairs remained at 10,000ft to give top cover as the Barracudas began their dives. Hellcats and Wildcats, led by Lieutenant Commander J W Sleigh DSC RN of Admiral Bisset's staff, dived low enough for the hills to hide their approach from anti-aircraft fire but kept *Tirpitz*'s foretop in sight as a marker. They flew together down the hillsides and strafed shore batteries and *Tirpitz* with their front guns. German records revealed that *Tirpitz*'s gunnery was disorganised by this classic opening move and her captain reported that the fighters strafed the ship in great numbers, coming from so many directions that it was impossible to allocate flak groups against them all and that by the time the first bomb fell '… the main flak battery with both forward flak fire controls had already been put out of action by gunfire'.

At 0529 the Barracudas commenced their dive-bombing attacks and a minute later they were over. Bombs were released between 3,000 and 1,200ft and hits were seen by several Barracuda crews. *Tirpitz*'s W/T aerials were put out of action in the first seconds, preventing her from reporting that she had been attacked for eighty minutes. Internal communications

Tirpitz as the strafing fighters first saw her with smoke generators in action but not yet effective. (*Author's collection*)

were also destroyed and neither damage nor casualty reports could reach the command centre on the bridge. Succeeding hits added to the confusion and the captain had to turn over command of *Tirpitz* to his second in command when he was wounded by splinters. Only one Barracuda was shot down by anti-aircraft fire, which was described by Baker-Faulkner

One of *Tirpitz*'s multiple 20mm anti-aircraft mountings in action. The complete lack of protection for the gun crews led to high casualties from the fighters' strafing attacks. Two of this crew are not even wearing helmets. (*Author's collection*)

Although not in sharp focus, a steeply diving Barracuda can be seen at the top centre of this image as *Tirpitz* is hit. Note how ineffective the smokescreen was at this stage. (*Author's collection*)

as 'considerable but inaccurate'. This was 'M' of 830 NAS flown by Sub Lieutenant (A) T C Bell RNVR, Sub Lieutenant (A) RN Drennan RNVR and Leading Airman Burns. The aircraft was seen to be in a controlled glide after the attack by others as they withdrew and there were hopes that Bell might have pulled off a forced landing but, sadly, all three were killed. They were subsequently buried in the Commonwealth War Graves Commission Cemetery at Tromsø. One Hellcat had its hook damaged by enemy fire and ditched close to the task force rather than risk a crash on deck. Its pilot was rescued by *Algonquin*.

When the aircrew were debriefed on their carriers, it became clear that the attack had been a considerable success. In *Victorious*, 827 NAS aircrew had confirmed a number hits, including some of the big 1,600lb bombs, and several near misses. Most aircraft had dived at 50 to 55 degrees and attacked along the line of the ship. In *Furious* the aircrew of 830 NAS, which had followed 827 NAS into the attack, also confirmed hits by bombs of various sizes and during their getaway they had seen *Tirpitz*'s superstructure enveloped in smoke with orange flame appearing through it at intervals. 'G' had a 1,600lb bomb that failed to release and had to return to the ship with it. As the last aircraft of the first strike and their escort climbed to the north-west and headed towards the carriers at point PP for their recovery, the second strike force was already on its way, following an identical route.

The second strike force comprised the following aircrew listed in the order pilot, observer and then TAG:

52 TBR Wing

829 NAS flown off *Victorious*
L Lieutenant (A) M Meredith RNVR
   Lieutenant Commander V Rance RN
   CPO Airman T L Cridland
B Sub Lieutenant (A) A Hamersley RNVR
   Sub Lieutenant (A) E R Shipley RNVR
   Leading Airman T Harding
F Lieutenant P Hudson RN
   Sub Lieutenant (A) I D C Cooksey RNVR
   Leading Airman R T Knight
H Sub Lieutenant (A) S C Taylor RNZNVR
   Sub Lieutenant (A) N Harrison RNVR
   Leading Airman A B Sim
A Lieutenant Commander D Phillips RN
   Sub Lieutenant (A) H Ashford RNVR
   Chief Petty officer Airman E J W Sherlock
K Lieutenant (A) G W Grindred RNVR
   Sub Lieutenant (A) P Hollis RNVR
   Leading Airman I Kitley
P Sub Lieutenant (A) M C Farrer RNZNVR
   Sub Lieutenant (A) S A Erratt RNVR
   Leading Airman R Bacon
G Lieutenant (A) N B Hurstwick RNZNVR
   Sub Lieutenant (A) E Stacey RNVR
   Leading Airman T Spencer
R Sub Lieutenant (A) A N Towlson RNVR
   Sub Lieutenant (A) L J Ryan RNZNVR
   Leading Airman W Firth
Q Sub Lieutenant (A) E C Bowles RNVR
   Lieutenant (A) J P Whittaker RNVR
   Leading Airman C J Colwell
M Sub Lieutenant (A) H H Richardson RNVR
   Sub Lieutenant (A) A G Cannon RNVR
   Leading Airman E Carroll

831 NAS flown off *Furious*

A   Lieutenant Commander (A D Brooks RN
    Lieutenant (A) D S Miller RNVR
    Petty Officer Airman T W Halhead
K   Lieutenant (A) C G Hurst RNVR
    Lieutenant (A) W S Lindores RNVR
    Leading Airman D Robinson
G   Sub Lieutenant (A) P H Abbott RNVR
    Sub Lieutenant (A) L W Peck RNVR
    Leading Airman V Gallimore
C   Sub Lieutenant (A) N H Bovey RNVR
    Sub Lieutenant (A) W Smith RNVR
    Leading Airman V Watkins
F   Lieutenant (A) G Russell-Jones RNVR
    Sub Lieutenant (A) J Cartwright RNVR
    Leading Airman G S McRae
L   Sub Lieutenant (A) R N Robbins RNVR
    Sub Lieutenant (A) J Coe RNVR
    Leading Airman T Ward
B   Sub Lieutenant (A) T M Henderson RNVR
    Sub Lieutenant (A) V Hutchinson RNVR
    Leading Airman V Smyth
H   Sub Lieutenant (A) M M Bebbington RNVR
    Sub Lieutenant (A) G J Burford RNVR
    Leading Airman R R Rankin
M   Sub Lieutenant (A) P Hunter RNVR
    Sub Lieutenant (A) E M King RNVR
    Leading Airman W A Allen

One of 829 NAS' Barracudas failed to start, reducing the number of aircraft in the strike at the outset to twenty, and 'Q' from the same squadron crashed shortly after take-off, killing its three crew members and reducing the size of the strike force still further. The remaining nineteen Barracudas set heading for *Tirpitz* following the same track as the first strike and escorted by thirty-nine fighters. These comprised ten Corsairs from 1836 NAS led by Lieutenant Commander (A) C C Tomkinson RNVR; eight Wildcats of 896 NAS led by Lieutenant Commander (A) L A Hordern RNVR; ten Hellcats of 804 NAS led by Lieutenant Commander (A) S G Orr RNVR and eleven Wildcats of 898 NAS led by Lieutenant Commander (A) G R Henderson RNVR. The three CVE squadrons were led as a cohesive tactical force by Lieutenant Commander (A) M F Fell RN.

The weather remained excellent with a calm sea, which helped the fifty-nine aircraft to fly off in only nine minutes. One 896 NAS Wildcat suffered engine trouble shortly after take-off but managed to return to *Pursuer* and land on. Once the force had climbed to 10,000ft, Lieutenant Commander Rance saw the smokescreen around *Tirpitz* from 40 miles away but reported that it made no difference to the Barracuda crews' ability to see and attack the target, although it must have considerably hampered the aim of the enemy's close-range weapons. The strike aircraft began to descend slowly as they approached Kaa Fjord and they saw that *Tirpitz* was still floating but appeared to have swung across the fjord with her stern practically aground. German records revealed that she was anticipating a second attack and was actually under way and trying to re-enter her net defences without the aid of a tug, which could not be seen in the smoke. As in the first strike, the Corsairs remained high to give top cover and the Hellcats strafed heavy anti-aircraft positions ashore. The Wildcats flew low over the mountains and strafed the ship's exposed positions as the Barracudas began their dives. Again, the whole attack was over in less than a minute.

This time the anti-aircraft guns had fired a box barrage round the target, with every gun firing blind through the smoke, but all fire had ceased by the time the last bomb was dropped. A single Barracuda, 'M' of 829 NAS, was shot down and was seen to crash into a mountainside, probably after releasing its bomb over the target. Several other aircrew thought they saw the crew bale out but both Richardson and Cannon were killed; they too are buried in Tromsø but Carroll survived and it may have been his parachute that was seen. As with the first strike, the aircrew confirmed seeing hits by several types of bombs at their debriefs. They described the smokescreen as covering the area but leaving *Tirpitz* clearly visible. 'M' was seen to go down with its port wing broken and on fire and many of them described *Tirpitz* on fire with a dull red glow on the port side amidships. The first of 831 NAS' aircraft to attack was 'A', which did so from the port quarter and its crew reported seeing a large fire burning on the port side by the bridge structure and then a second fire breaking out in a similar position to starboard. Others saw *Tirpitz*'s stern within 30yd of the shore, a fire near 'X' turret and a large orange flame billowing from the funnel, an explosion near the bow and a fire amidships.

The aircraft climbed away to the north-west and fighters engaged any targets that presented themselves in or near the fjords over which they passed, but there was still no German air opposition. The strike force located the carriers in position PP without difficulty and the two destroyers that had been placed closer to the coast for air-sea rescue duties if required gave useful assistance to the aircraft by acting as signposts

Wildcats of 898 NAS landing on *Searcher* after the Tungsten strike. Other fighters can just be seen returning in the distance. A pilot who has already landed and parked his aircraft forward in Fly 1 is in the foreground walking towards the island. (*Author's collection*)

with their forward guns trained in the direction of the task force. By 0758 all the surviving aircraft had landed on safely; of the 121 aircraft that had taken part in the two attacks only two Barracudas had been shot down by the enemy, a third had ditched after engine failure and a Hellcat had been forced to ditch near the fleet because its arrester hook had been damaged by enemy gunfire. The reaction in the fleet was exhilaration and as the task force moved away from the Norwegian coast Admiral Moore considered the question of carrying out a repeat attack on the next morning, 4 April. As details of numerous hits emerged from the aircrew debriefings, however, and on learning of their natural reaction after successfully completing such a major and dangerous operation, he decided to return to Scapa Flow. Both US and British experience had shown that post-action fatigue had a lowering effect on efficiency and this was clearly the right decision under the circumstances. The force arrived in Scapa Flow on 6 April and were given a rousing reception by the C-in-C, who had arrived in *Duke of York* a day earlier, and by all the other ships in harbour. In his report on Tungsten, Admiral Moore wrote that:

> Great credit is due to Rear Admiral Bisset ... and the commanding officers of the fleet and escort carriers for the efficiency and team

work which was achieved in so short a time, and for the smoothness with which the operation was carried out. But above all, I wish to express my admiration for the brilliant and daring attack carried out by the aircrews themselves, most of whom were having their first experience of enemy action.

The Admiralty carried out a preliminary examination of the probable hits on *Tirpitz* based on the debriefing of aircrew and the assessment of photographs taken during the strike. It was concluded that she had certainly been hit by eight bombs with five probables and possibly by as many as seventeen. In the circumstances, with multiple bomb bursts in a short period of time with a thickening smokescreen, this was a reasonable interpretation of what had happened. German records, when analysed, showed that *Tirpitz* had actually been hit fourteen times. One 1,600lb bomb had hit but failed either to detonate or penetrate the armoured deck. Another hit was by a 500lb bomb that had only partially exploded. It was also assessed that some bombs had been dropped from heights below those briefed and that this would have limited their ability to penetrate the armoured deck. The effectiveness of the lighter bombs on anti-aircraft guns and structure above the armoured deck can be gathered from German casualty lists, which amounted to 121 dead and 316 wounded, the latter figure including the captain. A more thorough assessment by Admiralty experts across several disciplines of the probable effect of Tungsten on *Tirpitz* led to the conclusion that she needed repair work that would certainly prevent her from putting to sea for three months and that it was unlikely she would be operational in less than five.[17] She actually recovered her operational status on 1 July, two days earlier than the predicted three months.

After analysing Tungsten the Admiralty took note of a number of lessons. The importance of preliminary practices and rehearsals for a set-piece strike like this was obviously of paramount importance. The importance of meticulous aircrew briefings with the aid of models, photographs and accurate maps was also clear. Captain Denny wrote covering *Victorious'* action reports that officers had been informed, under conditions of strict secrecy, about the intended operation some days previously and were thus able to make themselves acquainted with the available intelligence material. Detailed briefing of squadrons separately was completed on 1 April, when the TAGs were told of the plan for the first time. Officers' briefings prior to Tungsten had lasted up to ten hours. The element of surprise was also recognised as being of fundamental importance and strict orders were laid down for the preservation of radio silence on the outbound legs. Even then, however, some aircrew had broken the rule before they even

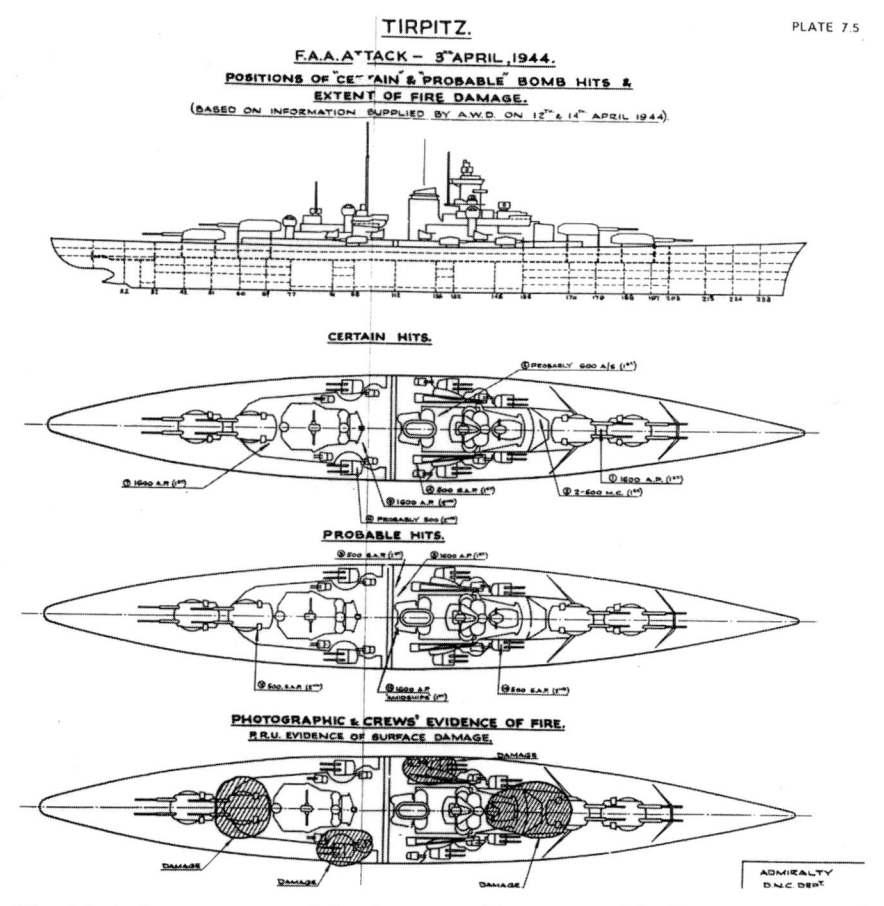

The Admiralty assessment of the damage to *Tirpitz* caused by Tungsten prepared by the Director of Naval Construction. It was based on aircrew reports and photographs. (*Admiralty – Crown Copyright*)

reached the coast. Strafing the target and outlying anti-aircraft positions on shore had proved an important part in softening up the defences and was to be included in every future strike operation. On the other hand, the Admiralty commented that, however commendable pilots' aggression had been, weapons must, in future, be released as close as possible to the briefed parameters if they were to achieve the necessary effect.

Maintaining deck parks of aircraft at night under Arctic weather conditions was recognised as a possible cause of unserviceability unless special precautions were taken but it was accepted that this was the only way of embarking sufficient aircraft for major operations of this type. The employment of three different types of carrier, five types of

When *Victorious* returned to Scapa Flow after Tungsten she was visited by His Majesty King George VI and Queen Elizabeth. He is seen here on the flight deck with Admiral Sir Bruce Fraser, C-in-C Home Fleet, to the left and Captain M M Denny CB CBE RN, captain of *Victorious*, on the right. King George VI qualified as a pilot before the war and proudly wore his Fleet Air Arm wings on his left sleeve. (*Author's collection*)

aircraft and four types of bomb had complicated the air plan and made co-ordination difficult but it had worked. This was greatly to the credit of the many young air and maintenance crews who were in action at sea for the first time and the aircraft handlers who had made it all happen. The relatively minor number of bomb failures experienced was to the credit of armourers, who had to work quickly in unpleasant conditions.

Further strikes against Tirpitz by the Home Fleet

A Repeat of Tungsten, designated Operation Planet, was planned for 26 April but was cancelled because of forecast bad weather.[18] On 15 May a further strike, designated Operation Brawn, was carried out in which twenty-seven Barracudas from *Victorious* and *Furious* were flown off escorted by twenty-eight Corsairs, four Seafires and four Wildcats. However, as they neared the Norwegian coast they encountered full cloud cover down to 1,000ft and had no choice but to abort. A similar planned attack on 28 May, Operation Tiger Claw, also had to be abandoned because of weather but three days later the same force was able to attack shipping south of Aalesund. On 17 July the Home Fleet attempted a further strike, Operation Mascot,[19] with the fleet carriers *Furious*, *Formidable* and *Indefatigable*, the latter only recently completed and in action for the first time. This time the weather was fine but the Germans had established an observation post on a mountain top from which the smokescreen could be triggered and defensive fire controlled as soon as the approaching aircraft were detected. The strike force this time comprised forty-four Barracudas escorted by eighteen Corsairs, eighteen Hellcats and, for the first time, twelve Fairey Fireflies from *Indefatigable*. At 0204 the observation post alerted the defences and anti-aircraft gun crews manned their weapons. Within ten minutes they were ready and the smokescreen was well established. The Barracudas were just too slow to reach the target and begin their attack against defences that were already

A Corsair taking off from *Formidable* during Operation Goodwood. Note the calm sea surface and the propeller tip vortices caused by the humid atmosphere. (*Author's collection*)

alert when they began their dives at 0220 and the target was almost entirely obscured by smoke. *Tirpitz* felt the detonation of a near miss at 0221 but no other bombs fell near her. Strafing Corsairs sank a 500-ton armed trawler and damaged the destroyer Z33, however.

The Home Fleet's strike power continued to increase through 1944 as a growing number of carriers and naval air squadrons were commissioned and a series of large set-piece strikes on *Tirpitz* were carried out in August designated Operation Goodwood I, II, III and IV. *Tirpitz* had completed post-Tungsten repairs in July and on 31 July she sailed for two days of exercises with other German warships, the last time she was able to do so. The Goodwood attacks were carried out by the fleet carriers *Formidable*, *Furious* and *Indefatigable* supported by the CVEs *Nabob* and *Trumpeter*, which were to provide CAP fighters over the task force together with anti-submarine patrols.

Operation Goodwood – aircraft complements

Formidable
1841 NAS	18 Corsair (6 Naval Fighter Wing)
1842 NAS	12 Corsair (6 Naval Fighter Wing)
826 NAS	12 Barracuda
828 NAS	12 Barracuda

Furious
801 NAS	12 Seafire FIII
880 NAS	12 Seafire LIIC
827 NAS	9 Barracuda

Indefatigable
887 NAS	9 Seafire FIII (24 Naval Fighter Wing)
894 NAS	12 Seafire FIII (24 Naval Fighter Wing)
1840 NAS	12 Hellcat
1770 NAS	12 Firefly
820 NAS	12 Barracuda

Nabob
852 NAS	12 Avenger + 4 Wildcat

Trumpeter
846 NAS	8 Avenger + 4 Wildcat

The frequency with which Barracuda squadrons moved between carriers and naval air stations by this stage meant that they were no longer trained or embarked as part of a TBR wing and from this operation onwards they operated as single squadrons. The first two attacks were carried out on 22 August and differed in that some of the fighters were armed with bombs in the hope that their higher speed would allow them to gain hits and disable the anti-aircraft defences before the smokescreen became effective. The ability to arm Hellcats and Corsairs with bombs of up to 1,000lb showed their quality and they began to assume the dive-bombing duties only carried out previously by TBR aircraft. In Goodwood I low cloud prevented the Barracudas and their escort from reaching *Tirpitz* but Hellcats did manage to carry out an attack at low level and claimed two hits with 500lb bombs. That evening a further sortie by six Hellcat fighter-bombers from *Indefatigable* attacked again at low level and claimed two further hits. However, German records revealed that no hits had been made in either attack. On the afternoon of 22 August *Nabob* was struck aft by an acoustic torpedo fired by *U-354*, which blew a hole 50ft long by 40ft high below the waterline and bent the single propeller shaft. Damage control parties did a superb job of shoring up the after bulkheads and kept her afloat. Despite being well down by the stern, she even managed to fly off two Avengers on an anti-submarine patrol while she made her way slowly, but under her own steam, to Scapa Flow.[20] Emergency work was carried out by the Fleet Maintenance Group in Orkney to keep her afloat but there was insufficient industrial capacity in the UK to repair

Nabob down by the stern after being hit aft by an acoustic torpedo on 22 August 1944. She is making her own way back to Scapa Flow with Avengers parked right forward in Fly 1 to counterbalance the weight of flooding in the after compartments. Remarkably, she managed to fly off aircraft in this state. (*Author's collection*)

Barracuda 'M' of 830 NAS becomes airborne from *Furious* with a 1,600lb bomb for a strike against *Tirpitz* in July 1944. Like the modern ski-jump, the wooden ramp on the forward part of the flight deck was intended to give the effect of lengthening the take-off run available for heavily loaded strike aircraft. In fact, a close study of this photograph shows that this aircraft's wheels have already left the deck inches before it reached the ramp. (*Author's collection*)

her and she was decommissioned on 30 September and left in nominal reserve on a mud bank on the south shore of the Firth of Forth. Her loss was felt keenly by the RCN, which had provided most of her seaman department to gain experience of carrier operations prior to taking over one of the new light fleet carriers. Her air department was provided by the RN and many of the aircrew in 852 NAS came from New Zealand, so some adjustments had to be made to pay scales to avoid friction between the different Commonwealth navies that made up her ship's company.[21]

On the afternoon of 24 August the fleet carriers flew off a further strike against *Tirpitz*, Goodwood II, in which thirty-three Barracudas took part. Each of them carried a 1,600lb armour-piercing bomb as these American weapons were now available in greater quantities, and ten Hellcats each carried a single 500lb bomb. Five of the twenty Corsairs carried a single 1,000lb armour-piercing bomb and the ten Fireflies were briefed to use their four 20mm front guns to suppress anti-aircraft guns. The lessons from Tungsten had been well taken on board and, although the Barracudas approached at 10,500ft, the fighter-bombers closed in at low level from all

Armourers rolling out 1,600lb bombs on modified torpedo trolleys to arm Barracudas on *Formidable* for one of the Goodwood strikes. Corsairs are also being ranged by aircraft handlers. (*Author's collection*)

directions and effectively confused the gunnery control. The alarm was given to the German defences at 1547 and as the aircraft arrived over the target the smokescreen was not yet effective. The attacking aircraft achieved both success and bitter disappointment in this attack. A 500lb bomb hit the top of 'B' turret and its detonation depressed its armoured roof and destroyed the quadruple 20mm mounting on it. It also damaged the elevating mechanism of the starboard 15in gun. The other hit was by a 1,600lb bomb, which penetrated the upper deck and the 5.75in armoured deck below it, finally coming to rest in the lower platform deck but failing to detonate. This was the only 1,600lb bomb to penetrate the armour and German records revealed that when bomb disposal experts managed to extract the fuse they found that the explosive content was only 100lb rather than the designed 215lb. Had it detonated in the position where it was found it would have wrecked the main fire control room and switchboard as well as causing serious flooding. *Tirpitz* would have been rendered useless as a fighting ship and, potentially, even sunk. The German records studied by the Admiralty after 1945 stated that:

> ... the attack of 24 August 1944 was undoubtedly the heaviest and most determined so far. The English showed great skill and dexterity

in flying ... during the dive-bombing, fighter planes attacked the land batteries which, in comparison with earlier attacks, suffered heavy losses. The fact that an armour-piercing bomb of more than 1,540lb did not explode must be considered an exceptional stroke of luck, as the effects of that explosion would have been immeasurable.

Losses on 24 August amounted to a Hellcat and three Corsairs. The Corsair losses included two pilots from 1842 NAS, Sub Lieutenants (A) J H French and E W Thornbury RNVR. The third Corsair pilot was Sub Lieutenant (A) C E Woodward RNZNVR of 1841 NAS; all three were from *Formidable*. The Hellcat pilot who was lost was Lieutenant Commander (A) A R Richardson RNZNVR, the commanding officer of 1840 NAS in *Indefatigable*.

The German naval command in north Norway ordered the time taken for the smokescreen to be deployed to be reduced from ten minutes to seven. Alternate gales and fog delayed a further strike until 29 August, when the last attack of the Goodwood series was carried out. This was another large strike with sixty aircraft flown off *Formidable* and *Indefatigable*; her low fuel state having forced *Furious* to return to Scapa Flow. Four out the seven Hellcats were fitted with target markers, bright flares that were intended to mark *Tirpitz* sufficiently well for the Barracudas to dive-bomb it through the smoke. This was another innovative idea but on this day the battleship was completely obscured by smoke and the aircraft were forced to bomb blind. The aircrew thought hits might have been scored but there were none. A Firefly of 1770 NAS from *Indefatigable* was shot down and its crew, Sub Lieutenants (A) N J Smith and R D Viney RNVR, were both killed. A Corsair of 1842 NAS was also lost and its pilot, Sub Lieutenant (A) J G Walker RNVR from *Formidable*, killed.

In June 1944 Admiral Moore relieved Admiral Fraser as the C-in-C Home Fleet and he wrote a summary for the Admiralty of the carrier strikes he had led against *Tirpitz*. He emphasised the difficulty of forecasting Arctic weather conditions off north Norway sufficiently far ahead to allow a carrier task force to sortie from Scapa Flow with a reasonable expectation of being able to carry out the planned strike. The solution, as the BPF was to find during 1945, was to move away from the flawed RN concept of 'tip-and-run' strikes and embrace under way replenishment, allowing task forces to remain at sea until a suitable weather window opened. It would also allow the force to carry out multiple strikes and dominate a given area of sea for extended periods. The concept was nearly realised when RFA tankers were deployed to refuel destroyers escorting the Russian convoys but its wider application to keep an entire task force in action long enough to achieve its aim if adverse weather was encountered seems to have been a step too far for the Home Fleet staff in 1944. The Fleet Air Arm attacks had caused considerable damage and come agonisingly close to inflicting more with the 1,600lb bomb that did not detonate but from September RAF Bomber Command was tasked with attacking *Tirpitz* using the newly developed 12,000lb Tallboy bombs. Kaa Fjord was beyond the radius of action from the UK of Lancaster bombers armed with Tallboys and so a force of thirty-three Lancasters deployed to Yagodnik, from where they were to carry out an attack. On 15 September twenty-one bombers armed with tallboys and a further six armed with twelve 400lb mines bombed *Tirpitz* through the smokescreen. Norwegian Resistance discovered that a single Tallboy had hit the forecastle about 50ft aft of the stem; it passed through the decks to emerge below the waterline on the starboard side before exploding. Her machinery was shaken by the shock wave and there was considerable flooding forward. This hit ended her operational career and a conference in Berlin on 23 September decided that it was no longer possible to make the ship ready for sea. She was to be moved to Tromsø and grounded as a gun battery to defend the port. *Tirpitz* moved under her own power for the last time on 15 October to be positioned over a spoil bank deposited off Haakoy Island so that she could only sink by about a foot if she was attacked again. Tromsø was just within the radius of action of Tallboy-armed Lancasters flying from Lossiemouth and an attack by thirty-two aircraft was made on 12 November. This caused her to roll over on the spoil bank and she came to rest with much of her lower hull above the water. Of the 1,700 men on board at the time, about 1,000 were drowned despite the order to abandon ship having been given. Holes were cut in the ship's bottom, which allowed eighty-seven men to be rescued. Though she had not been sunk, *Tirpitz* now lay irrecoverably on her side in shallow water.

Convoy RA 59

The crippling of *Tirpitz* in Operation Tungsten gave the Home Fleet the opportunity to convoy the merchant ships assembled in north Russia back to the west in convoy RA 59, the last Arctic convoy until the autumn. It also meant that no heavy covering force was required but an escort force commanded by CS 1, Rear Admiral Sir Rhoderick McGrigor KCB DSO in the cruiser *Diadem* sailed from Scapa Flow for the Kola Inlet on 19 April to rendezvous with the convoy and escort it home. The operation was designated FZ by the Home Fleet and the escort included the CVEs *Activity*, still commanded by Captain Willoughby who remained senior officer escort carriers, and *Fencer*, commanded by Captain W W R Bentinck RN. The force also included sixteen destroyers and four frigates. The outbound passage began only five days after *Activity* had returned from escorting RA 58 but proved uneventful. During the carrier's few days in harbour, however, all her experienced Swordfish crews had been reappointed to squadrons that were due to fly in support of Operation Neptune, the naval element of the Normandy landings in June. They were replaced by three pilots straight from training, who carried out their first deck landings during the outbound passage at the end of a dawn patrol. These did not go well and gave Captain Willoughby grave misgivings about their usefulness during the return passage with the convoy. During his own flying career he had crashed on his second night deck landing in 1931 and was very aware of the skill needed to land on a carrier. One of the Swordfish pilots had to be instructed to ditch after breaking his arrester hook during his first attempt to land on and another demolished his aircraft's undercarriage with an extremely heavy landing. However, *Activity*'s 819 NAS still had three Wildcat pilots left with experience from the previous convoy and these were augmented by five others from 816 NAS, which had done well in JW/RA 57 two months earlier. The squadron embarked with three Swordfish and seven Wildcats. *Fencer* was in better shape, with most of her 842 NAS' experienced crews remaining, albeit with some dilution, but this was her first Arctic operation.[22] It embarked with eleven Swordfish and nine Wildcats. Captain Bentinck was another aviation specialist, having qualified with Number 14 Observer Course in December 1928. His promotion from commander to acting captain to take up this appointment is a strong indication of the Admiralty's desire to place aviation specialists in command of carriers.

Activity anchored in Scapa Flow with Swordfish and Wildcats of 819 NAS on deck. (*Author's collection*)

The pre-sailing plan was for *Activity* to take on the majority of fighter sorties and run the air defence plot while *Fencer* would concentrate on anti-submarine patrols and run the U-boat plot. Each ship was ready to back up the other and, during quiet periods, they could operate watch and watch about. During the outbound passage there was a heavy swell, no wind and patches of fog and it was these unpleasant conditions that had caught out *Activity*'s new Swordfish pilots on their first attempts at deck landing. *Fencer* did most of the flying without sighting any U-boats and also attempted to intercept a suspected shadower with no result. One of her Swordfish crashed on deck, an indication that conditions were far from easy, even for pilots with more experience. This aircraft had to have a new engine and propeller, two new wings and a new undercarriage but all were available on board and the aircraft was serviceable again, albeit without a swung compass, when the ship sailed from Kola, a remarkable achievement under very difficult circumstances. Apart from the disastrous sorties to see how her new pilots would cope with deck landing, *Activity* did no other flying on the outbound voyage. On arrival in Kola on 23 April they had to anchor in Vaenga Bay for several days and they were entertained by an all-male Russian naval concert party of fifty, which reportedly gave an excellent performance.

RA 59 sailed on 28 April and, as in the previous convoys, U-boats were appreciated to be the principal threat with only a minimal threat from aircraft. The focal point of the anti-submarine organisation was the HF/DF plot maintained in *Fencer*, which showed that whenever bad weather interrupted flying U-boat bearings showed them moving into advantageous attacking positions on the surface. In good weather they were kept down by air patrols, their low dived speed forcing them to drop astern. Enemy shadowers, when they did appear, were few in number and on the two occasions when they attempted to close they were driven off by *Activity*'s Wildcats, with one Bv 138 shot down by Lieutenant (A) J G Large RNVR. A second Bv 138 was so badly damaged that it was heard transmitting an SOS saying that its engines had stopped and so it too may have been destroyed. Flying operations were hampered by poor R/T conditions, snowstorms, a following wind, continuous daylight and high seas. Both carriers at one time had 6in of snow on their flight decks and this proved especially difficult for *Activity*, which lacked steam heating needed to clear it quickly. Aircraft handlers had to resort to fire hoses, shovels and brooms. *Fencer* had steam jets for this very purpose and took over all flying while the handlers on *Activity* struggled. She flew anti-submarine patrols despite considerable deck movement during stormy conditions but had no incidents because they were all flown by experienced pilots who had been on board for nine months. Three new crews, fresh from training, were not flown at all because their inexperience risked damage to aircraft that was not acceptable. Once more sonar conditions were bad and aircraft proved to be the most potent anti-U-boat weapons.

When the convoy arrived, *Fencer*'s report modestly claimed one U-boat probably sunk, one damaged and three probably damaged but when they were studied, German records revealed that three boats had been sunk: *U-277*, *U-674* and *U-959*. Over the period in which these sinkings took place *Fencer* kept up anti-submarine patrols for seventy-two hours with only a short break and with additional sorties flown against any promising reports of contact. In this critical period there were sixty-two sorties totalling 150 hours' flying time and fifteen U-boat sightings. Her aircraft might have done even better if they had been armed differently according to Captain Bentinck, who said in his report that:

> ... this may have been due to bad luck or it may be that U-boats decide on their course of action as soon as they can see whether depth charges or R/Ps are carried ... standard procedure was for the latter to be carried by patrol aircraft and this was intended [but] ... at first there was insufficient wind for Swordfish to fly off with R/Ps ... only enough for two depth charges. U-boats remained on the surface as if to fight but dived before the arrival of the strike and pilots returned complaining 'if only we had had R/Ps'. During the middle phase R/Ps were carried but U-boats dived immediately on being sighted and pilots complained 'if only we had had depth charges'. Patrolling in pairs was the only solution but this would have meant two pairs in the air all the time if both ahead and astern sectors [of the convoy] were to be adequately protected.

Once Coastal Command Catalinas were able to take on some of the escort function from 2 May, *Fencer*'s Swordfish did indeed fly in differently armed pairs. Difficulties of communication, however, prevented task force direction officers from guiding the Catalinas towards U-boats that were working their way past the convoy to get into attacking positions ahead of it. Once he had returned to Scapa Flow, CS 1 sent some of his staff officers to the RAF base at Sullom Voe from which the Catalinas operated to explain to the aircrew, in simple terms, the principles of fixing U-boats by HF/DF bearings and the subsequent direction of aircraft to attack them. CS 1 noted in his report that neither RAF aircrew nor their controllers seemed to fully understand naval tactics. They were very keen, however, and willing to co-operate but lacked experience of working with the Home Fleet. That this meeting was deemed necessary after the two services had been working together for four and a half years of war can only be described as disappointing. CS 1 was not the first to recommend that Coastal Command aircrew must receive naval training to make their operations fit for purpose. Nor was he the last.

Captain Willoughby commented that 'a feature of the carrier operations with RA 59 was the extremely high standard of *Fencer*'s deck landing operations. At times she had a great deal of movement on her and in my nineteen years of working in and with carriers, *Fencer*'s showing was as good as, if not better than, I have ever seen before.' Praise from an expert who knew the degree of difficulty they had overcome. Admiral McGrigor[23] wrote that as the threat from the first U-boat concentration of about seven boats built up on the evening of 30 April, when the only merchant ship in RA 59 was torpedoed, HF/DF bearings were received in *Activity*'s plot at the rate of fifteen a minute. Much credit was, he felt, due to the communications and plotting staff in all ships but he had managed to maintain situational awareness with the help of a direction officer 'borrowed' from *Activity* who helped him to keep in touch with the carriers and co-ordinate the activities of destroyers with those of aircraft. He strongly recommended that in future flagships should be given an extra direction officer and this was acted upon for all future Arctic convoys. Whenever possible CVE action information rooms were also brought up to the full standard envisaged by the Admiralty. Communications between direction officers was to be by VHF R/T and it was recommended that this should be used in preference to visual signals to report shadowers to all ships in a task force in order to save time, the slight risk of the transmission being intercepted being acceptable.

By 2230 on 3 May the HF/DF plot showed that the last of the U-boats had dropped well astern and CS 1 ordered *Fencer* to proceed to the Clyde. *Activity* parted company with the escort force and returned to Scapa Flow on 6 May. Only one merchant ship had been lost from RA 59 and set against this the enemy had lost three U-boats and one or probably two reconnaissance aircraft. All had been destroyed by carrier-borne aircraft, which had themselves suffered no losses in action, only the Swordfish that had to be ditched after the unfortunate deck landing episode. *Activity*'s aircraft had flown a total of thirty-five and a half hours and *Fencer*'s exactly 200 hours. When the combat reports from FZ were examined within the Admiralty, NAD criticised the decision to operate *Fencer*'s aircraft close to the convoy; they rarely flew more than 12 miles from it even after the enemy obviously knew the convoy's location. The Admiralty view was that patrols should have been flown to a greater depth. Captain Bentinck made no specific mention in his report of the reason for this restriction in patrol depth but it is reasonable to conclude that the bad weather had much to do with it. There is also the likelihood, given the prevailing conditions, that a strike force flown off on receipt of a sighting report could reach the scene more quickly and stand a better chance of carrying out an effective attack. NAD's criticism was, of course, made before it became aware of the true scale of U-boat losses *Fencer*'s aircraft had achieved; her tactics might not have been perfect but they had a devastating impact on the enemy.

Operation Neptune

Three CVEs, *Emperor* with 800 and 804 NAS embarked with Hellcats, *Pursuer* with 881 and 896 NAS embarked with Wildcats and *Tracker* with 846 NAS embarked with both Avengers and Wildcats, operated in the western part of the English Channel during the initial landing phase to prevent light surface craft and U-boats[24] from interfering with it. They actually encountered little enemy activity and they were soon returned to other tasks. From May a number of naval air squadrons operated from bases ashore at various times and for varying periods while they were disembarked. They provided cover over the English Channel and the convoy routes from the northern UK as Allied forces were built up in Normandy before breaking out into a series of offensive operations to liberate Europe. These included 811, 816, 819, 838, 842, 846, 848, 849, 850, 854 and 855 NAS. During the critical period in June and July ten of

Swordfish of 816 NAS armed with 3in rocket projectiles in D-Day recognition stripes operating from Perranporth in May 1944. (*Author's collection*)

these squadrons were detached on these duties but as their parent carriers needed them to embark they were gradually withdrawn. The planners had thought it possible that attacks might be mounted on invasion traffic from both the west and east and to counter the former squadrons were based at RAF airfields in Cornwall. In fact, most enemy intervention came from the east along the Dutch and Belgian coastlines and the squadrons based in the south-east of England saw the most action.[25] Two squadrons, 811 and 846 NAS, operated on convoy protection tasks from RAF Limavady in Northern Ireland during June and July while disembarked. A collision between *Tracker* and HMCS *Teme* on 10 June meant that the CVE had to be repaired and 846 NAS became available at very short notice. During September and October 811, 825 and 850 NAS moved to Limavady for the same tasking, moving to RAF Mullaghmore in November and December.

Naval air squadrons operated from airfields ashore in support of Operation Neptune

811 NAS	12 Swordfish	Lieutenant Commander (A) E B Morgan RANVR
816 NAS	12 Swordfish	Lieutenant Commander P Snow RN
819 NAS	12 Swordfish	Lieutenant Commander (A) P D T Stevens RNVR
825 NAS	12 Swordfish	Lieutenant Commander (A) F G B Sheffield DSC RNVR
827 NAS	12 Barracuda	Lieutenant Commander (A) K H Gibney DSC RN
838 NAS	12 Swordfish	Lieutenant Commander (A) J M Brown DSC RNVR
842 NAS	12 Swordfish	Lieutenant Commander (A) G F S Hodson RNR
846 NAS	12 Avenger	Lieutenant Commander (A) R D Head DSC RN
848 NAS	12 Avenger	Lieutenant Commander A P Boddam-Whetham RN
849 NAS	12 Avenger	Lieutenant Commander (A) K G Sharp RN
850 NAS	12 Avenger	Lieutenant Commander (A) B White DSC RNVR
854 NAS	12 Avenger	Lieutenant Commander W J Mainprice DFC RN
855 NAS	12 Avenger	Lieutenant Commander J B Harrowar RNR

On 20 April 816 NAS moved to RAF Perranporth under the control of 19 Group Coastal Command and remained there until 7 August,

when it was disbanded. On the same day 849 NAS moved from RNAS Machrihanish to Perranporth and remained there until it was redeployed to the BPF in *Rajah* in September. The third Perranporth unit was 850 NAS, which arrived on 23 April and remained until 1 September, when it moved to RAF Limavady.[26] Another unit, 838 NAS, moved from RNAS Machrihanish to RAF Harrowbeer north of Plymouth on 20 April to operate under the control of 156 Wing, Coastal Command, during the assault phase of Neptune. It remained there until 8 August, when it redeployed to RNAS Worthy Down. Two squadrons operated from RAF Hawkinge; the first was 854 NAS, which arrived on 23 May from RNAS Machrihanish and it remained there until August, when it was redeployed to the BPF for embarkation in *Illustrious*. The other was 855 NAS, which arrived on 26 May. It redeployed to several other RAF airfields from 3 August before being disbanded on 21 October. After disembarking from *Activity*, 819 NAS lost its Wildcat flight and took its Swordfish to RAF Manston on 20 April to operate under the control of 155 Wing Coastal Command. Its aircrew proved particularly proficient in night patrols off the enemy coastline looking for and attacking anything that moved. The other Manston squadron was 848 NAS, which arrived on 20 April and remained until moving to RAF Thorney Island on 14 June, after which it embarked in *Formidable*.

In August several squadrons were redeployed to cover different areas; 849 NAS was the only squadron left at Perranporth, although its aircraft also

Sub Lieutenant (A) R Banks RNVR of 896 NAS in close on his leader flying CAP over escort groups in the south-west approaches to the UK on 9 June 1944. (*Author's collection*)

operated from St Eval. Although based mainly at Harrowbeer, 838 NAS split its flying activities between there and RAF Long Kesh in Northern Ireland. Later, 854 and 855 NAS split their operations between Thorney Island and Hawkinge; 819 NAS operated from both Swingfield and Lee-on-Solent and 848 NAS operated from Thorney Island. During September 855 NAS operated from RAF airfields at Docking, Bircham Newton and Thorney Island and 819 NAS split its time between Bircham Newton and Swingfield. Nos 811, 825 and 850 NAS all operated from Limavady at some stage. The last to arrive had been 825 NAS, which had disembarked from *Vindex*. It moved to Mullaghmore in November before re-embarking in *Vindex* in December. Other later arrivals included 842 NAS, which operated Swordfish from Benbecula, Stornoway, Mullaghmore and Thorney Island from August before being disbanded at the end of the year.

A montage prepared for the Admiralty's aviation journal *Flight Deck*, August 1944 edition, to mark D-Day. The title on the facing page read 'THIS WAS D-DAY AND 886 NAS WAS THERE'. (*Admiralty – Crown Copyright*)

An expansion of the convoy escort task in northern UK waters led to 838 NAS operating from RAF airfields at Benbecula, Dallachy and Fraserburgh from mid-September. The number of squadrons employed on these tasks decreased in October, with 819 NAS operating from Bircham Newton; 825 and 850 NAS operating from Limavady; 838 NAS from Fraserburgh and Dallachy and 842 NAS from Benbecula. A single Barracuda squadron, 827 NAS, disembarked from *Furious* in October with twelve aircraft and operated from RAF airfields at Beccles and then Langham under the control of 16 Group Coastal Command. In November 825 and 850 NAS moved to Mullaghmore. By December there were only five squadrons left on these detached duties ashore. Of these 819 NAS was still based at Bircham Newton but deployed aircraft to forward landing strips B-63 at St Croix, B-65 at Maldeghem and B-83 at Knokke-le-Zoute. The remaining four were 825 and 850 NAS at Mullaghmore and 838 with 842 NAS at Thorney Island.

The naval air squadrons' tasking included sea control over the French, Belgian and Dutch coastlines, anti-submarine patrols and convoy escort. Many flights lasted for several hours and were both arduous and unspectacular but they made a significant contribution to the security of the Normandy landings and later to the opening of the Scheldt and the consequent use of Antwerp to resupply the advancing Allied armies. German records confirmed that these squadrons had achieved a number of successes with a total of twenty-three ships sunk between May and October.[27]

Naval Air Tactical Note Number 5 had been issued by NAD to all the TBR squadrons operating in the English Channel during Neptune. It advised that aircraft should normally operate individually, have a serviceable ASV radar and would be best operated under shore-based radar guidance until the enemy was detected on radar or sighted visually. Contact by ASV IIN would normally be at about 10 miles from a search height of 3,000ft and a ten-minute interval between individual attacks should be the aim. The 100lb A/S bomb was accepted as the lightest that would deal effectively with an E-boat and aircraft should be loaded with as many as possible. Sticks of five or six, fused with a timed detonation of 0.025 seconds after impact, appeared likely to give optimal results and should be considered normal, giving each aircraft the potential for two attacks. With good radar control and reasonable visibility, flare illumination was seldom necessary, particularly when targets were moving at high speed. When they were used, strike aircraft generally used their own but had to ensure that they were not dropped in such a position that they silhouetted themselves. Height on passage to the target depended on weather but should allow good VHF radio contact with the radar control station and 3,000ft was considered ideal. After detecting the enemy, aircrews were advised to manoeuvre into a position where the target was silhouetted against the lightest part of the sky and then attack without delay. Under these conditions the relative line of approach in the dive or run-in would be determined by the amount of natural light but an attack along the line of the target was usually the simplest. A shallow dive was acceptable because the target's length allowed for moderate range errors and deflection errors could be corrected more easily. When attacking across the target the dive should be as steep as practicable, making ranging less liable to error while moderate deflection errors would be taken care of by the width of the target presented. If flares were needed, they were to be laid at right angles and across the target's course in a single stick so that enemy avoiding action could be allowed for. Whether the flares were laid ahead or astern depended on the intended direction of attack but, in either case, allowance had to be made for target speed and surface wind. An attack from ahead with flares laid astern would be less likely to make the target take violent avoiding action and offer a better chance of success. A flame float dropped after the last bomb helped the next aircraft to locate the target.

Squadrons sent monthly summaries of their operations to the Admiralty, where they were used by NAD to compile the CB 3053 *Naval Aircraft Progress* series of publications. They were also used to create the squadrons' own record books. These were maintained by junior officers and varied in quality depending on the authors' skill and the degree of interest shown by their commanding officers. Some were outstanding, others were not.[28] Fortunately, 849 NAS' monthly report for July has survived[29] and it describes how the squadron flew coastal defensive anti-submarine patrols up to 9 July and then offensive anti-submarine patrols in the area west of Brest. No sightings were made and on 21 July the squadron began flying six aircraft anti-shipping sweeps around the Channel Islands in which every aircraft carried four 500lb bombs, which were tail fused with a 0.01-second delay. The first sighting was made at 2030 on 28 July, when three minesweepers and four landing craft were seen leaving St Malo; the leading ship had just passed through the boom defences. Since the harbour was known to be defended by both light and heavy anti-aircraft batteries, the leader decided against carrying out an immediate dive-bombing attack while the ships were mostly still in harbour and he led his aircraft on towards Normandy at 3,500ft. After nearing Granville he turned on to a reciprocal course and arrived over the enemy force, which was now clear of St Malo, at 2050. The aircraft moved into line astern formation and then turned to attack the ships from the beam in a 40-degree dive from 3,500ft. The whole attack from the first to the last bomb drop was over in one minute and left one landing craft

The German convoy attacked by 849 NAS on 28 July 1944. (*Author's collection*)

sinking and two minesweepers surrounded by near misses, one of them shown in photographs to be completely enveloped in smoke and water. This was also considered to have been sunk and later reconnaissance found that the survivors had turned back to St Malo. Every bomb had released satisfactorily but one aircraft, JZ 300, had been hit and damaged by anti-aircraft fire. Its port tailplane and elevator were shot away and there was damage to the port side of centre fuselage, port mainplane and tailfin. Unfortunately the damage to the fuselage resulted in the death of the observer, Lieutenant (A) J J Nixon RNVR. The pilot, Sub Lieutenant T D White RNVR, was slightly wounded in the back but was considered fit to fly again by the end of the month.

Bombardment spotting

Bombardment spotting on D-Day and the subsequent offensive to break out of the Normandy bridgehead was carried out by a composite air unit totalling 143 British and United States pilots. The RN contribution to this effort was Number 3 Naval Fighter Wing led by Commander N G 'Buster' Hallett DSC RN, who had a distinguished career as a fighter pilot with seven air victories.

Number 3 Naval Fighter Wing – RNAS Lee-on-Solent – June 1944
Commander N G Hallett DSC RN

808 NAS	12 Seafire LIIC	Lieutenant Commander (A) J F Rankin DSC RN
885 NAS	12 Seafire LIII/FIII	Lieutenant Commander (A) S L Devonold RN
886 NAS	12 Seafire LIII	Lieutenant Commander P E I Bailey RN
897 NAS	12 Seafire LIIC	Lieutenant Commander (A) W C Simpson DSC RN

The naval wing was grouped with two RAF Spitfire squadrons, 26 and 63, and a single squadron of the US Navy, VCS-7, at Lee-on-Solent and tasked with bombardment spotting. VCS-7 had replaced its Vought Kingfisher OS2U floatplanes with Spitfires from RAF stocks for this operation. When on task the aircraft worked in pairs, one of which made spotting corrections while the other watched for enemy fighters. On 6 June twenty different VHF bombardment frequencies were in use at any one time and the force was briefed to carry out 528 sorties, of which 435 were flown. On this day and on D + 19 when the Cherbourg Peninsula was bombarded, most targets were pre-arranged and each mission was briefed for two targets. On other days the majority of targets were impromptu. Three Army Liaison Sections, each consisting of two Army officers, were available to 3 Wing but they were pooled with the RAF squadrons' liaison

Commander N 'Buster' Hallett DSC RN at RNAS Lee-on-Solent in June 1944. Note the bombed out hangar in the background. (*Author's background*)

officers and their resources shared by all the spotting aircraft. Spotting procedures allowed two different techniques. The preferred option was to report the fall of shot using the clock code and the majority were carried out using this method. The spotter imagined a clock face with its centre on the target and twelve o'clock to its north. The direction of shell bursts from the target were called using the 'clock time' with distance information in yards, for instance 'three o'clock 250' for a shell burst 250yd east of the target. The alternative required the pilot to control the shoot using line of fire corrections in a method known as air control, which was not as popular with ships' gunnery officers. In this method the pilot told the gunners what to do next, up 500, right 400 for instance, with just a few guns firing until the target was bracketed. When it was, the pilot would order 'fire for effect'. If he was correct and the gunners had adjusted their sights as instructed, several broadsides would fall on the target. The RN and USN pilots were not trained in tactical reconnaissance and did not carry cameras but a great deal of valuable tactical information was nevertheless derived from their debriefing, especially on D-Day and during the advance towards Cherbourg.

Number 3 Wing's pilots were specifically trained in bombardment spotting techniques for HM ships in the weeks before D-Day and it was emphasised that this was their primary role. However, the Admiralty appreciated that this task could only be carried out after they had gained control of the airspace in which they operated and that they might have to fight to do so effectively. Air combats over the landing areas fully justified this policy, with most taking place in the first three days of the operation; only one group of Bf 109s attempted to interfere after that. All 3 Wing's Seafires had been fitted with gyro lead-computing gunsights and Commander Hallett wrote in his report that although the period allocated for training had been just sufficient, it had left no time to spare.

Lieutenant (A) R Crosley DSC RNVR flew with 886 NAS as one of the bombardment spotters on 6 June. Fortunately he kept his own diary and left a vivid word picture of events in his book *They Gave Me a Seafire*,[30] in which he described how 'Buster' Hallett had taken over command of the wing in April and made immediate improvements in both equipment and preparation. The Gyro Gunsight Mark IID had only been brought into service in May. It had two 'rings' projected onto a head-up display collimated to infinity in the pilot's line of sight. One was a fixed, 4-degree ring but the second moved. If the pilot kept the pipper at the centre of the moving ring on his target, a gyro mechanism in the sight laid off the correct aim ahead to hit a crossing target. The aim ahead, or deflection angle, varied according to the target's crossing speed but the gyro, which was spinning at constant rpm on a universal fitting known as a Hook's Joint after its inventor, took no account of target speed unless its tilt could be altered to take range into account.[31] A range-finding facility was, therefore, incorporated, which required the pilot to recognise the target type and set its known wingspan on a dial below the head-up display. This was graduated in feet but most pilots painted marks on it for known targets such as the Bf 109 or Fw 190 to make quick selection easier in action. By turning a twist grip on his throttle the pilot expanded or contracted the eight graticules that formed the moving ring so that they just covered the target's wingtips while he kept the pipper on the aiming point, usually its cockpit. By carrying out these actions smoothly and accurately, the ideal aim off was calculated constantly but harsh handling or a big deflection could cause the gyro to topple, in which case the moving ring ceased to function until a further period of smooth tracking allowed it to recover. This was why the fixed ring was retained as a back-up. The sight fitted in the Seafire LIII was ideally suited to long-range fire when smooth tracking was possible and great accuracy was required. It could also be used for rocket firing and bomb dropping with the appropriate settings painted on to the graduated dial. It took out all line of flight errors in the attacking aircraft and computed the actual, not apparent, flight path of the target. It was also designed to allow for the drop in the bullets' line of flight due to gravity and the reduction in bullet velocity over longer ranges. It provided the best means yet devised to overcome the gyroscopic yaw effect of the fighters' propeller disc in a high-powered turning fight. Its one drawback in the Seafire was its size; four times the volume of the sight it replaced. It was only 8in from the pilot's face and made it more difficult for him to bale out.

Another of Hallett's innovations was the removal of the outer 2ft of the Seafires' elliptical wings. This gave them a significantly faster rate of roll without adversely affecting the low-level turning circle. The decreased wing area reduced drag and made the aircraft lighter, which led in turn to a slight increase in speed. Weight was reduced even further by removing the two outboard 0.303in machine guns, which were of little value, and reducing the number of rounds carried for the remaining guns. Even though it had the weight and complication of the wing-fold mechanism, these changes meant that at 3,000ft the Seafire LIII was a better gun platform with more horsepower in a lighter airframe than the Spitfire IX, the latest type in RAF service. The LIII could out-accelerate, out-turn, out-roll and out-climb the Spitfire IX at all altitudes up to 10,000ft. At last the Fleet Air Arm had a fighter that could outperform its RAF contemporary, albeit across a narrow height band.

About the events on D-Day itself, Mike Crosley wrote:

... Don [his wing man, Sub Lieutenant (A) D Keene RNVR] and I flew three times over France spotting for 'Spunyarn' (Warspite) flying a total of six hours – fifty [minutes]. Cloud was rather low and this meant that we had to go down well below light flak height to do our spotting. Four blokes were consequently knocked down. Metcalf of Tiny Devonald's squadron, 885 NAS, managed to bale out over the Isle of Wight on the way back with only a broken arm as the damage. Sub Lieutenants (A) A H Bassett and HA Coghill RNVR were shot down and killed. Lieutenant Wallace was shot down and force-landed in France. My first flight took off at 0735 ... We spent forty-five minutes over France spotting on a heavy gun position near the coast at Trouville. The shoot was fairly accurate by the clock method but the broadsides had no effect as the [enemy] guns could be seen still firing at the same time through the clouds of white concrete flung up by Warspite's shells. Keene was a good number two and let me know where the flak was.

The second shoot was at an impromptu target, taking off at lunch time. Warspite's R/T was better but she wasn't ready to start until it was time for us to go home. On the way home we shot up what could have been a German staff car. This overturned in a field off the road. One occupant got out and ran away. We also strafed and stopped a lorry about to enter a village. It was smoking badly when we left it ... one unexpected worry was the extent of the danger from our own AA [anti-aircraft fire] and fighter aircraft. We had been told, of course, that we would be well protected from the German Luftwaffe not only by our own number twos guarding our tails but by 150 fighters on CAP overhead stacked up to 30,000ft. However, what we had not realised was how boring it must have been for all those RAF and USAAF fighters without an effective air direction room to tell them where to go for the first seventy-two hours and nothing in sight. They naturally looked down to see what was happening and could see us in twos circling over the beach head and countryside. Sometimes we were up to twenty miles inland. They could see that we had square wing tips. They naturally thought, therefore, that we were Bf 109s in spite of the huge black and white ['invasion'] stripes on our wings and around our fuselages and they leapt on us in large numbers. Nothing we said or did for the first three days seemed to be able to stop them.

... we hoped that our bombardment ships would reply at the appointed times to our radio calls. After some minutes of calling, I might receive a reply and managed after a few tries to note down on my knee pad the map reference of the chosen target. The next thing to do was to find the right Army ordnance map in the cockpit somewhere, fold it so that the target's six figure map reference was uppermost and then fly in that direction. Having identified it, to say 'Target Ready' to 'Spunyarn'. While submerged in maps with eyes on the ground and trying to find the target ... the next problem might be a warning from Don over the R/T that there were Spitfire IXs in the area looking aggressive. Eventually things might settle down; 'Spunyarn' this is Red 1 – begin – over.

This is 'Spunyarn' – shot ten (seconds) – over.

This is Red 1 – Roger. Out.

This is 'Spunyarn' (eight seconds later) – Splash – Over.

Then after several more corrections which I would give to their ranging shots:

This is 'Spunyarn' – firing for effect – over.

Splash, splash, splash – over.

This is Red 1 – seen – target obliterated – smoke and corruption everywhere – good shooting – over.

This is 'Spunyarn' – thanks – out.

In addition to flying in pairs for bombardment spotting, Number 3 Wing also carried out fighter sweeps near enemy airfields to prevent fighters from attacking the spotters while they were on task. The formation normally flown in the combat area during these sweeps was the standard naval fighter formation. On long sweeps Commander Hallett led sixteen, twenty-four or thirty-two aircraft. The most commonly used number was twenty-four and these were disposed in three groups of eight aircraft, each further sub-divided into sections of four with the leader's two sections flying at 8,000ft. The second group of eight would fly stepped down into sun at approximately 6,000ft, all sixteen aircraft flying loosely in 'battle' or 'finger-four' formation with the second sections slightly astern of the leaders' sections. The remaining eight aircraft flew in very open line abreast at 2,000 to 3,000ft above the leader's section, their task being to spot and attack any aircraft about to 'bounce' the lower flights. The formation chosen for this flight was intended to make the top flight very difficult for enemy aircraft to spot, allowing it to get into attacking positions quickly and to give them complete freedom of tactical manoeuvre.

Whilst engaged on fighter sweeps west of the River Orne during the early days of the operation, Number 3 Wing pilots spotted several enemy 'human torpedoes', which they strafed with their cannon and destroyed. They were all moving at slow speed on the surface at the time and proved extremely vulnerable to fighters. Overlord was the first time four RN fighter squadrons had operated together either from a carrier or a shore base and it was decided from the outset that it would be more effective to centralise maintenance rather than have each squadron plan its own. Under this new system, all trades were responsible to the senior Air Engineering Officer, who was himself responsible to Commander Hallett. A full range of Seafire stores were obtained and held by Lee-on-Solent to support the wing, together with sufficient stores to support the two RAF Spitfire squadrons and those of VCS-7. In order to cope with the amount of extra work this entailed, Lee's air supply staff was itself reorganised into a single, centralised unit tasked with supporting the bombardment spotting aircraft to the best of their ability. The operation lasted for about six weeks and the centralised storage and maintenance systems worked admirably. Even after the first three days, when a daily total of more than 600 sorties had to be flown, the standard of maintenance was so high that no restrictions had to be placed on the wing's tasking.

Strike operations in the Norwegian littoral
The growing Home Fleet campaign against enemy traffic in Norwegian coastal waters was intended to interdict German logistic support, thus weakening the enemy's hold on Norway. It should not be judged merely on the number of ships sunk or damaged because many more had to be held in port for fear of attacks by carrier aircraft. The strikes also stretched German defences to their limit and encouraged the Norwegian resistance movement. At first the dissemination of Norwegian shipping intelligence to the Home Fleet staff had been slow. This led the Admiralty to establish a Norwegian shipping plot kept by officers lent for the purpose from ACOS, Coastal Command and the Admiralty's operational intelligence centre, and dissemination became much quicker as 1944 progressed. It was agreed that Coastal Command should attack shipping south of Stadlandet and the Home Fleet's carrier-borne aircraft would carry out strikes further north. However, as accurate minelaying tactics by carrier

aircraft progressed, narrow channels south of Stadlandet were mined by RN aircraft to force enemy shipping out into the open sea, where Coastal Command aircraft were better able to attack them. Admiral Moore, who succeeded Admiral Fraser as C-in-C, wrote that co-operation between the two organisations was now excellent.

Operation Ridge Able

Carried out on 26 April, Ridge Able was an attack on enemy shipping in and around Bodø by two Home Fleet task forces designated as Forces 7 and 8. Force 7 was commanded by VA 2 BS in *Anson* with *Victorious*, *Furious*, *Kent* and seven destroyers. Force 8 was commanded by RAEC in *Royalist* with *Searcher*, *Emperor*, *Pursuer*, *Striker* and *Jamaica* with a further seven destroyers. As in Tungsten, the assault carriers were gaining experience before their planned deployment to the Mediterranean. The attack was carried out by two air striking forces; the first comprised eighteen Barracudas from 8 TBR Wing with aircraft from both *Victorious* and *Furious* escorted by four Wildcats from *Pursuer*'s 896 NAS and a further eight Wildcats from *Searcher*'s 882 NAS. Twelve Hellcats from *Emperor*'s 800 and 804 NAS provided top cover. The second comprised nine Barracudas from 52 TBR Wing, again drawn from both fleet carriers, escorted by four Wildcats from 881 NAS and four from 896 NAS in *Pursuer* and eight Wildcats from *Searcher*'s 898 NAS. Twelve Corsairs from 1834 and 1836 NAS in *Victorious* provided top cover. Each Barracuda was armed with three 500lb

Wildcats of 881 and 882 NAS with two Hellcats from 804 NAS set heading having formed up near *Searcher* for a strike sortie off the Norwegian coast. (*Author's collection*)

bombs. Aircraft from *Furious* and *Striker* were flown off to provide CAP and anti-submarine patrols around the forces.

Both strikes were flown off from single ranges in their respective carriers, joining up once they were airborne. Strike I was briefed to set heading directly for Bodø to attack shipping in the anchorage, while Strike II was briefed to search the leads north and south of Bodø to attack any shipping found under way. Strike I's leader was to report shipping seen leaving the anchorage to the leader of Strike II. Departure times from the form-up areas were briefed as thirty-five minutes after the first aircraft was catapulted from *Victorious* for Strike II and forty-five minutes for Strike I. Strike I formed up 4 miles from the CVEs on the side away from an imaginary line between the fleet and escort carriers. Strike II formed up 4 miles from the fleet carriers on the imaginary line joining the two forces.[32] The fighters joined the Barracudas once they had formed up and were ready to set heading. The plan stipulated that zero hour would be the time at which the first Barracuda was catapulted from *Victorious* and this proved to be 0432. The weather was poor with a bitter westerly wind at 18 knots causing a slight sea and a short, moderate swell. Visibility was assessed as 8 miles in the clear patches between snowstorms, with complete cloud cover at 1,500 to 2,500ft, but the freezing level was at only 500ft. The first aircraft catapulted off *Victorious* was Lieutenant Commander Rance in the leading Barracuda of 52 TBR Wing, followed quickly by three more Barracudas and *Victorious*' Corsairs, but from then onwards the form-up went slowly and Strike II did not set heading until 0510. Lieutenant Commander Baker-Faulkner was airborne at 0445 to lead 8 TBR Wing and his Strike I was formed up much more quickly by 0455. The actual, rather than planned, departure times caused some confusion in RAEC's staff, which assumed that the aircraft taking departure first had become Strike I. An unnecessarily complicated plan limited the attack's effectiveness, with Strike I taking departure first at 0506, eleven minutes earlier than the time laid down in the signalled plan. Strike II followed between 0510 and 0513, five minutes later than in the signalled plan. This confused the fighter escorts as they attempted to join the Barracudas. Red flight of 896 NAS from *Pursuer* joined Strike I when it should have joined Strike II. *Searcher*'s Wildcats also experienced difficulty in joining up with Strike I, possibly due to the Barracudas not forming up in the briefed position but more probably due to the bad visibility and the distance of the form-up position from the CVEs. These misunderstandings are difficult to comprehend from combat reports read long after the event, but it is easy to imagine how difficult the situation must have appeared to the pilots at the time as they flew under low cloud between snow showers.

After frequent southerly alterations of course to avoid snow squalls, Strike I made landfall 38 miles south-west of Bodø at 0540 and turned up the coast towards their briefed target. As they emerged from a snow squall near Arn Island, Baker-Faulkner sighted a convoy of five merchant ships heading south escorted by one or two flak ships. The cloud base was at 2,400ft with heavy, intermittent snow. He led his force up to the cloud base and then into a diving attack while the fighters strafed the flak ships. Hits were claimed on three large merchant ships and a smaller one was claimed to have been sunk. None of the aircraft in Strike I carried out their briefed mission to attack shipping in Bodø, no enemy fighters were encountered and the force returned to the fleet for recovery. One Barracuda of 827 NAS was lost and its crew were all killed. They were Sub Lieutenant (A) J D Herrold DSC RNZNVR, his observer Sub Lieutenant (A) G Alexander RNVR and TAG Leading Airman W Murray. A Hellcat and its pilot, Sub Lieutenant (A) B F Brine RNVR of 804 NAS, were lost together with a Wildcat from which the pilot survived.

Strike II made landfall at 0546 at Ness, which was well south of Bodø, and turned north to search the leads. The leader of Strike I's escort, who was with Strike II by mistake, flew on to Bodø in an effort to re-join his planned force but failed to make contact and eventually returned to the fleet with neither. A beached and derelict merchant ship was sighted at 0550 and the starboard column broke away to attack it without orders. Two of the aircraft heard their leader's call not to attack this ship and complied but in the prevailing conditions of snow and low cloud they failed to find and re-join the port column of this strike force. They made their way separately to Bodø with four fighters as escort. Once over the harbour they saw and attacked a merchant ship but were not sure if they had hit it. At 0601 the remainder of Strike II came across the convoy attacked previously by Strike I. It appeared to consist of three merchant vessels, one ashore and on fire, one stopped close inshore and one picking up survivors covered by the two flak ships. The leader felt that there was little chance of penetrating into Bodø anchorage and so he ordered an attack on the remaining merchant ships and their escort at 0624. Several near misses were claimed but two Corsairs were lost. Their pilots were rescued and the remaining aircraft all recovered safely to their carriers, although by the time they arrived overhead the weather had deteriorated and the sea state had got worse, causing violent motion on the CVEs.

Although a convoy had been targeted, NAD minuted that shipping in Bodø had not been attacked effectively and this had been the primary objective of Strike I. Had Strike I adhered to its briefing and left the convoy to Strike II both objectives could have been achieved. Several lessons were drawn out of aspects of this operation that had clearly not gone well. Future plans must make clear beyond all doubt how rendezvous and form-up instructions were to be carried out with no margin for misunderstanding.

They should never require two streams of aircraft to take-off and then cross over each other's flight path, and NAD stated emphatically that if two strike forces with different briefed objectives were to be flown off there must be a gap of at least fifteen minutes between them. A repeat strike operation by the same forces later in the day, designated Ridge Baker, was cancelled because the weather continued to deteriorate. Six Corsairs of 1834 NAS were flown off *Victorious* in the afternoon, however, briefed to carry out an armed reconnaissance of beaches and landing grounds in the Narvik area to encourage enemy suspicions that the Allies were planning to land in Norway. This sortie was designated as Operation Veritas and timed to coincide with the passage of convoy RA 59. Further strikes, planned to combine attacks by carrier-borne and RAF aircraft and designated as Operations Pitchbowl I and II, were cancelled because of continuing bad weather.

Operation Croquet

Croquet was carried out by *Furious*, *Searcher* and *Berwick* with six destroyers on 6 May. It had been intended to carry out the operation a day earlier but when the force reached the flying off position the weather over the target area was forecast as unsuitable and the force stood out to sea in the hope that the weather would improve. The flying off position was regained at 0630 on 6 May and the planned attack went ahead. Its object was the destruction of enemy shipping between the leads off the Norwegian anchorage at Bud and the island of Smolen. The strike force comprised eighteen Barracudas from 827 and 830 NAS in *Furious* flown off in two ranges, escorted by twenty Wildcats from 882 and 898 NAS in *Searcher*. Eight of the Barracudas were armed with torpedoes and the remaining ten were each armed with three 500lb MC bombs filled with Torpex and fused for a 0.4-second delay. The Wildcats were briefed to give fighter cover to the Barracudas and to support their attacks by smothering anti-aircraft fire from the escorts.[33] Fighter protection over the fleet was provided by 880 NAS Seafires from *Furious*. Ten Barracudas of 827 NAS began to fly off *Furious* at 0642 and at the same time *Searcher* flew off ten Wildcats. At 0720 *Furious* flew off the second range, this time of eight Barracudas, and the first Seafire CAP as *Searcher* flew off a further ten Wildcats. They joined up with the aircraft already airborne and on this occasion the strike formed up quickly and efficiently before taking its departure at 0725.

The aircraft flew at 50ft to remain below enemy radar cover but started to climb when the coast was sighted 20 miles away. When the leader estimated they were 10 miles off the coast they turned north to fly parallel to it at 4,000ft and almost immediately two merchant vessels escorted by two flak ships were seen heading south. Four Barracudas, three of them armed with bombs and one with a torpedo, were detached to attack them with four Wildcats. The latter dived immediately to strafe the escorts and the Barracudas followed them, obtaining a probable torpedo hit and a certain bomb hit on one of the merchant ships, which was seen to break up and sink. This was the first operational torpedo attack to be carried out by a Barracuda with its Type F analogue computer system and clearly it worked very well. After the war this ship was identified as the *Almora*. The smaller ship was damaged by near misses. One Barracuda was shot down from this group.

The remainder of the strike force continued to fly up the coast and soon sighted another convoy, this one comprising three merchant ships in line ahead escorted by two flak ships on either beam and a destroyer ahead of them. They were attacked from 0808 in the face of intense anti-aircraft fire, which shot down a second Barracuda. Unfortunately most of the Wildcats went after two Bv 138s that were orbiting the convoy, leaving too few to suppress the enemy fire effectively. Both enemy aircraft were shot down but the TBR pilots found their attacks made more difficult by the volume of enemy fire. Nevertheless, a large freighter was hit by two bombs and a torpedo. A tanker, later identified as the *Saarburg*, suffered one bomb and two torpedo hits that left it stopped and severely damaged. The bombs had been released at an average height of 1,600ft and the torpedoes, which all ran correctly, were dropped at a range of 1,000yd. Once the attack was over the strike force returned to the carriers and their recovery was completed by 0944. The crews of both Barracudas were lost; Sub Lieutenant (A) J R Brown RNVR of 827 NAS with his observer Sub Lieutenant (A) D L Pullen RNVR and TAG Leading Airman W H A Reynolds;[34] Sub Lieutenant (A) J A Grant RNVR of 830 NAS with his observer Sub Lieutenant (A) A C P Walling RNVR and TAG Leading Airman B P Bussey.

Throughout both attacks the weather had remained clear, although the light wind forced *Furious* to steam at high speed to launch the heavily laden Barracudas, causing her to become widely separated from *Searcher*, which had no problem launching its Wildcats. No enemy fighters were encountered throughout the operation, a sign of growing German weakness. On the strike's return, one Wildcat was unable to lower its arrester hook but was saved from having to ditch by landing on *Furious*, which worked up to her maximum speed to give 34 knots of wind over the deck, allowing the pilot to brake to a stop in the amount of flight deck available. Apart from the fighters' concentrating on the Bv 138s rather than their briefed task of flak suppression, Croquet was a model of its kind that acted as an example for future operations in the Norwegian littoral. It also confirmed how effective the Barracuda, with its computerised sighting system, was as a torpedo aircraft, but by mid-1944 there were few targets left for it.

Operation Hoops

On completion of Croquet her limited endurance forced *Furious* to return to Scapa Flow but *Searcher* was joined off the Norwegian coast by *Emperor* and *Striker* to carry out attacks on enemy shipping between Gossen and Kristiansand North, together with oil tanks and a fish oil factory at Fossevag. Hoops was carried out on 8 May in clear weather with a 35-knot wind at sea level and good visibility. Two strikes were flown off, the first of which comprised eight Hellcats from 800 NAS embarked in *Emperor*, each armed with a single 500lb MC bomb, with eight Wildcats from 882 NAS from *Searcher* as escort. Swordfish and Sea Hurricanes of 824 NAS were embarked in *Striker* to provide anti-submarine patrols and CAP over the task force. As soon as these aircraft had been flown off, a second strike force was ranged in *Emperor* and *Searcher*. This comprised eight Hellcats from 804 NAS, each armed with a single 500lb MC bomb, with eight Wildcats of 898 NAS as escort. The two groups sighted and attacked an enemy convoy of nine ships escorted by six flak ships and the Hellcats attacked it using a glide-bombing technique while the escorting Wildcats strafed the flak ships, attempting to suppress their fire.[35] Two Wildcats were shot down and one of their pilots, Sub Lieutenant (A) J A Cotching DSC RNVR, was killed. Enemy fighters arrived at the height of the action and of these one Fw 190 and two Bf 109s were shot down, together with two Bv 138 flying boats that had been escorting the convoy. Unfortunately two Hellcats were shot down and their pilots killed, Sub Lieutenant (A) R A Cranwell RNZNVR of 804 NAS and Sub Lieutenant (A) R L Thompson RNVR of 800 NAS. One patrol vessel, later identified as *V 5704*, was seen to be on fire after the Hellcat attack but no other ships were damaged.

Operations Potluck A and B

Six days after Hoops, aircraft from *Emperor* attacked shipping at Rørvik and the fish oil factory at Fossevag in further strikes designated as Potluck A and B. Anti-submarine patrols and CAP were again flown by the Swordfish and Sea Hurricanes of 824 NAS in *Striker*; this was one of the last occasions in which Sea Hurricanes were flown operationally and they were replaced by Wildcats in 824 NAS Fighter Flight later in the month. Potluck A was carried out on 14 May and began with two Hellcats of 800 NAS being flown off to carry out a reconnaissance of the coastal waters off Rørvik.[36] When they located enemy shipping in the harbour, a strike force of eight Hellcats from 804 NAS was flown off, each armed with a single 500lb MC bomb, escorted by seven Hellcats from 800 NAS. Three enemy merchant ships were assessed as having been hit by bombs and German records revealed that *Tyrifjord* had been severely damaged in Rørvik. An attempt to interfere with the attack by several Bf 110 fighters was driven off without loss on either side but four He 115 floatplanes at their moorings in the harbour were destroyed by the Hellcats. One of 800 NAS' Hellcats was lost and its pilot, Sub Lieutenant (A) R Hollway RNVR, was killed.

Potluck B was carried out early on the morning of 15 May, briefed to destroy the fish oil factory. It comprised eight Hellcats from 804 NAS, each armed with a single 500lb bomb, escorted by nine Hellcats from 800 NAS. The weather on this day was worse with the cloud base down to 800ft in places, which made the results difficult to assess. There was no enemy interference, however, and all the aircraft were recovered safely by 0545 as the carriers withdrew towards Scapa Flow. Despite the lack of any outstanding success in these operations, the Admiralty noted with satisfaction after studying the combat reports that bomb-armed fighters were now the most efficient means of carrying out strikes of this nature. They were able to close their targets more quickly than TBR aircraft and once they had dropped or jettisoned their bombs they were able to engage enemy fighters if necessary. The balance of air group composition was continuing to shift towards larger numbers of fighter-bomber aircraft such as the Hellcat and Corsair with TBR aircraft now specialising in minelaying and anti-submarine work.

Two projected operations, Proteus and Cambridge, on 15 May were cancelled because of the low cloud. These had been intended as an armed reconnaissance of the Narvik area as a feint before the Normandy landings began, hoping to convince the Germans that an amphibious assault in the north of Norway was imminent.

Operation Lombard

When bad weather forced the cancellation of Operation Tiger Claw, a set-piece attack on *Tirpitz* in Kaa Fjord, the task force centred on *Victorious* and *Furious* remained at sea until the weather improved in order to carry out Operation Lombard when the weather improved. This was to be an attack on shipping known to be at Aalesund and the coastal waters near it, and it was eventually carried out on 1 June. The attacking force comprised sixteen Barracudas, each armed with three 500lb bombs, made up from 829, 831, 827 and 830 NAS in the two fleet carriers escorted by twenty-two Corsairs from 1834 and 1836 NAS in *Victorious* as mid and high cover. Twelve Seafires from 801 and 880 NAS in *Furious* provided close cover while others remained on CAP over the task force. The ability of Seafires to carry larger drop tanks meant that, at last, they could be used for longer-range missions in support of strike forces, although they never achieved a radius of action comparable with the Hellcat and Corsair. The weather was good with minimal cloud cover and limitless visibility.

A enemy convoy of three merchant ships with their escort was located and attacked off Kram Island. German records showed that two ships were sunk, *Leonhart* and the flak ship *Sperrbrecher 181*. *Florida* was badly damaged and run aground, later becoming a total loss, together with another, smaller, vessel. The convoy escort and two other flak ships were strafed by fighters and their fire suppressed. One Corsair and one Seafire were shot down, the pilot of the latter, Sub Lieutenant (A) K R Brown RNVR of 801 NAS, being killed. Another projected attack on shipping in the Norwegian leads by aircraft from *Victorious* and *Furious*, designated Operation Kruschen, was to have been carried out on 8 June but was cancelled because of bad weather. The number of operations cancelled or aborted because of bad weather, even during summer, in the waters off Norway are indicative of how bad operating conditions could be.

Operations Wanderers and Blues

Between 20 and 23 June *Striker* and *Fencer* joined *Sheffield* and six destroyers in a search for U-boats in north Norwegian waters designated as Operation Wanderers. Its aim was to force the Germans to retain U-boats in the north, from where they could not oppose the Normandy landings. It was also intended to maintain the fiction that the Allies were about to carry out a major amphibious landing in north Norway and, as if that were not enough, to simulate the passage of a Russian convoy covering force. Continuous anti-submarine patrols were carried out by the Swordfish of 842 NAS in *Fencer* with Wildcats from the same squadron's fighter flight maintaining CAP together with those of 824 NAS in *Striker*. No confirmed contacts were made and the impact of the operation on the enemy's plans was probably minimal.

A similar operation further south was carried out by *Furious* on 22 June, intended to give the impression of an imminent amphibious assault as well as simulating an anti-submarine sweep. Six Barracudas of 827 NAS were flown off, each armed with three depth charges, escorted by three Seafires of 801 NAS. They were briefed to fly to the limit of their endurance towards the Norwegian coast at low level, then break W/T silence and carry out three mock attacks on U-boats before climbing as they returned to the carrier to ensure that they were detected by German radar. The mission was carried out exactly as briefed but again it probably had very little impact, although it did demonstrate that even a small carrier task force could now operate with impunity off the enemy-held coast, even when it deliberately showed off its presence.

Operation Turbine

Turbine was a further attack on enemy shipping planned to take place on 3 August. Its two aims were to provide combat experience for the air group of the new fleet carrier *Indefatigable* and to maintain pressure on German forces in Norway to prevent them being withdrawn for operations in France and the Low Countries. *Furious* also formed part of the task force.[37] *Indefatigable* operated one of the largest air groups yet formed for a British carrier and for this operation it comprised Number 24 Naval Fighter Wing with 887 and 894 NAS, each with twelve Seafire FIIIs; 1840 NAS with twelve Hellcats; 1770 NAS with twelve Fireflies and both 820 and 826 NAS, each with twelve Barracudas, for a total of seventy-two aircraft. For this operation she also had CS 1 embarked. *Furious* retained the twenty-one Barracudas of 827 and 830 NAS together with the twenty-four Seafires of 801 and 880 NAS. Unfortunately, when the force arrived at the flying off position the weather was too bad to undertake anything but a low-level fighter sweep. Sixteen Seafires were flown off *Indefatigable* and eight from *Furious* but they found fog in all the leads they attempted to enter. They did, however, find several enemy gun positions and radio masts near Holmen Graa and strafed them before being forced to return to the carriers as the weather deteriorated still further. The results of the attacks could not be observed and, since the weather forecast showed no sign of improvement, the operation was abandoned.

Operation Offspring

This was the Home Fleet's largest air mining operation of the Second World War and the task force that carried it out included *Indefatigable*, *Trumpeter* and the RCN-manned *Nabob*. CS 1 was embarked in *Indefatigable* again but her air group was slightly reduced by the disembarkation of 826 NAS' Barracudas to RNAS Grimsetter in Orkney. *Trumpeter* had 846 NAS embarked with eight Avengers and four Wildcats, while *Nabob* had 852 NAS embarked with twelve Avengers and four Wildcats. By this stage of the war the CVE air groups underwent frequent changes. The Admiralty recognised that squadrons had become expert in differing roles and they were moved between ships at short notice for specific tasks. The aim of Offspring was to lay a minefields in Haarhamsfjord and Lepsorev intended to disrupt coastal shipping used to support German garrison troops. The opportunity was also taken to carry out a diversionary fighter sweep against Gossen airfield and other targets of opportunity.[38]

The Avengers and Barracudas each carried a single Type A Mark I mine and between them they laid forty-seven mines in two strikes. The amount of shipping sunk by the minefields was never known for certain but its avoidance caused considerable disruption and German records revealed that the minesweeper *R-89* was sunk during attempted clearance operations. Fighter sweeps strafed a W/T station on Vigra Island and set fire to an oil tank. The airfield at Gossen was well strafed with at least six Bf 110 fighters destroyed on the ground and barracks left burning. One Avenger, one Firefly and three Seafires were shot down. The 846 NAS Avenger crew lost were Sub Lieutenant (A) J A Gaunt RNVR, Sub Lieutenant (A) A Salisbury RNVR, his observer, and Petty Officer Airman J H Ashton, his TAG. The Firefly crew from 1770 NAS were Lieutenant (A) J A Davies RNVR and his observer Sub Lieutenant (A) D R Bennet RNVR. The Fleet Air Arm Roll of Honour does not list any Seafire pilots lost on this day so it appears that the pilots of the three Seafires were rescued.

Operation Begonia

After the Goodwood series of strikes against *Tirpitz* in August and September, the Home Fleet resumed air mining operations in the Norwegian leads. Begonia was carried out on 12 September by *Furious* and *Trumpeter*. By then *Furious*' elderly machinery was deteriorating rapidly and her experienced engineering staff were desperately needed for the large number of light fleet carriers being brought into service. After her return from Begonia she was paid off into reserve on 15 September. The occasion was marked by signals from the Admiralty and the C-in-C Home Fleet, which paid tribute the ship's unique contribution to the development of naval aviation over more than a quarter of a century. After a brief spell as an accommodation ship, she was towed to Loch Striven, near Rothesay, where she was used for bombing trials and investigations into the effects of bomb near misses on her hull and machinery. She was sold to the British iron and Steel Corporation in 1948 for scrap, although not finally demolished until 1954 at Troon. For Begonia she had retained the same air group as in the earlier strikes. With *Nabob* damaged and taken out of service in Goodwood I, 852 NAS was added to 846 NAS in *Trumpeter*'s air group.

Begonia's aim was for the Avengers to lay a minefield off Vaagso and attack any shipping targets of opportunity. One of the eighteen Avengers flown off was hit by flak and jettisoned its mine after suffering a hydraulic failure;[39] the other seventeen laid their mines successfully. Sixteen Seafires of 801 and 880 NAS from *Furious* provided close and top cover for the strike aircraft and were briefed to strafe any vessels encountered after the lay was complete. They found an enemy minesweeper in Aramsund Channel and sank it with cannon fire. They also sank two other vessels identified from German records as *VP-5307* and *VP-5105*. One Seafire was lost and its pilot, Sub Lieutenant (A) M A Glennie RNVR, killed. Three Seafires and four Avengers were damaged by anti-aircraft fire.

Two further air minelaying operations by the Home Fleet, designated Operations Divan and Tenable, were planned for 19 and 30 September but had to be cancelled because of bad weather.

Operation Lycidas

Trumpeter and *Fencer* carried out two further minelaying strikes on 14 and 15 October. They had Avengers and Wildcats of 846 and 852 NAS distributed between to lay mines off Haarhamsfjord, Lepsorev and Ramsoysund and to attack shipping known to be in Frohavet. In the first strike eleven Avengers were flown off *Trumpeter* with an escort of eleven Wildcats, four from *Trumpeter* and seven from *Fencer*. Unfortunately a navigational error in *Fencer*'s launch position resulted in aircraft making a landfall too far to the south and the mines intended for Haarhamsfjord on 14 October were actually laid in deep water off Sando that was seldom used by enemy coastal traffic and in Aramsund Channel in positions close to those laid a month earlier.[40] A day later, on 15 October, a second strike by eleven Avengers laid eleven mines successfully in Ramsoysund without meeting any opposition. Later on the same day seven Avengers from *Trumpeter*, each armed with three 500lb MC bombs, attacked a medium-sized merchant ship In Frohavet. They were escorted by three Wildcats from *Trumpeter* and five from *Fencer*. There were two flak ships close to the vessel, which put up intense light anti-aircraft fire but this was cut down by persistent strafing attacks on them by the fighters. The Avengers carried out a glide-bombing attack on the merchant ship in which they scored one definite hit and a very near miss. German records revealed that *Olga Traber* had been damaged and the coaster *Christiania* was damaged in the minefield several days later.

In August the new fleet carrier *Implacable* began to work up with 828 and 841 NAS embarked with Barracudas. In September 1771 NAS embarked with Fireflies but the Seafire wing intended for her was still being re-equipped with new aircraft after serving in *Furious*. She joined the Home Fleet in Scapa Flow on 7 October and sailed on 18 October with a destroyer escort for an unnamed operation to locate *Tirpitz*, which was

Implacable photographed shortly after her completion carrying out sea trials off Arran. (*Author's collection*)

Tirpitz located and photographed off Haakoy Island, Tromsø, by Fireflies of 1771 NAS on 16 October 1944. The white dots are tracer rounds being fired at the aircraft taking the photograph. (*Author's collection*)

known to have moved from Kaa Fjord to Tromsø. A section of Fireflies located and photographed her anchored south of Haakoy Island and her captain, Captain L D Mackintosh DSO DSC RN, sought permission to launch a Barracuda strike against it armed with torpedoes. The C-in-C Home Fleet rejected the proposal, however, because of the lack of fighters to escort the strike aircraft. This decision must have galled Captain Mackintosh, who had commanded *Eagle* during the Pedestal convoy and then *Victorious* while she served with the US Navy in the Pacific during 1943. He knew that Fireflies could provide a strike escort but would be unable to match single-seat fighters if they were encountered. In fact, the Luftwaffe had few fighters available to defend the battleship and lacked the inclination to use the ones it did have for this purpose but no one in *Implacable* or the Home Fleet knew that. Fireflies did carry out a series of armed reconnaissance sorties, however, and used their cannon armament to good effect. One He 115 was destroyed at its mooring in Soreisen and a Bv 138 badly damaged. Two aircraft were destroyed on the ground at Bardufoss and a vessel later identified as *Levante* was damaged at Mosjøen. There was no enemy air opposition but one Barracuda of 841 NAS was lost carrying out an anti-submarine patrol and its crew killed, Lieutenant (A) R M Goodfellow RNZNVR, his observer Sub Lieutenant (A) G A Hall RNVR and TAG Petty Officer Airman P W Maitland.

Operation Hardy

A further attempt to mine Haarhamsfjord and Lepsorev was made on 24 October by Avengers of 846 and 852 NAS in *Trumpeter*. This time *Campania* joined them with 813 NAS embarked, a composite squadron equipped with twelve Swordfish for task force anti-submarine protection and eight Wildcats. The first lay was carried out by eight Avengers escorted by Wildcats and was achieved accurately without interference by enemy fighters despite an enemy radar station at Vigra detecting them. Once the mines were laid the Wildcats strafed the enemy airfield at Gossen, where one Wildcat was damaged by anti-aircraft fire and forced to ditch but its pilot was rescued. A second lay by a further eight Avengers was also successful. The force waited in the vicinity for a further day in the hope that another anti-shipping strike would be possible but the weather deteriorated, further activity was cancelled and the task force returned to Scapa Flow. The new minefield was known to have sunk at least one vessel, the coaster *Ira*, and German records confirmed that the Wildcat attacks on Gossen had damaged an equipment depot significantly.[41]

Operation Athletic

On the same day as Hardy, *Implacable* sailed from Scapa Flow flying the flag of Admiral Moore, now C-in-C Home Fleet, with *Mauritius* and six destroyers to continue attacks on enemy shipping, particularly vessels known to be moving German troops out of Norway to Germany. This time *Implacable* had her full air group embarked comprising the twenty-four Barracudas of 841 and 828 NAS, which constituted Number 2 TBR Wing; twenty-four Seafires of 887 and 894 NAS, which constituted Number 24 Naval Fighter Wing, and twelve Fireflies of 1771 NAS. At 0835 on 26 October she flew off eight Barracudas, each armed with three 500lb MC bombs, and eleven Fireflies to search the leads from Melofjord to Sandnessjøen. Within forty-five minutes a convoy comprising three LCTs and a coaster was located and attacked. One LCT was sunk by bombs and the remaining two set on fire by the Fireflies' 20mm cannon. The coaster was driven ashore and all nineteen aircraft returned to the carrier safely. A second strike was flown off from 1418 to carry out an armed reconnaissance in the Rørvik area. This was intended to consist of five Barracudas with nine Fireflies as escort but unfortunately one Barracuda crashed into the sea on take-off and its TAG, Petty Officer J W Bone of 828 NAS, was killed. The remainder of the force carried on to Rørvik, however, where they found and attacked a warship believed to be a destroyer, two merchant ships and an aircraft tender. The tender was sunk and the other ships were all seen to be damaged by bomb near misses and strafing. Unfortunately one Firefly was shot down and its pilot, Sub

The new C-in-C Home Fleet, Admiral Sir Henry Moore, visited *Implacable* in autumn 1944. He is seen here on the flight deck in front of Seafires of Number 24 Naval Fighter Wing in the centre of a group with, from right to left, Captain C C Hughes-Hallett RN, Captain of *Implacable*, a visiting USN captain in his 'aviation green' uniform, the Captain of the Fleet, the Flag Lieutenant and Commander C L G Evans DSO RN, the ship's Commander 'Air'. (*Author's collection*)

A Firefly of 1771 NAS taxiing forward of the barriers in *Implacable* with Barracudas that had landed before it parked folded in Fly 1. (*Author's collection*)

Lieutenant (A) R M Shaw RNZNVR, was listed as killed in action; his observer was not listed as killed and was presumably rescued.

Early on the morning of 27 October four Fireflies were flown off to search the leads between Støttvaer and Rørvik while a larger strike force was ranged. They found a U-boat escorted by what was described as a frigate and a merchant vessel at anchor together with several small craft. They were strafed but in the process one Firefly was shot down and its pilot, Sub Lieutenant (A) S A W Waters RNVR, was listed as killed in action. Again there is no mention in the report of his observer, who presumably survived. A strike force comprising thirteen Barracudas armed with three 500lb MC bombs each, five Seafires to act as escort and three Fireflies was flown off as soon as the sighting report was received. On reaching the target area, six Barracudas attacked the merchant ship and saw it surrounded by bomb splashes, and soon afterwards a heavy explosion was seen near its bridge. The U-boat was strafed by the Fireflies, whose aircrew saw an explosion forward of the conning tower. They were followed closely by seven Barracudas, whose bombs were seen to fall just astern of it. The U-boat was driven aground and seen to roll onto its beam ends as it was abandoned by its crew. German records identified it as *U-1060*. The attacking aircraft also sank an 'M'-class minesweeper, *M-433*, and an air-sea rescue ship as well as damaging five minor vessels.[42]

A fighter sweep comprising ten Seafires and two Fireflies was flown off from 1410 briefed to search the leads near Bodø for targets of opportunity. Landfall was made too far to the south, however; when they reached Bodø the defences were wide awake and they were opposed by dense anti-aircraft fire. They did, however, locate and strafe a merchant ship off Fugl Island and three smaller ships in the harbour were also set on fire. Another small ship was attacked on the return flight to the carrier. All these aircraft returned safely but, unfortunately, one Seafire of 894 NAS crashed over the side while landing on and its pilot, Petty Officer E Barrow, was killed.

Lodingen was the briefed target area for a strike that left *Implacable* at 0830 on 28 October. It comprised fourteen Barracudas, each armed with three 500lb MC bombs, with five Fireflies and five Seafires as escort. As they approached the target area, the Barracudas split into two sections and, supported by the Fireflies, dived out of the sun from 8,500ft to attack the shipping found in the harbour, five merchant ships, a tanker, two escorts and a minesweeper. A direct hit was seen on the tanker, which was then strafed and seen to blow up. Hits resulted in fires and damage on all the remaining ships. The top-cover Seafires had no enemy fighter opposition to counter and all the aircraft from this strike returned safely to the carrier. That afternoon eight Barracudas armed with torpedoes

Barracudas from *Implacable* carried out the Royal Navy's last operational airborne torpedo attack on 28 October 1944, sinking a number of enemy ships and damaging others. *U-1060*, seen here, was left aground and abandoned on a reef after the attack. (*Author's collection*)

were flown off briefed to finish off the shipping damaged in the earlier strike. They were escorted by six Fireflies and four Seafires. One ship, identified as *Karmoy* in German records, was seen to blow up and sink after a torpedo hit, and a further hit damaged *Karmattan*. Both these ships had been ferrying German troops and it was believed that there were heavy losses when they sank. During this attack an enemy armed trawler tried to lay a smokescreen but was set on fire and driven ashore by the Fireflies. One aircraft was slightly damaged by anti-aircraft fire but otherwise there were no casualties and all aircraft returned safely. After they had landed on the task force retired and arrived at Scapa Flow on 30 October.

Operation Counterblast

On 13 November Home Fleet cruisers attacked and destroyed the major portion of an enemy convoy south-east of Egersund. *Pursuer* formed part of the task force and Wildcats of 881 NAS provided CAP but none of them attacked shipping on this occasion. Two minesweepers, three anti-submarine vessels and the merchant ships *Cornouaille* and *Grief* were sunk by the fleet's gunfire and the one surviving minesweeper damaged.

Operation Steak

Wildcats from *Pursuer* took part in a further strike, designated Operation Steak, on 14 October. Twelve Wildcats were flown off from 1105, each armed with two 250lb SAP bombs, to attack shipping in the leads. A search of Vingvaagen anchorage revealed nothing but two Norwegian ships and an armed trawler were found in Trondheim leads. The trawler opened fire and was promptly dealt with by four aircraft that left it on fire and sinking; German records showed it to have been *VP 6413*. The strike then re-formed and headed for Titran radar station, which it bombed and strafed from low level. Light anti-aircraft fire was encountered that damaged six aircraft slightly but they all recovered safely. All bombs were seen to hit the radar site compound, leaving it on fire.

Operation Handfast

On 20 November *Premier* and *Pursuer* carried out Handfast, a minelaying strike in Salhusstrommen near Haugesund. Eight Avengers of 856 NAS embarked in *Premier* carried out the lay escorted by sixteen Wildcats of 881 NAS from *Pursuer*, which also provided a CAP over the task force.[43] Seven mines were laid successfully and accurately but one Avenger was hit by anti-aircraft fire and had to jettison its mine. Though damaged, it was recovered safely. Strafing damaged two small coasters and various targets of opportunity were shot up by the fighters. Intelligence sources reported that the minefield held up the movement of enemy shipping for at least a week.

Operation Provident

The original intention of Provident was for aircraft from *Implacable*, *Premier* and *Pursuer* to carry out a combined attack on U-boat depot ships at Kilbotn and the airfield at Bardufoss. They sailed from Scapa Flow at 1615 on 22 November in two task forces. Force 7 comprised *Implacable* flying the flag of the C-in-C Home Fleet with *Dido* and six destroyers; Force 8 comprised *Premier* and *Pursuer* with *Devonshire* and five destroyers. However, a storm developed on 23 November with wind reaching Force 10 from the south-east, backing to the north-east. Speed had to be reduced to 7 knots but large waves caused damage to the forward parts of both CVEs' flight decks. Force 8 was, therefore, ordered to return to Scapa Flow at 1138 on 24 November. It appeared that the centre of the low-pressure system would continue to move to the north-east, making the area off the Lofoten Islands untenable for the planned operation, and so at 1400 the C-in-C ordered Force 7 to alter course towards Trondheim. However, the weather intervened again and early on 25 November this alternative plan also had to be abandoned.

Force 7 stood away from the coast until 1545 and then returned with the intention of operating between Sandnessjøen and Rørvik but once more the weather was too bad for flying operations and, after waiting hopefully for a few hours, the force stood out to sea again. At 2030 on 26 November it closed the coast once more and found the weather to be suitable. Two reconnaissance sorties, each comprising a single Firefly of 1771 NAS and two Seafires of 880 NAS, were flown off at 0900 on 27 November. One went north to Mosjøen, where three coasters were seen in the harbour with an LCT on the point of entering. They encountered heavy, accurate anti-aircraft fire that damaged one Seafire. Next they found a vessel anchored in Sandnessjøen. Further south in Alst Fjord they found a convoy of five merchant ships at anchor. Sighting reports were made and then this team searched to the south, where they found the southern reconnaissance aircraft attacking a merchant vessel after making landfall south of Rørvik and then flying north. In Rørvik two small ships had been seen at anchor and at Gravik a large merchant ship was found at anchor. After they made their sighting reports they strafed the latter vessel.[44] The reconnaissance aircraft from the north joined in and the ship was left on fire.

When the contact reports were received in *Implacable*, a strike force of eleven Barracudas from 828 NAS, each armed with three 500lb MC

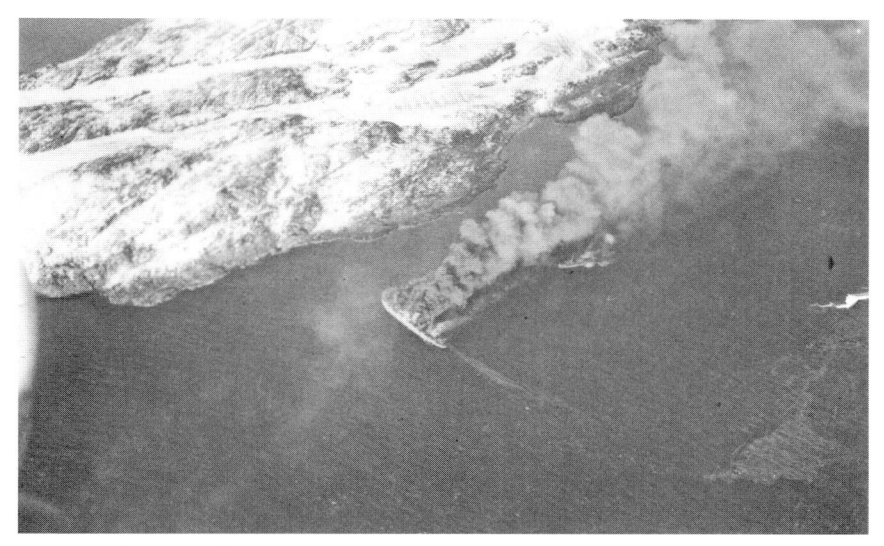

MV *Rigel* aground and burning after an attack by *Implacable*'s aircraft on 27 November 1944. She had been carrying troops back to Germany and an armed trawler is closing her, surprisingly from downwind, to take off survivors. (*Author's collection*)

A Firefly of 1771 NAS from *Implacable* strafing the German steamer *Korsnes* off the Norwegian coast. (*Author's collection*)

bombs, and ten Fireflies from 1771 NAS were flown off from 1005, followed at 1025 by eight Seafires from 880 NAS, which overtook them to act as close escort. Two miles from the convoy, which had now got under way, the Fireflies and four of the Seafires increased speed and began a strafing attack to silence the anti-aircraft defences. Behind them, the Barracudas deployed into two flights; one of four aircraft carried out a glide-bombing attack on a ship later identified as *Rigel* and obtained hits that set it on fire. The other flight attacked a ship later identified as *Korsnes* and it too was seen to be hit and set on fire. As the last of the strike aircraft withdrew, both ships were seen to be beached, down by the stern and burning furiously with about 100 survivors, probably soldiers, in the water near them. The fighters strafed the other two ships with their cannon and they were also assessed as being total losses. An armed trawler that arrived on the scene and attempted to rescue survivors was riddled with cannon shells and left derelict.

Three Seafires and six Fireflies still had ammunition left in their front guns and so, leaving four of the latter to cover the Barracudas' withdrawal, the remainder flew to Sandnessjøen, where the Seafires strafed oil tanks. North-east of Alsten the Fireflies strafed a vessel later identified as *Spree* and then continued up Vefsen Fjord to Mosjøen, where they found and attacked an LCT and a small coaster despite encountering intense anti-aircraft fire. The other four Fireflies remained with the Barracudas until they were well clear of the coast and then broke away to fly south down the leads. They found the vessel that had been attacked by the reconnaissance aircraft still on fire with a smaller vessel alongside, which was apparently attempting salvage operations. Two armed trawlers were seen approaching from the south. Both the trawlers and the salvage vessel were strafed and left smoking. One Firefly was damaged but by 1300 all the strike aircraft and their escort had been recovered safely in *Implacable*. Operations on 28 November were prevented by a very deep depression moving in from the west that compelled Force 7 to withdraw towards Scapa Flow. A day later conditions were worse with winds of over 50 knots and sea state 8; even *Implacable* suffered some weather damage but she arrived at Scapa Flow safely with the rest of the force at 1400 on 29 November.

Operation Urbane

On 7 December *Premier* and *Trumpeter* carried out Urbane, another minelaying operation off Salhusstrommen. Twelve Avengers of 856 NAS from the former carried out the lay escorted by fourteen Wildcats of 881 NAS from the latter. Ten mines were known to have been laid successfully; one was definitely known to have been dropped in a 'safe' condition and the reliability of another was doubtful after it was seen that its parachute had not deployed correctly.[45] A gun battery at Avaldsnes and another near a lighthouse together with a radar station were strafed by the fighter escort.

A day later *Implacable* joined the Urbane force and a combined strike of twelve Fireflies from 1771 NAS and nine Wildcats of 881 NAS from *Trumpeter* carried out an armed reconnaissance looking for shipping targets of opportunity. They found and attacked two merchant ships and left them on fire, then found and attacked self-propelled barges. They too were left on fire. An R-boat, *R-56*, was sunk in Bommelnfjord and another damaged. When they had finished, the aircraft withdrew towards the fleet below 100ft to keep below enemy radar coverage and they were all recovered on board safely.

Operation Lacerate

On 14 December *Premier* and *Trumpeter* carried out Lacerate, the last Home Fleet air mining operation of the year. Six Avengers escorted by eight Wildcats from each carrier took part; the former comprising aircraft of 846 and 856 NAS and the fighters from 881 NAS. Twelve mines were laid successfully in Ramsoysund in the briefed area and the close escort fighters shot up a gun battery on Halten Island together with oil storage tanks. The low cover fighters strafed a gun battery on Ramsoysund and an observation post identified on Kya Island. During the course of this operation the Luftwaffe intervened and three attacks were directed at the force by Ju 88 torpedo bombers. One was shot down by anti-aircraft fire from the task force and the others were all driven off without inflicting any damage.[46] The weather began to deteriorate at this stage and so, since the enemy obviously knew about the task force and the element of surprise had been lost, a planned further mine lay was abandoned and the force returned to Scapa Flow.

Operation Fretsaw

The last strike operation carried out by the Home Fleet in Norwegian waters during 1944 was an attack on shipping off Stadtlandet on 21 December, designated Operation Fretsaw. *Trumpeter* was the only carrier involved and she flew off a force of nine Avengers from 846 NAS with eight of the squadron's own Wildcats as close escort. A further five Wildcats of 881 NAS were flown off as medium cover. No enemy shipping was found during a search of the designated area and, with the obvious absence of enemy activity, the force returned to Scapa Flow.

The resumption of convoys to and from North Russia

A new cycle of convoys began on 15 August when JW 59 sailed with *Vindex*, commanded by Captain H T T Bayliss RN, an observer who had qualified with number 4 course in 1923, and *Striker*, commanded by Captain W P Carne RN, as part of its escorting force. The return convoy that followed it on 28 August was designated RA 59A since RA 59 had already been used by the return convoy in April. The cover and escort operations for the August convoys were designated Operation Victual by the Home Fleet. *Vindex* embarked the Vice Admiral 10 CS, Vice Admiral Sir Frederick Dalrymple-Hamilton, and sailed with *Striker*, *Jamaica* and six destroyers to join the convoy and its close escort on 16 August. *Vindex* had 825 NAS embarked with twelve Swordfish and six Sea Hurricane IICs with two further Sea Hurricanes as reserves. *Striker* had 824 NAS embarked with twelve Swordfish, ten Wildcats and two Wildcats as reserves.

Constant anti-submarine patrols were flown except for a period on the evening of 18 August when visibility deteriorated badly.[47] At 1800 on 20 August the escorts obtained a HF/DF fix on a U-boat and both Swordfish and Sea Hurricanes were vectored towards the position but failed to find anything. The sloop *Kite* was torpedoed and sunk by a homing torpedo fired by *U-344* at 0650 on 21 August 220 miles south-west of Bear Island. She went down almost immediately and only nine men were rescued but an extensive search by aircraft and surface vessels near her sinking position failed to locate the U-boat. Intelligence reports indicated that there were six U-boats in the vicinity of the convoy at dawn on 22 August and a Bv 138 shadowing aircraft was detected on radar. The Wildcat CAP was vectored on to it and it tried to use cloud cover to escape but was pursued relentlessly and eventually shot down after an hour's chase. By 0835 the convoy was north of Bear Island heading east when a Swordfish from *Vindex* south of the convoy sighted and attacked a U-boat as it surfaced. Depth charges were released from only 50ft and fell along the starboard side of the boat, one close to the quarter, a second abeam and the third struck and lodged in the forecastle. Their detonation sank the boat, later identified as *U-354*.

From 1000 searches were only flown in the sectors ahead and to starboard of the convoy since U-boats could not operate in the pack ice to port. This policy was vindicated at 1100 when an 824 NAS Swordfish sighted two fully surfaced U-boats 70 miles from the convoy centre bearing 130 degrees. They were estimated

Swordfish and Sea Hurricanes of 825 NAS ranged on *Vindex* in Scapa Flow during 1944. Parking the fighters on outriggers and Swordfish close to the starboard deck edge left a clear take-off run to port. Two Swordfish are ranged aft ready for take-off with their wings spread and all appear to be fitted with rocket rails. (*Author's collection*)

to be 5 miles apart and were subjected to a series of attacks by aircraft during the next hours but without any observed result. Meanwhile, escorts gained HF/DF bearings on a U-boat that appeared to be following a course parallel to the convoy 30 miles south of it. An 824 NAS Swordfish was vectored on to it and saw it at 1450 but it dived before it could be attacked. Voice radio had been used without restriction after it became clear that the enemy had located the convoy and aircraft were directed to saturate the area to the south for the remainder of the day to keep U-boats dived and limit their attack options. Aircraft from 824 NAS' saw two U-boats and forced them to dive. On 23 August Swordfish of 825 NAS sighted a U-boat on the surface at 0001 52 miles from the convoy's centre on its starboard quarter. A strike was flown off *Striker* but again it dived before it could be attacked. At 1332 a Swordfish sighted another U-boat, which remained on the surface to put up a considerable amount of anti-aircraft fire as the aircraft approached. It then dived only fifteen seconds before the aircraft released its depth charges but no result was seen. The sea was calm and visibility from the air extremely good; U-boat wakes were visible at distances up to 15 miles, although aircraft could only be seen from U-boat conning towers at about 8 or 9 miles. The remainder of the outward passage was uneventful and there were no convoy losses. On 24 August a second U-boat, later found to be *U-344*, the boat that had sunk *Kite*, was attacked and sunk by 825 NAS' Swordfish together with *Mermaid*, *Loch Dunvegan*, *Keppel* and *Peacock*.

On 28 August the forty-five merchant ships of RA 59A sailed with the same escort. CAP and anti-submarine patrols were flown but there were no U-boat sightings until 0925 on 1 September when two Wildcats saw a U-boat on the surface 40nm north-east of the convoy. They strafed it as it dived and shortly afterwards a Swordfish dropped depth charges at the furthest-on position from the dive datum but found no evidence that the boat had been destroyed. Escorts continued to gain HF/DF bearings throughout the day that indicated the presence of four or five U-boats between 40 and 60nm astern of the convoy and on its quarters transmitting shadowing reports. At 0620 on 2 September an 825 NAS Swordfish saw a surfaced U-boat 48nm from the convoy and attacked it with RP and depth charges. The depth charges failed to explode but the rockets damaged it and the aircraft remained on the scene until a surface action group comprising *Mermaid*, *Keppel*, *Whitehall* and *Peacock* arrived and these sank the boat at 1945. German records identified it as *U-394*. After that the U-boat threat diminished but Swordfish were kept airborne and fighters were held ready at deck alert. A total of 529 hours were flown by the two CVEs during the outbound convoy and 549 with the return convoy. This was by far the largest number flown in any Russian convoy operation.

The next outbound convoy was JW 60 with thirty-one merchant ships. It sailed on 16 September and again two CVEs formed part of the escort; *Campania*, commanded by Captain K A Short RN, who had qualified as an observer in Number 22 Course in 1933. She was the task force flagship with VA 1 CS, Vice Admiral Sir Rhoderick McGrigor, a future 1SL, embarked. Her squadron was 813 NAS with twelve Swordfish Mark III, four Wildcats and, for the first time, three Fulmar NF II night fighters. The latter were fitted with the metric AI Mark VI air-intercept radar and were lent from 784 NAS, the RN night fighter development unit at RNAS Drem, and demonstrated that, at last, progress was being made in night fighter capability. The Swordfish issued to 813 NAS were Mark IIIs, among the first to be fitted with the centimetric ASV XI radar, a specialised anti-submarine variant of the type with the scanner fitted in a radome between the oleos that allowed it to rotate through 360 degrees. It had an average range of 10 miles against a surfaced U-boat and up to 40 miles against a medium-sized warship. The extra equipment meant that this variant was flown with a two-man crew: pilot and observer, with no room for the telegraphist air gunner. The radome prevented a torpedo being carried but depth charges and 3in R/Ps could be attached under the wings. They only operated from escort carriers and to help them fly off in low wind conditions, provision was made for RATOG. The remainder of the escort force on this occasion comprised *Striker*, still commanded by Captain Carne, with *Rodney*, *Diadem* and their escorting destroyers. Cover and escort for the outbound and return convoys was designated Operation Rigmarole by the Home Fleet.

The passage to north Russia encountered constant bad weather and low visibility, and only thirty-three hours were flown before JW 60 arrived in the Kola Inlet on 23 September with no sign of enemy activity. RA 60 sailed on 28 September amid Russian reports of periscopes sighted by aircraft near the entrance to the inlet and so close anti-submarine patrols and clearance searches were flown off immediately and two Swordfish were maintained on patrol throughout the night.[48] During the early hours of 29 September enemy transmissions indicated that at least two and possibly three U-boats were in the vicinity but none were

A Swordfish Mark III landing on with two unused depth charges. Note the radome between the main undercarriage legs that prevented this mark from carrying a torpedo. (*Philip Jarrett collection*)

located by air search or sonar. Further searches produced no results but at 1632 two merchant ships in the starboard wing column were torpedoed simultaneously. Extra anti-submarine patrols were flown off but there was still no contact with the enemy before the weather deteriorated again and stopped flying. Conditions improved by 0400 on 30 September and flying resumed but one of the aircraft briefed to search the stern sector failed to return. It was flown by 813 NAS' commanding officer Lieutenant Commander (A) C A Allen RNVR and his observer Lieutenant (A) K H Tilley RNVR; both were reported as missing presumed killed.

On 30 September 824 NAS Swordfish carried out two unsuccessful depth charge attacks on U-boats as they dived but success was achieved at 1830, just after sunset, when an 813 NAS Swordfish gained ASV radar contact on a surfaced U-boat 35 miles astern of the convoy. The boat was seen at just over a mile and attacked. Only one depth charge released but this was seen to fall 40ft ahead of the boat's dive position and 10 degrees to starboard of its track. The aircraft remained over the datum point and found that the depth charge must have caused damage because contact was regained on radar in less than an hour at a range of only 3 miles and at 1927 its conning tower broke surface. The U-boat lay stopped as the Swordfish attacked again, this time with its four RPs. The U-boat fired back and both darkness and return fire prevented the crew from seeing the result of their attack but it was accurate and German records showed that *U-921* had been sunk. The rest of that night passed without incident and the numerous searches flown in all directions during the next day, together with the lack of HF/DF fixes, gave confidence that the enemy was no longer in contact.

The escorting force for the next convoy sequence, JW 61 outbound and RA 61 return, sailed from Scapa Flow on Trafalgar Day, 21 October, designated as Operation Trial by the Home Fleet with Vice Admiral Dalrymple-Hamilton, CS 10, in command again embarked in *Vindex*, which was still commanded by Captain Bayliss. It was the first escort force to include three CVEs; the other two were *Tracker*, commanded by Captain J H Huntley RN, and *Nairana*, commanded by Captain H N Surtees RN. *Vindex* and *Nairana* were British conversions and reflected opinion within the Admiralty that their riveted hulls were better able to withstand Arctic sea conditions than the less robust welded hulls of US conversions such as *Tracker*. *Vindex* had 811 NAS embarked with twelve Swordfish IIIs and four Wildcats; *Tracker* had 853 NAS embarked with ten Avengers and six Wildcats and *Nairana* 835 NAS with fourteen Swordfish IIIs and six Wildcats. The remainder of the escorting task force comprised *Dido*, *Nubian*, *Undaunted* and close escort groups lent from Western Approaches Command. The convoy comprised thirty merchant ships destined for the Kola Inlet[49] and as usual it had gathered in Loch Ewe in western Scotland. The Commodore of both convoys, Rear Admiral M W S Boucher, had commanded *Courageous* before the war, taken a keen interest in the development of the Fleet Air Arm and been the first Director of Air Material at the Admiralty. The escort plan was to use the carriers in three watches of eight hours each as duty carrier, standby carrier and available carrier,[50] the latter allowing a rest period for aircrew, command personnel and aircraft handlers with this CVE taking station in one of the convoy columns instead of being in the flying 'box'. This sound arrangement had to modified in practice because only *Vindex* and *Nairana* could operate their aircraft at night, each of them becoming duty carrier for half the hours of darkness.

Weather conditions became so bad after a dawn patrol on 24 October that no further flying was attempted until late on 25 October, when continuous anti-submarine patrols commenced. The outbound journey was without incident until a HF/DF fix close to the convoy was gained at midnight on 26 October, followed by several further fixes indicating that at least three U-boats were in contact. Alterations of course were ordered by Admiral Dalrymple-Hamilton and hunter groups of escorts

Aircraft handlers clearing snow from *Fencer*'s flight deck. Swordfish and Wildcats are ranged aft. Awful as these conditions were, flying operations had to continue. (*Author's collection*)

were detached but an Avenger of 853 NAS gained first contact at 1118 on 27 October in the grain of the convoy at 60 miles. The crew saw it on the surface heading towards the convoy and it appeared not to have seen the aircraft at first but eventually dived without opening fire as the Avenger began its attacking run. A homing torpedo, known for security reasons as a Mark XXIV mine, was dropped thirty seconds after the boat disappeared under the surface but although the attack parameters had been good, an electrical malfunction in the aircraft prevented the torpedo's engine from starting and no result was achieved. However, the aircraft remained over the datum until surface escorts arrived on the scene thirty-five minutes later. There was no further contact with the enemy and the whole convoy arrived safely at its destination on 28 October. Flying was largely confined to Avengers by day and Swordfish by night, with German shadowing aircraft conspicuous by their absence. Fighters were only flown off to intercept 'bogeys' on two occasions and both turned out to be Russian Catalinas that had forgotten to switch on their IFF.

RA 61 comprised thirty-three merchant ships and the escort joined it at 1530 on 2 November. *Vindex* detected the sound of a running torpedo on her sonar soon after leaving the Kola Inlet and its track was seen some distance away. Constant anti-submarine patrols were flown and one of these sighted a U-boat on the surface in the grain of the convoy about 50 miles from it. The sighting was made with binoculars at a range of about 10 miles and before the aircraft could get into an attacking position a Russian Catalina flew past the U-boat and it dived while the Avenger was still 8 miles from it. The remainder of the voyage was devoid of incident and the task force returned to Scapa Flow. The aircraft of 811 had flown a total of seventy-six hours, forty-two of which were at night; 853 NAS had flown a total of 150 hours, all of them in twilight or daylight conditions, and 835 NAS had flown a total of 104 hours, almost all of them at night. Calm conditions, unusual for the time of year, meant that many Swordfish take-offs had to be made with the assistance of RATOG.

Flying operations had not all gone well. *Nairana* was on her first Arctic operation but 835 NAS, commanded by lieutenant Commander (A) F V Jones RNVR, was experienced in night operations and well able to cope. Its pilots commented on how lucky they were to be doing the majority of the night flying as they thought that the ship had less movement at night. There was probably just as much movement but they were unaware of it in the dark as they concentrated their attention on obeying the signals of the deck landing control officer. *Nairana*'s only three deck landing accidents occurred during daylight and CS 10 commented in his report on the squadron's skill and good teamwork. Unfortunately the same could not be said of 811 NAS, which had been commanded since 27 July by

Nairana under way slowly in the Clyde in January 1944. (*Author's collection*)

Lieutenant Commander (A) E E G Emsley RNVR. This unit had replaced 825 NAS but despite carrying out a work-up in UK waters prior to Operation Trial, its flying had not been impressive and it went to pieces during its first Arctic operation. To make matters worse, *Vindex*'s two air staff officers, responsible for planning flying operations, had also been changed. The first two Swordfish flown off got lost in poor visibility and had to be homed by D/F bearings, forcing *Vindex* to break W/T silence. One of these was airborne for four and three-quarter hours when it landed on with only 2 gallons of avgas left. The squadron's standard of deck landing deteriorated as morale dropped and there were a series of crashes in which Lieutenant (A) D L Walsh RNVR with Sub Lieutenant (A) W E Carr RNVR were killed on 28 October and Sub Lieutenant (A) D Evans RNVR was killed on 3 November. Eight Swordfish were written off or damaged beyond the ship's ability to repair them. This was why the squadron's total number of flying hours was so much lower than the squadrons in the other two carriers. Two Wildcats were also damaged; one broke free of its lashings during a heavy roll and the other turned upside down but remained on deck. Captain Bayliss wrote in his report that '... even by day a safe landing became an occasion for relief. I am of the opinion that the TBR portion of this squadron is at present unfit to go on another operation.' It was disbanded soon afterwards.

The failure of 811 NAS to measure up to the standard required illustrates the extreme toughness, both moral and physical, required of all naval aircrew. The need for more realistic training was accepted by the Admiralty, helped by the fact that sufficient resources were now available to achieve it, and NAD noted that graduation from previous convoy

A Wildcat and Fulmar storm ranged on *Searcher*'s flight deck. Note the extent to which the ship is rolling, the wind-blown spray and the number of lashings holding down the two aircraft. Engine and cockpit covers are lashed in place and the air mechanics working on the rear aircraft are in significant danger. Unfortunately this print was damaged at some stage but its subject value makes it worthy of inclusion. (*Philip Jarrett collection*)

protection activities in the Atlantic produced the best results in squadrons that were redeployed to the Arctic. Working up periods in the Clyde or Irish Sea were not sufficient to harden squadrons for the rigours of flying in bad visibility and long Arctic nights. Tougher training did not just apply to flying; aircraft handling, particularly the heavy Avenger, in rough conditions required both skill and a determination to succeed no matter what conditions were like on the flight deck. This could only be achieved under active service conditions, which were probably worse in the Arctic than in any other theatre of operations. Captain Huntley wrote that his Avenger pilots had found it particularly difficult to taxi into position for a catapult launch when the deck was rolling through 32 degrees.

Convoys to and from north Russia were planned some weeks in advance and when a small one had to be added at short notice it was identified as JW 61A. The opportunity was taken to bring back a return convoy identified as RA 61A. The outbound convoy was the most unusual of the series and it sailed from Liverpool on 31 October with just two fast personnel ships, *Empress of Australia* and *Scythia*. Their purpose was to return 11,000 Russian soldiers to the Soviet Union who had been captured fighting for the Germans by Allied forces in Normandy. Their eventual reception by the communist authorities in Murmansk can only be imagined.[51] The return convoy comprised the same two ships bringing Soviet sailors to the UK, where they were to man British ships being lent to the Soviet Navy including the battleship *Royal Sovereign*. They also brought back the British guards who had secured the Russian prisoners on the outbound voyage.

The operation to escort both convoys was designated Operation Golden by the Home Fleet and the ocean escort comprised *Campania* with *Berwick* and six destroyers; they replaced the local escort on 2 November and *Berwick* also carried Norwegian troops to be put ashore in Murmansk to join Soviet forces entering northern Norway in an endeavour on the part of the exiled Norwegian government to ensure its sovereignty over territory liberated from the Germans. Two further destroyers ferried Norwegian troops to the Kola Inlet independently after bad weather prevented them being flown as planned. After landing them the destroyers joined the escort of RA 61A and returned with it. There was no contact with enemy U-boats in the fast passage of either convoy and *Campania*'s aircraft only flew for a total of nine hours; one Bv 138 shadower was shot down by Wildcat interceptors during each passage.

The last Russian convoy operation of the year, JW/RA 62, was designated Operation Acumen by the Home Fleet and the ocean escort included *Campania* and *Nairana* with a destroyer escort. *Campania* had 813 NAS embarked with twelve Swordfish III, two Fulmar NF II night fighters and four Wildcats. *Nairana* had 835 NAS embarked with fourteen Swordfish III and six Wildcats. They sailed from Scapa Flow on 30 November and joined the thirty-one merchant ships that had sailed from Loch Ewe on 1 December. Weather was bad at first and very little flying was carried out until the morning of 4 December, when anti-submarine patrols began. On 6 December HF/DF fixes indicated that several U-boats were in the approaches to the Kola Inlet and two Swordfish were flown off to search on either bow out to 60 miles. One of these gained a radar contact and homed on to it. Flares were dropped and illuminated the boat sufficiently for a depth charge attack in which the third hit the water 50ft ahead of the conning tower as it submerged and underwater flashes followed the explosions of the other two. The observer saw what might have been a dinghy in the water by the light of a flare but there was no indication that the U-boat had been sunk or damaged so he marked the datum and the aircraft remained overhead. The area continued to be covered by patrols but no further contact was made and the convoy arrived in the Kola Inlet unmolested on 7 December.

Nairana sailed with destroyers from Vaenga on 9 December to search the approaches to the inlet and the thirty merchant ships of RA 62 sailed with *Campania*, *Bellona* and the remainder of the escort force at 0800 on 10 December. Anti-submarine patrols commenced at 1145 but the weather deteriorated and the last patrol was recalled at 1810, landing on successfully in a snowstorm. During the night HF/DF fixes showed that a U-boat was shadowing astern of the convoy and at 0602 on 11 December the destroyer *Cassandra* was torpedoed by *U-365* on the convoy's port quarter. Her bow was blown off forward of 'B' gun mounting and casualties were heavy. She managed to return to Kola, however, arriving on 14 December and the damaged portion of hull was cut away in a dry dock and temporary repairs carried out. She finally sailed for the UK in June 1945.[52]

By 0900 on 11 December the weather was so bad that flying was limited to the most experienced pilots but 835 NAS maintained patrols astern of the convoy where the shadower had been fixed.[53] At 1116 one of these saw a surfaced U-boat and attacked it with R/Ps but the boat continued to dive and no wreckage was seen. Flying was abandoned at 1440 when a heavy swell added to the problem of low visibility in snowstorms but it was resumed at 2044. At 2222 a Swordfish gained radar contact at 8 miles but severe clutter caused by sea returns prevented contact being held inside 4 miles and it was not detected visually. Between 0034 and 0138 on 12 December the convoy was shadowed by a Bv 138. A second aircraft was detected at 0810, intercepted and shot down by an 835 NAS Wildcat. As the convoy passed south-west of Bear Island, a small group of Ju 88 torpedo bombers were detected closing the convoy and *Nairana* flew off two 835 NAS fighters to intercept them. This was the first time in more than a year that Luftwaffe torpedo bombers had attempted to attack a Russian convoy. Another shadowing aircraft closed the convoy from the east, where the ships were silhouetted against the fading light in the west, and guided Ju 88s into attacks at 1350 with one group approaching from the south-west and another from the north-west in order to drop torpedoes on either bow. They were broken up by gunfire from the screen, however, and emergency turns allowed both convoy and escort to comb the torpedoes' tracks. Later a second attack by an estimated twelve Ju 88s developed from the west, north and south but again heavy defensive gunfire broke up the enemy formations and the convoy was manoeuvred successfully to counter each attack. None of the ships was hit but two Ju 88s were shot down and others probably damaged. *Nairana*'s fighters were recalled at 1550 and one of them landed on safely but the other, last seen on the tail of an attacking Ju 88, failed to return and its pilot, Sub Lieutenant (A) I L T Miller RNVR, was reported as having been killed.

On 13 December HF/DF bearings enabled an 835 NAS Swordfish to be vectored on to two U-boats, which were seen and attacked without result, but at 1730 one of two Swordfish returning in formation gained radar contact at 12nm and both aircraft homed on to the target. The aircraft with the contact had no depth charges left and the other had suffered a radar failure, so success depended on their close co-operation. Radar contact was held down to 1½ miles and flares were dropped, which illuminated a surfaced U-boat. The aircraft without weapons remained within their pool of light to gain the enemy's attention while the other Swordfish set up an attack out of the darkness on the other side using a 20-degree glide technique. Depth charges spaced at 30ft intervals straddled the U-boat; one fell to port, one to starboard and the third hit the casing, rolled off and exploded as the boat began to dive. When next seen, the U-boat's stern was well clear of the surface with both propellers and rudder visible. Within thirty seconds it sank at an angle of 45 degrees, leaving a large and rapidly expanding patch of oil and other debris plainly visible as the last flare burnt out. German records identified it as *U-365*, the boat that had torpedoed *Cassandra*.

Later that night one of 813 NAS' Swordfish carried out another attack and at 0240 on 14 December an 835 NAS Swordfish found a U-boat on the surface off the convoy's port quarter and attacked it with depth charges. In neither case was evidence of damage or destruction seen and German records revealed no further losses. After that the weather began to deteriorate rapidly and no further flying was attempted. Overall 813 NAS had flown for 180 hours, of which seventy were at night, and 835 NAS had flown for 162 hours, which were nearly all at night. RA 62 reached the UK without loss on 18 December.

One further convoy, JW 63, sailed on 30 December but the greater part of its passage took place in January 1945 and it will be described in the next chapter.

9
1945

From late 1944 the Royal Navy's attention was focused on building up the BPF and Eastern Fleet for operations against Japan. The Home Fleet was reduced in size and significant changes were being made in the number and training of aircrew.

The state of the Fleet Air Arm in 1945

By January five of the six fleet carriers of the *Illustrious* group had already joined the BPF and the last, *Implacable*, sailed from the UK on 16 March. The first three light fleet carriers left the UK on the same day to work up in the Mediterranean before joining the BPF. The fourth commissioned on 21 February and sailed for the BPF on 14 May. Two of the three maintenance carriers were already with the BPF, with the third due to join it on her completion in August. The British-converted escort carrier *Pretoria Castle* was being used in home waters as a trials carrier.

Until the end of the European war in May the Home Fleet retained *Premier*, *Trumpeter*, *Nairana*, *Campania*, *Puncher*, *Queen*, *Vindex* and *Searcher* for anti-shipping and minelaying operations in the Norwegian littoral and for the continued support of convoys to north Russia.[1] Other CVEs were engaged in a variety of strike, anti-submarine, training, ferry and replenishment roles across the world. *Battler*, *Smiter* and *Ravager* were used on a continuous basis until May as deck landing training carriers with reduced ships' companies. At the beginning of the year Western Approaches Command included fifteen merchant aircraft carriers, MAC ships, of which two were Dutch manned. Their operations fall outside the scope of this book but, of interest, the last operational flight of a Fairey Swordfish was from *Empire Mackay* on 27 June when the three aircraft of her 836 NAS R Flight disembarked to RNAS Maydown to disband. The Swordfish finally ceased to be an operational aircraft with the end of the European war, having remained in service since before 1939 virtually unchanged except for its equipment fit; it had excelled in both the anti-ship and anti-submarine roles and deserves recognition as one of the greatest warplanes of all time.

In 1945 *Ravager* was used as a dedicated deck landing training carrier. This view of her hangar shows Fulmars, Hellcats, Avengers and Barracudas embarked for use by pilots under training. The Fulmar in the right foreground is a night fighter with the four 0.5in machine gun armament and shields aft of the exhaust stubs to prevent the pilot being blinded by their glare at night. (*Author's collection*)

Operations from shore bases under RAF Coastal Command control continued until May and five naval air squadrons were detached at various times for anti-shipping and anti-submarine patrols in the Western Approaches, English Channel and off the Belgian and Dutch coasts. During the period from January to March 819 NAS operated from advanced landing grounds in Belgium to protect Allied logistic shipping in the Scheldt estuary.

By 1945 the Admiralty was finding it difficult to recruit the numbers required to fill every kind of specialisation but especially aircrew. In January 1945 the RN had 2,650 pilots available for front-line duties with a further 1,336 undergoing operational training. There were 2,154 undergoing basic training, all in Canada or the USA and a further 674 pilots who could only be used on second-line tasks. By July 1945 there were 3,243 pilots available for front-line duties. As the European war drew to a close, the Admiralty asked the Air Ministry, responsible then as now for all UK flying training, to move all RN pilot training from Canada to the UK. The Air Ministry agreed and the new arrangements were to have come into effect from December but the unexpectedly early end of the Pacific war in August led to a significant reduction in numbers as the changeover to peacetime training was made. The move from Canada had been expected to shorten the time taken to train a naval pilot by four months since it removed the need for travel and time spent in pool squadrons acclimatising to European conditions.

The increase in the number of single-seat fighters and the decrease in the number of TBR squadrons led to a significant reduction in the number of observers required. With 1,843 available for front-line duties, there was actually a surplus and the Admiralty decided to cease observer training on a temporary basis. The Observer School at RNAS Piarco in Trinidad was run down and closed. There were 1,353 observers under training in January but only 596 in July and observer training was not resumed until after the war when post-war requirements were clarified. The same thing applied to TAGs; there were 2,102 in July but the number under training dropped from 1,797 in January to only four in July. The training school in Canada at RCAF bases Dartmouth and Yarmouth were run down and the number required continued to drop as aircraft such as the Barracuda were modified for operation by a crew of two rather than three. The Admiralty stressed, however, that the roles of observers and TAGs 'were not dying'; rather their numbers were being reduced because the contemporary naval aircraft required them in significantly smaller numbers.

An RNVR officers' course photographed at the Royal Naval College, Greenwich, in 1945. Almost half the men in this photograph are Canadian ex-RCAF pilots. (*Author's collection*)

With carrier operations now recognised as the focal point of naval operations and what was expected to be a long campaign in the Pacific, the Admiralty wanted to get pilots into operational squadrons as quickly as possible. An approach to the Air Ministry in September 1944 led to 360 surplus RAF pilots being transferred to the RN. Of these 250 were granted naval commissions and the remainder served as petty officers or higher rates commensurate with their former RAF status. They underwent the Divisional Course at RNC Greenwich before moving on to fly, the majority going to fighters but some to TBRs. Their treatment was the same as that for new entry RN pilots. There was a considerable surplus of RAF, RAAF, RCAF and RNZAF pilots reaching the end of their operational training when the war in Europe ended and an agreement was reached that many of these could, if they volunteered, transfer to the RN. These could be trained to operate naval aircraft and taught the basics of naval air warfare far more quickly than newly entered recruits who could not complete their training before the end of 1946. Eventually 700 pilots were transferred to the RN under the scheme agreed in 1944 and a further 1,400 under another scheme agreed in 1945. Of the latter, 550 transferred from the RAF, 500 from the RCAF, 250 from the RNZAF and 100 from the RAAF. Of interest, many of the Canadian and Australian pilots accepted under this scheme went on after the war to form the core of the fleet air arms set up by the RCN and RAN with RN assistance.[2] Since these men were no longer required by their air forces, many had to be transferred more rapidly than they could be absorbed by the RN operational flying schools in mid-1945 and these were soon filled to capacity. Those who could not be trained immediately were appointed to a series of courses arranged to enable them to carry out their duties as naval officers or ratings more efficiently and give them insight into how the Navy was run. To help the unprecedentedly large number of naval air squadrons reach the high standards required by the Admiralty, steps were taken to ensure that every unit had a qualified flying instructor, QFI, in its scheme of complement, a concept that has continued into the twenty-first century. Plans had already been agreed within the Admiralty that every fighter and strike squadron should have at least one air warfare instructor, AWI, in their schemes of complement.

In early 1945 the Admiralty made several changes to improve aircrew conditions of service in the light of operational experience. Operational tours for individual pilots and observers were limited to fifteen months under normal circumstances, with an absolute maximum of eighteen to be followed by a period of ten months in a second-line squadron or 'behind a desk'. Tour lengths for TAGs were expected to match these parameters but were subject to review given the reduced number of aircraft that required

Training for flight deck officers was relatively sophisticated by 1945. These students are using carrier techniques to launch Barracudas from the dummy deck at RNAS Easthaven. Note the bus rebuilt to simulate a carrier's island parked by the deck. It even had a mast to fly appropriate flag hoists. (*Author's collection*)

them. Reduced age limits for aircrew in operational squadrons were laid down in AFO 3717/45, intended to make it clear to outstanding younger officers that they had good prospects of attaining command appointments. The rapid expansion in the number of fighter pilots made possible by the transfer of trained pilots from the Commonwealth air forces allowed the Admiralty to overbear pilot numbers in fighter squadrons by 50 per cent as it wanted.

After the German surrender anti-submarine training was reduced drastically but to keep the art alive four Barracuda crews per month continued to be trained in the role. After completing their deck landing training on type at RNAS Easthaven, the pilots were joined by observers at RNAS Ronaldsway to complete the two-month anti-submarine course. This was followed by a specialised anti-U-boat course at RNAS Maydown. Another major shift was the decision to cease training Barracuda crews in the torpedo attack role at RNAS Crail. This had the effect of shortening the training period on this type, which was now centralised at RNAS Ronaldsway. There was thus a gap before the first Firebrand TF IV squadron was due to form in autumn 1945, during which there was no operational requirement for the British 18in Mark 15/17 torpedo and its support facilities at Crail were mothballed. Avenger training was centralised at Crail and limited support for the USN 22.4in Mark 13 torpedo was retained there. However, the Admiralty did intend to keep British 18in aircraft torpedoes in its air weapon inventory. They had achieved the highest percentage of hits of any weapon in service in 1945, assessed as 224 hits out 615 torpedoes dropped operationally. The Firebrand was reaching the end of its protracted development as a torpedo-fighter and a small number of pilots for these would require training. The Sea Mosquito TR.33 was entering production and it was also designed as a torpedo strike aircraft. The most economical policy would have been a drastic cut in torpedo facilities and training followed by a slow build-up to the planned post-war establishment but the Admiralty believed that once the highly effective torpedo training organisation created over the past six years was lost it would be very difficult to rebuild and so it was decided to retain a nucleus organisation in being to cater for future requirements. Similarly, mobile air mining sections were run down at the end of the European war but a small organisation was retained to restore, if needed, the capability of laying up to fifty mines per week from carrier-borne aircraft.

A night fighter organisation had been created at last with suitably equipped Fulmars embarked in CVEs on Russian convoy duties in late 1944. Training was carried out at RNAS Drem on both two-seat Fireflies and single-seat F6F-5N Hellcats, the latter obtained through Lend-Lease arrangements. Replacement crews were trained at the rate of six crews per month for Fireflies and five pilots per month for Hellcats. The former were converted on to the Firefly at RNAS Lee-on-Solent, given operational training at RNAS Inskip and then a two-month night fighting course at Drem. Initially Hellcat pilots were trained on type at RNAS Yeovilton, completing their training with the two-month course at Drem. Later courses were expected to carry out their whole day and night training course in a five-month course at Drem and activity there increased significantly during 1945 but it was found very difficult to maintain the necessary number of sorties because the airfield surface deteriorated in winter conditions. For this reason the Admiralty decided to move night fighter training to RNAS Burscough but the end of the war brought significant changes as the front-line force was largely demobilised. Planned night fighter squadrons included 1790, 1791 and 1792 with Firefly NF Is and 891, 892 and 893 with F6F-5Ns, known as Hellcat NF IIs in RN service. The light fleet carrier *Ocean* was to be completed as a night fighter carrier for the BPF in 1945 and, although delayed, she was to carry out important night fighter trials during 1946 with 1791 and 892 NAS embarked.

Air intercept radar was the most important element of night fighter development and several types reached operational status in 1945. The USN-supplied AN/APS-4 was fitted in the Firefly NF I and, with British modifications, gave intercept ranges of either 2 or 6 miles when the observer locked on to a target or selections of 5, 10, 20, 50 or 100 miles in the search mode. It had a sea clutter elimination facility for use on low-level interceptions to prevent the target disappearing into the clutter before the pilot could gain visual contact through his gunsight. The first squadron fitted with AN/APS-4 was 1790 NAS and it achieved good

Night fighter Hellcats of 892 NAS and Fireflies of 1792 NAS ranged on *Ocean* in late 1945. They evaluated night carrier operations and the difference in capability between single and two-seater night fighters. (*Author's collection*)

results working up at Burscough. They were also fitted with the Gyro gunsight GGS Mark IID, Series III, which could be used to aim R/P as well as guns. This mark of Firefly also had AN/APS 13 tail warning radar and provision to carry two 1,000lb bombs for the all-weather strike role. Hellcat NF IIs were fitted with AN/APS-6 radar in a pod on the leading edge of the starboard wing clear of the propeller arc. The first unit equipped with this variant was 892 NAS, which worked up at Drem. A British modification was under development in 1945 to give head-up displays for pilots of both types of night fighter. They proved successful but the end of hostilities took the urgency out of the work.

Although referred to as night fighters, these aircraft were also needed for adverse weather operations by day. In both cases, flying off the carrier was relatively straightforward but recovery depended upon getting the aircraft into a position from which the pilot could see the batsman and flight deck in the final stages of his approach. Important work on what were known at first as blind approach aids were carried out on the trials carrier *Pretoria Castle*. After the war these became known as carrier controlled approach aids, CCA, an important element of every carrier's systems. The first of these was Type 93, a beacon that provided the pilot with audio indications through his headset that guided him on to a narrow approach path. By 1945 the system worked well but further

The AN/APS-6 radar screen and controls in the cockpit of a Hellcat F6F-5N. The screen was ideally positioned below the reflector gunsight and alongside the artificial horizon. With only six controls, APS-6 was well-designed for operation by pilots who had to devote much of their attention to flying the aircraft at night or in bad weather. (*Author's collection*)

trials were required to examine the effect of the carrier yawing in rough weather on the average pilot's ability to maintain himself within the approach path. The first operational Type 93 was fitted in *Ocean*. The production carrier controlled approach aid that followed was the Type 961, a modified version of ASV Mark XI fitted inside a weather-proof radome. It allowed a controller sat at a screen to talk down a pilot until he was close enough to see the batsman in azimuth while passing him advisory information about height. Typical calls would be, 'You are at half a mile, you should be passing 400ft; you are at a quarter of a mile, you should be at 200ft, look up for the batsman.' This system proved to be a great success and Type 961 remained in use until the early 1970s. There were also considerable improvements in radio communications.

The convoys to North Russia continued

The covering force for convoys JW/RA 63 sailed on 30 December 1944, designated Operation Greystoke by the Home Fleet. *Vindex*, with 825 NAS embarked, provided the only air element with twelve Swordfish

III and seven Wildcats.[3] There was no contact with the enemy on the outbound voyage and on the return passage the weather was so bad that flying was hardly possible. There were no losses to the thirty-five outbound and thirty homeward-bound merchant ships and the escort force returned safely to Scapa Flow on 11 January. Overall 825 NAS flew for 110 hours, of which eighty-six were at night.

The Admiralty had appreciated that the enemy now seemed to be concentrating schnorkel-fitted U-boats in the approaches to the Kola Inlet, where they could lie in wait for convoy traffic, rather than in the Barents Sea. The Luftwaffe had deployed Ju 88 torpedo bombers back to Norway and had used them against JW/RA 62. These attacks had been unsuccessful but they were repeated in February during JW/RA 64, designated as Operation Hotbed by the Home Fleet. Convoy protection over the next four months represented the zenith of convoy work in terms of flying skill, escorting technique and the mass handling of the ships. The carriers deployed in Hotbed were *Campania* and *Nairana*, each with the same commanding officer and embarked squadrons as before. Rear Admiral R R McGrigor, CS 1, was embarked in *Campania* and the force sailed on 3 February. After JW/RA 62 *Campania* had been fitted with Type 277 air warning radar, which was to prove invaluable during Hotbed. Shortly after the carriers joined JW 64, a CAP was flown off in the hope of intercepting the Trondheim weather reconnaissance aircraft, whose W/T transmissions had been detected by *Campania*'s Y Party. No interception resulted but it was considered that this aircraft had probably picked up the convoy and reported it because on the afternoon of 6 February a Ju 88 appeared and began to shadow.[4] Its time on task was short-lived, however, as it was promptly shot down by 813 NAS' Wildcats. Unfortunately, one Wildcat was shot down by return fire and its pilot, Lieutenant (A) R J Smyth RNVR, was lost.

On the morning of 7 February another shadower was detected and from information gathered about its transmissions by the Y Party it was anticipated that an attack by torpedo aircraft was imminent. Admiral McGrigor kept his screening forces in their night cruising disposition, therefore, which formed two concentric circles of escorts around the convoy. At 0745 a number of enemy aircraft were detected at low level by *Campania*'s Type 277 and shortly afterwards they were seen to comprise two groups, each consisting of six Ju 88 torpedo bombers. One was promptly shot down by the corvette *Denbigh Castle* and the convoy was turned through 90 degrees towards the dawn, which put the enemy's most favourable attacking sector astern. None of the Ju 88s pressed home their attack, however, and they withdrew by 0900 without inflicting any damage on either convoy or escort. *Nairana*'s Wildcats were scrambled at 0810 but failed to intercept the Ju 88s in the poor light conditions and low cloud. The rest of the day was comparatively quiet, although 835 NAS' Wildcats intercepted and seriously damaged another shadower.

On 8 and 9 February further enemy shadowers were detected and appeared to be homing U-boats on to the convoy. Air searches and patrols were flown by Swordfish throughout the day and night on 8 February in an effort to locate the U-boats but none were found. Swordfish from 813 NAS were armed with four R/P and two depth charges by day and three depth charges at night. From the escort's HF/DF bearings it appeared that the convoy, which was slightly to the north of its planned route, had probably passed around the flank of a U-boat patrol line. Only one Fulmar night fighter had been embarked with 813 NAS this time but it was found to be in poor condition. Its maintenance party tried hard to make it serviceable and it carried out two maintenance test flights around the convoy by day in good weather. It was flown off against an enemy shadower at 1730 on 8 February but electrical and radar failures forced it to return ninety minutes later. Frustratingly it had closed to within 3,000yd of its prey when the failures occurred. Landing on in the dark in what were described as rather difficult conditions, it crashed so heavily into *Campania*'s barrier that it was irreparable on board.

Queen joined the Home Fleet in 1945 and took part in a series of strikes against targets in Norwegian waters. (*Author's collection*)

On the evening of 9 February the weather deteriorated to the point where all flying had to cease but, after further shadowers were detected in the middle watch, conditions improved and flying was resumed at 0810 on 10 February when two Swordfish were flown off. At 1000 a single aircraft was detected on radar closing the convoy and it was thought that it might be Russian. The light was poor with a full cloud cover at low level, frequent rain squalls and a surface visibility of about 5 miles. The aircraft continued to close and was identified as a Ju 88 at 1010 when it dropped a torpedo near *Sioux*. It turned away with one engine on fire after being hit by the fleet's gunfire and the destroyer successfully evaded the torpedo.

Wildcats that were scrambled to intercept it failed to make contact when it evaded into cloud. The convoy and its escort were now thoroughly alerted and in their anti-aircraft stations when *Campania*'s Type 277 picked up further contacts at 1020. They were reported as approaching at sea level from the starboard bow. Moments later *Whitehall*, the right-hand ship of the extended screen, and then *Lark* saw two formations of about eight Ju 88s and opened such an effective fire on them that they broke up. Three aircraft made an attack on *Whitehall* but one made off damaged, the second was shot down and destruction of the third was shared with *Lark*. All their torpedoes were evaded successfully. Two more Ju 88s were shot down by 835 NAS Wildcats and a sixth was shared by them with escorts' gunfire. Admiral McGrigor had made 90-degree emergency turns to head the convoy away from the attacking aircraft and more fighters were flown off to counter the remaining Ju 88s, which had broken their formations to approach from all directions. All the torpedoes they dropped were successfully evaded by further emergency turns, a remarkable tribute to the convoy's clever handling. It was noticed that several torpedoes exploded in the ships' wakes. At least one more Ju 88 was shot down by the escort's gunfire and fire from the merchant ships themselves but some Wildcats were hit by the convoy's own anti-aircraft fire and so badly damaged that they only just managed to land on and crashed as they did so. One less fortunate pilot of a damaged Wildcat was forced to ditch astern of his carrier but he was rescued by an escort's sea boat. Several Swordfish returning from their anti-submarine patrols were also fired on and since the convoy had been warned on R/T beforehand of their return using the correct recovery procedures, this indiscriminate firing revealed an inexcusably bad standard of aircraft recognition and fire discipline.

The self-inflicted damage meant that 813 NAS only had one Wildcat left serviceable, so it was fortunate that there was a lull between 1110 and 1130, but after that several Ju 88s made a half-hearted attack that did no damage to the convoy, all their torpedoes being dropped at long range outside the screen. A further Ju 88 was shot down by the combined efforts of 835 NAS' fighters and ships' gunfire, raising the total number destroyed to seven certain, four probable and eight estimated as damaged out of the twenty-five enemy aircraft that had taken part in the two attacks. Although a number of fighters had been damaged, only one had been a total loss and no ships had been hit.

The convoy was two days out from the Kola Inlet but fortunately there were no further attacks by either aircraft or U-boats. Icing conditions put a stop to all flying operations from the afternoon of 10 February. They were resumed early on 11 February but further icing conditions forced them to be stopped again in the afternoon. The weather improved on 12 February, allowing close anti-submarine patrols to be resumed while other Swordfish searched the approaches to Kola Inlet for U-boats. These were the last sorties during JW 64 and they found no sign of the enemy. The convoy entered the inlet during the middle watch in pitch darkness and anchored in a snowstorm; all twenty-six merchant ships had arrived safely. The carriers anchored off Vaenga where, during the next few days, a number of Soviet officers paid visits to them, a welcome change from the previous frigid attitude to the British by Soviet officials. *Denbigh Castle* was torpedoed just outside the entrance; she was towed in and beached but subsequently rolled on to her side and became a constructive total loss. Two merchant ships arriving from the White Sea to join RA 64 were torpedoed in the same position, one of which was lost, and it was clear that the convoy would have to fight its way through a U-boat concentration at the mouth of the inlet when it sailed. Russian countermeasures were limited to day flying and a few small patrol craft, and so Admiral McGrigor countered the threat by sending a surface hunting group to search the approaches up to 35 degrees East on the night before RA 64 sailed. He decided not to send one of his carriers with the hunting group because flying conditions were limited by the intense cold, Arctic smoke and fog, which were difficult to forecast for any reasonable time ahead. *Lark* and *Alnwick Castle*, both part of the hunting group, sank *U-425* in the approaches to the inlet. Whilst in Vaenga, the two carriers had put considerable effort into repairing their damaged aircraft and when they sailed on 17 February, 813 NAS had managed to make nine Swordfish and two Wildcats serviceable. The Fulmar was a write-off. No. 835 NAS had fourteen Swordfish and six Wildcats serviceable but one Swordfish crashed on take-off when the first anti-submarine patrol was flown off. Its crew was rescued. Unfortunately *Lark* was torpedoed as the carriers and *Bellona* left harbour but was brought back under tow. An hour later a merchant ship was also torpedoed before taking up its allotted position in the convoy. It was abandoned immediately and sank but Admiral McGrigor thought that it might have been possible for her, too, to have regained harbour if her crew had remained with her. That afternoon the corvette *Bluebell* on the inner screen was torpedoed and blew up with only one survivor. Thereafter RA 64 and its escort drew clear of the Arctic smoke and *Campania* began to fly anti-submarine patrols, while a number of Russian fighters covered the convoy's passage. *Nairana* took over flying duties for the dog watches and the two carriers flew turn and turn about through the night and into the next day until 1530 on 18 February, when rapidly deteriorating weather brought an end to flying.

By midnight on 18 February there was a gale blowing with wind speeds recorded by the carriers' meteorological staff at over 60 knots. By 19 February the convoy was scattered and remained so for twenty-four hours. An enemy shadower was thought to have located it but no attack developed. Shadowing continued but by 0900 on 20 February there were only four stragglers out of the remaining thirty-one merchant ships; a tribute to the work of the escorts that had rounded them up. The re-concentration was only just in time; at 1000 groups of up to eight enemy aircraft were detected ahead of the convoy as it steamed due west. The sea was still rough and the wind high but *Nairana* flew off two Wildcats at 1010 to intercept the enemy, now plotted 12 miles away. One Ju 88 was attacked and flew off with both its engines emitting white smoke. It was assessed as a probable kill. At 1025 two further Wildcats were flown off *Nairana* and the convoy was turned 90 degrees to port in two emergency turns that put most of the enemy aircraft on its quarter. The majority approached from this direction but some were detected coming from ahead. A few attacks were pressed home fairly well but most enemy aircraft left the convoy alone and went after the four stragglers, only one of which was actually attacked but not hit. A number of enemy torpedoes exploded in the rough water or in ships' wakes and none of the convoy or its escort were hit. The Wildcats of 835 NAS shot down one Ju 88; the destroyers *Onslow* and *Zealous* shot down one each and a probable was shared between the fighters and the escort. Two others were seen to have been damaged. Overall there had been three certain kills and two probables out of the estimated twenty-five enemy aircraft that had attacked. Admiral McGrigor considered that the highest credit was due to *Nairana* and her Wildcats, which had operated with great success and landed on safely in a rough sea with a wind over the deck of over 50 knots. On the other hand, some of the merchant ships had inexcusably opened fire on the returning fighters yet again, despite R/T warnings of their return. This time, however, no aircraft were damaged.

The rest of 20 February passed quietly and three additional escorts arrived from Scapa Flow. By the last dog watch only two stragglers remained out of position but the weather remained bad and no anti-submarine patrols could be flown during the night. Early on 21 February two shadowing aircraft were detected, which transmitted a series of 'A's, presumably to home U-boats, but there were no attacks. By 1600 the weather improved sufficiently to allow *Nairana* to fly off Swordfish to search for the stragglers. One was found 18 miles to the south-east but nothing was seen of the second and nor was it heard from until 27 February, when it reported its position 300 miles astern of the convoy.

It was lucky to reach the UK unharmed. Shortly after midnight on 22 February another shadower was heard reporting the convoy and HF/DF bearings were made on U-boats to the east. A heavy swell across the wind direction prevented flying and an even stronger gale with winds of 70 to 80 knots developed from ahead. By the evening conditions had deteriorated still further and the convoy began to break up again. *Campania* was rolling through 45 degrees either side of the vertical and had to heave to. There was little respite on 23 February and another shadower found the badly scattered convoy, but when the weather moderated slightly, *Campania*, with several merchant ships, was able to join the Convoy Commodore's group. By the dog watches the convoy had re-formed and resumed its course. No enemy attack developed during the rounding up process but a torpedo striking force of Ju 88s did find the last straggler, the merchant ship *Henry Bacon*. It was torpedoed at 1420 and reported that it was sinking. Despite the weather, *Nairana* flew off a section of Wildcats, which were directed down the bearing of the ship's transmissions. They found her and climbed to allow the carrier to obtain an accurate fix on the sinking ship's position 47 miles to the east. The nineteen Ju 88s had disappeared by then but the survivors, which included Norwegian women and children, said that they had possibly shot down two of them. The gale persisted with winds occasionally reaching 70 knots but, unfortunately, the exact wind over the deck was not recorded when these two Wildcats landed on. It must have been in excess of 50 knots. The carrier's log did describe conditions as wind from the south-south-west force 8–9 with extensive cloud cover, below which visibility was 5 miles. These conditions were further described as being 'the worst weather in which flying was possible'.

Early in the forenoon of 24 February two RAF Liberator maritime patrol aircraft arrived and escorted RA 64 for the remainder of the day. Unfortunately, in Admiral McGrigor's words 'each Liberator in turn chose to orbit calling loudly on convoy R/T and acting as a beacon for the enemy. It took some time to stop them talking … clearly they were not aware that radio silence was in force …' The enemy appeared to be unaware of the convoy's position by then and having the RAF broadcast it to them must have been particularly galling. The convoy's speed of advance had been reduced to 3.5 knots in the bad weather and the fuel situation became serious. All but four escorts had to be detached to the Faroe Islands to refuel. Normal flying patrols were out of the question and neither carrier flew any of its aircraft for the remainder of Hotbed. At 1830 *Campania*, *Nairana*, *Bellona* and four destroyers were detached directly to Scapa Flow, where they arrived on 27 February. Their passage from Kola Inlet had taken them ten days and the convoy itself took twelve.

In his summary of this convoy cycle Admiral McGrigor wrote that enemy shadowers had flown in adverse weather, mainly at night. By day they never stayed for long, driven by a healthy respect for the carriers' fighters. He also stressed the extreme importance of Type 277 radar and good communications in the flagship since he relied on both to manoeuvre the convoy, direct the fighter interceptions and control the screen's gunfire. The shortage of fighters in the two carriers was a cause for concern since they were wasting assets in the appalling conditions. McGrigor considered it vital that every CVE should carry as many fighters as they were capable of embarking. He did accept, however, that a compromise was necessary in the Arctic convoys between TBR aircraft and fighters since it was never clear in advance whether aircraft or U-boats would constitute the greater threat. The need to keep air direction plots up to date was imperative but with large numbers of friendly and enemy aircraft, mostly at or near sea level within 20 miles of the convoy, this required both skill and concentration from the radar plotters. An indication of how aircraft direction had developed can be drawn from the excellent report compiled by *Campania*'s direction team in which they explained that they had constantly been required to:

(a) direct their own fighters.
(b) supply *Nairana* with sufficient information for her to direct her fighters.
(c) keep the command accurately informed about the air situation and any other threat that was developing.
(d) keep all escorts and merchant ships in touch with the air situation.
(e) watch the Swordfish patrols and vector them clear if they were threatened.

Type 277 radar gave the most valuable data, while the earlier Type 281 in other ships was rarely of much use. *Campania*'s set had a blind arc of 25 degrees either side of her stern and so *Denbigh Castle* outbound and *Alnwick Castle* on the return passage were placed in positions where their Type 277s covered the gap. During the JW/RA 64 cycle 813 NAS flew seventy-five hours, of which seventeen were at night, and 835 NAS flew for 148, of which forty-six were at night. Captain Short reported that some Ju 88 attacks had demonstrated a 'deplorable' lack of skill and that enemy torpedoes were clearly unsuited to rough sea conditions judging from the number that exploded prematurely. He also recommended that a stock of spare aircraft should be kept at Vaenga to make good losses on outbound convoys. The lack of such a facility is surprising when it is recalled that spare aircraft and pilots had been maintained in north Russia for CAM ships, although these were, of course, one-shot systems.

There were three more convoys cycles to north Russia, the last of which took place after the German surrender on 8 May. Operation Scottish was the designation given by the Home Fleet to the JW/RA 65 cycle.[5] This time the escort included *Campania*, again with the twelve Swordfish and seven Wildcats of 813 NAS embarked, and *Trumpeter* commanded by Captain K S Colquhoun RN, a graduate of Number 18 Observer Course in 1930. She had 846 NAS embarked with eight Avengers and eight Wildcats. JW 65 sailed on 11 March and was routed outside a radius of 300 miles from the enemy-held airfields at Bardufoss and Trondheim. There were no losses until the convoy entered Kola Inlet, where a concentration of U-boats sank two merchant ships. The remaining twenty-two arrived safely. On the return passage, which began on 23 March, the weather was good throughout but there were no losses and the twenty-five merchant ships all arrived safely. The carriers and their escort returned to Scapa Flow, 813 NAS having flown for eighty-seven hours during this cycle, of which nineteen were at night, and 846 NAS having flown for ninety-five hours, all of them in daylight.

The last fighting convoys of the series, JW/RA 66, were designated Operation Roundel and the carriers that covered them were *Vindex*, now commanded by Commander J D L Williams DSC RN, and *Premier*, which was commanded Captain R J Gardner RN. *Vindex* embarked 813 NAS, which had been modified after the lessons learnt in recent cycles to comprise eight Swordfish and twelve Wildcats. These numbers were intended to balance 856 NAS embarked in *Premier*, which had twelve Avengers but no fighters. The passage of JW 66 began on 17 April and passed without incident; all twenty-five merchant ships arriving safely in Kola Inlet. RA 66 sailed on 29 April and saw more action, with one U-boat sunk by the escort and another damaged. One of the escorts was sunk as the convoy cleared Kola Inlet, the frigate *Goodall* torpedoed by *U-968* at 2038. A magazine explosion blew the forward part of the ship away and it had to be abandoned and scuttled.[6] Another escort was damaged but there was no other interference by the enemy as RA 66 made its way back to the UK and all twenty-four merchant ships arrived safely.

The last convoy cycle of the series, JW/RA 67, was designated Operation Timeless by the Home Fleet. There was only one CVE, *Queen* commanded by Captain K J D'Arcy RN. It had been planned before the German surrender on 8 May and the Admiralty decided to continue with it, fearing that some U-boats might try to carry on the fight from northern Norway. The attitude of some German officers interviewed when they surrendered reinforced this view but the U-boats still at sea obeyed their orders and there was no attack on either convoy. Both convoys comprised twenty-three ships and both arrived at their destinations safely. *Queen*

Wildcats of 853 NAS at alert on *Queen*. The men in the cockpits are fitters, who will start the engines so that they can warm up while the pilots make their way from the ready room after briefing. Parking fighters on outriggers like this allowed them to remain on deck while keeping a clear space for take-off. (*Author's collection*)

sailed on 12 May with 853 NAS embarked comprising eight Avengers and eight Wildcats. Between them they flew for 281 hours in daylight before returning to Scapa Flow. Overall the Royal Navy had escorted 771 merchant ships to and from north Russia, of which 746 had arrived at their destination, a remarkable achievement. Nine U-boats had been sunk by aircraft with a further five shared with surface escorts. Twenty-four enemy aircraft had been shot down by carrier fighters with a further five probables but the elements, enemy action, crashes on deck and friendly fire incidents had taken their toll. The carriers that had escorted the Russian convoys had lost forty-two Swordfish, twenty-one Wildcats, eight Sea Hurricanes, five Avengers and one Fulmar; a total of seventy-seven aircraft.

Further strike operations in the Norwegian littoral

Attacks on Norwegian targets by aircraft of the Home Fleet began with Operation Sampler, an attack on shipping in and near Vaagso. *Nairana* sailed on 1 January but the weather was bad and, with no improvement forecast, the operation was cancelled and she returned to Scapa Flow on 5 January. On 12 January *Premier* and *Trumpeter* sailed from Scapa Flow for Operation Spellbinder, the provision of anti-submarine patrols and air cover for a surface action group, SAG, attacking an enemy convoy off Egersund. *Premier* had the Avengers of 856 NAS embarked together with four Wildcats of 881 NAS. *Trumpeter* had the Avengers and Wildcats of 846 NAS embarked together with the remaining Wildcats of 881 NAS. The SAG sank an enemy minesweeper and damaged a merchant ship off Nord Byfjord. Wildcats shot down a Ju 88 shadower but two of their number were shot down while suppressing enemy anti-aircraft fire. Both pilots were recovered. Another Wildcat had to carry out an emergency landing after its pilot received a head wound from anti-aircraft fire.

On 13 January the same carriers carried out Operation Gratis, minelaying by their Avengers off Haugesund after covering the withdrawal of the SAG. The weather was perfect and the lay was carried out by six Avengers of 846 NAS, each armed with a single Type A Mark I mine, with eight Wildcats as escort and a further six Avengers of 856 NAS, also with eight Wildcats as escort.[7] Three unserviceable Wildcats in *Premier* were repaired by spare parts flown across from *Trumpeter*. Eleven mines were laid successfully but one was unfortunately dropped in a safe condition by one of *Premier*'s aircraft. All twelve Avengers dropped from heights of between 200 and 500ft at 170 knots. As the strike force withdrew, fighters strafed the enemy radar and W/RT station at Utsira but were unable to estimate what damage they had done and no post-strike photographic reconnaissance was available. No aircraft were lost.

A further operation to replace the cancelled Sampler, designated Operation Winded, was carried out on 28 January. *Campania*, *Premier* and *Nairana* took part in this night attack on shipping between Stadtland and Aalesund carried out by Swordfish IIIs from *Campania* and *Nairana*. Fighters from *Premier* provided cover during daylight. The Swordfish were armed with eight 3in R/Ps with 25lb solid warheads or with four 250lb bombs. The weather was clear with a full moon, although there was overcast at 5,000ft near the coast. This was the first night shipping strike by Home Fleet carriers and it was estimated[8] that two merchant ships had been hit by rockets and left stopped and that a larger ship had been hit by both bombs and rockets and damaged. Another ship had been attacked with unseen results. German records failed to confirm these estimates but by this stage of the war they were neither comprehensive nor accurate.

Fighter cover for the withdrawal of another SAG was provided by *Premier* and *Puncher* on 12 February as part of Operation Selenium.

Premier retained the same air group as before and *Puncher* had the twelve Barracudas of 821 NAS embarked. On the same day the two carriers carried out a second phase, designated Selenium II, in which mines were laid off Skatestrommen near the lighthouse at Skaten. Seven Avengers of 856 NAS carried one mine each with a close escort of four 856 NAS Wildcats and top cover provided by twelve Wildcats of 881 NAS. One Avenger was forced to return shortly after it flew off and had to jettison its mine. The others made a successful landfall and released their mines as briefed, except for one aircraft that could not release its mine and eventually had to jettison it in a safe condition. The channel was effectively blocked, however, and the close escort Wildcats strafed an anti-aircraft battery at Rugsundo together with gun emplacements at Skarsten and Berdle. One

As an aid to navigation over Norwegian coastal waters, the Admiralty produced a booklet for observers that described every lighthouse and its signal. This is a small part of it showing the degree of detail it contained. (*Author's collection*)

Wildcat was slightly damaged by enemy fire and a second inadvertently fired its guns as it caught an arrester wire, damaging two other Wildcats and a Barracuda. Thankfully nobody was hurt; the pilot had obviously failed to switch his guns to 'safe' before entering the landing pattern.

Two operations were combined on 22 February, designated Operations Shred and Groundsheet and, once again, *Premier* and *Puncher* took part. Shred was a sweep of the narrows leading to Salhusstrommen and Groundsheet a mine lay in the channel by Barracudas of 821 NAS. When they arrived at the flying off position the visibility was poor with haze up to 4,000ft[9] and Shred was cancelled. Groundsheet went ahead and nine Barracudas were flown off with eight Wildcats as close cover and a further eight as top cover. Landfall was made at Stavanger but it was mistaken for Rovaersholmen Light. The strike leader altered course to starboard and ordered both the close escort and top cover to break off. They did so but, before returning independently to their carriers, they strafed buildings on Stavanger waterfront, a W/T station on Feistein Island and two Do 24s at their moorings at the southern end of Hafrsfjord. One of the latter was left on fire. The Barracudas continued unescorted to the Karmoy Channel, meeting intense light anti-aircraft fire from Stangaland onwards. Two aircraft were shot down and their crews killed but the remainder laid their mines successfully in Karmoy Sound. The lost crews were Lieutenant (A) L W E Maffey RNZNVR with his observer Sub Lieutenant (A) D M King RNVR and TAG Leading Airman H J Brooks, and Lieutenant (A) A D L Payne RNVR with his observer Sub Lieutenant (A) J B Watson RNVR and TAG Leading Airman N F W Smee.[10]

The last minelaying sortie, designated Operation Cupola, was carried out on 20 March. *Searcher*, *Premier* and *Queen* took part, although aircraft from the latter did not join in the mine lay itself. Bad weather delayed the take-off until the afternoon, when the cloud base lifted to 2,000ft. Eight Avengers of 856 NAS were flown off *Premier* with twenty Wildcats of 882 NAS from *Searcher* providing both close escort and top cover. They were briefed to drop their mines in Oranesund and no enemy aircraft were sighted during the approach. Gun positions were attacked by the fighters as the Avengers laid their mines and only one anti-aircraft position was able to open fire. Seven mines were dropped successfully but one Avenger was unable to release due to a technical malfunction. All the aircraft returned safely to land on but there was a heavy swell and two Wildcats were damaged. Once the Avengers had completed their runs, the Wildcats strafed targets of opportunity, causing damage to enemy coastal batteries and a patrol vessel.

The four remaining strike operations of the European war were all attacks on shipping. The first of these was Operation Prefix on 26 March with Admiral McGrigor embarked in *Searcher* accompanied by *Queen* and *Puncher*. A night strike by *Nairana*'s Swordfish designated Operation Muscular was to have followed but the weather deteriorated and it was cancelled. The first part of Prefix was an attack on shipping known to be in Trondheim leads heading towards Kristiansand North. It was carried out by nine Avengers of 853 NAS, each armed four 500lb MC Mark VII bombs, escorted by nineteen Wildcats of 882 NAS with a further four 882 NAS Wildcats as top cover. The weather was good and the strike force approached the coast at 300ft. Two ships proceeding up Tustna/Stablen Fjord were seen and attacked by two flights of Wildcats. They were identified as a tanker escorted by a minesweeper but the fighters' front guns did little damage to them. Eight to ten Bf 109Gs intercepted the force and a combat ensued with two flights of Wildcats in which three enemy aircraft were shot down. Two of these were destroyed by Lieutenant Commander R A Bird RN and the third by Sub Lieutenant (A) A F Womack RNVR. Two other Bf 109s were assessed as having been damaged. One Wildcat was badly damaged in this fight but the pilot managed to carry out a perfect deck landing on his return. While all this was going on, the Avengers found no further targets and jettisoned their bombs as they returned to the task group.

The bad weather continued throughout 27 March but the task force remained off the coast waiting for it to clear. A further strike, still deemed to be part of Prefix, was carried out by fifteen Wildcats of 882 NAS, seven of which were armed with two 250lb SAP bombs. The weather was better but still not good and they were led to Aalesund by a Firefly night fighter of 746 NAS from *Nairana*. They made a feint into Smolafjord to simulate a minelaying sortie, after which they made an accurate landfall despite rain, sleet and poor visibility. Two merchant ships were seen alongside a quay and attacked from low level but, despite the determination with which this was pressed home, no hits were observed. The fighters strafed a W/T station on Vikero Island as they withdrew and left it on fire.[11]

The next strike, designated Operation Newmarket, was to be an attack on U-boat depot ships in Kilbotn, near Harstad, by aircraft from *Puncher*, *Queen*, *Searcher* and *Trumpeter*. It was due to take place on 6 April but bad weather prevented any aircraft flying off.[12] The task force cruised off the Lofoten Islands for several days hoping for better conditions but when there was no improvement Newmarket was abandoned. A replacement air attack on the depot ships in Kilbotn, designated Operation Judgement[13] was scheduled for 4 May, this time with *Trumpeter*, *Searcher* and *Queen* taking part. The task force was designated as Force 1 with Admiral McGrigor in command but this time he flew his flag in the cruiser *Norfolk* rather than a carrier. His force also included the cruiser *Diadem* with five

Operation Judgement II, the attack on Kilbotn on 4 May 1945. The depot ship *Black Watch* with *U-711* alongside it is in the centre of the image surrounded by bomb splashes. She is already burning. This was the Royal Navy's last strike operation of the European war. (*Philip Jarrett collection*)

destroyers and left Scapa Flow at 1100 on 1 May. This time the weather conditions were perfect when the force arrived in the flying off position opposite the Lofoten Islands, with visibility over 60 miles, patches of cloud at 3,000ft and a light wind. The strike force included aircraft from all three carriers and comprised eight Avengers of 846 NAS, each armed with four 250lb MC Mark VII bombs, and a further eight from 853 NAS with the same weapons. Sixteen Wildcats, eight of which were fitted with one 250lb MC bomb, were flown off to suppress the defences and four Wildcats from each of the composite Avenger/Wildcat squadrons acted as close escort for their bombers. Four Wildcats of 846 NAS acted as top cover. Having flown off and formed up quickly in the ideal conditions, they set heading for Kilbotn at 1623. Landfall was made at Skoger, where the Avengers and defence suppressers continued towards the harbour at 5,000ft with the top cover and dive bombers climbing to 8,000ft. The attack had been carefully orchestrated and the first step was for one flight of the anti-flak escort to deploy during the final approach to attack the anti-aircraft cruiser *Harald Haarfagre*. Next, one section of the second flight strafed heavy anti-aircraft positions ashore and a flak barge while the other attacked the submarine depot ship *Black Watch* and a ship that was thought to be the torpedo supply ship *Admiral Von Hering* but later identified as a cargo ship. Simultaneously, from different angles, the dive-bombing Wildcats attacked from immediately above their targets. One flight released its bombs on *Harald Haarfagre*, while other aircraft bombed gun positions, the flak barge, *Black Watch* and the cargo ship. The timing of the two attacks was so perfectly judged that that the first anti-flak bombs dropped immediately after the strafers had passed over their respective targets.

The close escort strafed ahead of the Avengers, which began their glide-bombing runs from up sun, crossing their targets from port quarter to starboard bow and thus allowing them to make their getaway to seaward around Rogla Island. Avengers of 846 NAS released their bombs on *Black Watch*, while those of 853 NAS attacked the cargo ship. One 853 NAS pilot found his target obscured by spray from bomb bursts and, since he could see *Black Watch*, he attacked that instead. No enemy air opposition was encountered but the perfect visibility had limited the element of surprise and intense, accurate, medium and light anti-aircraft fire continued throughout the attack from ships and shore batteries. Pilots also reported fire from Rogla Island, which had been thought to be undefended. RN losses included one Wildcat that was seen to receive a direct hit from the flak ship and one Avenger that failed to return. The Wildcat pilot was Lieutenant (A) H Morrison RNZNVR of 882 NAS. He is buried in Narvik New Cemetery in a grave administered by the CWGC. The Avenger crew comprised Lieutenant F J Gahan RNVR, his observer Sub Lieutenant (A) A D H Elder RNVR and TAG Leading Airman P B Mansfield of 846 NAS. Their bodies were also recovered and are buried at Sorvik Churchyard, details of which can be found through the CWGC website.

The results achieved by this strike were outstanding. The strafing aircraft achieved numerous hits on *Black Watch*, the cargo ship and *Harald Haarfagre*. The fighter-bombers secured two hits on *Harald Haarfagre* and one on the stern of *Black Watch*. Avengers of 846 NAS gained at least three direct hits on *Black Watch* and the Avenger of 853 NAS that also attacked it another probable. She was seen to explode, break in two and sink. A U-boat alongside it, later identified at *U-711*, also sank either as a result of a bomb hit or the depot ship's explosion. The cargo ship, later identified as *Senja*, also sank after receiving several hits and near misses. *Harald Haarfagre* was left badly damaged and on fire. The strike landed on from 1805, including one Wildcat that was so badly damaged that it was deemed to be beyond repair, and the Force returned to Scapa Flow. This was the last offensive operation by the Home Fleet before hostilities ceased on 8 May and Admiral Sir Henry Moore wrote that 'the complete

The batsman gives the 'cut' signal to a Wildcat returning after the Kilbotn strike. (*Philip Jarrett collection*)

success of this operation ... is a fitting ending to the Home Fleet offensive operations in the European War. The result may well have persuaded the German Naval High Command that continued U-boat warfare from Norway was not worth-while.'

The end of the war in Europe

Fears that some German units might not heed the order to cease hostilities led to these CVEs returning to sea immediately after their return to Scapa Flow in order to escort British naval forces on their way to liberate Copenhagen between 6 and 8 May. This short-notice deployment was designated as Operation Cleaver.[14] Anti-submarine patrols and CAP were maintained during daylight hours by the same squadrons that had carried out Judgement II. By 1900 on 8 May the operation was deemed to be complete as British warships, including the cruiser *Birmingham*, successfully passed through German minefields to arrive off Copenhagen. The carriers returned to Scapa Flow but with the unconditional German surrender due at 2200 GMT[15] on 8 May they had to deal with a significant amount of German activity while on passage. Two Ju 88s were detected at 0727 and Wildcats of 882 NAS were vectored to intercept them. One was engaged and damaged but the other indicated its surrender by firing a red Very light and it was escorted to an airfield in Denmark, where it landed at 0945. A further eight Ju 88s were detected at 1110 and shadowed by Wildcats as they made their way harmlessly to Oslo, where they

A German surrender delegation of senior naval officers at RNAS Drem in May 1945 standing next to the Luftwaffe Ju 52 transport aircraft that brought them to the UK. (*Author's collection*)

landed. The Home Fleet ended the war with a number of CVEs that had carried out strike operations off Norway, escorted convoys to Russia and provided deck landing training for new pilots. Their numbers ran down rapidly as ships and personnel were transferred to the Far East, the Home Fleet bearing the brunt of manpower reductions as wartime reservists and long-serving personnel from the Royal Fleet Reserve were demobilised. The rapid reduction in the size of the RN after 1945 is described in *The British Carrier Strike Fleet after 1945*[16] but a brief look at how the Home Fleet's CVE force was run down is illustrative.

After disembarking her aircraft, *Trumpeter* was refitted from 15 May and sailed to join the Eastern Fleet on 7 July.[17] *Searcher* was also refitted from 15 May and sailed to join the Eastern Fleet on 1 July. When *Queen* returned to Scapa Flow after the JW/RA 67 convoy cycle she was reallocated to Rosyth Command on 7 June and then refitted. After further modifications from 18 September she sailed for Portsmouth Dockyard on 18 November to be prepared for duty as a troop transport to and from Australia. *Puncher* had defects rectified from 21 April and then joined Rosyth Command for a brief period to provide deck landing training for 1790 and 1791 NAS' Firefly night fighters. When this was completed on 25 June and she was modified with bunks in the hangar for trooping duties to and from the UK and Canada, which continued until early 1946.

Nairana had begun a major refit in Belfast on 31 March but hit a jetty while being manoeuvred out of dry dock on 7 August. Repairs took until October, after which she was used a deck landing training ship. In March 1946 she was lent to the Royal Netherlands Navy for two years and renamed *Karel Doorman*. *Premier* was refitted from 21 May and then used as a deck landing training carrier from 24 July until September.

Campania was the only RN escort carrier to see longer-term service. She was refitted from 7 April but was damaged on being taken out of a dry dock on 5 June. Repairs were carried out from 10 June and then she was allocated to the Nore Command for trooping duties from 11 August. In her case she worked between Trinidad and the UK before being laid up in Category B reserve at Rosyth on 30 December. In 1950 she was brought forward for use as a civilian-manned exhibition ship to tour the UK in support of the Festival of Britain during 1951 and in 1952 she was fitted out as the headquarters ship for the British atomic bomb tests carried out at Monte Bello Island off north-west Australia. She had a small air group of Sea Otter amphibians and Dragonfly helicopters. On return in 1953 she was laid up in reserve and finally scrapped in 1955. *Vindex* was refitted from 17 May. On 1 July she sailed to join the BPF as a replenishment carrier, arriving in Brisbane in August, only days before VJ-Day.

The naval air squadrons that had been embarked in these carriers were, in large part, disbanded so that their aircrew could be retrained for service in the BPF or demobilised. British aircraft types such as the Swordfish had no further use and even other types such as the Barracuda and Seafire were available in larger numbers than were now required. Older airframes were, therefore, concentrated at selected naval air stations and sold for scrap. More than 250 Barracudas were gathered at RN Air Stations Crail and Dunino in Fife to await their fate. American aircraft such as the Wildcat were not needed by the BPF and even the war-weary Home Fleet Corsairs, Hellcats and Avengers were of little use since newer airframes were being delivered from the USA in large numbers. Aircraft that had been delivered to the RN under Lend-Lease arrangements had now to be paid for in dollars, returned or destroyed. Payment was out of the question and large-scale returns would have been expensive. Most were taken to sea and dumped around the world as hostilities ended in the various theatres of war.

The CVE squadrons did not last long. On 8 May 813 NAS was disembarked from *Vindex* to RNAS Hatston, where it was disbanded a week later on 15 May.[18] In July 821 NAS embarked in *Trumpeter* for passage to the Eastern Fleet but the war ended before it could take part in operations. Its personnel were brought home in September without their aircraft and, after re-equipment with Barracudas at RNAS Rattray, the unit was disbanded in 1946. On 7 April 825 NAS disembarked from *Campania* to RNAS Machrihanish, where it was disbanded on 12 April. Similarly, 835 NAS was disembarked from *Nairana* to RNAS Hatston on 29 March, where it was disbanded on 1 April. The fighter flight of 846 NAS was disbanded at RNAS Stretton on 23 May 1945 but the Avengers lasted a little longer. After short spells at RN Air Stations Hatston, Twatt, Crail and Machrihanish, it was renumbered as 751 NAS on 22 September. *Queen*'s 853 NAS disembarked to RNAS Hatston on 30 May and was disbanded there with immediate effect. The personnel of 881 NAS were redeployed to RNAS Wingfield near Cape Town in South Africa but with the end of the war they returned to the UK to be disbanded in October. After a period disembarked at RN Air Stations Grimsetter, Machrihanish and Ayr, 882 NAS re-embarked in *Searcher* and deployed to the Eastern Fleet, disembarking to RNAS Katukurunda in what was then Ceylon on 20 August. With the end of the war its personnel were brought back to the UK in *Searcher* to be disbanded formally on 9 October. By October 1945 the Home Fleet was a smaller force that differed radically from the fleet that had commenced hostilities six years earlier.

10

Retrospection

The Fleet Air Arm units that operated as part of the Home Fleet and ashore in UK airfields were never large and the Admiralty struggled in the early war years to provide them with an adequate supply of aircraft. This had been because the MAP, created at a time of national emergency, failed at first to comprehend the RN's legitimate need for aircraft. It not only reduced the number of naval aircraft coming off the production lines; it stopped the development of new fighter and TBR aircraft such as the Firefly and Barracuda. The results of this policy were seen in the reduced carrier air groups deployed in 1941–42 and the continued use of obsolescent designs such as the Swordfish. The Home Fleet remained a constant, powerful force but its full strategic capability was shown in the reinforcement it provided to the Mediterranean, Atlantic convoy escort, Middle and Far East with heavy units whenever necessary. Examples include *Victorious* being lent to the Mediterranean for Operation Pedestal and to the US Pacific Fleet. Despite this, it retained sufficient strength to counter any attempt to break out into the Atlantic by enemy capital ships. The continuous achievement of both tasks was a considerable success. It would be unfair to compare the Fleet Air Arm's performance too closely with the American and Japanese naval air arms, neither of which had the administration of their training and aircraft procurement regimes forced on them for nearly two decades by an organisation that was not only institutionally averse to specialised naval aviation but saw no value in it. Furthermore, both America and Japan were able to concentrate on single-ocean strategies, whereas the Fleet Air Arm was committed to operations around the world.

The RAF had insisted upon non-specialised training and the fact that RN observers had to be lent to both Coastal and Bomber Commands to instruct crews in naval warfare speaks volumes about the failure of that concept. Throughout the era of split control the Admiralty had fought to retain operational control of its aircraft and this stood it in good stead on the outbreak of war. As with other new technologies, especially radar, however, the tactical employment of carrier-borne aircraft took time to develop. Early fleet doctrine had centred upon preparation for a decisive sea battle but experience soon led to a policy of containment and the need to defend against attacks by the Luftwaffe. The extent to which the Home Fleet was able to counter enemy air operations over Norway with inadequate Skua fighters is testimony to the skill and determination of their pilots, especially Lieutenant Lucy, the first British fighter pilot of the war to shoot down five or more aircraft. Naval pilots invariably had to fight against enemy aircraft in greater numbers and of superior quality but the courage of men such as Lieutenant Commander Esmonde and his contemporaries shone through and they deserve to be remembered with pride by the generations that follow them.

As the war progressed men from Canada, New Zealand and Australia filled the gaps in Fleet Air Arm aircrew numbers and after 1941 it was not unusual to have men from New Zealand who had undergone basic flying training in Canada before their operational training in the UK in many naval air squadrons. Inevitably the bulk of aircrew trained in the war years were members of the RNVR Air Branch or its Commonwealth equivalents. There were too many calls on the limited number of career RN officers passing out of Dartmouth to provide more than a small percentage of the pilots and observers that were required for the expanding front line. The bulk of aircrew in 1940 had been RN or RN (A) but by 1944 this had changed. Taking the Barracuda pilots that took part in Operation Tungsten as an example of Fleet Air Arm structure, thirty were RNVR, six were RNZNVR, four were RN or RN (A) and one was RCNVR. There was a similar situation in the ratings' structure, with the majority of technical ratings and aircraft handlers joining under emergency national service regulations. After the end of the war it would take some time to establish the Fleet Air Arm on a permanent basis but the process was aided by a number of men who volunteered for regular commissions or engagements. A significant number of RNVR officers had become experts in air warfare with outstanding service in command of naval air squadrons. While many had to accept an initial drop in rank, a number went on to have noteworthy careers with several reaching flag rank.

From its inception the British Air Ministry had always claimed that the RAF could provide whatever air power was needed to support joint forces in any kind of operation. The real experience of warfare could not have been more different and it was the RN that had to provide the air dimension, either directly with carrier-borne aircraft deployed to the point of contact with the enemy or by ferrying RAF aircraft to Norway, Malta, West Africa and the Far East. Despite the desperate shortage of trained aircrew to form new naval air squadrons and replace combat losses, the RN never hesitated to lend aircrew to its sister service when appeals were made. On frequent occasions the RN had to suspend its own operational plans to enable the RAF participation in operations; a fact that must never be lost sight of by those who study history.

The key advantages demonstrated by the Fleet Air Arm were its strategic mobility, the ability to deploy aircraft and the support needed to operate them effectively at the point of contact with the enemy, and the value of having all its people trained as part of the wider naval service, sharing its skills, values and aims. These were more closely comparable with the USN and IJN, as were the series of carrier strike operations carried out in the Norwegian littoral from 1944 onwards. In 1940–41 aircraft such as the Grumman F4F-4 Martlet/Wildcat were purchased from the USA using Britain's rapidly diminishing dollar reserves but from 1942 the gaps were filled with USN aircraft types provided by Lend-Lease arrangements. Most of these were a generation later than the British types that had been delayed by the MAP but the delay led to both entering service at the same time. The deployment of its larger carriers to reinforce other fleets led to the extensive use of CVEs for strike operations and cover for the Russian convoys. Once these became available in sufficient numbers to meet the needs of both Western Approaches Command and the Home Fleet their achievements were impressive.

Set-piece strike operations such as Operation Tungsten, the *Tirpitz* strike, and Operation Judgement II, the attack on Kilbotn, were models of their kind that stand comparison with any other air attack during this period by any air arm. The scale of potential enemy fighter defences forced the attack on Taranto to be carried out at night; both the *Tirpitz* strikes and Kilbotn were carried out in daylight with first-class fighter escorts hoping that the enemy would react so that he could be engaged and defeated. The operations carried out in support of the Russian convoys, often in atrocious weather conditions, were also models of their kind and are examples of how new and evolving technologies could be mastered to take the fight to the enemy. Some of the experiences set down as 'lessons' were arguably not lessons at all and reflected the lessons that had already been learned by the RNAS before 1918. It is interesting to note how quickly politicians can forget things once wars are over.

The strategic mobility of the Royal Navy's aircraft carriers and their embarked air groups are as fundamentally important to Great Britain today as they were when the events described in this book took place, even in the current digital era with its new combat domains. I hope that this book will prove to be a source of information for those who knew little about the achievements of naval aviation in this theatre and a source of pride to those whose knowledge of, and affinity with, the Fleet Air Arm have been enhanced by reading it.

Notes

Chapter 1 Introduction
1 David Hobbs, *The Royal Navy's Air Service in the Great War*, Barnsley, Seaforth Publishing, 2017, Chapters 13 and 14 describe the political arguments that led to the RNAS being subsumed into the new RAF. **2** David Hobbs, *The Dawn of Carrier Strike*, Barnsley, Seaforth Publishing, Chapters 1, 2 and 8 describe the period of 'Dual Control' between 1918 and 1939 and the decision by Sir Thomas Inskip, the Minister for Defence Co-ordination, that full control of naval aviation should be returned to the Admiralty. **3** *The Dawn of Carrier Strike*, p. 21. **4** *The Dawn of Carrier Strike*, p. 131ff. **5** Thomas C Hone, Norman Friedman & Mark D Mandeles, *American & British Aircraft Carrier Development*, Annapolis, Naval Institute Press, 1999, p. 106ff. **6** David Hobbs, *Taranto and Naval Air Warfare in the Mediterranean 1940–1945*, Barnsley, Seaforth Publishing, 2020.

Chapter 2 The structure of the Fleet Air Arm in 1939
1 J David Brown, *Carrier Operations in World War II*, Barnsley, Seaforth Publishing, 2009, p. 14. **2** Theo Ballance, Lee Howard & Ray Sturtivant, *The Squadrons and Units of the Fleet Air Arm*, Staplefield, Air Britain Publishing, 2016. **3** Wing Commander John A MacBean & Major Arthur S Hogben, *Bombs Gone – The Development and Use of British Air-Dropped Weapons from 1912 to the Present Day*, Wellingborough, Patrick Stephens, 1990. **4** Lieutenant Commander Ben Warlow RN, *Shore Establishments of the Royal Navy*, Liskeard, Maritime Books, 2000 edition. **5** Admiralty, *The Navy List*, London, HMSO, August 1939 edition. **6** Admiralty, CB 3053 (1), *Naval Aircraft Periodical Summary* No. 1, London, Naval Air Division, Naval Staff, September 1940. **7** Admiralty, Unpublished Naval Staff History, *The Development of Naval Aviation 1919–1945*, Appendix VIII, copies of which are in the author's archive and the Naval Historical Branch in Portsmouth. **8** David Hobbs, *The Dawn of Carrier Strike*, Barnsley, Seaforth Publishing, 2018, p. 139ff. **9** Geoffrey Till, *Air Power and the Royal Navy 1914–1945 – a Historical Survey*, Jane's Publishing, London, 1979, p. 55 et seq. **10** Ray Sturtivant with Dick Cronin, 'Fleet Air Arm Aircraft, Units and Ships 1920 to 1939'. Air Britain (Historians) Ltd, Tonbridge Wells, 1998, p. 306.

Chapter 3 The first weeks of conflict
1 David Hobbs, *The Dawn of Carrier Strike*, Barnsley, Seaforth Publishing, 2019, p. 196ff gives more detail. **2** J David Brown, *Carrier Operations in World War II*, Barnsley, Seaforth Publishing, 2009, Edited by David Hobbs, p. 12ff. **3** J David Brown, *Warship Losses of World War II*, London, Arms & Armour Press, 1995, p. 27. **4** W S Hewison, *This Great Harbour Scapa Flow*, Stromness, The Orkney Press, 1985, p. 233ff. **5** Admiralty, *Naval Staff History of the Second World War, The Development of British Naval Aviation 1919–1945*, Volume 1, 1954, p. 160. **6** All aircraft data in this book has been taken from documents in the author's archive. As always, research has revealed considerable variations in the data produced by manufacturers and Admiralty documents and the figures presented above are an attempt to rationalise them.

Chapter 4 1940
1 David Hobbs, *The Dawn of Carrier Strike*, Barnsley, Seaforth Publishing, 2019, p. 213ff. **2** Ibid., p. 218ff. **3** Ibid., p. 258ff. **4** Geoffrey Till, *Air Power and the Royal Navy*

1914–1945, London, Macdonald and Jane's Publishers, 1979, p. 13. **5** For a more detailed account of the German assault on Norway on 9 April 1940, the reader is directed to *The Dawn of Carrier Strike*, p. 222ff, and the Naval Staff History of the Second World War, Battle Summary Number 17, *Naval Operations of the Campaign in Norway*. The German plan is given a wider perspective in BR 1840(1) *The German Campaign in Norway*. **6** *The Dawn of Carrier Strike*, p. 251. **7** Twenty-two years earlier in 1918 seven RNAS Sopwith 2.F1 Camels had been launched to attack the German airship sheds at Tondern with bombs from the same ship before her conversion to a flush-deck carrier. They could not land back on board and those that returned had to ditch near the fleet. **8** For a detailed account of military operations ashore during the Norwegian campaign, the reader is recommended to study Geirr H Haarr's three books, *The Gathering Storm*, *The German Invasion of Norway* and *The Battle for Norway*, all published in Barnsley by Seaforth Publishing. **9** 400yd. **10** HMS *Furious* 4/320 April 1940 in the Naval Historical Branch archive, a copy of which is held in the author's archive. **11** *The Dawn of Carrier Strike*, Chapter 15. **12** *The Dawn of Carrier Strike*, Chapter 16. **13** *The Dawn of Carrier Strike*, p. 257. **14** *The Dawn of Carrier Strike*, p. 222 et seq. **15** T K Derry, *History of the Second World War: The Campaign in Norway*, London, HMSO, 1952, p. 173. **16** CAB 84/13 f 125 Memoranda 131–179 in the National Archive at Kew. **17** CAB 21/1471 Operation Paul: Minelaying in the Gulf of Bothnia in the National Archive at Kew. **18** CAB 84/2 f 132 and WO 106/1873, Minutes of the JPSC. **19** Naval Historical Branch, Admiralty Library, Portsmouth, Admiralty Signal 1655/5 June 1940. **20** WO 106/1873 contains a copy of Admiralty signal 0043/8 June 1940 at the National Archive, Kew. **21** Admiralty Library. Naval War Diary entry for Sunday, 6 June 1940. **22** Wing Commander H R Allen DFC RAF, *Who Won the Battle of Britain?* London, Arthur Barker, 1974, p. 181 et seq. **23** Paul Beaver, *Forgotten Few – Naval Fighter Pilots in the Battle of Britain*, Clatford, Beaver Westminster, 2019, p. 78. **24** Ibid., pp. 4 and 5. **25** Ibid., p. 78. **26** Anthony J Cumming, *The Royal Navy and the Battle of Britain*, Annapolis, Naval Institute Press, 2010, p. 150 et seq. **27** Sir Hugh Dowding, 'The Great Lesson of this War; Sea-Air Power is the Key to Victory', London, *Sunday Chronicle*, 29 November 1942. **28** David Hobbs, *British Aircraft Carriers, Design, Development and Service Histories*, Barnsley, Seaforth Publishing, 2013, p. 90. **29** Ibid., p. 48. **30** Ibid., p. 42. **31** Admiralty, CB 3053 (2) *Naval Aircraft Periodical Summary* # 2, London, February 1941, paragraphs 60 to 62. **32** CB 3053 (2) paragraphs 69 to 73. **33** CB 3053 (2) paragraphs 83 to 87. **34** CB 3053 (2) paragraph 97. **35** Admiralty, *Naval Staff History of the Second World War, The Development of British Naval Aviation* 1919–1945 Volume 1, London, 1954, p. 110ff. **36** CB 3053 (2) paragraphs 98 to 101. **37** G A (Hank) Rotherham, *It's really Quite Safe*, Belleville Ontario, Hangar Books, 1985, p. 153ff.

Chapter 5 1941

1 David Hobbs, *Aircraft Carrier Victorious Detailed in the original builders' plans*, Barnsley, Seaforth Publishing, 2018, p. 8. **2** Admiralty, *Naval Staff History of the Second World War, The Development of British Naval Aviation 1919–1945* Volume I, London, 1954, p. 206ff. **3** Ibid., p. 208ff. **4** Admiralty, *Naval Staff History of the Second World War, The Development of British Naval Aviation 1919–1945* Volume II, London, p. 25ff. **5** Rheinübung translates as Rhine Exercise. **6** David Hobbs, *British Aircraft Carriers – Design, Development and Service Histories*, Barnsley, Seaforth Publishing, 2013, p. 91ff. **7** Admiralty, *Naval Staff History of the Second World War, Battle Summary Number 5, The Chase and Sinking of the Bismarck*, BR 1750 (3/50), London, 1950. **8** Martin Marylands were used on reconnaissance by the RAF from Malta, most notably to photograph the Italian Fleet in Taranto before the attack by Swordfish from *Illustrious* in November 1940. **9** He had been a member of Number 22 Observer Course, which started in October 1932, and had many flying appointments before being promoted to commander. **10** G A (Hank) Rotherham, *It's Really Quite Safe*, Belleville Ontario, Hangar Books, 1985, p. 195ff. **11** Unlike electrical intercom systems, voicepipes never fail, even if they are damaged. **12** The flagship's buoy at her mooring in Scapa Flow was fitted with a cable that connected it to the Admiralty telephone network. **13** The silhouettes of the two ships were very similar, especially when viewed at over 10nm in the Arctic dawn. **14** Derek Howse, *Radar at Sea*, Basingstoke, MacMillan Press, 1993, Appendix F, p. 307ff. **15** Admiralty, CB 3053(4) *Naval Aircraft progress and Operations Periodical Summary Number 4*, London, December 1941, section 120, p. 22ff. **16** Sunset was at 0052 on 25 May 1941. **17** *Battle Summary*, p. 17ff. **18** John

Hoare, *Tumult in the Clouds – A Story of the Fleet Air Arm*, London, Michael Joseph, 1976, p. 93ff. **19** *Radar at Sea*, p. 91. **20** Michael Apps, *The Four Ark Royals*, London, William Kimber, 1976, p. 185ff. **21** David Mearns and Rob White, *Hood And Bismarck, the Deep Sea Discovery of an Epic Battle*, Basingstoke, Channel 4 Books, an imprint of Pan Macmillan Ltd, 2001, p. 176ff. **22** J David Brown, *Carrier Operations in World War II*, Barnsley, Seaforth Publishing, 2009, p. 18ff. **23** Michael Apps, *Send Her Victorious*, London, William Kimber, 1971, p. 50. **24** CB 3053 (4), section 151, p. 27ff. **25** Peter C Smith, *Eagle's War – The War Diary of an Aircraft Carrier*, Manchester, Crecy Books, 1995, p. 121ff. **26** B B Schofield, *The Russian Convoys*, London, Batsford, 1964, p. 7ff. **27** *The Development of British Naval Aviation*, Volume II, p. 168ff. **28** There is some confusion about whether 809 NAS provided eight or nine escort Fulmars. The text of the naval staff history contains later amendments than CB 3053 (4) but it, too, gives different numbers on pages 169 and 170. I believe that the higher number is based on the original combat reports and I have, therefore, used it in my narrative. **29** CB 3053 (4), section 181, p. 32. **30** *Furious* landed on twenty-one aircraft, some of them in damaged condition, in forty-three minutes without mishap. A good achievement given her age and the state of the art in 1941. **31** Used by 701 NAS' Walrus for maintenance during the brief 1940 Norwegian campaign. **32** *The Development of British Naval Aviation*, Volume II, p. 176ff. **33** Arnold Hague and Bob Ruegg, *Convoys to Russia 1941–1945*, Kendal, World Ship Society, 1992, p. 20ff. **34** *British Aircraft Carriers*, p. 42.

Chapter 6 1942

1 Peter Kemp, *The Escape of the Scharnhorst and Gneisenau*, Shepperton, Ian Allan, 1975, p. 9ff. **2** Admiralty, *Naval Staff History, The Development of British Naval Aviation 1919–1945* Volume II, London, 1956, p. 41ff. **3** Admiralty, CB 3053 (5) *Naval Aircraft Progress and Operations Summary* Number 5, London, June 1942, sections 105 to 119, p. 15ff. **4** It was to be demonstrated on many occasions throughout the conflict that committing untrained aircrew to operations in order to make up numbers was unlikely to be successful and would lead only to excessive losses. **5** Terence Robertson, *Channel Dash – The Drama of Twenty-four Hours of War*, London, Evans Brothers, 1958, p. 68ff. **6** I am indebted to Terence Robertson for his research into precisely what happened on that fateful day. It has allowed me to quote, verbatim, some of the exchanges that took place on the telephone between Constable-Roberts and Esmonde. Constable-Roberts retired from the RAF as an Air Commodore in 1958 and died in 1991. **7** It may be significant that Constable-Roberts had served with the Fleet Air Arm between 1927 and 1934. He had been a member of 481, 442 and 441 (Fleet Spotter Reconnaissance) Flights as well as 823 NAS from 1933 to 1934. In 1937 he elected to remain with the RAF when the Admiralty resumed full control of naval aviation after the Inskip Award and from 1940 to 1941 he commanded 206 Squadron RAF flying Hudsons. **8** Chaz Bowyer, *Eugene Esmonde VC DSO*, London, William Kimber, 1983, p. 138ff. **9** Ray Sturtivant with Mick Burrow, *Fleet Air Arm Aircraft 1939 to 1945*, Tunbridge Wells, Air Britain (Historians), 1995, p. 87ff. **10** Which he described in his report as 'balls out right through the gate'. **11** *Escape of the Scharnhorst & Gneisenau*, p. 64ff. **12** Published by Authority. *The London Gazette*, London, Third Supplement to the edition of 27 February 1942, dated 3 March 1942, pp. 1007–1008. **13** Bunce was a temporary leading airman but appears in the *London Gazette* as a naval airman. He was later confirmed in the higher rate and, since he flew on that fateful day as a leading airman, I have used that rate throughout this book. **14** Who commanded the Spanish Armada in 1588. **15** Admiralty/Air Ministry, *Report of the Board of Enquiry appointed to enquire into the circumstances in which the German battlecruisers Scharnhorst and Gneisenau and the cruiser Prinz Eugen proceeded from Brest to Germany on 12 February 1942 and on the operations undertaken to prevent this movement*, London, His Majesty's Stationary Office, March 1946, pp. 22 and 23. **16** *The Development of British Naval Aviation*, Volume II, p. 181ff. **17** *The Development of British Naval Aviation*, Volume II, p. 46ff. **18** C-in-C Home Fleet Report contained in M.050801/42 (under the old National Archive cataloguing system). **19** CB 4499(B), *Tirpitz* log, a copy of which is held in the Naval Historical Branch archive in Portsmouth Naval Base. **20** Vice Admiral E Weichold, *German Surface Ships: Policy and Operations in the Second World War* quoted on p. 188 of *The Development of British Naval Aviation* Volume II. **21** Percy Corry, *Our World was the Stage – A Personal History of Watts and Corry, Theatrical Contractors*, Manchester, Neil Richardson, 1984, p. 38ff. **22** Ibid., p. 41. **23** Admiralty, CB 3053 (6) Naval Aircraft Progress and Operations, Periodical Summary Number 6, period ended 31 December 1942, London dated February 1943, Section 129ff, p. 25ff. **24** *The Development of British Naval Aviation*, Volume II, p. 256ff. **25** Bob Ruegg and Arnold Hague, *Convoys to Russia*, Kendal, The World Ship Society, 1992, p. 34ff. **26** TNA Case 7607 quoted in *The Development of British Naval Aviation*, Volume II, p. 191. **27** *The Development of British Naval Aviation*, Volume II, p. 194ff. **28** Report M.051890/42 quoted in *The Development of British Naval Aviation*, Volume II, p. 195. **29** One of the Skua pilots who had attacked and sunk the German cruiser *Königsberg* on 10 April 1940. He had been 800 NAS' White section leader. **30** Cannon-armed Mark IIC Sea Hurricanes were first used in Operation Torch later in 1942 during the North African landings. **31** M.051890/42and TSD 1309/42 in Case 8196 at the National Archive, Kew, quoted in *The Development of British Naval Aviation*, Volume II, p. 201ff.

Chapter 7 1943
1 David Hobbs, Barnsley, Seaforth *British Aircraft Carriers – Design, Development and Service Histories* Publishing, 2013, p. 136. **2** Ibid., p. 132. **3** J David Brown, *Carrier Operations in World War II*, Barnsley, Seaforth Publishing, 2009, p. 23. **4** Bob Ruegg and Arnold Hague, *Convoys to Russia 1941–1945*, Kendal, World Ship Society, 1992, p. 55. **5** Admiralty, *Naval Staff History – The Development of British Naval Aviation 1919–1945*, Volume II, London, 1956, p. 269ff. **6** AP 2382, *Pilot's Notes for Hellcat I & II*, 2nd Edition, 1945. **7** Owen Thetford, *British Naval Aircraft Since 1912*, London, Putnam, 1962 edition, p. 68ff. **8** *The Development of British Naval Aviation*, Volume II, p. 230. **9** J David Brown, *Fairey Barracuda Marks I–VI*, Aircraft Profile 240, Windsor, Profile Publications, 1972, p. 121ff. **10** Bill Gunston, *Rolls Royce Aero Engines*, Yeovil, Patrick Stephens, 1989, p. 90ff. **11** From which the Lancaster with its four Merlin engines was derived. **12** Now London's Heathrow Airport. **13** Admiralty, CB 3053 (8), *Naval Aircraft Progress and Operations, Periodical Summary Number 8,* Period ended 31 December 1943, February 1944, section 289ff, p. 42ff.

Chapter 8 1944
1 HMS *Victorious*, December 1942 to September 1943. **2** The numbering of convoys to north Russia had been changed in December 1942 from the PQ/QP sequence to a new JW/RA sequence beginning with JW 51 and the contemporary RA 51. **3** Bob Ruegg and Arnold Hague, *Convoys to Russia 1941–1945*, Kendal, World Ship Society, 1992, p. 62ff. **4** Admiralty, *Naval Staff History Second World War, The Development of British Naval Aviation 1919–1945* Volume II, London, 1956, p. 205ff. **5** Admiralty, CB 3053 (9), *Naval Aircraft Progress and Operations*, Periodical Summary Number 9, Period ended 30 June 1944, London, September 1944, section 299ff, p. 47ff. **6** A word subsequently described by the Naval Historical Branch as 'monstrous'. It was used in contemporary official documents to denote modifications, alterations and additions made to ships to render them fit for service in the Arctic. **7** Ripley Registers, *Seedie's List of Fleet Air Arm Awards 1939–1969*, Tisbury, Ripley registers, 1990, p. 18. **8** *The Development of British Naval Aviation*, Volume II, p. 208ff. **9** Quoted in *The Development of British Naval Aviation*, Volume II, p. 210 with the original National Archive reference of Case 9069. **10** Standardised patrol and search measures listed in Appendix I to Atlantic Convoy Instructions. They were allocated the code names Cobra, Viper, Adder, Python, Mamba, Lizard, Frog, Alligator and Crocodile. **11** Orders reproduced from *The Development of British Naval Aviation*, Volume II, Appendix IX, p. 303ff. **12** *The Development of British Naval Aviation*, Volume II, p. 213. **13** Ibid., p. 215. **14** J David Brown, *Carrier Operations in World War II*, Barnsley, Seaforth Publishing, 2009, p. 24. **15** Theo Ballance, Lee Howard & Ray Sturtivant, *The Squadrons and Units of the Fleet Air Arm*, Staplefield, Air-Britain Publishing, 2016, relevant squadron entries. **16** Admiralty, CB 3081 (20), Battle Summary Number 27, *Naval Aircraft Attack on the Tirpitz, Operation Tungsten, 3 April 1944*, London, Admiralty, November 1944, section 2, p. 2ff. **17** Admiralty Signal 181413 of 18 April 1944 to C-in-C Home Fleet info VA 2BS. **18** Gervis Frere-Cook, *The Attacks on the Tirpitz*, Shepperton, Ian Allan, 1973, p. 73ff. **19** *Carrier Operations in World War II*, p. 28. **20** David Hobbs, *British Aircraft carriers – Design, Development and Service Histories*, Barnsley, Seaforth Publishing, 2013, p. 162. **21** In 1947 the USN, who still owned her under the Lend-Lease deal, sold her to a shipyard in Rotterdam, which rebuilt her as a merchant ship. **22** *The Development of British Naval Aviation*, Volume II, p. 222ff. **23** A future First Sea Lord. **24** David Hobbs, *British Aircraft Carriers – Design, Development and Service Histories*, Barnsley, Seaforth Publishing,

2013, pp. 136, 145 and 156. **25** Admiralty, CB 3053 (10) *Naval Aircraft Progress and Operations*, Periodical Summary Number 10, Period Ended 31 December 1944, London. March 1945, section 8, paragraphs 445ff. **26** Theo Ballance, Lee Howard and Ray Sturtivant, *The Squadrons and Units of the Fleet Air Arm*, Staplefield, Air-Britain Publishing, 2016, gives details of every squadron location. **27** *The Development of British Naval Aviation*, Volume II, Annex XXVII, p. 349ff. **28** At the end of the war many squadrons were hastily disbanded without squadron record books being given the historical importance they were due. Some found their way back to the Admiralty, some were kept as souvenirs by the record book officers when they were demobilised and others, sadly, were lost. Some eventually found their way to the National Archive, The Imperial War Museum and the Fleet Air Arm Museum. Sadly, when their keepers died many were thrown away by families who did not appreciate their historical importance. **29** Monthly Progress Report – 849/22/3 dated 3 August 1944. **30** Commander R 'Mike' Crosley DSC RN, *They Gave Me a Seafire*, Shrewsbury, Airlife Publishing, 1986, p. 118ff. **31** This account of how the GGS worked also takes into account the notes I took when I was lent to the Day Fighter/Ground Attack School at RAF Chivenor flying the Hawker Hunter FGA 9. **32** Admiralty, CB 3053 (9) *Naval Aircraft Progress and Operations – Periodical Summary* Number 9, London, period ended 30 June 1944, dated September 1944, section 242ff, p. 36ff. **33** Ibid., section 285ff, p. 40ff. **34** Fleet Air Arm Roll of Honour, copies of which are in the author's archive and the Royal Naval Museum at RNAS Yeovilton. **35** *The Development of British Naval Aviation*, Volume II, Appendix X, p. 305. **36** Ibid., p. 306. **37** CB 3053 (10). Section 302, p. 43. **38** *The Development of British Naval Aviation*, Volume II, Appendix X, p. 306. **39** CB 3053 (10). Section 356, p. 52. **40** CB 3053 (10). Section 357, p. 52. **41** Ibid., section 358, p. 52. **42** Ibid., section 337, p. 48ff and *The Development of British Naval Aviation*, Volume II, Appendix X, p. 308. **43** *The Development of British Naval Aviation*, Volume II, Appendix X, p. 308. **44** CB 3053 (10), Section 344ff, p. 50ff. **45** Ibid., Section 360, p. 53. **46** Ibid., Section 361, p. 53. **47** CB 3053 (10), Section 364ff, p. 54ff. **48** Ibid., Section 381ff, p. 56ff. **49** Ibid., Section 390ff, p. 57. **50** *The Development of British Naval Aviation*, Volume II, p. 231ff. **51** *Convoys to Russia*, p. 68ff. **52** John English, *Obdurate to Daring, British Fleet Destroyers 1941–1945*, Windsor, World Ship Society, 2008, p. 120ff. **53** CB 3053 (10), Section 396ff, p. 57ff.

Chapter 9 1945
1 Admiralty, CB 3053 (11), *Naval Aircraft Progress and Operations*, Periodical Summary Number 11, Period ended 30 June 1945, London, Admiralty, September 1945. **2** David Hobbs, *The British Carrier Strike Fleet After 1945*, Barnsley, Seaforth Publishing, 2020, Chapter 3, p. 76ff. **3** Admiralty. *Naval Staff History, The Development of British Naval Aviation 1919–1945*, Volume II, Appendix VIII, p. 300ff. **4** Ibid., p. 234ff, which quotes from 1 CS' 544/9/8 dated 28 February 1945. **5** *The Development of British Naval Aviation*, Volume II, Appendix VIII, p. 300. **6** J David Brown, *Warship Losses of World War Two*, London, Arms & Armour Press, 1990, p. 149. **7** *The Development of British Naval Aviation*, Volume II, Appendix XI, p. 310ff. **8** CB 3053 (11) section 411, p. 63. **9** Ibid., section 409, p. 63. **10** Fleet Air Arm Roll of Honour. **11** CB 3053 (11), section 412ff, p. 63ff. **12** *The Development of British Naval Aviation*, Volume II, Appendix XI, p. 311. **13** Confusingly this was also the operation name that had been allocated to the air strike on the Italian battle fleet in its harbour at Taranto on 11 November 1940. There were several instances throughout the war where operation names were recycled. **14** *The Development of British Naval Aviation*, Volume II, Appendix XI, p. 312. **15** 2301 Central European Time. **16** David Hobbs, *The British Carrier Strike Fleet after 1945*, Barnsley, Seaforth Publishing, 2020, Chapter 1. **17** David Hobbs, *Royal Navy Escort Carriers*, Liskeard, Maritime Books, 2003, is the source for the data used in this paragraph. **18** Theo Ballance, Lee Howard & Ray Sturtivant, *The Squadrons and Units of the Fleet Air Arm*, Stapleford, Air-Britain Publishing, 2016.

Bibliography

Primary Sources
CB 3307(1), Naval Staff History of the Second World War, *The Development of British Naval Aviation 1919–1945* Volume I, London, Naval Historical Branch, Admiralty, 1954.
CB 3307(2), Naval Staff History of the Second World War, *The Development of British Naval Aviation 1919–1945* Volume II, London, Naval Historical Branch, Admiralty, 1956.
Flight Deck, the Admiralty restricted journal on naval aviation matters, Volume I number 1 August 1944 to Volume II number 5 January 1946, London, Naval Air Division, Admiralty.
CB 3053(1), *Naval Aircraft Periodical Summary* Number 1, period ended 20 September 1940, London, Naval Air Division, Admiralty, October 1940.
CB 3053(2), *Naval Aircraft Periodical Summary* Number 2, period ended 3 February 1941, London, Naval Air Division, Admiralty, February 1941.
CB 3053(3), *Naval Aircraft Periodical Summary* Number 3, period ended 13 July 1941, London, Naval Air Division, Admiralty, July 1941.
CB 3053(4), *Naval Aircraft Progress and Operations Periodical Summary* Number 4, period ended 25 December 1941, London, Naval Air Division, Admiralty, December 1941.
CB 3052(5), *Naval Aircraft Progress and Operations Periodical Summary* Number 5, period ended 30 June 1942, London, Naval Air Division, Admiralty, June 1942.
CB 3053(6), *Naval Aircraft Progress and Operations Periodical Summary* Number 6, period ended 31 December 1942, London, Naval Air Division, Admiralty, February 1943.
CB 3053(7), *Naval Aircraft Progress and Operations Periodical Summary* Number 7, period ended 30 June 1943, London, Naval Air Division, Admiralty, August 1943.
CB 3053(8), *Naval Aircraft Progress and Operations Periodical Summary* Number 8, period ended 31 December 1943, London, Naval Air Division, Admiralty, February 1944.
CB 3053(9), *Naval Aircraft Progress and Operations Periodical Summary* Number 9, period ended 30 June 1944, London, Naval Air Division, Admiralty, September 1944.
CB 3053(10), *Naval Aircraft Progress and Operations Periodical Summary* Number 10, period ended 31 December 1944, London, Naval Air Division, Admiralty, March 1945.
CB 3053(11), *Naval Aircraft Progress and Operations Periodical Summary* Number 11, period ended 30 June 1945, London, Naval Air Division, Admiralty, September 1945.
CB 3305(2), Battle Summary Number 17, *Naval Operations of the Campaign in Norway*, Admiralty, 1951.
BR 1736, Battle Summary Number 27, *Naval Aircraft Attack on the TIRPITZ* (Operation Tungsten) 3 April 1944, Admiralty, 1945.
BR 1736 (3/50), Battle Summary Number 5, *The Chase and Sinking of the BISMARCK*, Admiralty, 1950.
BR 1736(32), Battle Summary Number 41, *The Evacuation from Dunkirk – Operation Dynamo*, Admiralty, 1949.
BR 1840(1), *The German Campaign in Norway – Origin of the plan, execution of the operation, and measures against Allied counter-attack*, Admiralty, 1948.
AP(N) 71, *Manual of Naval Airmanship*, London, Admiralty, 1949 edition.
AP(N) 144, *Naval Aircraft Handbook* (London, Admiralty, 1958 edition).
Milner F, Captain RN & Shercliff, R F, Captain RN, *The Fleet Air Arm Roll of Honour*, created in association with the Naval Historical Branch and the Fleet Air Arm Museum, 2011.

Published Secondary Sources

Apps, Michael, Lieutenant Commander, *Send Her Victorious* (London, William Kimber, 1971).

Apps, Michael, Lieutenant Commander, *The Four Ark Royals* (London, William Kimber, 1976).

Ballance, Theo with Howard, Lee & Sturtivant, Ray, *The Squadrons and Units of the Fleet Air Arm* (Staplefield, Air-Britain Publishing, 2016).

Barker, Ralph, *The Hurricats* (London, Pelham Books, 1978).

Barringer, E E, *Alone on a Wide, Wide Sea – The Story of 835 Naval Air Squadron in the Second World War* (London, Leo Cooper, 1995).

Bowyer, Chaz, *Eugene Esmonde VC DSO* (London, William Kimber, 1983).

Boyd, George, Lieutenant (A) RNVR, *Boyd's War – The Story of a Royal Navy Volunteer Reserve Fighter Pilot during the Second World War* (Newtownards, Colourpoint Books, 2002).

Brown, D K, *Nelson to Vanguard – Warship Design and Development 1923–1945* (London, Chatham Publishing, 2000).

Brown, Eric M, CBE DSC AFC RN, Captain, *Wings on My Sleeve* (London, Weidenfeld & Nicolson, 2006 revised edition).

Brown, Eric M, CBE DSC AFC RN, Captain, *Duels in the Sky – World War II Naval Aircraft in Combat* (Annapolis, Naval Institute Press, 1988).

Brown, Eric M, CBE DSC AFC RN, Captain, *Wings of the Navy* (London, Jane's Publishing, 1980).

Brown, Eric M, CBE DSC AFC RN, Captain, *Wings of the Luftwaffe – Flying the captured German aircraft of World War II* (Manchester, Hikoki/Crecy Publishing, 2010).

Brown, J David, (Edited by David Hobbs) *Carrier Operations in World War II* (Barnsley, Seaforth Publishing, 2009).

Brown, J David, *Fairey Fulmar Marks I & II*, Aircraft Profile 254 (Windsor, Profile Publications, 1973).

Brown, J David, *Carrier Fighters* (London, Macdonald & Jane's, 1975).

Brown, J David, *Aircraft Carriers – WW2 Fact Files* (London, Macdonald & Jane's, 1977).

Brown, J David, *The Seafire* (London, Greenhill Books, 1989 edition).

Brown, J David, *Warship Losses of World War Two* (London, Arms and Armour Press, 1995 edition).

Crosley, R, DSC, Commander RN, *They Gave Me a Seafire* (Shrewsbury, Airlife, 1986).

Cull, Brian and Galea, Frederick, *806 Naval Air Squadron – The FAA's top-scoring fighter squadron in the Second World War* (Stroud, Fonthill Media, 2019).

Dickens, Peter, *Narvik* (Shepperton, Ian Allan, 1974).

Ellis, Paul, *Aircraft of the Royal Navy* (London, Jane's Publishing, 1982).

Fletcher, R G, *Front Line Avenger Squadrons of the FAA* (Bury St Edmunds, Self-Published, 1995).

Frere-Cook, Gervis, *The Attacks on the Tirpitz* (Shepperton, Ian Allan, 1973).

Friedman, Norman, *British Carrier Aviation* (London, Conway Maritime Press, 1988).

Gunston, Bill, *Rolls-Royce Aero Engines* (Patrick Stephens Limited, 1989).

Haar, Geirr, *The German Invasion of Norway April 1940* (Barnsley, Seaforth Publishing, 2009).

Haar, Geirr, *The Battle for Norway April – June 1940* (Barnsley, Seaforth Publishing, 2010).

Hadley, Dunstan, *Barracuda Pilot* (Shrewsbury, Airlife Publishing, 1992).

Harrison, W A, *Fairey Swordfish and Albacore* (Marlborough, The Crowood Press, 2002).

Hibbert, Edgar, *HMS Unicorn – The Versatile Air Repair Ship* (Ilfracombe, Arthur H Stockwell, 2006).

Hill, Michael, *Duty Free – Fleet Air Arm Days* (Deal, Hovellers Press, 2003).

Hoare, John, *Tumult in the Clouds – A Story of the Fleet Air Arm* (London, Michael Joseph, 1976).

Hobbs, David, *Aircraft Carriers of the Royal and Commonwealth Navies* (London, Greenhill Books, 1996).

Hobbs, David, *Royal Navy Escort Carriers* (Liskeard, Maritime Books, 2003).

Hobbs, David, *British Aircraft Carriers – Design, Development and Service Histories* (Barnsley, Seaforth Publishing, 2013).

Hobbs, David, *The Dawn of Carrier Strike* (Barnsley, Seaforth Publishing, 2019).

Holmes, Robin, *The Battle of Heligoland Bight 1939 – The Royal Air Force and the Luftwaffe's Baptism of Fire* (London, Grub Street, 2009).
Hore, Peter, *Bletchley Park's Secret Source – Churchill's Wrens and the Y Service in World War II* (Barnsley, Greenhill Books, 2021).
Horsley, Terence, Lieutenant Commander RNVR, *Find, Fix and Strike – The Story of the Fleet Air Arm* (London, Eyre & Spottiswoode, 1943).
Howarth, Stephen and Law, Derek, Editors, *The Battle of the Atlantic 1939–1945* (London, Greenhill Books, 1994).
Howse, Derek, *Radar at Sea – The Royal Navy in World War 2* (Basingstoke, Macmillan Press for the Naval Radar Trust, 1993).
Jenkins, C A, Commander, *HMS Furious Part II 1925–1948* – Warship Profile 24 (Windsor, Profile Publications, 1972).
Jones, Ben, Editor, *The Fleet Air Arm in the Second World War* (Farnham, Ashgate Publishing for the Navy Records Society, 2012).
Kealy, J D F, & Russell, E C, *A History of Canadian Naval Aviation* (Ottawa, The Queen's Printer, 1967).
Kemp, Peter, *Escape of the Scharnhorst and Gneisenau* (Shepperton, Ian Allan, 1975).
King, H F, *Armament of British Aircraft 1909–1939* (London, Putnam, 1971).
Lamb, Gregor, *Sky Over Scapa 1939–1945* (Orkney, Byrgisey, 1991).
Lehan, Mike, *Flying Stations – A Story of Australian Naval Aviation* (St Leonard's, New South Wales, 1998).
Lenton H T & Colledge J J, *Warships of World War II* (Shepperton, Ian Allan, 1968 edition).
Lenton, H T, *German Submarines 1* (London, Macdonald, 1965).
Lenton, H T, *German Submarines 2* (London, Macdonald, 1965).
Lenton, H T, *British Battleships and Aircraft Carriers* (London, Macdonald, 1972).
MacBean, John A, Wing Commander & Hogben, Arthur S, Major, *Bombs Gone – The development and use of British Air-dropped weapons from 1912 to the present day* (Wellingborough, Patrick Stephens Limited, 1990).
Macintyre, Donald, *Narvik* (London, Evans Brothers, 1959).
Macintyre, Donald, *Wings of Neptune – The Story of Naval Aviation* (London, Peter Davies, 1963).
Mackenzie, Hector, *Observations* (Bishop Auckland, The Pentland Press, 1997).
Masters, A O 'Cappy', *Memoirs of a Reluctant Batsman – New Zealand Servicemen in the Fleet Air Arm 1940–1945* (London, Janus Publishing, 1995).
McCart, Neil, *HMS Victorious 1937–1969* (Cheltenham, Fan Publications, 1998).
McCart, Neil, *Three Ark Royals 1938–1999* (Cheltenham, Fan Publications, 1999).
Partridge, R T, DSO RM, Major, *Operation Skua* (Yeovilton, Friends of the Fleet Air Arm Museum, 1983).
Payne, Donald, *Swordfish* – From the Cockpit 10 (Ringshall, Ad Hoc Publications, 2008).
Phillips, Lawrie, TD RD, Lieutenant Commander RNR, *The Royal Navy Day by Day* (Stroud, the History Press, 2018 edition).
Poolman, Kenneth, *Ark Royal* (London, William Kimber, 1956).
Poolman, Kenneth, *The Catafighters and Merchant Aircraft Carriers* (London, William Kimber, 1970).
Poolman, Kenneth, *Escort Carrier 1941–1945* (Shepperton, Ian Allan, 1972).
Poolman, Kenneth, *Escort Carrier* (London, Secker & Warburg, 1983).
Popham, Hugh, *Into Wind – A History of British Naval Flying* (London, Hamish Hamilton, 1969).
Reece, Michael, Colonel, *Flying Royal Marines* (Eastney, Royal Marines' Historical Society, 2012).
Robertson, Terence, *Channel Dash – The Drama of Twenty-four Hours of War* (London, Evans Brothers, 1958).
Roskill, Stephen, Captain RN, History of the Second World War – *The War at Sea*, Volumes I to Volume III Part II, Her Majesty's Stationary Office.
Ross, Andrew T & Sandison James M with a forward by Jack McCaffrie, *A Historical Appreciation of the Contribution of Naval Air Power*, Papers in Australian Maritime Affairs Number 26 (Canberra, Sea Power Centre – Australia, 2008).
Rowe, Anthony, *Seedie's List of Fleet Air Arm Awards 1939–1969* (Chippenham, Ripley Registers, 1990).

B B Schofield, Vice Admiral, *The Russian Convoys* (London, Batsford, 1964).
B B Schofield, Vice Admiral, *Loss of the Bismarck* (Shepperton, Ian Allan, 1972).
B B Schofield, Vice Admiral, *Operation Neptune* (Shepperton, Ian Allan, 1974).
Smith, Peter C, *Skua! – The Royal Navy's Dive-Bomber* (Barnsley, Pen & Sword Aviation, 2006).
Soward, Stuart E, *Hands to Flying Stations – A Recollective History of Canadian Naval Aviation 1945–1954* (Victoria BC, Neptune Developments, 1993).
Spencer, H J C, *Ordinary Naval Airmen* (Tunbridge Wells, Spellmount, 1992).
Stott, Ian G, *Fairey Swordfish Marks I to IV*, Aircraft profile 212 (Windsor, Profile Publications, undated).
Sturtivant, Ray, *British Naval Aviation* (London, Arms & Armour Press, 1990).
Sturtivant, Ray with Burrow, Mick, *Fleet Air Arm Aircraft 1939 to 1945* (Tunbridge Wells, Air-Britain (Historians), 1995).
Taylor, H A, *Fairey Aircraft since 1915* (London, Putnam, 1974).
Thetford, Owen, *British Naval Aircraft since 1912* (London, Putnam, 1982 edition).
Thomas, Andrew, *Royal Navy Aces of World War 2* (Oxford, Osprey Publishing, 2007).
Till, Geoffrey, *Air Power and the Royal Navy 1914–1945 a historical survey* (London, Jane's Publishing, 1979).
Willis, Matthew, *Blackburn Skua & Roc* (Redbourn, Mushroom Model Publications, 2007).
Woods, Gerard A, *Wings at Sea – A Fleet Air Arm Observer's War 1940–1945* (London, Conway Maritime Press, 1985).

Index

Abbott, P H, Sub Lieutenant (A) RNVR, 229
Acasta, HMS, 61
Achates, HMS, 87, 94
Active, HMS, 92
Activity, HMS, 204–206, 208, 209, 211–213, 241–243, 245, 248
Admiral Scheer, German Armoured Ship, 85, 154
Adventure, HMS, 12
Admiralty, 1, 2, 4–7, 14–18, 24–28, 32–35, 43, 45, 49, 53, 61, 63–68, 70, 75–88, 90–92, 94, 101, 103, 111, 113, 115, 117, 128–131, 133, 135, 136, 145, 148, 151, 153, 154, 156, 157, 160–162, 165, 175, 177, 178, 180, 181, 185, 189, 190, 202–204, 210, 218, 221, 232, 233, 239, 240, 245, 246, 250, 251, 253, 257, 261, 264, 266, 267, 282, 283, 285, 291–295, 298, 305, 308, 317
Airfields (non naval)
  Banak, 169
  Bardufoss, 57–60, 64, 274, 305
  Beccles, 249
  Benbecula, 249
  Biggin Hill, 138, 139
  Bircham Newton, 76, 77, 79, 163, 249
  Castle Bromwich, 18
  Coltishall, 137, 194
  Dallachy, 249
  Dartmouth, Nova Scotia, 292
  Desford, 18
  Detling, 75, 76
  Docking, 163, 249
  Elmdon, 18
  Exeter, 194
  Fraserburgh, 249
  Gravesend, 18
  Harrowbeer, 248, 249
  Hawkinge, 135, 136, 248
  Hornchurch, 138, 139, 142
  Hyeres, 18
  Knocke-le-Zoute, 249

Langham, 163, 249
Leuchars, 18, 137
Limavady, 247–249
Long Kesh, 249
Maldeghen, 249
Manston, 76, 131, 136–139, 142, 146, 149, 152, 164, 193, 194, 248
Middle Wallop, 164
Mullaghmore, 247, 249
Netheravon, 18
Perranporth, 246–248
Peterborough, 18
Rochester, 18
Shawbury, 18
Skaanland, 58, 64
St Croix, 249
St Eval, 133, 249
Stornoway, 249
Sullom Voe, 52, 79
Sumburgh, 90, 154, 156
Swingfield, 249
Sydenham, 18
Sywell, 18
Tangmere, 164, 194
Thorney Island, 133, 163, 248, 249
Vaenga, 124, 168, 304
Vaernes, 44, 45, 51, 61, 62
Wick, 26, 31
Yarmouth, Nova Scotia, 292
Yatesbury, 18
Ajax, HMS, 22
Albatross, HMS, 10
Alderdale, RFA, 120, 121
Alexander, A V, First Lord of the Admiralty, 68, 81
Alexander, G, Sub Lieutenant (A) RNVR, 223, 260
Algonquin, HMCS, 227
Allen, C A, Lieutenant Commander (A) RNVR, 282
Allen, W A, Leading Airman RN, 229
Alnwick Castle, HMS, 301, 304

Andalsnes, 43, 44, 47–52, 54, 55
Anson, HMS, 180, 205, 214, 217, 258
Antelope, HMS, 87
Anthony, HMS, 87
Appleby, S G J, Sub Lieutenant (A) RN, 37
Archer, HMS, 163
Ardent, HMS, 61
Arethusa, HMS, 87
Argus, HMS, 2, 18, 73, 74, 83, 86, 111, 120, 121, 124
Ark Royal, HMS, 8, 9, 12, 19, 22–25, 31, 33, 43–52, 54–62, 65, 66, 68, 73, 84–86, 101–107, 131, 134
Armitage, J B, Lieutenant (A) RNZNVR, 224
Armstrong, J W, Leading Airman RN, 88, 90, 91
Armstrong, T, Leading Airman RN, 155
Ashanti, HMS, 33
Ashford, H, Sub Lieutenant (A) RNVR, 228
Ashton, J H, Petty Officer RN, 267
Assiniboine, HMCS, 92
Aurora, HMS, 86, 92
Avenger, HMS, 167–170, 172–176, 178, 202, 203

Bacon, R, Leading Airman RN, 228
Bailey, P E I, Lieutenant Commander RN, 252
Baker-Faulkner, R S, Lieutenant Commander RN, 216, 218, 221, 223, 226, 259, 260
Baker, R, Leading Airman RN, 102
Baldwin, K G, Petty Officer RN, 48
Ballantyne, A E, Sub Lieutenant (A) RNVR, 209
Ball, J N, Lieutenant RN, 114, 115
Ball, W A, Leading Airman RN, 224
Barnard, A A, Leading Airman RN, 42
Barrow, E, Petty Officer RN, 272
Barrow, L E, Leading Airman RN, 113, 116
Bassett, A H, Sub Lieutenant (A) RNVR, 255
Battler, HMS, 290
Bayliss, H T T, Captain RN, 278, 282, 285
Beagle, HMS, 205, 210
Beardsley, J, Leading Airman RN, 116
Bear Island, 119, 120, 157, 200, 210, 211, 278, 279, 288
Bebbington, M M, Sub Lieutenant (A) RNVR, 229
Beech, J, Leading Airman RN, 200
Beer, C F, Leading Airman RN, 116
Belfast, HMS, 217
Bell, T C, Sub Lieutenant (A) RNVR, 224, 227
Bell-Davies, R, Vice Admiral, 62
Bellona, HMS, 287, 301, 303
Bennet, Sub Lieutenant (A) RNVR, 139
Bennet, D R, Sub Lieutenant (A) RNVR, 267
Bentinck, W W R, Captain RN, 215, 241, 242, 244, 245

Beresford, P J, Sub Lieutenant (A) RNVR, 200
Bergen, 33–35, 41, 42, 54, 87–92, 154
Berwick, HMS, 83, 154, 156, 261, 287
Beynon, W, Sub Lieutenant (A) RNVR, 141
Binney, Sir Hugh, Admiral, 151
Bird, R A, Lieutenant Commander RN, 181, 310
Birmingham, HMS, 12, 86, 87, 313
Bismarck, German Battleship, 85–87, 89, 92–98, 100–107
Bisset, A W LaT, Rear Admiral, 214, 217, 221, 225, 231
Biter, HMS, 163, 205
Blackburn Firebrand, 294
Blackburn Roc, 28, 29, 44, 54–56, 75, 82
Blackburn Skua, 8, 11, 12, 15, 17, 23, 27, 32, 33, 35, 41–48, 50–52, 54–59, 61, 62, 65, 66, 71, 73–76, 82, 83, 318
Black, J F, Petty Officer RN, 116
Black Prince, HMS, 198
Black Watch, German Depot Ship, 311, 312
Blake, A G, Sub Lieutenant (A) RN, 72
Bligh, P, Sub Lieutenant (A) RNVR, 139, 141
Bluebell, HMS, 301
Blue Ranger, RFA, 217
Boadicea, HMS, 201, 205
Boddam-Whetham, A P, Lieutenant Commander RN, 247
Bodo, 64, 124–126, 183, 258–260, 272
Bonaventure, HMS, 83
Bone, J W, Petty Officer RN, 270
Borrett, C S, Lieutenant Commander RN, 8
Bostock, R S, Lieutenant RN, 32, 50, 62
Boucher, M W S, Rear Admiral, 283
Bovell, H C, Captain RN, 113, 115, 119
Bovey, N H, Sub Lieutenant (A) RNVR, 229
Bowles, E C, Sub Lieutenant (A) RNVR, 228
Bramwell, H P, Lieutenant Commander RN, 46, 47, 50
Brest, 85, 86, 101, 102, 107, 128, 129, 133, 134, 251
Brewster Buffalo, 73
Brilliant, HMS, 107
Brind, E J P, Commodore RN, 90, 91
Brine, B F, Sub Lieutenant (A) RNVR, 260
Britton, J D, Sub Lieutenant (A) RNVR, 224
Brokensha, G W, Sub Lieutenant (A) RN, 46, 48, 50, 52, 53, 62
Bromwich, H F, Lieutenant Commander (A) RN, 215
Brooks, D, Lieutenant Commander (A) RNVR, 215, 229
Brooks, H J, Leading Airman RN, 309
Brown, D A, Sub Lieutenant (A) RNZNVR, 224
Brown, J M, Lieutenant Commander (A) RNVR, 247

INDEX

Brown, J R, Sub Lieutenant (A) RNVR, 223, 262
Brown, K R, Sub Lieutenant (A) RNVR, 265
Brown, L, Sub Lieutenant (A) RNVR, 160
Brown, W H G, Sub Lieutenant (A) RNVR, 158
Brown, W L M, Lieutenant Commander RN, 38
Brown Ranger, RFA, 217
Browse, A E, Sub Lieutenant (A) RNVR, 224
Bucknill, Sir Alfred, Judge, 151
Bunce, D A, Leading Airman RN, 141, 145, 150
Burch, A R, Captain RM, 35, 38, 39
Burford, G J, Sub Lieutenant (A) RNVR, 229
Burke, E S, Sub Lieutenant (A) RNVR, 116
Burnett, R, Rear Admiral, 169, 171–176
Burns, G J, Leading Airman RN, 224, 227
Burroughs, R A, Sub Lieutenant (A) RNVR, 119
Burton, A G, Leading Airman RN, 76
Burton, R D, Sub Lieutenant (A) RNVR, 224
Bussey, B P, Leading Airman RN, 224, 262

Calais, 77, 137, 142, 148, 164
Calcutta, HMS, 46
Callender, J R, Lieutenant (A) RN, 102
Cambell, B D, Lieutenant RN, 97
Cambell, D R F, Lieutenant Commander RN, 8, 23, 25
Camidge, C R, Sub Lieutenant (A) RNVR, 108
Campania, HMS, 270, 287, 290, 298–301, 303–305, 307, 315
Campbell, HMS, 146, 147
Campbell-Horsfall, C P, Lieutenant RN, 76
Cannon, A G, Sub Lieutenant (A) RNVR, 228, 230
Carne, W P, Captain RN, 278, 281
Carr, A E, Chief Petty Officer RN, 224
Carr, W E, Sub Lieutenant (A) RNVR, 285
Carroll, E, Leading Airman RN, 228, 230
Cartnell, T, Leading Airman RN, 223
Cartwright, J, Sub Lieutenant (A) RNVR, 229
Carver, R M P, Lieutenant RN, 55
Cassandra, HMS, 288, 289
Casson, J, Lieutenant Commander RN, 61, 62
Chance Vought Corsair, 186, 187, 213, 215, 221, 222, 225, 229, 230, 235–240, 259–261, 264, 265, 315
Chance Vought Kingfisher, 184
Charlton, P N, Lieutenant Commander (A) RN, 215
Chaser, HMS, 198–203, 210
Chatfield, Sir Ernle, Admiral of the Fleet, First Sea Lord, 6
Christian, J M, Lieutenant RN, 47, 99

Church, W C A, Lieutenant (A) RN, 51
Churchill, Winston, Prime Minister, 1, 63, 68, 73, 85, 109, 111
Clarabut, D S, Sub Lieutenant (A) RNVR, 224
Clare, Petty Officer RN, 76
Clarke, M L, Captain RN, 8
Clayton, A G, Petty Officer RN, 76
Clayton, A, Leading Airman RN, 58
Clinton, W J, Leading Airman RN, 141, 143, 144, 151
Coates, E C, Lieutenant Commander RN, 147
Cockburn, J C, Lieutenant Commander RN, 55, 56
Coe, J, Sub Lieutenant (A) RNVR, 229
Coghill, H A, Sub Lieutenant (A) RNVR, 255
Collett, D W, Sub Lieutenant (A) RNVR, 223
Colquhoun, K S, Captain RN, 305
Colthurst, A P, Commander RN, 169, 170, 172, 174, 176
Colwell, C J, Leading Airman RN, 228
Constable-Roberts, J, Wing Commander RAF, 136–140
Coode, T P, Lieutenant Commander RN, 103
Cooksey, I D C, Sub Lieutenant (A) RNVR, 228
Cooper, J, Sub Lieutenant (A) RN, 113
Cooper, J, Lieutenant Commander (A) RNVR, 215
Cork and Orrery, Lord, Admiral of the Fleet, 38, 61
Cork, R J, Sub Lieutenant (A) RN, 72
Corner, D W, Leading Airman RN, 116
Cosh, D R B, Lieutenant Commander RCNVR, 215
Coston, F, Leading Airman, RN, 53
Cotching, J A, Sub Lieutenant (A) RNVR, 263
Cotterill, C J E, Petty Officer RN, 25
Coulby, J, Leading Airman RN, 223
Courageous, HMS, 8, 10, 19, 22, 31, 283
Cranwell, R A, Sub Lieutenant (A) RNZNVR, 263
Crawford, W, Petty Officer RN, 48
Cridland, T L, Chief Petty Officer RN, 228
Crosley, R M, Lieutenant (A) RNVR, 254, 255
Cubitt, L A, Lieutenant Commander RN, 112
Curacoa, HMS, 47
Curlew, HMS, 49, 53
Curteis, A T B, Rear Admiral, 86

Dale, R F, Naval Airman RN, 38
Dalrymple-Hamilton, Sir Frederick, Vice Admiral, 205, 278, 282, 283
Dalyell-Stead, J, Lieutenant RN, 8

Daniel, C S, Captain RN, 63, 64, 68
D'Arcy, K J, Captain RN, 305
Darley, A T, Lieutenant RN, 40
Darling, P G, Lieutenant RCNVR, 223
Dasher, HMS, 163, 179, 180
Davies, G O C, Captain RN, 215
Davies, J A, Lieutenant (A) RNVR, 267
Davies, J J R, Sub Lieutenant (A) RN, 116
Dawson-Paul, F, Sub Lieutenant (A) RN, 72
Dean, F A, Leading Airman RN, 108
de Havilland Sea Mosquito, 294
Denbigh Castle, HMS, 298, 301, 304
Denington, P A, Sub Lieutenant (A) RNVR, 108
Denny, M M, Captain RN, 215, 218, 220, 232, 234
Devonald, S L, Lieutenant Commander (A) RN, 252, 255
Devonshire, HMS, 112, 119, 120, 274
Diadem, HMS, 205, 241, 281, 310
Dido, HMS, 274, 282
Dorsetshire, HMS, 101, 106, 107
Douglas Dauntless, 183
Dover, Straits of, 133, 135–138, 140, 148, 151, 164, 193, 194
D'Oyly-Hughes, G, Captain RN, 44
Drennan, R N, Sub Lieutenant (A) RNVR, 224, 227
Dubbie, A H, Sub Lieutenant (A) RNVR, 224
Duke of York, HMS, 153, 156, 165, 205, 214, 217, 231
Dunedin, HMS, 83, 107, 109
Dunkirk, 66, 68, 71, 75, 76
Dunworth, G, Sub Lieutenant (A) RNVR, 158
Dwyer, T, Naval Airman RN, 40

Eagle, HMS, 2, 17, 86, 107, 108, 269
Echo, HMS, 94, 112
Eclipse, HMS, 112, 120
Edinburgh, HMS, 94
Edwards, R A B, Captain RN, 91
Elder, A D H, Sub Lieutenant (A) RNVR, 312
Electra, HMS, 87, 94
Elias, P R, Sub Lieutenant (A) RN, 102
Ellis, R M, Captain RN, 100
Emerson, H R, Lieutenant (A) RNZNVR, 223
Emperor, HMS, 213–217, 221, 222, 246, 258, 263
Empire Lawrence, CAM-Ship, 167
Empire Mackay, MAC-Ship, 290
Empire Morn, CAM-Ship, 165, 175
Empire Tide, CAM-Ship, 167
Emsley, E E G, Lieutenant Commander (A) RNVR, 285
Erratt, S A, Sub Lieutenant (A) RNVR, 228

Escapade, HMS, 112, 120
Esk, HMS, 63
Esmonde, E, Lieutenant Commander (A) RN, 95, 96, 131, 134, 136, 138, 140–144, 146, 148, 149, 151–153, 318
Evans, C L G, Commander RN, 271
Evans, D, Sub Lieutenant (A) RNVR, 285
Eveleigh, R L, Sub Lieutenant (A) RNVR, 224
Everett, R N, Lieutenant RN, 51

Fabien, E P, Leading Airman RN, 116
Fairclough, J C, Sub Lieutenant (A) RNVR, 224
Fairey Albacore, 29, 30, 71, 77, 78, 80, 110–116, 121, 124, 126, 154–156, 158–160, 162, 164, 168, 180, 189, 190, 193–196
Fairey Barracuda, 161, 162, 165, 166, 189–192, 213, 215, 218–222, 225–227, 229–231, 235–240, 247, 249, 258–262, 264–266, 268–273, 275, 276, 291, 294, 309, 315, 317
Fairey Firefly, 187, 188, 235, 236, 238, 240, 266, 268–273, 275–277, 295, 296, 310, 314, 317
Fairey Fulmar, 27–29, 73, 80, 82, 91, 97–99, 103, 111–115, 117–119, 121, 124–127, 165, 190, 280, 286, 287, 291, 295, 299, 301, 306
Fairey Seafox, 13, 17, 22
Fairey Swordfish, 8–11, 17, 19, 22, 23, 27, 33, 35–39, 41, 44, 46, 51, 55, 56, 58, 64–66, 68, 71, 73, 74, 76–78, 82–84, 91, 94, 95, 97, 99, 101–109, 111–114, 131, 132, 137–146, 149, 152, 153, 163, 168–172, 174, 176, 178–180, 182, 189, 190, 193, 198–207, 209, 211, 212, 216, 242–249, 263, 265, 270, 278–285, 287–290, 297, 299–302, 304–307, 315, 317
Fancourt, H L StJ, Captain RN, 87, 88, 166
Farrer, M C, Sub Lieutenant (A) RNZNVR, 228
Faulkner, HMS, 174
Fell, M F, Lieutenant Commander (A) RN, 55, 217, 229
Fencer, HMS, 214–218, 221, 241–246, 265, 267, 268, 283
Fenton, J E, Lieutenant Commander RN, 8
Filmer, C H, Lieutenant RN, 47
Finch-Noyes, E D G, Lieutenant RN, 25, 48, 50, 62
Firth, W, Leading Airman RN, 228
Fison, J C, Lieutenant Commander RN (Ret), 10
Flamingo, HMS, 48
Forbes, Sir Charles, Admiral, 23–27, 33, 40, 47, 49, 54, 56, 61, 62, 68
Force H, 68, 84–86, 101–103, 105
Force K, 23, 84

INDEX

Force M, 120, 121, 124, 125
Force P, 111, 112, 115–119
Ford, P P, Leading Airman RN, 114
Formidable, HMS, 75, 80, 84, 86, 180–182, 214, 235, 236, 239, 240
Fortune, HMS, 33
Fossevag, 263
Fox, A, Leading Airman RN, 116
Franklin, D, Leading Airman RN, 200, 201
Franklin, L C, Sub Lieutenant (A) RN, 38
Fraser-Harris, A B, Lieutenant RN, 42, 45
Fraser, Sir Bruce, Admiral, 205, 213, 217, 234, 240, 258
French, J H, Sub Lieutenant (A) RNVR, 240
Fuller-Wright, E H, Sub Lieutenant (A) RNVR, 141
Furious, HMS, 4, 8, 9, 33–40, 57, 65, 66, 73, 74, 76, 83, 86, 109, 111–113, 115, 116, 118, 119, 125, 163, 178, 180, 181, 214, 215, 217, 218, 221, 222, 224, 227, 229, 235, 236, 238, 240, 249, 258, 259, 261–268
Furlong, F C, Lieutenant (A) RNVR, 97–100

Gahan, F J, Lieutenant (A) RNVR, 312
Galatea, HMS, 86, 92
Gale, H E K, Sub Lieutenant (A) RNVR, 223
Gallagher, L H, Midshipman (A) RN, 52, 62
Gallichan, F J G, Sub Lieutenant (A) RN, 116
Gallimore, V, Leading Airman RN, 229
Gardner, R E, Sub Lieutenant (A) RN, 72
Gardner, R J, Captain RN, 305
Gaunt, J A, Sub Lieutenant (A) RNVR, 267
George VI, HM The King, 234
Gibney, K H, Lieutenant Commander (A) RN, 215, 223, 247
Gibson, D C E F, Lieutenant RN, 55
Gledhill, J A, Sub Lieutenant (A) RNVR, 223
Gleeve, T, Wing Commander RAF, 137, 142, 149
Glennie, I G, Vice Admiral, 198
Glennie, M A, Sub Lieutenant (A) RNVR, 267
Glorious, HMS, 6, 17, 31, 33, 43–49, 54–61, 65, 66, 76
Gloster Sea Gladiator, 13, 17, 26, 44, 47, 49, 55, 56, 65, 73, 166
Glover, A H, Petty Officer RN, 58, 59
Gneisenau, German Battlecruiser, 61, 84–86, 128, 129, 136, 144, 146, 148, 151, 153
Goddard, N E, Lieutenant (A) RNVR, 88–91
Godfrey-Fausset, D F, Lieutenant RN, 51
Goodall, HMS, 305
Goodfellow, R M, Lieutenant (A) RNZNVR, 269
Goodger, M G, Sub Lieutenant (A) RNVR, 97
Graf Zeppelin, German Aircraft Carrier, 161

Graham, H R, Captain RN, 215
Grant, J A, Sub Lieutenant (A) RNVR, 224, 262
Gray, T E, Lieutenant RN, 58, 59
Green, E E, Sub Lieutenant (A) RNVR, 223
Grenade, HMS, 37
Grenfell, V C, Lieutenant Commander RN, 112, 113
Grieveson, J, Sub Lieutenant (A) RNVR, 223
Grindred, G W, Lieutenant (A) RNVR, 228
Grumman Avenger, 183, 192, 204, 206, 207, 209–213, 236, 237, 246, 247, 266–268, 270, 274, 277, 278, 282, 284, 286, 291, 294, 305–312, 315
Grumman Hellcat, 184, 185, 213, 216, 225, 227, 229–231, 235–238, 240, 246, 258, 260, 263, 264, 266, 291, 295–297, 315
Grumman Martlet/Wildcat, 5, 6, 26, 30, 73, 120, 124, 125, 180, 181, 183, 185, 187, 198, 200–207, 209–213, 216, 225, 229–231, 235, 236, 242, 243, 246, 248, 258–263, 265–268, 270, 273, 274, 277–280, 282, 283, 285–288, 298–303, 305–313, 315, 319

Haakoy Island, 241, 269
Hadley, J, Petty Officer RN, 48
Halhead, T W, Petty Officer RN, 229
Halifax, G W, Naval Airman RN, 52
Hall, G A, Sub Lieutenant (A) RNVR, 269
Hall, M, Leading Airman RN, 32
Hall, S J, Lieutenant Commander RN, 215
Hallett, N G, Commander RN, 252–257
Hamersley, A, Sub Lieutenant (A) RNVR, 228
Hammerfest, 119, 200
Hampden, G R, Sub Lieutenant (A) RN, 38
Hanson, M C E, Lieutenant RN, 23, 31, 34, 35, 42, 46, 47, 52, 58, 59
Harald Haarfagre, German Anti-Aircraft Ship, 311, 312
Harding, T, Leading Airman RN, 228
Hare, G, Lieutenant Commander RN, 35
Harris, L A, Lieutenant RM, 50
Harrison, N, Sub Lieutenant (A) RNVR, 228
Harrowar, J B, Lieutenant Commander RNR, 247
Hartley, J V, Sub Lieutenant (A) RN, 102
Harvey, D J R, Sub Lieutenant (A) RNVR, 155
Hawker Sea Hurricane, 5, 112, 113, 168, 170–174, 176, 179, 181, 202, 263, 278, 279, 306
Haworth, R B, Sub Lieutenant (A) RNVR, 119
Hay, R C, Lieutenant RM, 51
Hayes, H L, Lieutenant Commander RN, 10
Head, R D, Lieutenant Commander (A) RN, 205, 247

Henderson, G R, Lieutenant Commander (A) RNVR, 215, 229
Henderson, T M, Sub Lieutenant (A) RNVR, 229
Hermes, HMS, 2, 3, 10, 19
Hermione, HMS, 92
Herrold, J D, Sub Lieutenant (A) RNZNVR, 223, 260
Hilken, T J N, Captain RN, 215
Hipper, German Cruiser, 61, 83–85
Hoare, J E M, Sub Lieutenant RCNVR, 97–100
Hodgkinson, G B, Lieutenant Commander RN, 8
Hodson, G F S, Lieutenant Commander (A) RNR, 215, 247
Hogg, G S, Midshipman (A) RNVR, 76
Holland, C S, Captain RN, 44
Holland, L E, Vice Admiral, 86, 87, 92, 93
Hollis, P, Sub Lieutenant (A) RNVR, 228
Hollowood, S G, Leading Airman RN, 160
Hollway, R, Sub Lieutenant (A) RNVR, 264
Home Fleet, 6–8, 17, 19, 20, 23, 25, 26, 31, 33, 35, 37, 42, 43, 49, 59, 64–66, 68, 73, 79, 80, 86–88, 91, 92, 109–111, 117, 120, 127–129, 153, 156, 160, 165, 167–169, 178–180, 182–184, 197, 198, 205, 213, 220, 235, 236, 240, 241, 257, 258, 266–271, 273, 274, 278, 281, 282, 287, 290, 297–299, 305, 306, 312–314, 316–319
Hood, HMS, 23, 25, 86, 87, 92–94, 106
Hordern, L A, Lieutenant Commander (A) RNVR, 215, 229
Hoyte, H N, Leading Airman RN, 223
Hudson, P, Lieutenant RN, 228
Hughes, W L, Midshipman (A) RNVR, 108
Hughes-Hallett, C C, Captain RN, 271
Hughes-Williams, E E, Lieutenant (A) RNVR, 115
Humphreys, P W, Lieutenant Commander RN, 8
Hunter, E, Leading Airman RN, 223
Hunter, P, Sub Lieutenant (A) RNVR, 229
Huntley, J H, Captain RN, 205, 282, 286
Hurle-Hobbs, B H, Sub Lieutenant RN, 48, 50
Hurst, C G, Lieutenant (A) RNVR, 229
Hurstwick, N B, Lieutenant (A) RNZNVR, 228
Hutchinson, V, Sub Lieutenant (A) RNVR, 229
Hutton, F E P, Captain RN, 10
Huxley, N, Leading Airman RN, 102

Icarus, HMS, 63, 87, 94, 112
Iceland, 73, 79, 87, 92, 94, 99, 112, 125, 129, 154, 169, 180
Illustrious, HMS, 73, 75, 80.86, 181, 183, 248
Implacable, HMS, 197, 268–271, 273–275, 277, 290
Impulsive, HMS, 63, 198
Indefatigable, HMS, 197, 235–237, 240, 265, 266
Indomitable, HMS, 183
Inglefield, HMS, 92, 112, 120
Inskip, Sir Thomas, Minister for Defence Coordination, 1, 6, 82
Intrepid, HMS, 92, 112
Ivanhoe, HMS, 63

Jamaica, HMS, 180, 217, 258, 278
Javelin, HMS, 217
Johnson, A G, Petty Officer RN, 52, 53
Johnson, A L, Leading Airman RN, 138, 141, 143, 144, 151
Johnstone, M, Lieutenant Commander RN, 103
Jones, A G, Leading Airman RN, 75
Jones, F V, Lieutenant Commander (A) RNVR, 284
Jones, R C, Sub Lieutenant (A) RNVR, 160
Jouning, L J, Sub Lieutenant (A) RNVR, 223
Judd, F E C, Lieutenant Commander RN, 112, 119

Kaa Fjord, 213, 214, 218, 219, 221, 224, 230, 241, 264, 269
Keene, D, Sub Lieutenant (A) RNVR, 255
Kent, HMS, 258
Kenya, HMS, 86, 92, 98, 157
Keppel, HMS, 205
Kilbotn, 274, 310, 311, 313, 319
Kimber, H, Petty Officer RN, 51, 76
Kimberley, A M, Leading Airman RN, 223
King, D M, Sub Lieutenant (A) RNVR, 309
King, E M, Sub Lieutenant (A) RNVR, 229
King George V, HMS, 84, 86, 87, 91, 94, 101, 102, 106, 125, 126, 153, 154, 156, 157, 165
Kingdon, R D, Lieutenant Commander (A) RNVR, 215, 224
Kingsley-Rowe, C A, Lieutenant Commander RN, 8
Kingsmill, C M, Sub Lieutenant (A) RNVR, 141, 143–145, 150
Kirkenes, 109–115, 117–119, 121
Kite, HMS, 278, 280
Kitley, I, Leading Airman RN, 228
Knight, E D, Sub Lieutenant (A) RNVR, 224
Knight, R T, Leading Airman RN, 228
Kola Inlet, 109, 110, 180, 200, 212, 241, 243, 281, 283, 284, 287, 288, 298, 300, 301, 303, 305
Königsberg, German Cruiser, 34, 35, 42, 82

INDEX

Laing, D F, Sub Lieutenant (A) RNVR, 200
Lamb, R R, Sub Lieutenant (A) RN, 49
Lance, HMS, 92
Landles, J D, Sub Lieutenant (A) RNVR, 155
Larcom, C A A, Captain RN, 103
Large, J G, Lieutenant (A) RNVR, 243
Lark, HMS, 300, 301
Leach, J C, Captain RN, 93
Lee, E F, Sub Lieutenant (A) RNVR, 138, 141, 143–146, 149–151
Lee, R H, Leading Airman RN, 223
Legion, HMS, 92
Lett, W H, Sub Lieutenant (A) RNVR, 108
Lewin, E D G, Lieutenant Commander RN, 103
Lindley, Leading Airman RN, 158
Lindores, W S, Lieutenant (A) RNVR, 229
Lloyd, L M, Petty Officer RN, 45
Loch Dunvegan, HMS, 280
Loch Eriboll, 214, 217, 220
Lock, C M, Sub Lieutenant (A) RNVR, 223
Lock, S W, Petty Officer RN, 224
Lofoten Islands, 40, 64, 125, 126, 157, 310, 311
Luard, N S, Lieutenant Commander RN, 10
Lucas, W J, Lieutenant Commander RN, 158, 159
Lucy, W P, Lieutenant RN, 31, 32, 34, 35, 42, 44–49, 52, 53, 58, 59, 61, 318
Lulea, 63–69
Lützow, German Armoured Ship, 154
Lyster, A L StF, Rear Admiral, 117

Mackay, HMS, 146, 147
Mackintosh, L D, Captain RN, 213, 269
Maffey, L W E, Lieutenant (A) RNZNVR, 309
Magpie, HMS, 205
Mahratta, HMS, 199, 202
Mainprice, W J, Lieutenant Commander RN, 247
Maitland, P W, Petty Officer RN, 269
Makeig-Jones, W T, Captain RN, 8
Malaya, HMS, 11, 84
Manchester, HMS, 86, 87
Mansfield, P B, Leading Airman RN, 312
Maori, HMS, 33, 45, 106
Marmont, J P, Lieutenant RN, 55, 56
Marsh, P E, Sub Lieutenant RN, 49
Marshall, J, Midshipman (A) RNVR, 75
Martin Maryland, 88–91
Martyn, W H Lieutenant Commander (A) RN, 215
Mason, J F, Sub Lieutenant (A) RNVR, 200, 201
Matabele, HMS, 120
Matchless, HMS, 198
Mathew, H D, Lieutenant RN, 119
Mauritius, HMS, 270

McClintock, H V P, Captain RN, 198, 199, 201–204
McCormack, J, Sub Lieutenant (A) RNVR, 223
McEwen, B S, Lieutenant RN, 24, 25
McGrigor, Sir Rhoderick, Rear Admiral, 241, 245, 280, 298, 300–302, 304, 310
McIver, E D, Captain RM, 42
McKay, D R, Sub Lieutenant (A) RNVR, 116
McKay, G V, Petty Officer RN, 19
McKendrick, M G, Lieutenant RN, 115
McRae, G S, Leading Airman RN, 229
Meredith, M, Lieutenant (A) RNVR, 228
Mermaid, HMS, 280
Meteor, HMS, 198
Micklom, G M, Lieutenant RN, 223
Miller, D S, Lieutenant (A) RNVR, 229
Miller, I L T, Sub Lieutenant (A) RNVR, 288
Miller, T T, Sub Lieutenant (A) RN, 158
Mills, E A, Midshipman (A) RNVR, 116
Milne, HMS, 198
Milne, J D, Leading Airman RN, 88, 90, 91
Milwaukee, USS, 205, 213
Ministry of Aircraft Production, 80, 81, 317, 319
Monk, H A, Petty Officer RN, 32
Moore, Sir Henry, Admiral, 213, 217, 219, 231, 240, 258, 270, 271, 312
Morgan, E B, Lieutenant Commander (A) RANVR, 247
Morrison, H, Lieutenant (A) RNZNVR, 312
MTB 221, 138
Murmansk, 109, 124, 125, 165, 286
Murray, W, Leading Airman RN, 223, 260

Nabob, HMS, 236, 237, 266, 267
Nairana, HMS, 198, 282–285, 287, 288, 290, 298, 301–304, 306, 307, 310, 315
Namsos, 43, 46, 47, 54, 55
Narvik, 37, 38, 40, 57–59, 63, 66, 117, 201
Naval Air Squadrons
 700, 11, 79
 701, 57, 60, 73, 7
 710, 10
 746, 310
 751, 316
 761, 28, 127
 769, 8
 771, 88–90
 784, 280
 787, 191
 800, 8, 31, 32, 34, 42, 44, 46, 48, 50, 51, 53, 57, 61, 66, 112, 115, 116, 185, 215, 216, 221, 246, 258, 263–264
 800Z, 91, 98
 801, 8, 13, 31, 33, 41, 44, 46, 48–51, 53, 54, 57, 73–76, 83, 197, 215, 236, 264–267
 802, 44, 49, 55, 120, 124, 168, 171, 176

803, 8, 19, 23, 24, 26, 31, 34, 42, 44–49, 52, 53, 57, 58, 61, 66
804, 26, 31, 44, 49, 55, 70, 71, 73, 215, 216, 229, 246, 258, 260, 263
806, 73, 75
807, 103
808, 70, 71, 103, 252
809, 112–114, 116, 121, 124
810, 8, 44, 45, 51, 66, 103, 104
811, 8, 19, 163, 246, 247, 249, 282, 284, 285
812, 76–78, 112, 163
813, 270, 280–282, 287, 289, 298–301, 304, 305, 315
814, 10
815, 73, 76, 78
816, 8, 33, 35–37, 66, 73, 74, 163, 179, 198, 201, 242, 246, 247
817, 111, 112, 121, 124–126, 155, 156, 158
818, 8, 33, 35–38, 66, 78, 103, 104
819, 73, 163, 205, 209, 211, 212, 242, 246–249, 291
820, 8, 44, 45, 51, 66, 103, 104, 180, 236, 266
821, 62, 66, 308, 309, 315
822, 4, 8, 14, 22, 66, 132
823, 6, 62, 76, 164
824, 263, 265, 278, 279, 282
825, 6, 73, 74, 76, 91, 94, 95, 97, 100, 107, 131, 132, 134, 137–139, 141, 142, 144–146, 148, 153, 163, 168, 176, 178, 247, 249, 278–280, 285, 297, 298, 316
826, 77, 78, 195, 236, 266
827, 112, 114–116, 192, 215, 216, 223, 227, 236, 247, 249, 260–262, 264–266
828, 87, 88, 112, 115, 116, 236, 268, 270, 275
829, 78, 215, 216, 228–230, 264
830, 215, 216, 224, 227, 238, 261, 262, 264, 266
831, 215, 216, 229, 230, 264
832, 121, 124, 126, 154, 158, 160
832B, 164
835, 282, 284, 287–289, 299–302, 304, 316
836, 163, 290
838, 246–249
841, 164, 193–196, 268–270
842, 215, 216, 242, 246, 247, 249, 265
846, 205, 209–212, 236, 246, 247, 266, 267, 270, 277, 278, 305, 307, 311, 312, 316
848, 246–249
849, 246–248, 251
850, 246–249
852, 236, 238, 266, 267, 270
853, 282, 284, 306, 310–312, 316
854, 246–249
855, 246–249
856, 274, 277, 305, 307–309
880, 112, 119, 215, 236, 261, 264, 266, 267, 275, 276
881, 181, 215, 216, 221, 246, 258, 273, 274, 277, 278, 307, 316
882, 185, 201, 215, 216, 221, 258, 261, 263, 309, 310, 312, 313, 316
883, 168, 176
885, 180, 252, 255
886, 252, 254
887, 236, 266, 270
888, 180
891, 179, 295
892, 295, 296
893, 180, 295
894, 236, 266, 270
896, 215, 216, 229, 230, 246, 248, 258, 259
897, 252
898, 201, 215, 216, 229, 231, 258, 261, 263
1770, 187, 236, 240, 266, 267
1771, 268, 269–271, 275–277
1790, 295, 314
1791, 295, 314
1792, 295, 296
1830, 185
1834, 215, 216, 221, 258, 261, 264
1836, 215, 216, 229, 258, 264
1840, 236, 240, 266
1841, 236, 240
1842, 236, 240
3 Naval Fighter Wing, 252–254, 256, 257
6 Naval Fighter Wing, 236
7 Naval Fighter Wing, 217
8 TBR Wing, 216–218, 221, 223, 258
24 Naval Fighter Wing, 236, 266, 270, 271
47 Naval Fighter Wing, 216
52 TBR Wing, 216–218, 228, 258, 259
Naval Air Stations
  Arbroath, 16, 162
  Ayr, 316
  Burscough, 295, 296
  Campbeltown, 16, 33
  Crail, 16, 82, 161, 163, 294, 315, 316
  Donibristle, 13, 15
  Drem, 281, 295, 296, 314
  Dunino, 315
  Easthaven, 294
  Eastleigh, 15, 17
  Evanton, 33, 41
  Fearn, 162
  Ford, 15
  Grimsetter, 266, 316
  Hatston, 14, 15, 26, 27, 31, 34, 41, 42, 52, 54, 62, 64, 66, 68, 76, 87–91, 132, 165, 166, 315, 316

Inskip, 295
Lee-on-Solent, 15, 131, 142, 164, 249, 252, 257, 295
Machrihanish, 16, 162, 164, 248, 316
Maydown, 290, 294
Piarco, 28, 195, 292
Rattray, 316
Ronaldsway, 294
St Merryn, 16
Stretton, 192, 316
Twatt, 16, 316
Wingfield, 316
Worthy Down, 15, 248
Yeovilton, 16, 28, 82, 117, 127, 187, 295
Nelson, HMS, 23, 107
Neptune, HMS, 86, 107
Nestor, HMAS, 87, 92
Newcastle, HMS, 74
Newsom, A C, Captain RM, 45
Nixon, J J, Lieutenant (A) RNVR, 252
Norfolk, HMS, 86, 93, 94, 96, 97, 106, 107, 310
Nottingham, F C, Lieutenant Commander (A) RNVR, 198
Nubian, HMS, 282

Obedient, HMS, 198, 205
Ocean, HMS, 295–297
Offa, HMS, 198, 205
Onslaught, HMS, 198, 200
Onslow, HMS, 172, 205, 302
Operations
  Acumen, 287
  Alphabet, 66
  Athletic, 270
  Begonia, 267
  Blues, 265
  Brawn, 235
  Cambridge, 264
  Camera, 181
  Cleaver, 313
  Counterblast, 273
  Croquet, 261–263
  Cupola, 309
  Dervish, 120, 121, 125
  Divan, 267
  DX, 43, 44, 47, 54, 56
  EF, 111, 115–117, 120
  EG, 120, 124, 125
  EJ, 125, 127
  EV, 169, 170, 176, 177
  Fretsaw, 278
  Fuller, 130–132, 134–137, 139, 147, 153
  FX, 198, 201–204
  FY, 205, 213
  FZ, 241, 245
  Golden, 287
  Goodwood, 235–239
  Governor, 181
  Gratis, 307
  Greystoke, 297
  Groundsheet, 309
  Handfast, 274
  Hardy, 270
  Hoops, 263
  Hotbed, 298, 303
  Judgement II, 310, 311, 313, 319
  Kruschen, 265
  Lacerate, 277
  Leader, 183
  Lombard, 264
  Lycidas, 267
  Mascot, 235
  Muscular, 310
  Neptune, 242, 246, 248, 250
  Newmarket, 310
  Offspring, 266
  Overlord, 257
  Paul, 63, 64, 66–69, 77
  Pitchbowl I, 261
  Pitchbowl II, 261
  Planet, 235
  Post Horn, 197
  Potluck A, 263
  Potluck B, 263, 264
  Prefix, 309, 310
  Proteus, 264
  Provident, 274
  Ridge Able, 258
  Ridge Baker, 261
  Rigmarole, 281
  Roundel, 305
  Sampler, 306
  Scottish, 305
  Selenium I, 307
  Selenium II, 308
  Shred, 309
  Spellbinder, 307
  Steak, 274
  Strength, 120
  Tenable, 267
  Tiger Claw, 235, 264
  Timeless, 305
  Trial, 282, 285
  Tungsten, 205, 213–215, 217, 218, 221, 222, 231–236, 238, 241, 258, 318, 319
  Turbine, 265
  Urbane, 277
  Veritas, 261
  Victual, 278
  Wanderers, 265
  Wilfred, 63
  Winded, 307
Opportune, HMS, 205
Oribi, HMS, 198, 205
Orr, S G, Lieutenant Commander (A) RNVR, 215, 229
Orwell, HMS, 205

Oxley, O A G, Lieutenant Commander (A) RN, 205

Pardoe, A A, Lieutenant RN, 45
Parkinson, R L, Sub Lieutenant (A) RN, 141
Partridge, R T, Captain RM, 31, 32, 35, 42, 46, 48, 50, 62
Patton, J G, Sub Lieutenant (A) RNVR, 116
Payne, A D L, Lieutenant (A) RNVR, 309
Peacock, HMS, 280
Peck, L W, Sub Lieutenant (A) RNVR, 229
Penelope, HMS, 125
Pethick, H W, Sub Lieutenant (A) RNVR, 223
Petsamo, 109–112, 115, 118
Philip, G T, Captain RN, 215
Phillips, D, Lieutenant Commander RN, 228
Phillips, D W, Lieutenant Commander (A) RN, 215
Piorun, Polish Destroyer, 217
Pizey, C T M, Captain RN, 137, 146, 147, 153
Plover, HMS, 131, 132
Plugge, A J P, Lieutenant Commander RN, 154, 156, 158
Poole, N A F, Leading Airman RN, 223
Pound, Sir Dudley, Admiral of the Fleet, First Sea Lord, 64, 66, 68
Power, A J, Captain RN, 8
Premier, HMS, 274, 277, 290, 305, 307–309, 315
Prendergast, B J, Lieutenant RN, 114
Pretoria Castle, HMS, 290, 296
Priestly, G F, Leading Airman RN, 224
Prince of Wales, HMS, 86, 87, 92–94, 97
Prinz Eugen, German Cruiser, 85, 86, 92, 101, 107, 128, 136, 144–148, 154, 156
Pullen, D L, Sub Lieutenant (A) RNVR, 223, 262
Pullin, J A, Sub Lieutenant (A) RNVR, 181
Pumphrey, E N, Lieutenant Commander RN, 137, 138, 146, 153
Puncher, HMS, 290, 307–310, 314
Punjabi, HMS, 87, 92, 120
Pursuer, HMS, 214–217, 221, 222, 230, 246, 258, 259, 273, 274

Queen, HMS, 290, 299, 305, 306, 309, 310, 314

Rajah, HMS, 187, 248
Ramillies, HMS, 94
Ramsay, Sir Bertram, Vice Admiral, 130, 131, 133–138, 140, 145
Ranald, H C, Commander RN, 98
Rance, V, Lieutenant Commander RN, 216, 218, 228, 230, 259
Ranger, USS, 183, 184
Rankin J F, Lieutenant Commander (A) RN, 252
Rankin, R R, Leading Airman RN, 229

Ravager, HMS, 290, 291
Renown, HMS, 23, 84, 85, 102, 153, 156
Repulse, HMS, 23, 86, 87, 92
Resolution, HMS, 59
Revenge, HMS, 94
Reynolds, W H A, Leading Airman RN, 223, 262
Rice, F C, Petty Officer RN, 38
Richardson, A R, Lieutenant Commander (A) RNZNVR, 240
Richardson, H H, Sub Lieutenant (A) RNVR, 228, 230
Ritchie, A D, Sub Lieutenant (A) RNVR, 223
Robbins, R N, Sub Lieutenant (A) RNVR, 229
Robertson, I G, Sub Lieutenant (A) RNVR, 223
Robinson, D, Leading Airman RN, 229
Robinson, J B, Lieutenant (A) RNVR, 224
Rodney, HMS, 23, 24, 84, 94, 101, 106, 153, 281
Rorvik, 263, 270, 272, 275
Rose, B W, Sub Lieutenant (A) RNVR, 138, 139, 141, 143–145, 150, 151
Rosyth, 23, 25, 86, 153, 314, 315
Rotherham, G A (Hank), Commander RN, 79, 88–91
Rowe, D E, Sub Lieutenant (A) RNZNVR, 224
Royalist, HMS, 214, 217, 258
Royal Sovereign, HMS, 213, 287
Russell, G S, Leading Airman RN, 42
Russell-Jones, G, Lieutenant (A) RNVR, 229
Ryan, L J, Sub Lieutenant (A) RNZNVR, 228

Saguenay, HMCS, 92
Salisbury, A, Sub Lieutenant (A) RNVR, 267
Samples, R McC, Sub Lieutenant (A) RNVR, 141, 145, 150
Sanderson, D, Lieutenant Commander RN, 40, 112, 155
Saumarez, HMS, 205
Savage, HMS, 198
Scapa Flow, 25, 26, 31, 42, 43, 47, 49, 56, 58, 62, 66, 73, 87, 91, 109–112, 119, 120, 124–127, 153, 160, 165, 166, 169, 176, 179, 198, 202, 213, 214, 217, 220, 231, 234, 237, 240, 245, 263, 264, 268, 270, 273, 274, 277–279, 282, 284, 287, 298, 302, 303, 305–307, 311–314
Scharnhorst, German Battlecruiser, 61–63, 84–86, 128, 129, 136, 143, 145, 146, 148, 151, 154
Schonfeldt, P B, Lieutenant RN, 102
Scorpion, HMS, 205
Scylla, HMS, 169, 173, 174
Searcher, HMS, 185, 201, 214–217, 221, 222, 231, 258, 259, 261, 263, 286, 290, 309, 310, 314

Sellers, K A, Sub Lieutenant (A) RNVR, 223
Serapis, HMS, 198, 205
Seymour, B M, Petty Officer RN, 24
Sharp, K G, Lieutenant Commander (A) RN, 247
Sharples, F, Leading Airman RN, 116
Shaw, R M, Sub Lieutenant (A) RNZNVR, 272
Sheffield, F G B, Lieutenant Commander (A) RNVR, 247
Sheffield, HMS, 23, 102–105, 217, 265
Shephard, D J, Sub Lieutenant (A) RNVR, 160
Sherlock, E J W, Chief Petty Officer RN, 228
Short, K A, Captain RN, 280, 304
Shipley, E R, Sub Lieutenant (A) RNVR, 228
Sholto-Douglas, J, Lieutenant Commander (A) RN, 103
Shropshire, HMS, 120
Sim, A B, Leading Airman RN, 228
Simpson, J, Petty Officer RN, 19
Simpson, W C, Lieutenant Commander (A) RN, 252
Sinker, A J, Ordinary Seaman RN, 100
Sioux, HMCS, 299
Sivewright, C F, Leading Airman RN, 160
Skene, N R M, Captain RM, 8, 45, 51
Slattery, M S, Captain RN, 80
Sleigh, J W, Lieutenant Commander RN, 125, 225
Smee, N F W, Leading Airman RN, 309
Smeeton, B J, Lieutenant RN, 35
Smeeton, R M, Lieutenant RN, 49, 55
Smiter, HMS, 290
Smith, N J, Sub Lieutenant (A) RNVR, 240
Smith, R D, Sub Lieutenant (A) RNVR, 223
Smith, W, Sub Lieutenant (A) RNVR, 229
Smith, W G, Leading Airman RN, 141
Smyth, R J, Lieutenant (A) RNVR, 298
Smyth, V, Leading Airman RN, 229
Snow, P, Lieutenant Commander RN, 247
Somali, HMS, 24, 120
Somerville, Sir James, Vice Admiral, 102, 105, 107
Spearfish, HMS, 23
Spencer, T, Leading Airman RN, 228
Stacey, E, Sub Lieutenant (A) RNVR, 228
Starling, HMS, 205
Stavanger, 49, 64, 309
Stevens, P D T, Lieutenant Commander (A) RNVR, 247
Stewart-Moore, J A, Lieutenant Commander RN, 103, 112, 114
St Nazaire, 94
Stord, HNoMS, 205
Strange, R L, Lieutenant RN, 49
Street, D, Sub Lieutenant (A) RNVR, 200, 201
Striker, HMS, 258, 259, 263, 265, 278, 280, 281

Suffolk, HMS, 86, 92–94, 97, 100, 101, 112, 120
Supermarine Seafire, 165, 180, 186–188, 197, 215, 218, 222, 235, 236, 252, 254, 255, 261, 264–268, 270–273, 275, 276, 315
Supermarine Walrus, 8, 10–12, 17, 27, 57, 60, 74, 75, 79, 82, 84, 92, 93, 98, 112, 115, 119, 157
Surtees, H N, Captain RN, 282
Swift, HMS, 198
Sydney-Turner, P, Lieutenant Commander RN, 35–37

Talbot, A G, Captain RN, 116
Tapping, E, Leading Airman RN, 141
Tartar, HMS, 174
Taylor, S C, Sub Lieutenant (A) RNZNVR, 228
Taylour, E W, Lieutenant RN, 32, 50, 171
Teviot Bank, HMS, 63
Thompson, J C, Lieutenant (A) RN, 140–144, 151
Thompson, R L, Sub Lieutenant (A) RNVR, 263
Thomson, A H, Leading Airman RN, 224
Thornbury, E W, Sub Lieutenant (A) RNVR, 240
Tilley, K H, Lieutenant (A) RNVR, 282
Tilney, G A, Lieutenant Commander RN, 89
Tirpitz, German Battleship, 128, 154, 156–161, 167, 180, 205, 213, 214, 218–220, 224–226, 229, 230, 232, 233, 235–238, 240, 241, 264, 268, 269, 319
Tomkinson, C C, Lieutenant Commander (A) RNVR, 215, 229
Topliss, C, Chief Petty Officer RN, 223
Torry, G N, Lieutenant Commander RN, 8
Tovey, Sir John, Admiral, 86–88, 90, 94, 100–102, 107, 109, 111, 117, 125, 157, 160, 167, 171
Towlson, A N, Sub Lieutenant (A) RNVR, 228
Tracker, HMS, 204–206, 208, 209, 211–213, 246, 247, 282
Trident, HMS, 154, 156
Trinidad, HMS, 165
Tromso, 39, 57, 74, 119, 121, 154, 227, 230, 241, 269
Trondheim, 34–37, 43, 45, 46, 49, 51, 52, 57, 61, 62, 74, 156, 157, 274, 305, 310
Troubridge, T H, Captain RN, 33, 40, 41
Trumpeter, HMS, 236, 266–268, 270, 277, 278, 290, 307, 310, 314, 315
Tuckwood, C F, Ordinary Seaman RN, 100
Turnbull, F R A, Lieutenant Commander (A) RN, 216, 221
Tuscaloosa, USS, 168

U-29, 19, 22
U-30, 19
U-39, 19
U-64, 38
U-277, 244
U-288, 210, 211
U-344, 278
U-354, 237, 279
U-355, 210
U-365, 288
U-366, 200
U-369, 289
U-394, 280
U-425, 301
U-472, 200
U-589, 172
U-674, 244
U-703, 202
U-711, 311, 312
U-921, 282
U-959, 244
U-968, 305
U-973, 201
U-1060, 272, 273
Undaunted, HMS, 282
Unicorn, HMS, 181, 182
United States Naval Air Squadrons
   VCS-7, 252, 257

Valiant, HMS, 37, 55, 56
Venus, HMS, 205
Verulam, HMS, 198
Vestfjord, 38, 40, 60, 63, 64, 66, 125
Vian, P L, Rear Admiral, 101, 109, 110
Victorious, HMS, 80, 86, 87, 91, 94, 95,
   97–99, 101, 107, 109–114, 116, -121,
   124–127, 154, 156–158, 160, 165–168,
   178, 180, 188, 205, 213–215, 217–223,
   227, 232, 234, 235, 258, 259, 261, 264,
   265, 269, 317
Vigilant, HMS, 198
Vindex, HMS, 249, 278, 279, 282–285, 290,
   297, 305, 315
Viney, R D, Sub Lieutenant (A) RNVR, 240
Vivacious, HMS, 146, 147

Wade, H J R, Leading Airman RN, 116
Wake-Walker, W F, Rear Admiral, 86, 94,
   112, 113, 118, 120
Walker, F J, Captain RN, 205, 210
Walker J G, Sub Lieutenant (A) RNVR, 240
Walker, HMS, 205
Walling, A C P, Sub Lieutenant (A) RNVR,
   224, 262
Walpole, HMS, 146
Walsh, D L, Lieutenant (A) RNVR, 285
Warburton-Lee, B A W, Captain RN, 37
Ward, T, Leading Airman RN, 229
War Pindari, RFA, 40
Warspite, HMS, 11, 33, 38, 255

Washington, USS, 165
Wasp, USS, 165, 166
Waters, S A W, Sub Lieutenant (A) RNVR, 272
Waters, W E, Lieutenant Commander RN, 112
Watkins, V, Leading Airman RN, 229
Watkinson, F, Midshipman (A) RN, 35
Watson, J, Sub Lieutenant (A) RNVR, 223
Watson, J B, Sub Lieutenant (A) RNVR, 309
Wells, A C, Leading Airman RN, 224
Wells, Sir Lionel, Vice Admiral, 43, 47, 56,
   60, 61
Welshman, HMS, 131
Wheatland, HMS, 169, 174
Wheeler, H T A, Leading Airman RN, 141
Whimbrel, HMS, 205
Whirlwind, HMS, 59
White, B, Lieutenant Commander (A)
   RNVR, 247
White, T D, Sub Lieutenant (A) RNVR, 252
Whitehall, HMS, 280, 300
Whitshed, HMS, 146
Whittaker, J P, Lieutenant (A) RNVR, 228
Whitworth, W J, Rear Admiral, 38
Whyte, J Leading Airman RN, 224
Wild Goose, HMS, 205
Wilkinson, A E, Sub Lieutenant (A) RNVR,
   113
Wilkinson, D, Lieutenant (A) RNVR, 197
Williams, H E, Sub Lieutenant (A) RNVR,
   125
Williams, J D L, Commander RN, 305
Williams, R G, Sub Lieutenant (A)
   RNZNVR, 224
Williams, R R, Leading Airman RN, 223
Williams, W H, Lieutenant RN, 141, 144,
   151
Willis, D G, Sub Lieutenant (A) RN, 51
Willoughby, G, Captain RN, 204, 205, 209,
   241, 242, 245
Wills, N C, Leading Airman RN, 108
Wilton, HMS, 169
Windsor, HMS, 92
Womack, A F, Sub Lieutenant (A) RNVR,
   181, 310
Wood, C R, Sub Lieutenant (A) RN, 141
Woodward, C E, Sub Lieutenant (A)
   RNZNVR, 240
Wootton, D E, Leading Airman RN, 223
Worcester, HMS, 146, 147
Wren, HMS, 205
Wright, S G, Naval Airman RN, 58
Wroughton, J A D, Lieutenant Commander
   RN, 112

Yorke, G C, Lieutenant RN, 223

Zealous, HMS, 302
Zulu, HMS, 39
Z 33, German Destroyer, 236